MW01626278

30 AMERICANS

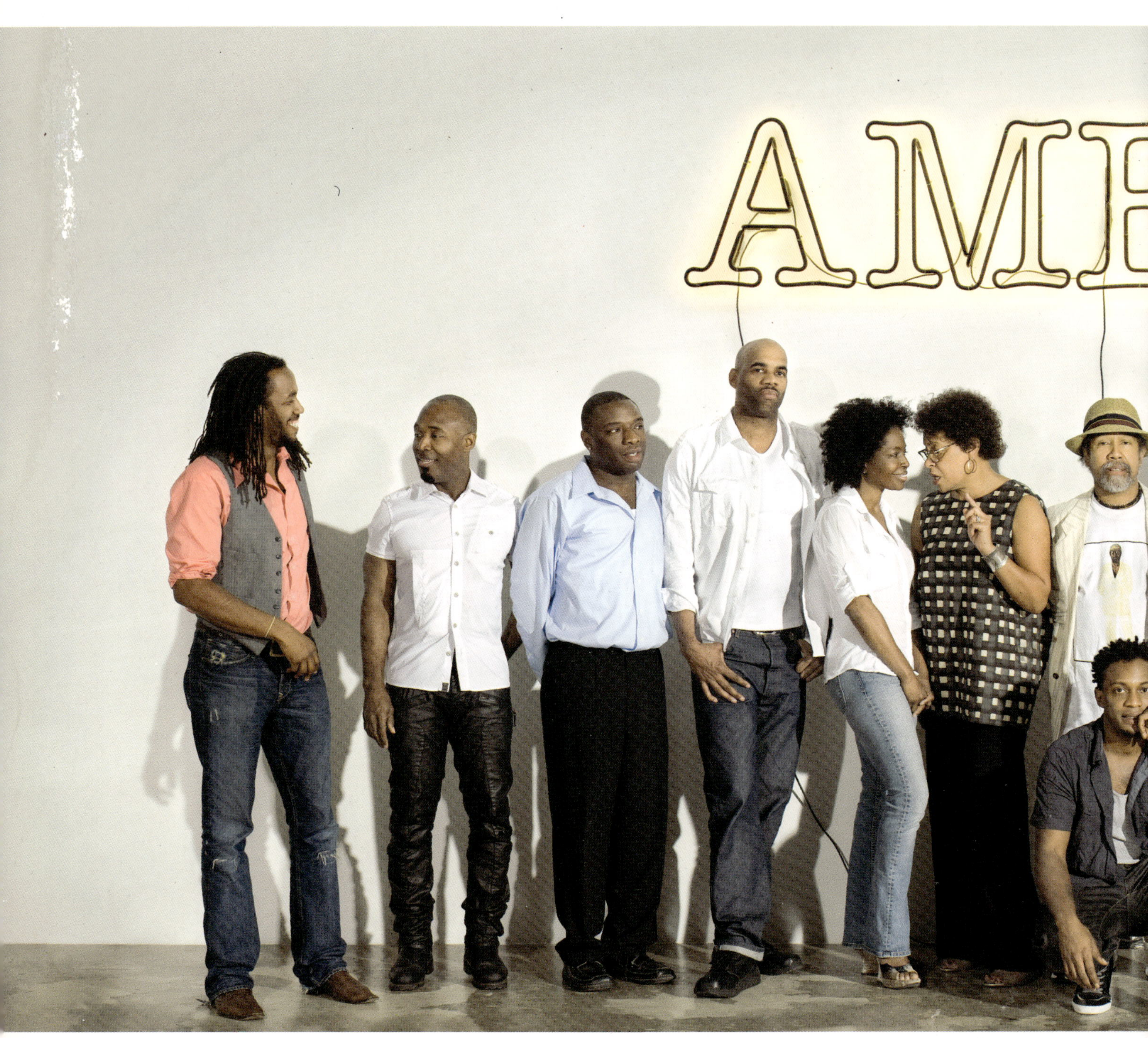

Left to right: Rashid Johnson, Nick Cave, Kalup Linzy, Jeff Sonhouse, Lorna Simpson, Carrie Mae Weems, Barkley L. Hendricks, Hank Willis Thomas (front row), Xaviera Simmons, Purvis Young, John Bankston, Nina Chanel Abney, Henry Taylor, Mickalene Thomas (front row), Kerry James Marshall and Shinique Smith

Photo credit: Kwaku Alston, December 5, 2008

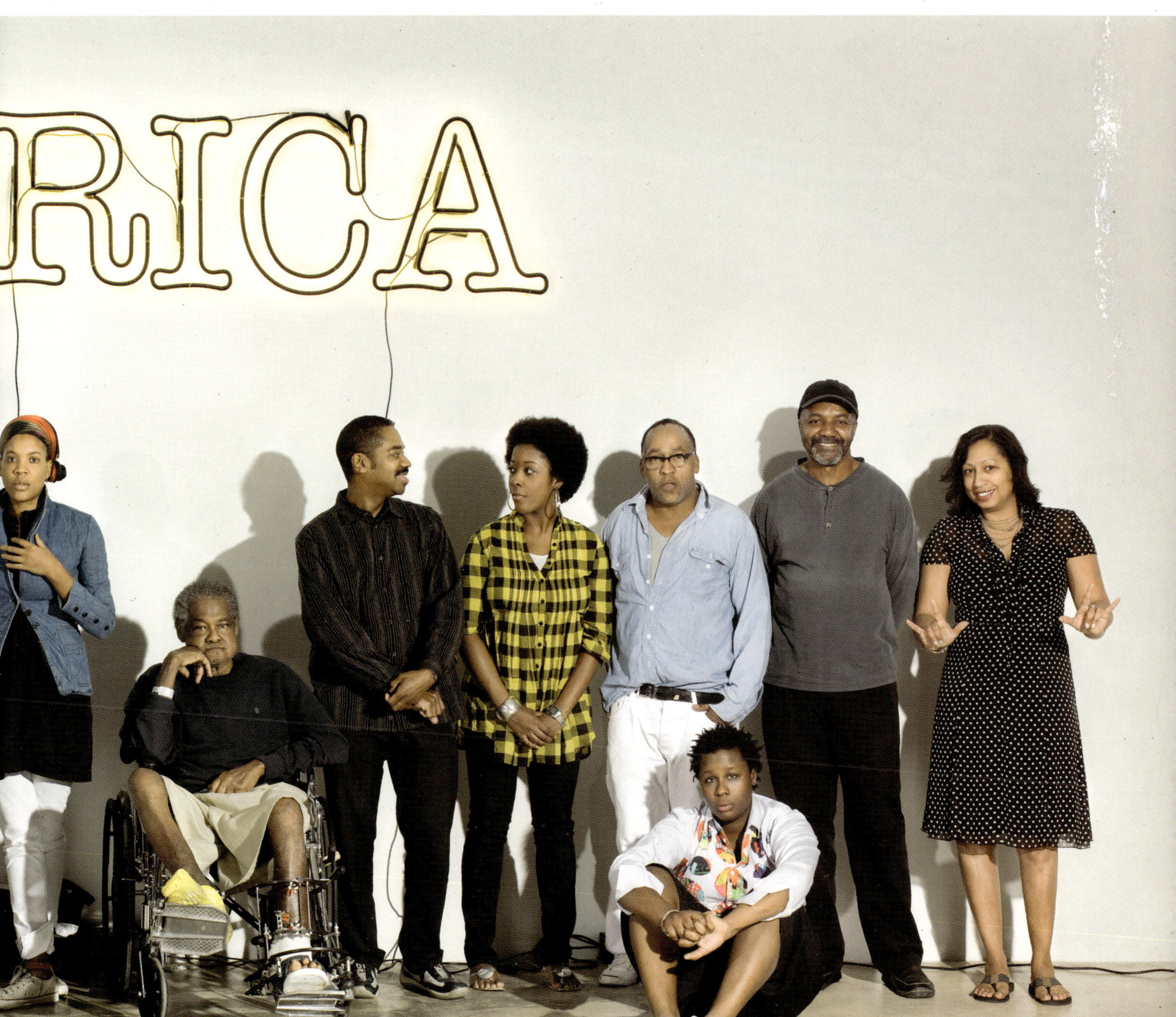
RICA

First published on the occasion of the exhibition *30 Americans*, organized by the Rubell Museum/Contemporary Arts Foundation

Rubell Family Collection, Miami
December 3, 2008 — May 30, 2009

North Carolina Museum of Art, Raleigh
March 20, 2011 — September 4, 2011

Corcoran Gallery of Art, Washington DC
October 1, 2011 — February 12, 2012

Chrysler Museum of Art, Norfolk
March 16, 2012 — July 15, 2012

Milwaukee Art Museum, Milwaukee
June 14 — September 8, 2013

Frist Center for the Visual Arts, Nashville
October 11, 2013 — January 12, 2014

Contemporary Arts Center, New Orleans
February 8, 2014 — June 15, 2014

Arkansas Art Center, Little Rock
April 9, 2015 — June 21, 2015

Detroit Institute of Arts, Detroit
October 18, 2015 — January 18, 2016

Cincinnati Art Museum, Ohio
March 19 — August 28, 2016

Tacoma Art Museum, Washington
September 24, 2016 — January 15, 2017

McNay Art Museum, San Antonio
February 8 — May 6, 2018

Juliet Art Museum, Charleston
April 1 — July 1, 2018

Tucson Museum of Art, Arizona
October 6, 2018 — January 13, 2019

Joslyn Museum of Art, Omaha
February — May, 2019

Nelson-Atkins Museum, Kansas City
May — August, 2019

Contributing writers: Robert Hobbs, Glenn Ligon, Franklin Sirmans and Michele Wallace

Fourth Edition, © 2017 Rubell Museum

ISBN: 978-0-9716341-2-1

Library of Congress Control Number: 2017953766

Rubell Museum
1100 NW 23 ST
Miami, Fl 33127
www.rfc.museum

Publication
Editor: Juan Valadez
Design & Photography: Chi Lam

Rubell Museum/Contemporary Arts Foundation
Director: Juan Valadez
Designer & Photographer: Chi Lam
Collection Manager: William Vargas
Archivist & Associate Registrar: Laura Randall
Installation Technician: Leyden Ayure, Giovanni Urrego Suaréz
Assistant Registrar: Katie Acosta
Visitor Services: Dieci Cai
Facility Technicians: Sonia Alvarez, Miriam Oliveras
Controller: Liliana Zarif
Office Manager: Marie Pena

Printed in China by Permanent Printing Limited

All rights reserved. No part of this publication may be reproduced or transmitted in any form or by any means—electronic, mechanical, photocopying, recording, or otherwise—without the prior written consent of the publishers and authors.

Cover: Rashid Johnson, *The New Negro Escapist Social and Athletic Club (Thurgood)*, 2008, Lambda print, ed. 2/5, 69 x 55 1/2 in. (175.3 x 141 cm)

We only show art we own. That is a founding principle of the Rubell Family Collection, a principle that gives us tremendous freedom and enormous constraints. When we set out to conceptualize a new exhibition, we know we will only get the depth and quality we seek if we already have a strong foundation of works by a core group of artists. Once the exhibition is determined, we then collect into it, buying works that we consider essential right up to the closing date for the catalogue, just one month before the opening of the show.

In general, the spark for a new exhibition begins in artists' studios. The artists often talk about earlier artists who influence or inspire them. When we start hearing the same names over and over, and many members of the more established generation are already well represented in our collection, we begin to think that there's a show to be done.

We then embark on a mission to both expand our commitment to the older generation—including some artists that we have only begun to understand through the eyes of the emerging generation—and collect this new generation in as much depth and breadth as possible. This entire endeavor is limited by the availability of great work, financial resources, and time. We depend on significant cooperation from artists, gallerists, curators, and the greater art community, and we have been moved by how willing everyone has been to help us create the very best show we can, every time. This process—conceptualizing the show, collecting additional works for it, curating it and publishing a catalogue—generally takes about three years.

Our shows are created in real time. These exhibitions are not comprehensive; each represents our family's personal view of what we are most excited about in art at this very moment, without the luxury or constraints of historical perspective. Because many of the artists are not broadly known, we make every effort to collect and exhibit each artist in the greatest depth possible. This becomes especially important as the show travels to various venues, particularly university museums, where students may be encountering most of the artists for the first time. We also publish a major catalogue to accompany each show, with critical essays that provide a framework through which students, artists, and the general public can gain a maximum understanding of the artists, the movements and the themes involved in a given exhibition.

Since we started collecting in the 1960s, we have always collected African-American artists as a part of our broader mission to collect the most interesting art of our time. Approximately three years ago, we found there was a critical mass of emerging African-American artists, and began the process of understanding what seemed to be a new movement. When we asked these artists about their influences, we heard some of the same names over and over: Robert Colescott, Renée Green, David Hammons, Barkley Hendricks, Kerry James Marshall, Gary Simmons, Lorna Simpson, Kara Walker, and Carrie Mae Weems. We had been collecting almost all of this older generation for decades. Perfect conditions for a new exhibition.

As we explored the possibility of a show, we were deeply influenced by a series of outstanding exhibitions around the country focusing on African-American artists, including the "Freestyle" and "Frequency" shows at the Studio Museum in Harlem; "Black Is, Black Ain't" at the Renaissance Society; the Barkley Hendricks show at the Nasher Art Museum at Duke University; the David Hammons show at P.S.1; and the museum retrospectives of Glenn Ligon, Kerry James Marshall, Lorna Simpson and Kara Walker.

We have spent the last three years traveling everywhere we can, speaking to as many artists, critics, and curators as we can, finding and acquiring the best work we can, and putting together the best possible portrait of contemporary African-American art that our physical, financial and intellectual limitations allow. The result is a show of more than 200 works of art, exhibited in 27 galleries occupying the entire 45,000-square-foot exhibition space of the Rubell Family Collection.

As the show evolved, we decided to call it "30 Americans." "Americans," rather than "African Americans" or "Black Americans" because nationality is a statement of fact, while racial identity is a question each artist answers in his or her own way, or not at all. And the number 30 because we acknowledge, even as it is happening, that this show does not include everyone who could be in it. The truth is, because we do collect right up to the last minute before a show, there are actually 31 artists in "30 Americans."

While watching a panel discussion on art and race, an audience member made the comment that today's African-American artists feel the need to assert their blackness. They feel the need to show how black they are in their work. One particular response resonated with me. Someone noted that, realistically, as soon as you depict a black person in your work, you are asserting your blackness whether you intend to or not. This notion of unintentionally asserting "blackness" piqued my interest, and inspired me to create a body of work that wasn't representational of stereotypical blackness. In my previous work, I was creating archetypes rather than individuals, so I began to explore portraiture. Portraiture demands to be accepted on its own terms, and for me it is the best way to capture truth.

For about a year, I painted the portraits of my family and friends. I had each person pose in minimal clothing. I didn't want any material object represented so as not allow the viewer to make a specific assumption about the individual based on stereotypes or popular culture. To create the environment, therefore, I considered the individual's personal life, personality and current hardships or struggles. I feel there isn't anything one could identify as "black" from the portraits. Therefore, the viewer is forced to look past race and focus on the subjects' facial expressions, the position of their bodies and hands, the colors of their clothing, and how they are painted to determine what type of person they may be.

I painted the figures in *Khaaliqua and Jeff* larger than life, facing the viewer, but not looking directly at the viewer. I wanted to create the impression that the viewer is being let in on an intimate moment, that the viewer personally knows those depicted. Because when you actually know someone personally, your opinion of that person is most likely based on inner qualities and personality traits rather than on race.

Class of 2007 [following page] was the last painting I completed as a graduate student. Therefore, I wanted the painting to be a kind of culmination of my entire experience at Parsons. I am interested in fusing multiple issues, so I set out to address the disproportionate number of white students in M.F.A. programs and the disproportionate number of African-American males in prison. I also wanted to address the idea of creating a work that is "universal." Over the course of my time at Parsons, several of my classmates noted that they felt as though they could not completely relate to my work. They commented on how they were unable to see their role in a painting about race. So I questioned what would make a work about race issues "universal" until I finally came up with an answer. I figured that I would paint my classmates as African-Americans, filtering them through my vision, I would be able to create a painting more understandable to them.

My entire time at Parsons, I found myself battling against the notion of "Black Art" and the expectations for a "Black Artist." I was the only African-American student in my class, and some of my classmates assumed that simply creating a class portrait would amplify that fact. They assumed the main objective of the portrait would be to show that I was the only black student in the class. But I'm not one to do the expected, so I led my classmates to believe that I would be creating a simple class portrait. Knowing that I would secretly switch everyone's race including my own, I insisted that the painting not be revealed until the installation of the show. I admittedly wanted a mixed response: some angry, some excited. I therefore did the best I could to take everyone's personality into account so as to determine what skin tone, hairstyle and accessories each student might be dissatisfied or pleased with.

During the big reveal, I got the unexpected: silence, then confusion, then laughter. Most seemed genuinely pleased, while some were visibly uncomfortable.

I had been searching my entire time in graduate school for what I consider the perfect balance: work that is conceptual, humorous and visually pleasing, while at the same time commenting on extremely uncomfortable race issues that can be experienced by anyone. With the creation of *Class of 2007*, I had finally begun to feel like I was within arms reach.

Nina Chanel Abney

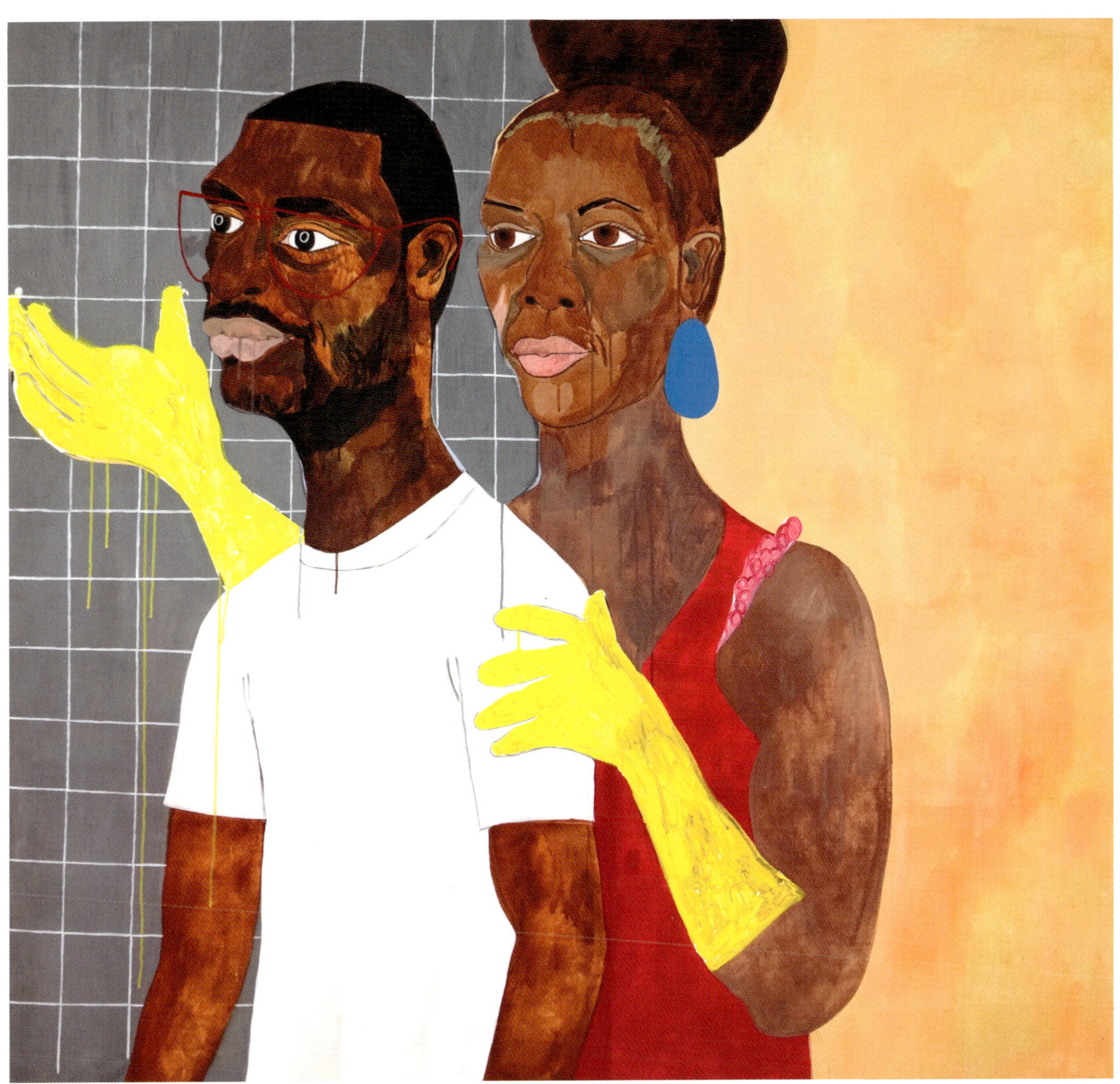

Khaaliqua & Jeff, 2007, acrylic on canvas, 61 x 63 3/4 in. (155 x 162 cm), acquired in 2007

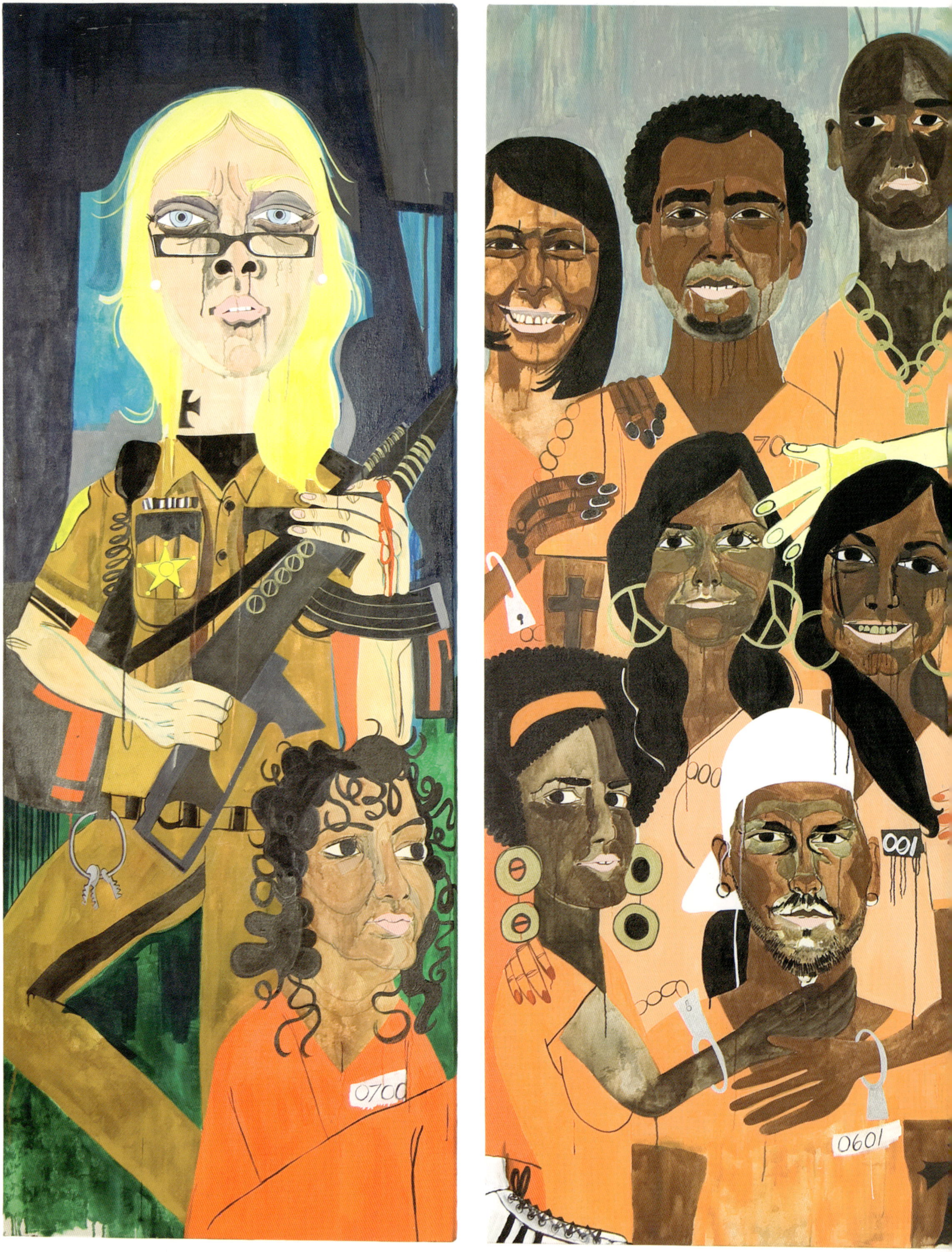

NINA CHANEL ABNEY

Class of 2007, 2007, acrylic on canvas, diptych, overall 114 x 183 in. (289.6 x 464.8 cm), acquired in 2008

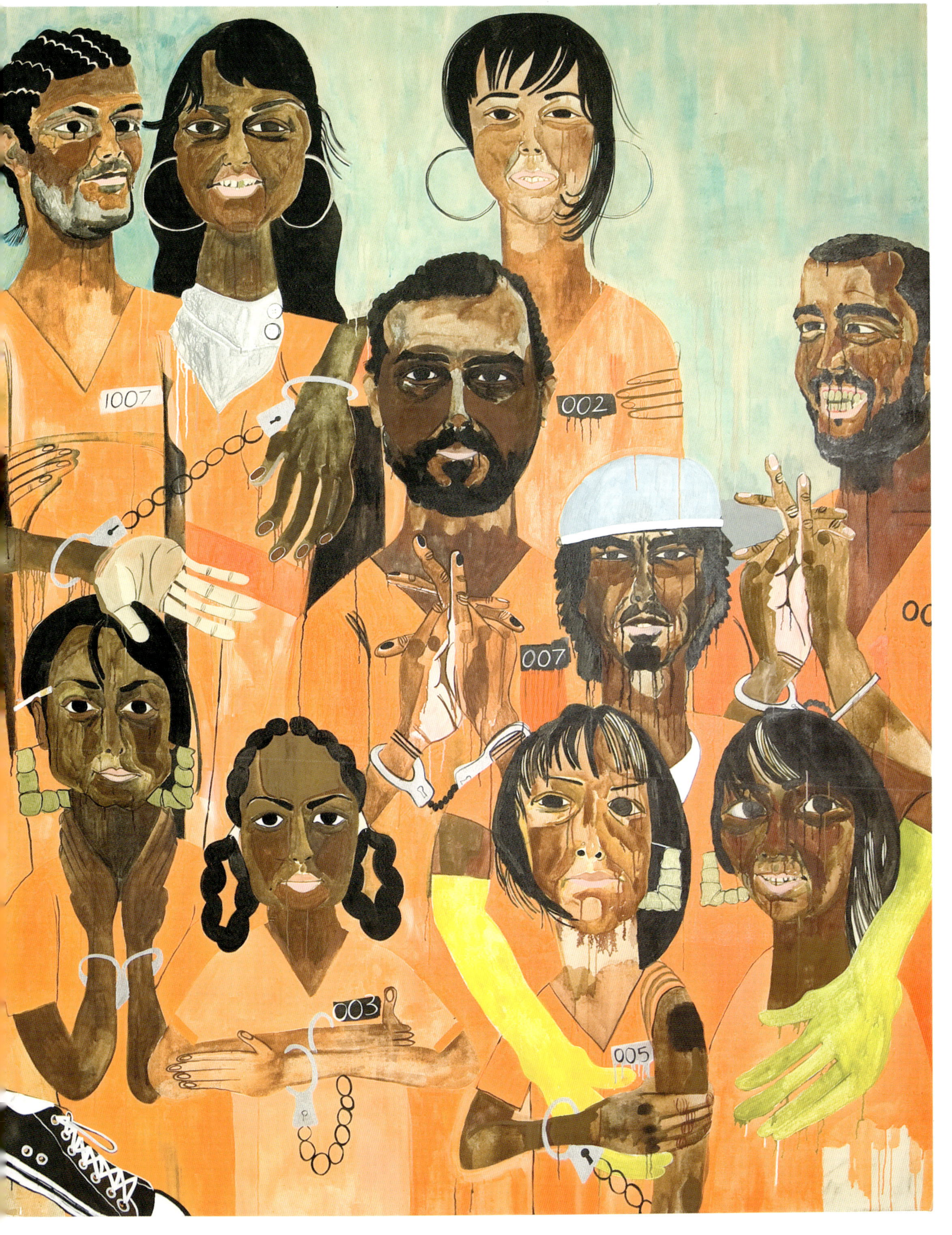
1007
002
007
003
005

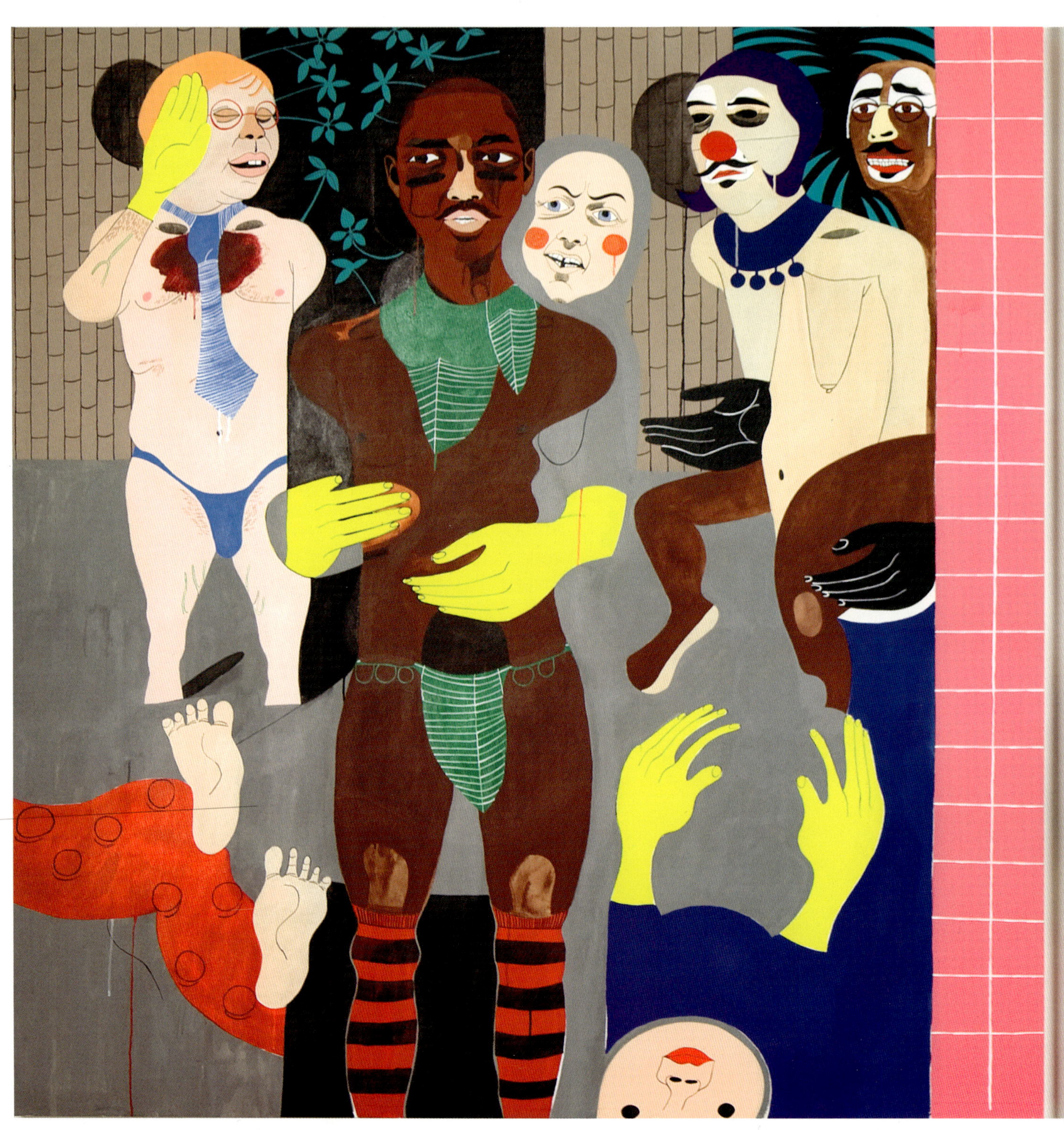

 NINA CHANEL ABNEY *The Boardroom*, 2008, acrylic on canvas, diptych, overall 77 x 156 in. (195.6 x 396.2 cm), acquired in 2008

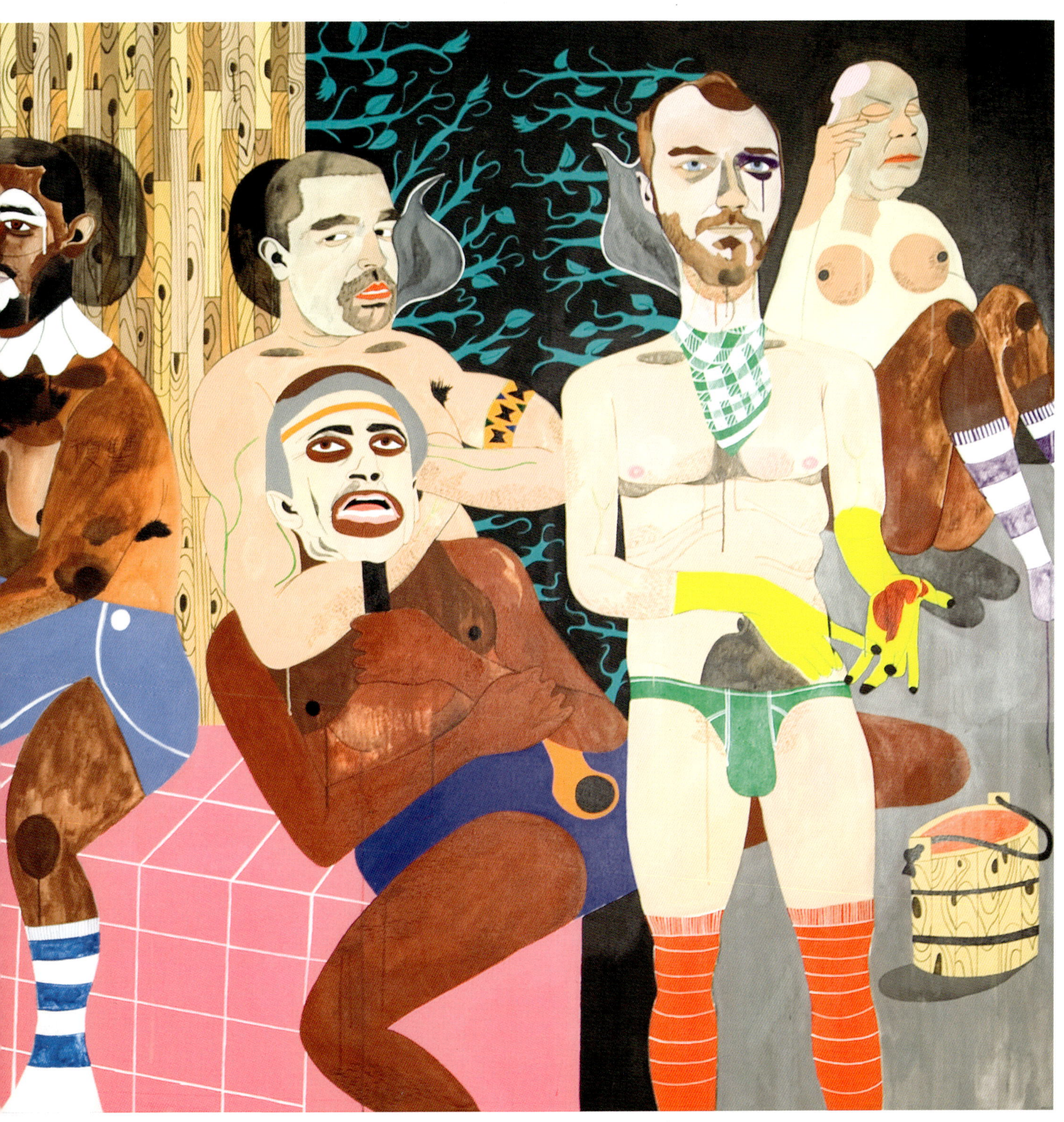

When I begin a painting, my first concern is how to integrate painting and drawing. In fact, my work is primarily concerned with the practices of painting – the technical aspects of moving paint around to create an image. But in doing that physical act I allow narrative into the work. The painting itself is a narrative of its making.

My work has involved an ongoing "visual novel," *The Capture and Escape of Mr. M.* This novel exists not as a printed book but in the form of drawings and paintings; the narrative is conveyed through small drawings or paintings. Large paintings represent key scenes from the storyline, which begins with the abduction of Mr. M by Mr. L. Held in Mr. L's leather lair (a cave in the Rainbow Forest), Mr. M eventually escapes with the help of various forest characters who wage war against Mr. L and his henchmen. The succeeding installments of the story follow Mr. M as he makes his way through this strange new land and manages to avoid the clutches of Mr. L.

The paintings in the Rubell Family Collection are from the chapter, "Man's Country." What interests me is the notion of a hyper masculine secret society. In this chapter, Mr. M, in his continual escape from Mr. L, comes to a clearing in the forest where there appears to be a circus. He discovers that the performers are also the audience and that the performances consist of dressing up and parading.

The setting for the work, Rainbow Forest, is a fantasy land – a place where the inhabitants are free to become the characters of their most secret desires. At the same time, the characters in the work are rooted in my day-to-day experience of life in San Francisco (perhaps a kind of fantasy land itself). The concept of "fantasy" is often thought to belong to the realm of escapism. But I like to think of fantasy as a way of re-imagining our world. It is a means of stepping outside one's known territory, a means of breaking boundaries.

The paintings and drawings engage the visual language of coloring books. Formally, this idiom allows for the integration of painting and drawing as well as figuration and abstraction. In the work, line is used to impose the boundaries of the forms. Color may describe the forms, but it does not always respect the boundaries of the line, as it can ooze and seep over the edges. I want the tension of "staying within the lines" to be seen literally and metaphorically.

In general, the work deals with transformation and identity. I approach these ideas from different levels. A coloring book page is about transformation. Through the act of applying color, the page goes from being a general image to a personal expression. I want the viewer to be aware of the "color" or ethnicity/identity of the characters in the work. I hope the viewer will think about a blank coloring page and the choices one makes when coloring the image. The images in the work are about people who have redrawn personal boundaries and have "colored" themselves outside the lines of received cultural norms. It is my hope that the viewer will be able to step into this fantasy world and for a moment live life "colored" outside the lines.

John Bankston

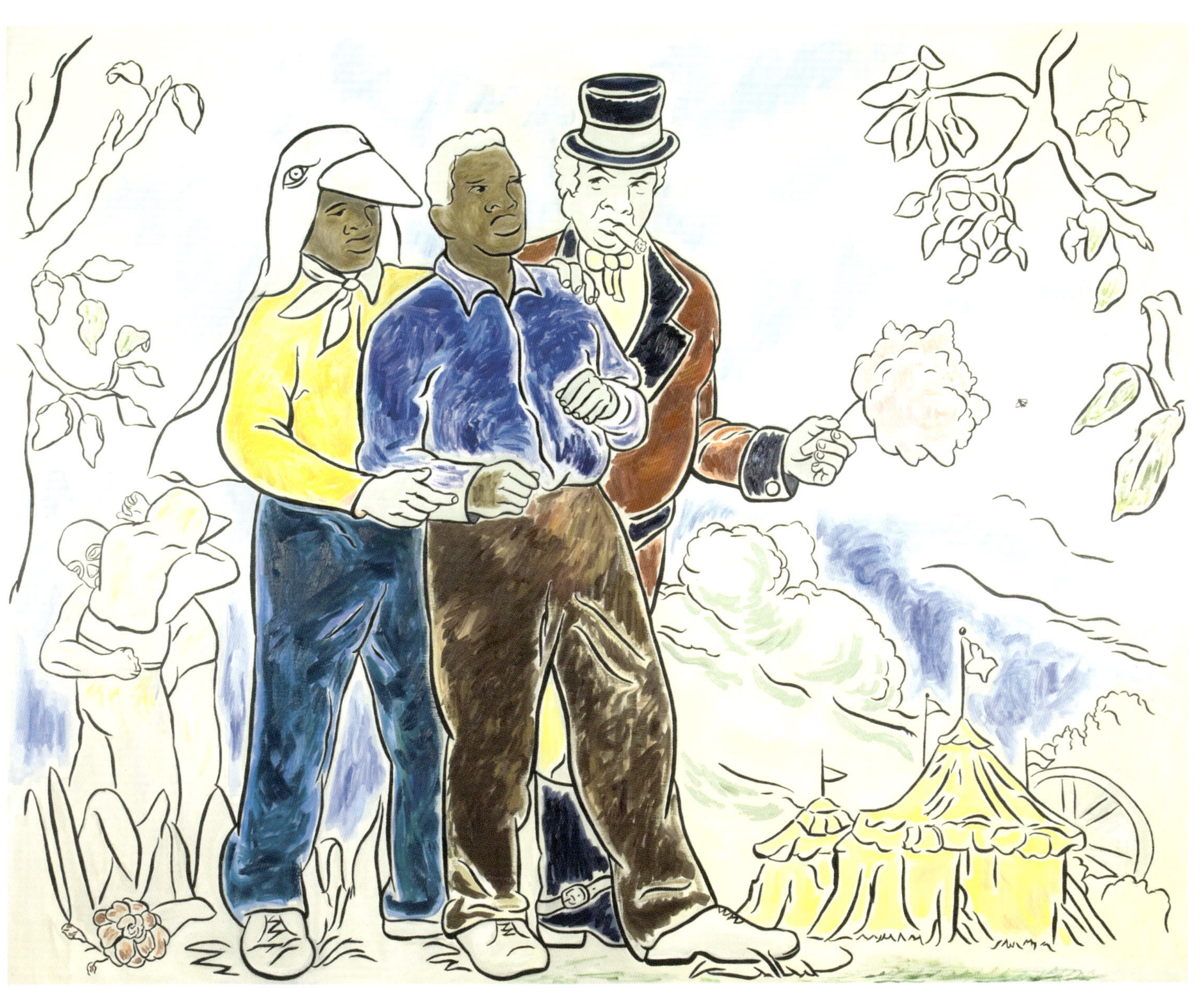

Man's Country II, 2004, oil on linen, 78 x 96 in. (198.1 x 243.8 cm), acquired in 2007

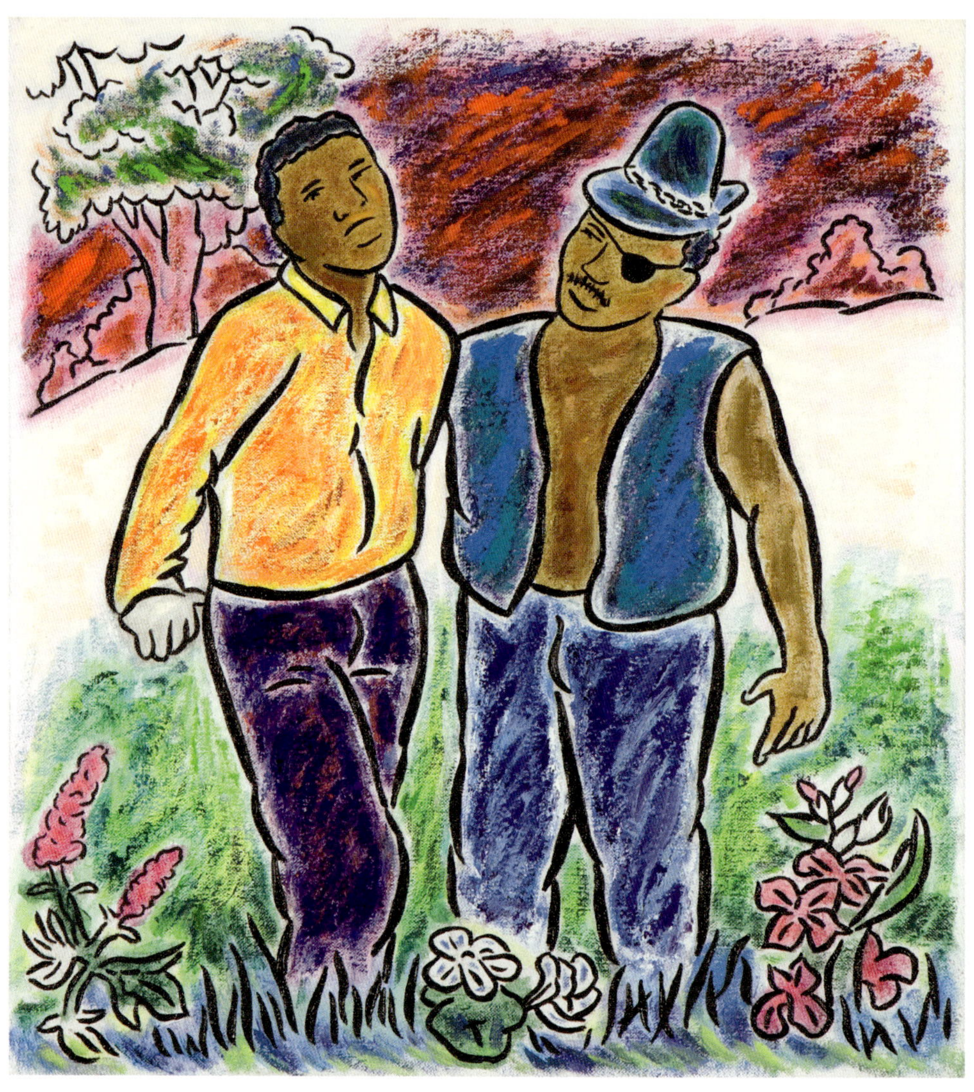

 JOHN BANKSTON *Beginning or End*, 2006-2007, oil and wax on linen, 20 x 18 in. (50.8 x 45.7 cm), acquired in 2007

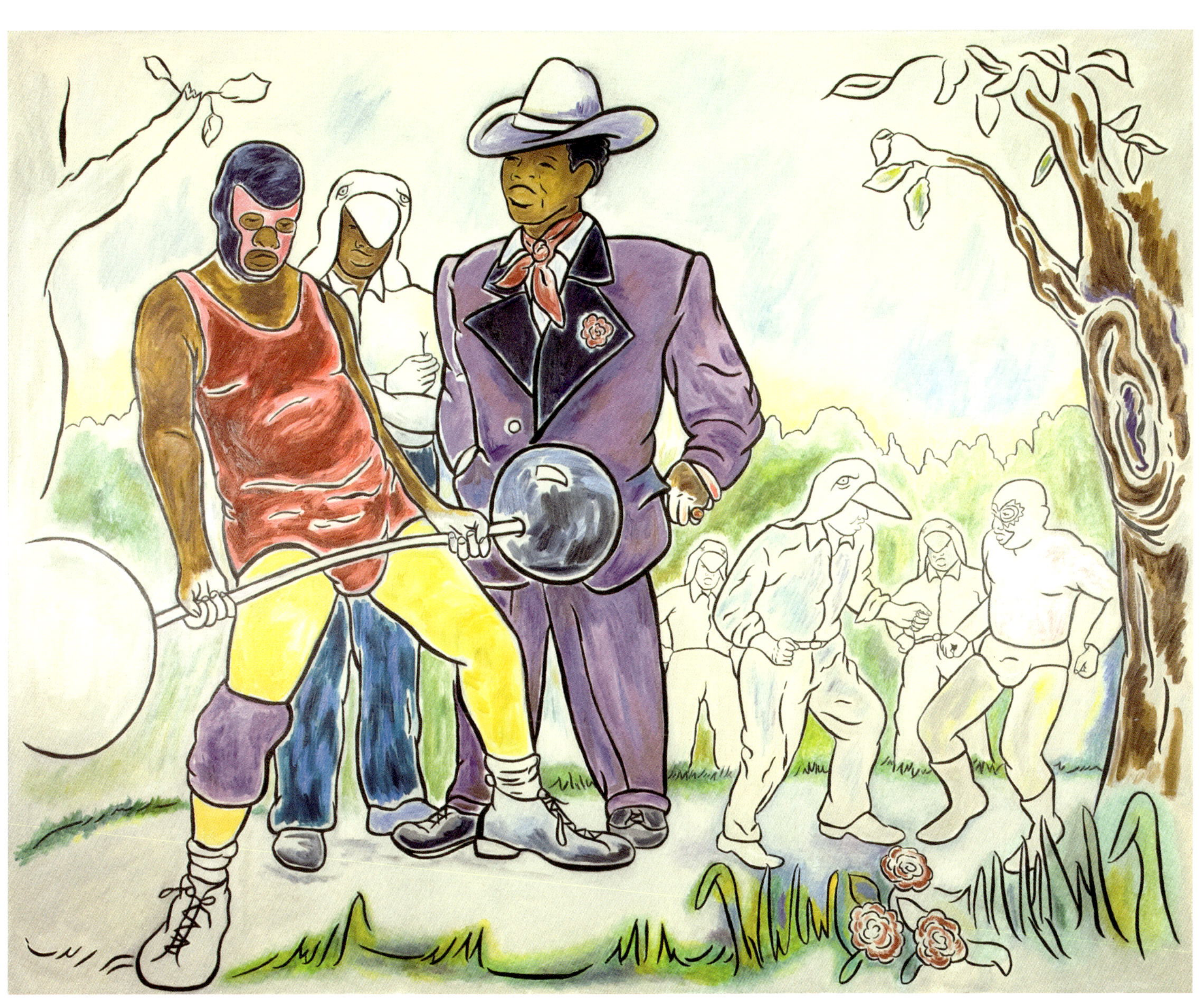

Man's Country I, 2004, oil on linen, 78 x 96 in. (198.1 x 243.8 cm), acquired in 2007

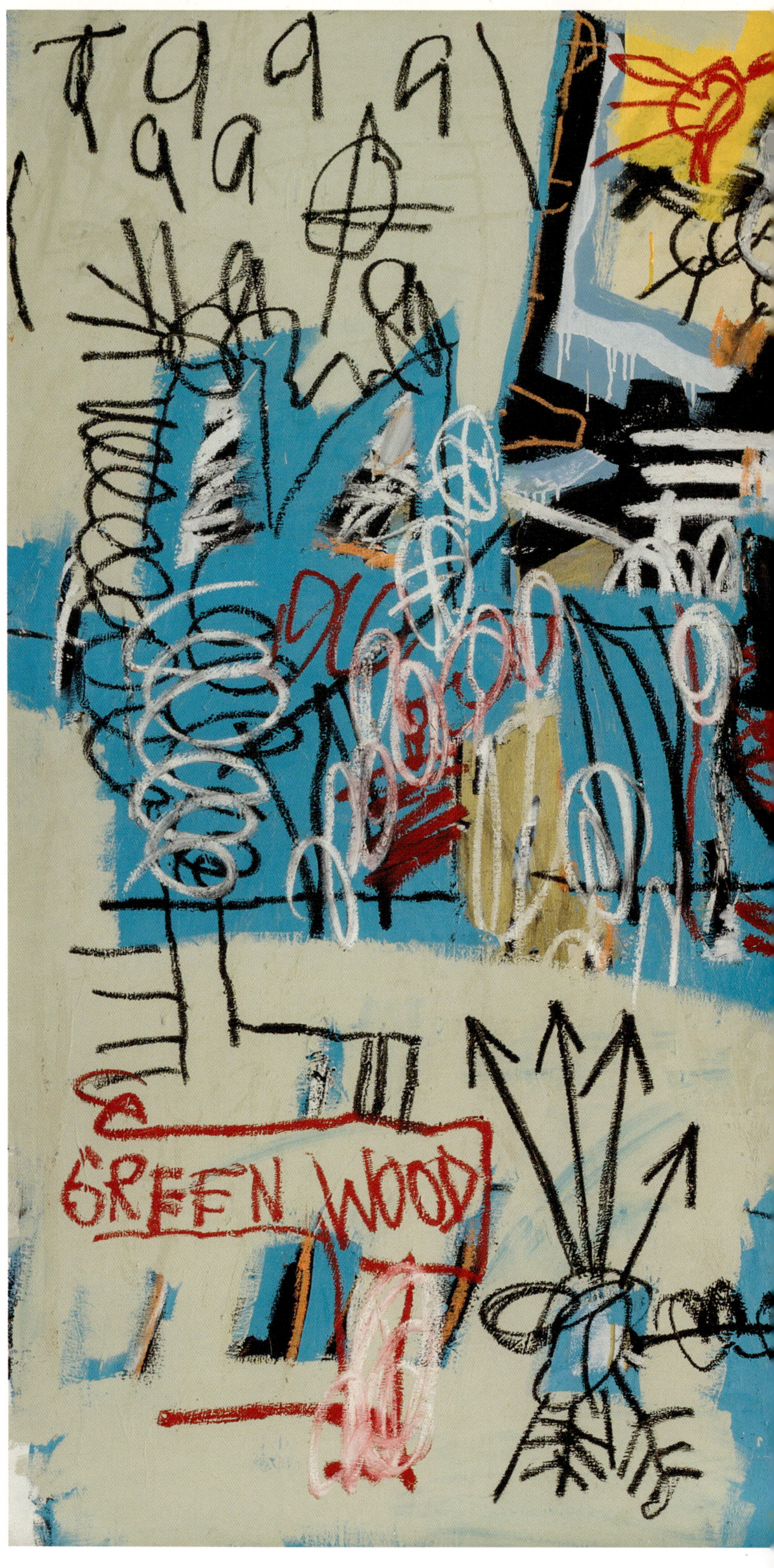

Bird On Money, 1981, acrylic and oil on canvas, 66 x 90 in. (167.6 x 228.6 cm), acquired in 1981

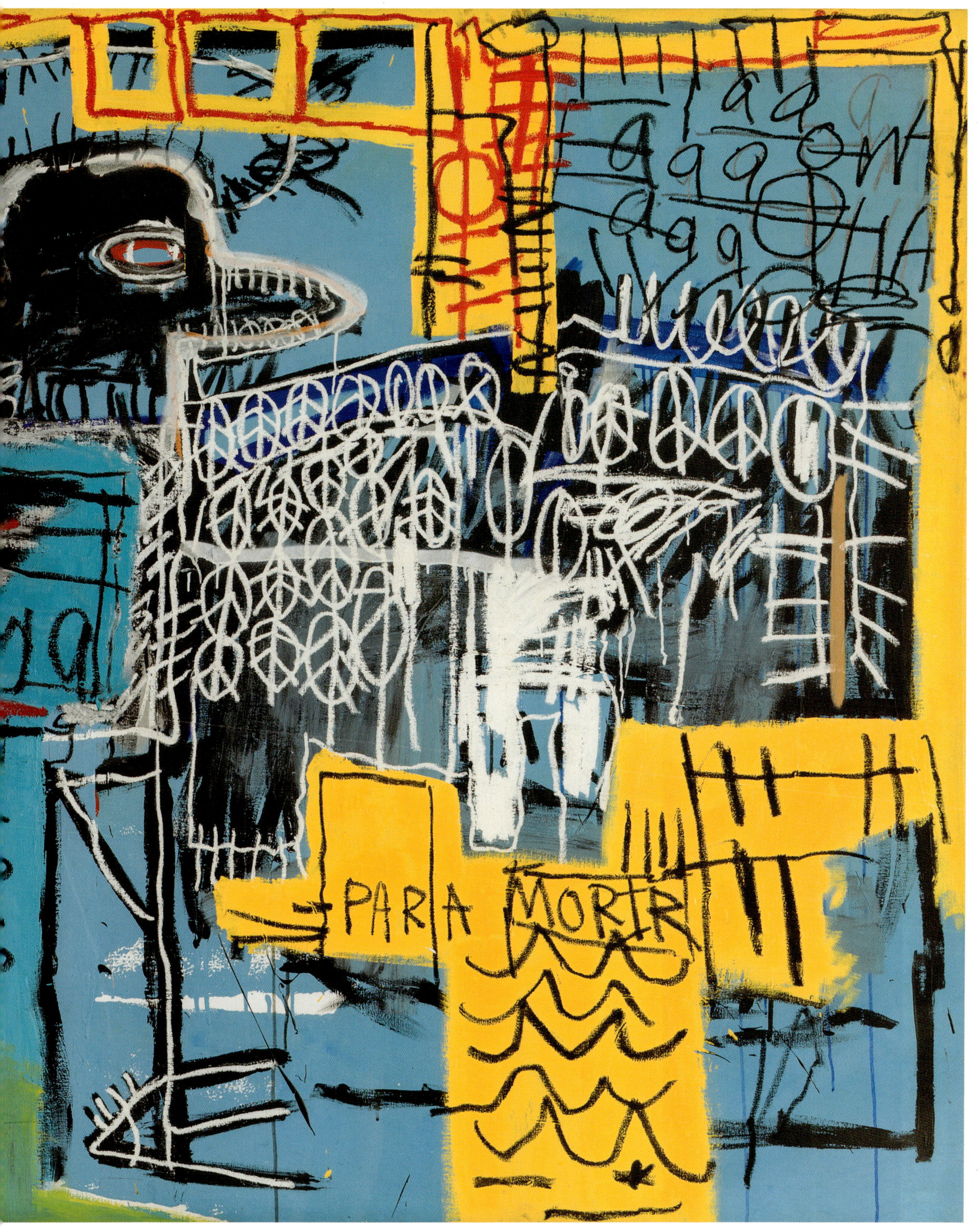
PARA MORIR

JEAN-MICHEL BASQUIAT

One Million Yen, 1982, oil on canvas with wood and jute, 60 x 58 x 3 3/4 in. (152.4 x 147.3 x 9.5 cm), acquired in 1982

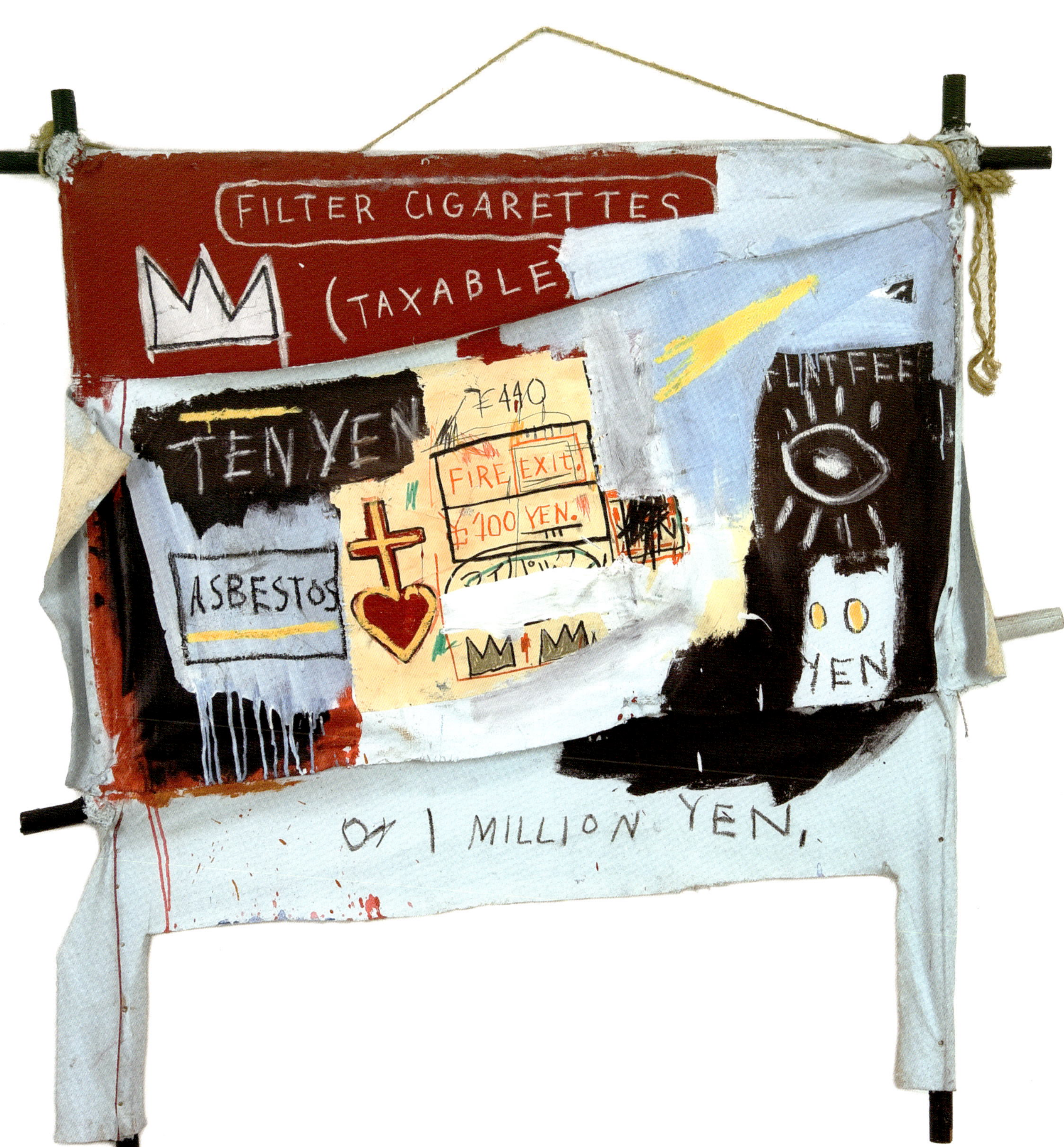

FILTER CIGARETTES
(TAXABLE)
TEN YEN
ASBESTOS
¥440
FIRE EXIT.
100 YEN.
YEN
1 MILLION YEN,

JEAN-MICHEL BASQUIAT

Untitled (Self-portrait), 1982-1983, oil on wood, 20 x 20 in. (50.8 x 50.8 cm), acquired in 1983

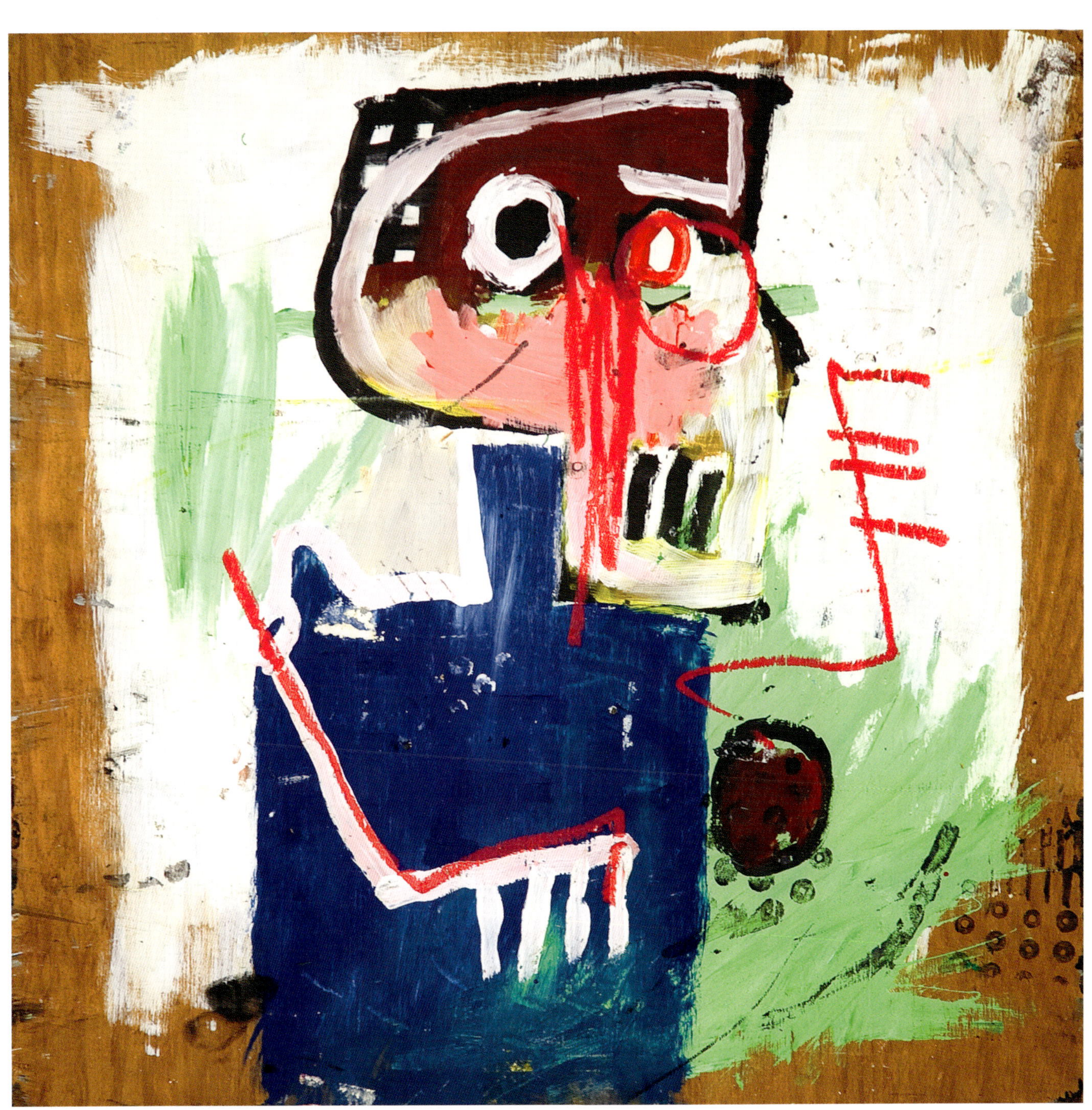

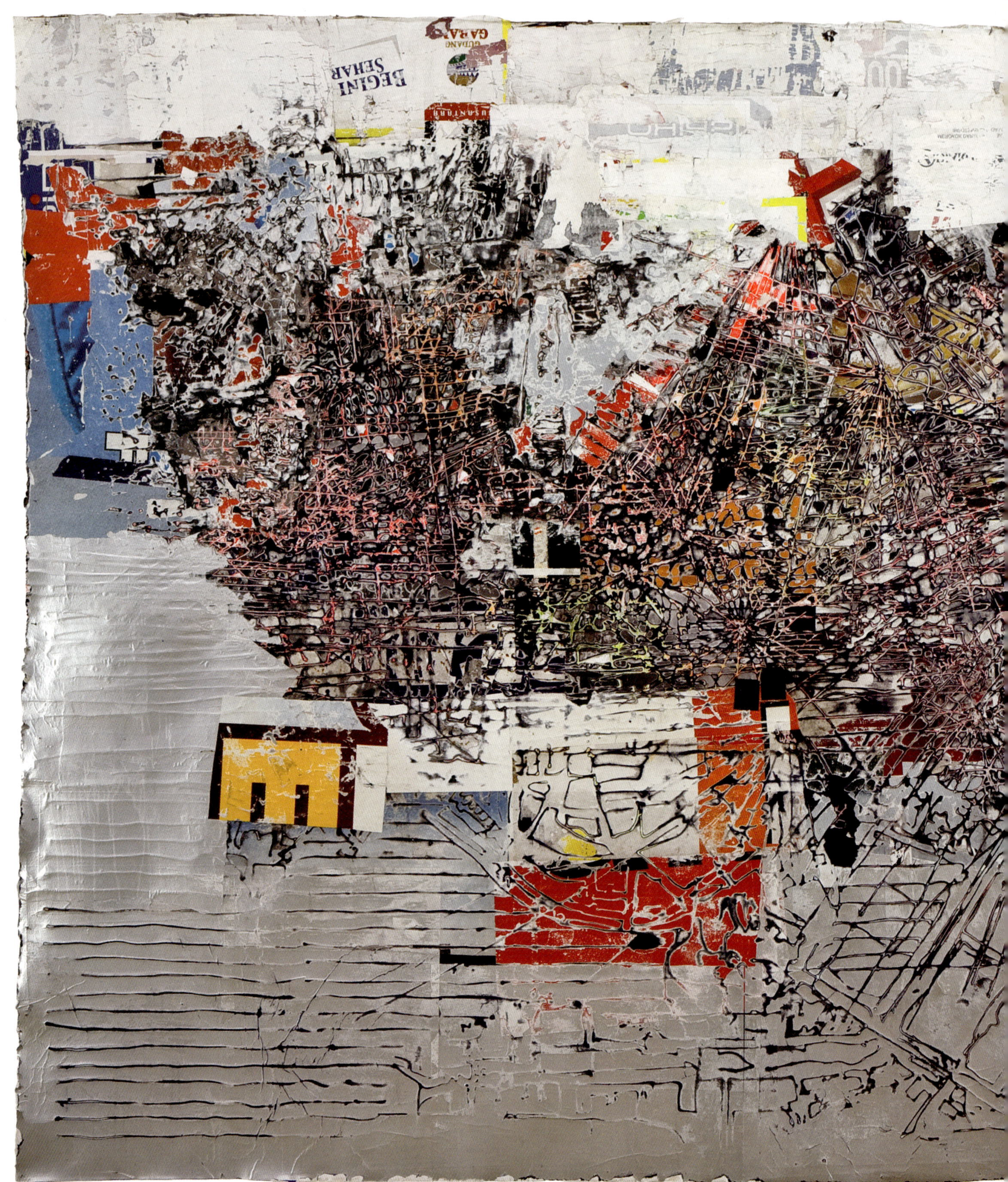

MARK BRADFORD *Whore in the Church House*, 2006, mixed media collage on canvas, 103 x 142 in. (261.6 x 360.7 cm), acquired in 2006

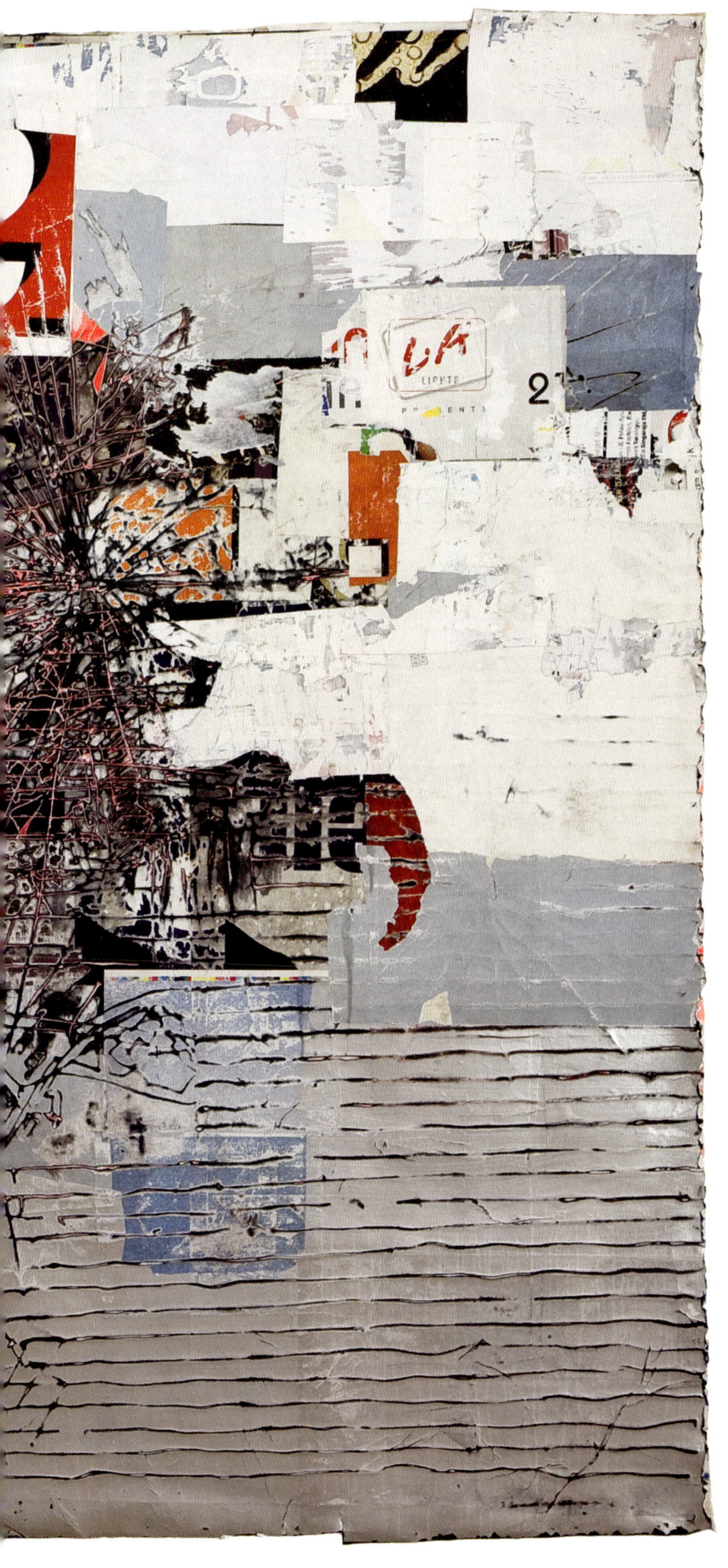

This painting is about the feelings I was having regarding my work within the larger context of painting and history. It felt like everything I was doing was kind of impure, and I had this desire to engage with painting; not collage, not found material, but with the history of paint. Since the early days of my art school education, I have wondered why the very first gesture, the material—paint—is never questioned nor critiqued. That interested me—why paint itself is so highly fetishized and discussions focus solely on the imagery within a painting. The fact that paint itself is never questioned is just another way of reinforcing hierarchic relationships. The way those relationships are constructed is connected to power. So I wanted to explore this problem. The materials I have always used were so impure, and using them felt at first like I was a whore in the holy church of modernism.

Mark Bradford

The works in the Rubell Collection are from my series of *Soundsuits*. This sculptural form is based on the scale of my body. It creates a camouflage, masking and forming a second skin that conceals race, gender, and class, forcing one to look without judgment. Three of the works in the Collection are in the shape of what I call an "A-frame." This form has many connotations that reference power, such as a bishop's mitre, a Ku Klux Klan uniform, a condom, or the head of a missile. As for the surfaces themselves, I treat them like collages, applying patterns that build on the surface. The piece that is made out of synthetic hair strips this down, using one material instead of many to create a visceral sensibility. The fourth piece, with the armature made of flowers, takes the baroque ornamental sensibility of the A-frame surfaces and brings it into an expanded dimensionality.

Nick Cave

 Soundsuit, 2008, fabric, fiberglass and metal, 102 x 36 x 28 in. (259 x 91.5 x 71 cm), acquired in 2008

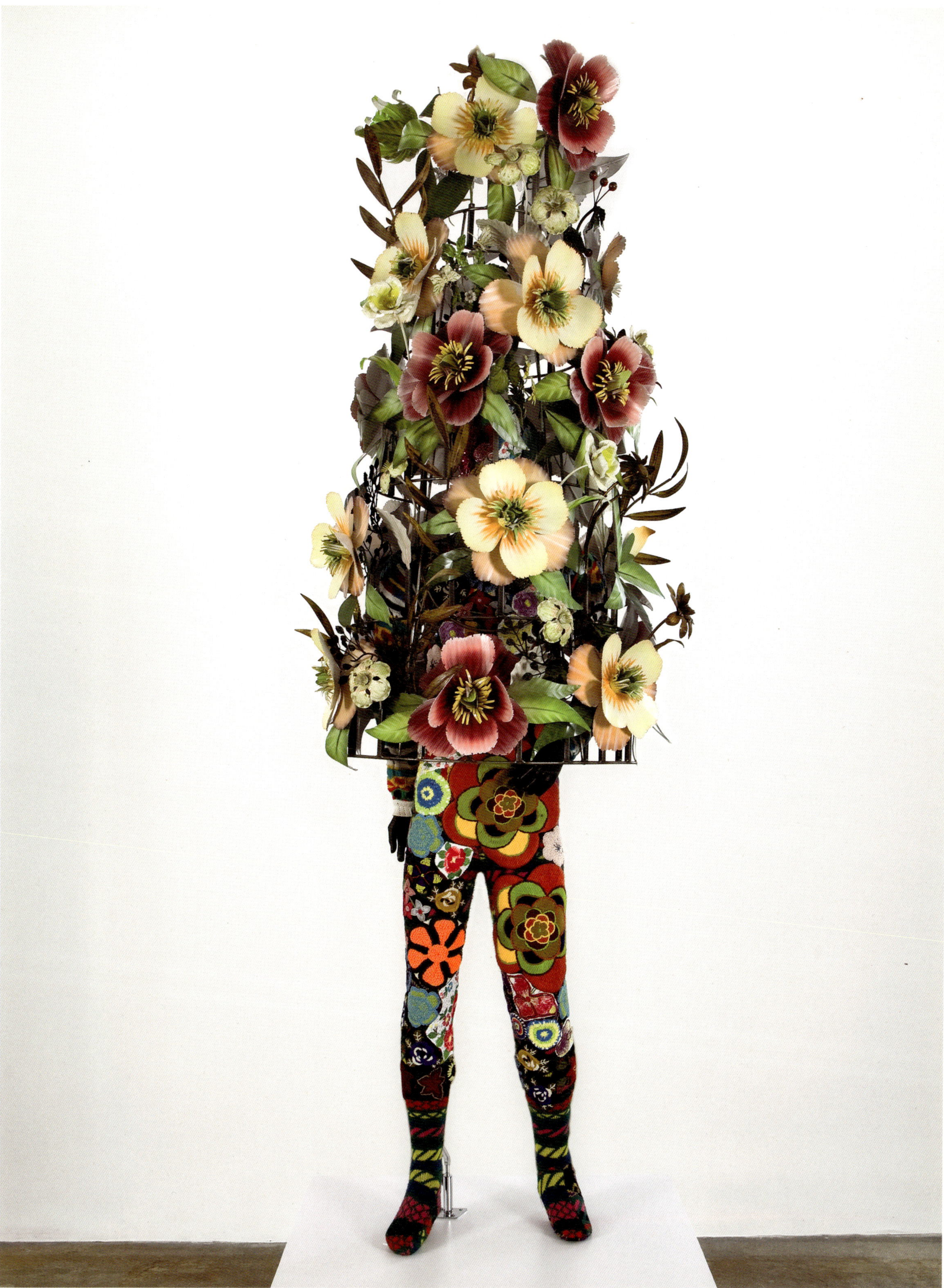

NICK CAVE

Soundsuit, 2008, synthetic hair, fiberglass and metal, 98 x 27 x 14 in. (248.9 x 68.6 x 35.6 cm), acquired in 2008

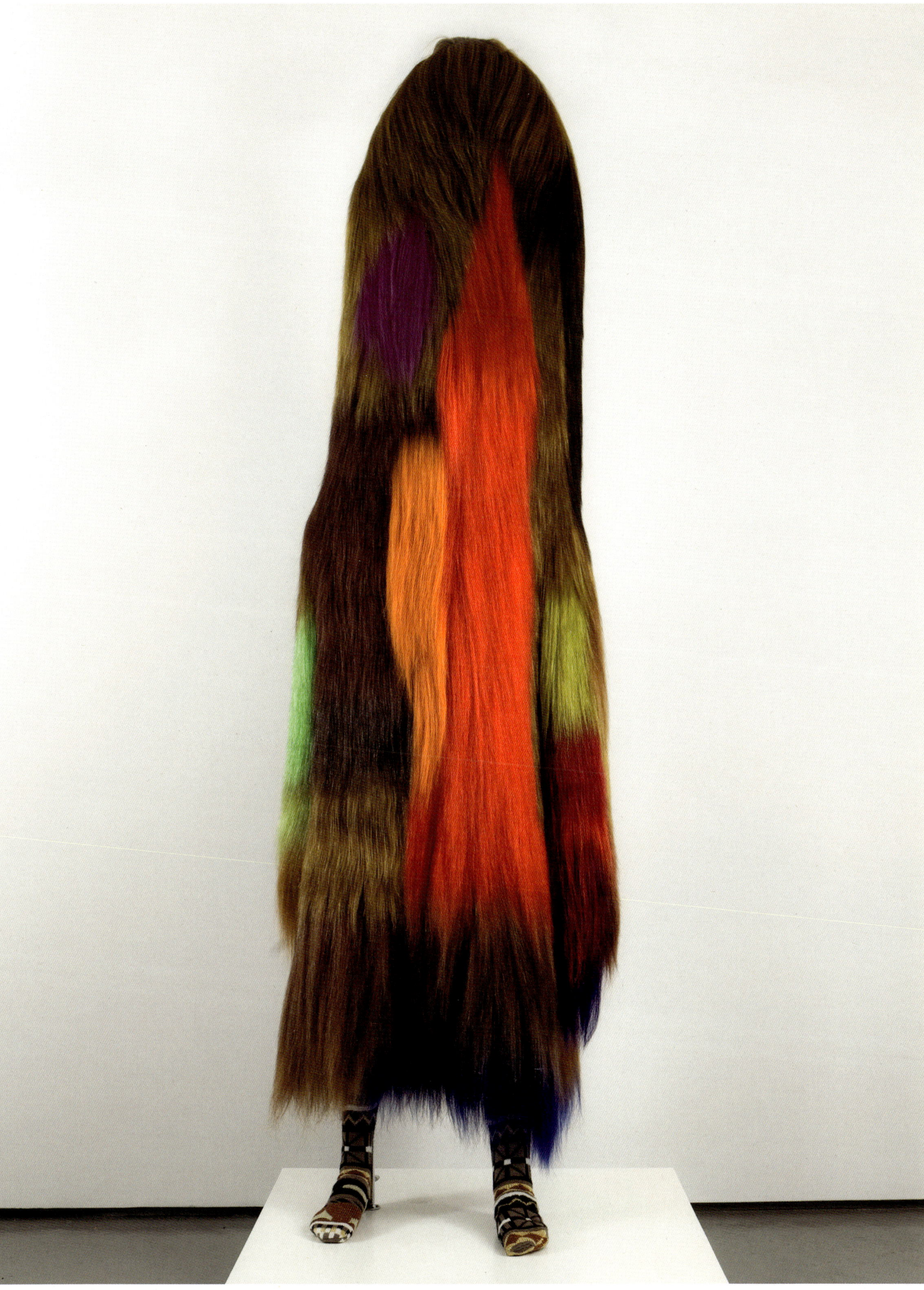

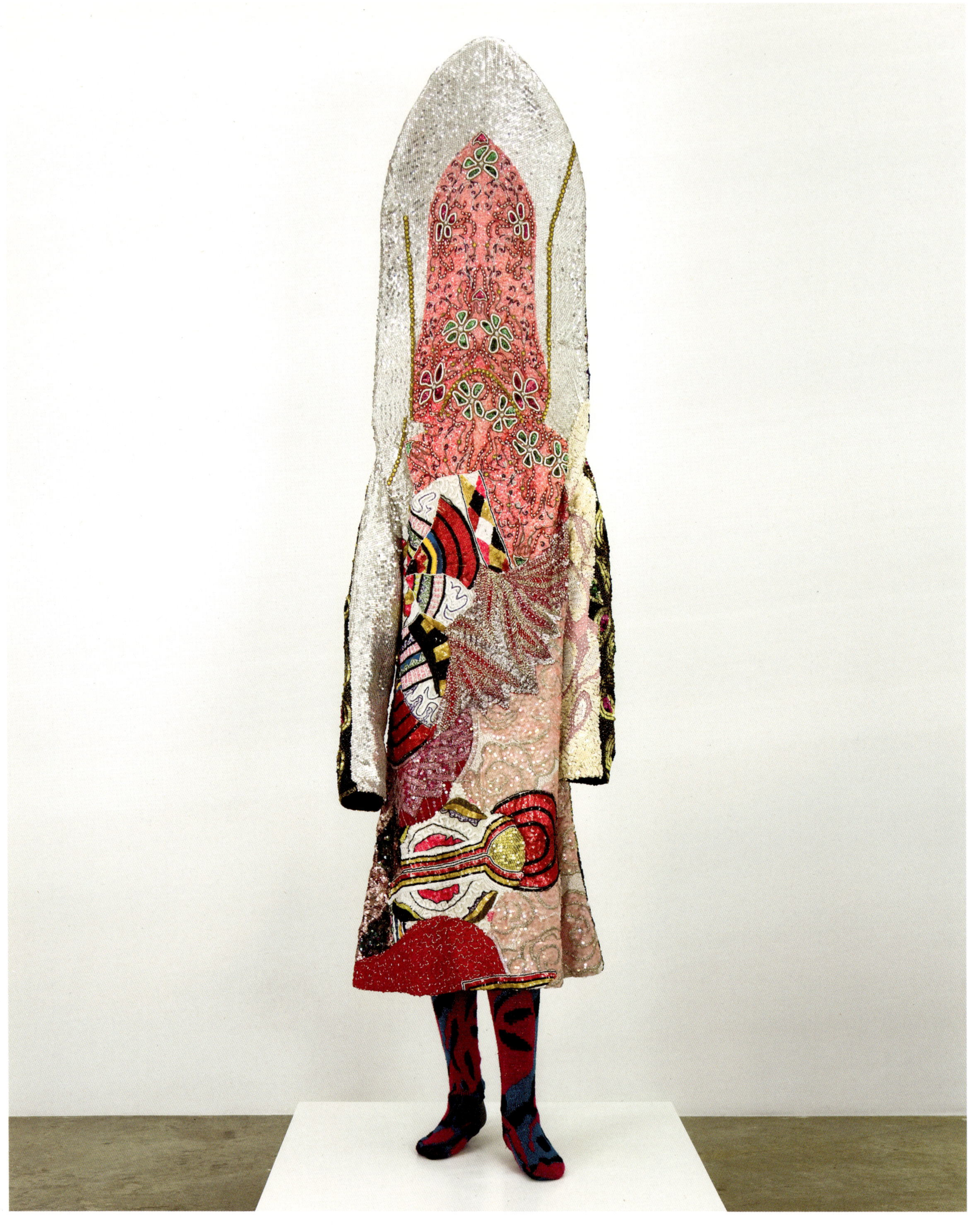

 NICK CAVE *Soundsuit*, 2008, fabric, sequins, fiberglass and metal, 100 x 25 x 14 in. (254 x 63.5 x 35.6 cm), acquired in 2008

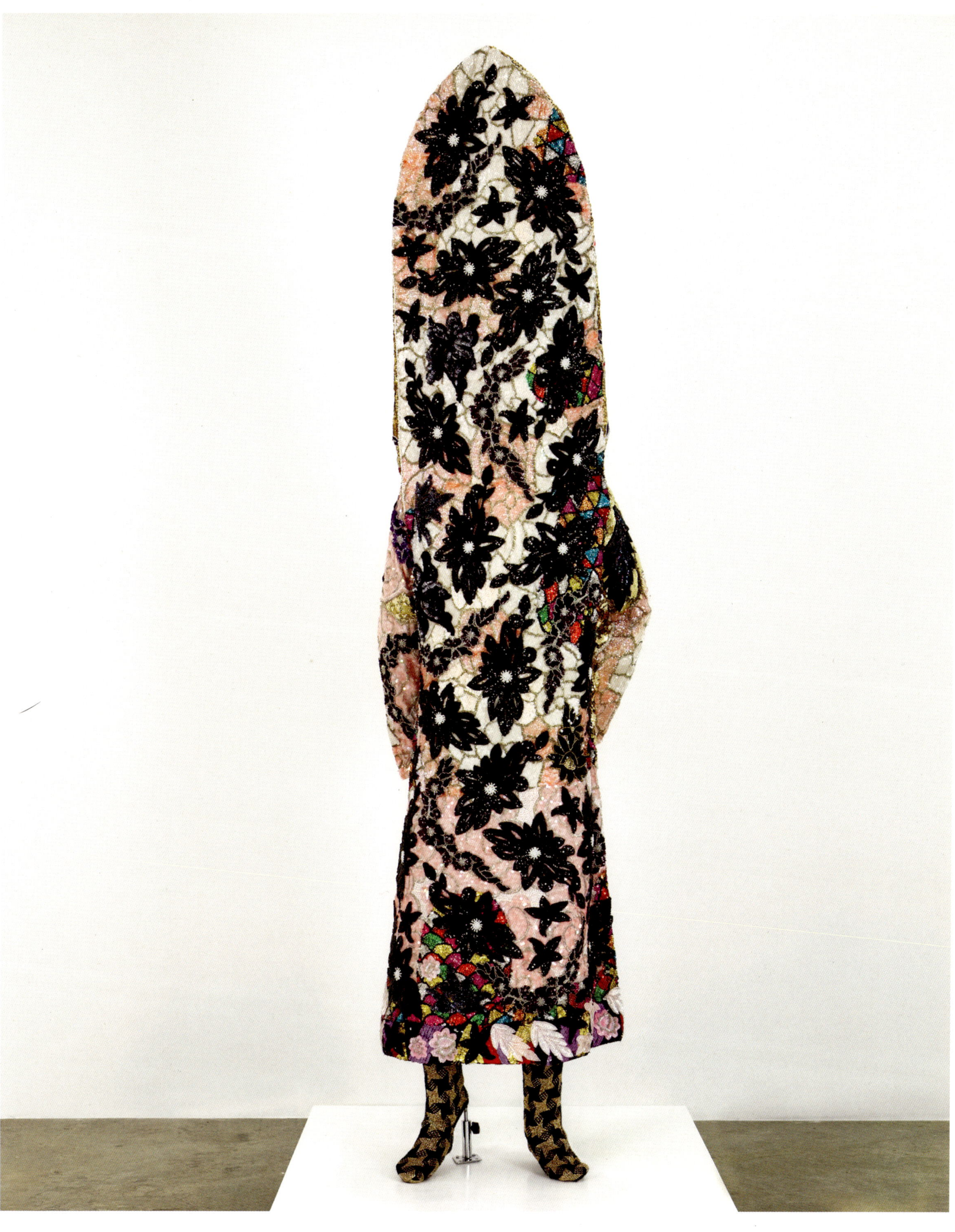

Soundsuit, 2006, fabric, sequins, fiberglass and metal, 100 x 26 x 13 in. (254 x 66 x 33 cm), acquired in 2006

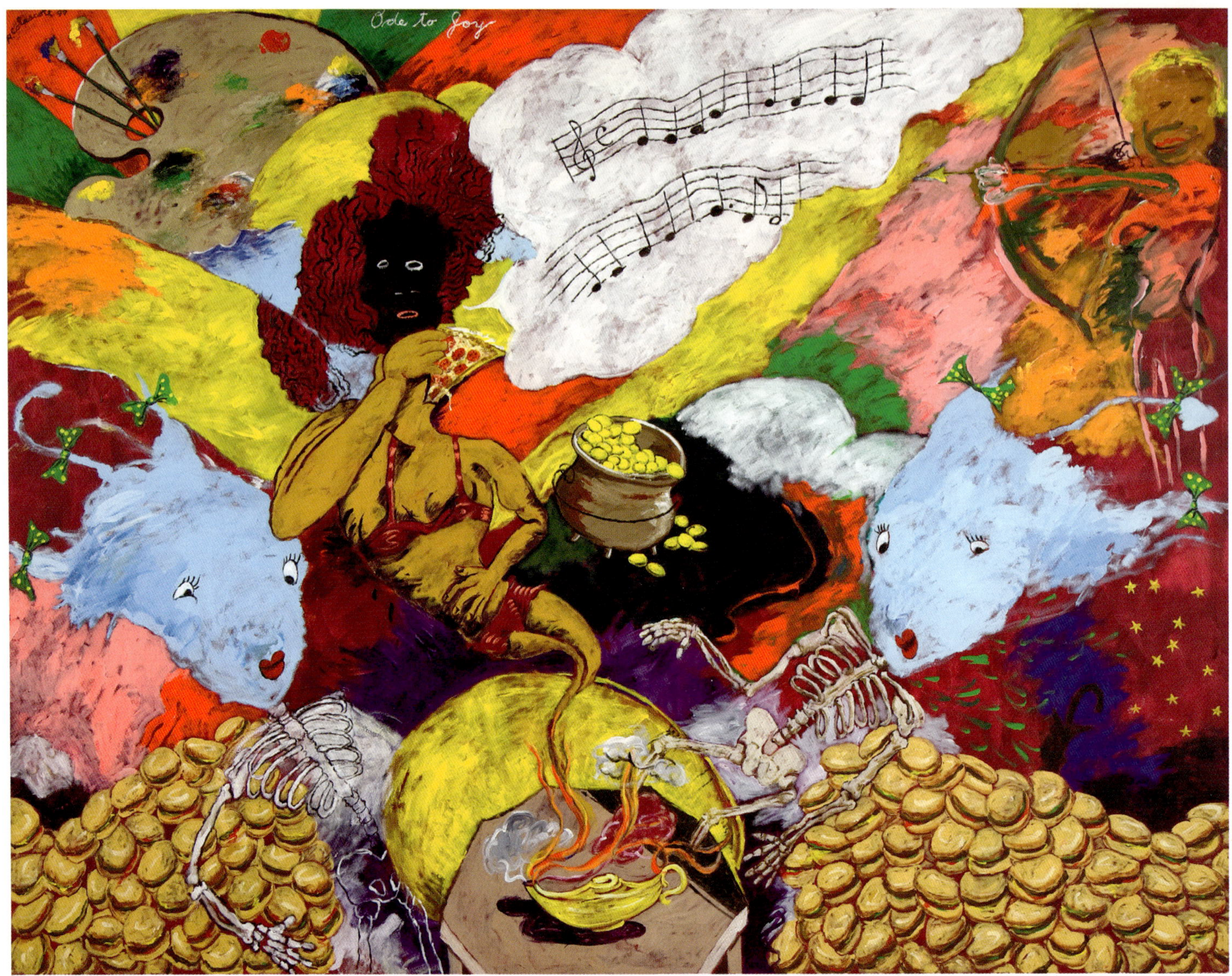

If there's one thing that black folks have it's a sense of humor. The lyrics in blues songs are often pretty rowdy, you know, and present a rather base expression of black arts. The guy that's supposed to be doing the old man on the mule, see. It's really funny. If you want to get acceptance within the community, just paint a couple of old men on mules, you know, or an old man on a mule and an old lady walking around. Some people will only be satisfied with that. And then some kind of heroic image which is very far from the truth. The heroic image where this guy looks like a . . . looks white with a sun tan, see . Any sense of exaggeration could be questioned. What I want to say about all this is sure, I've seen all that. And I've heard it all. But at the same time, right from the very beginning when I first started showing some of these works—a response to stereotyping—I had plenty of encouragement. And I was surprised at the vigor of the responses. And it just didn't break down on racial lines. There were white people who were offended because they felt guilty because their people had created these images. And so there were white people that felt threatened by these paintings, which monumentalized these perceptions.

We've already come to understand that it's about white perceptions of black people. And they may not be pretty. And they may be stupid. We didn't make up these images. So why should we take the heat? But it's satire. It's the satire that kills the serpent, you know?

Robert Colescott

 Ode to Joy (European Anthem), 1997, acrylic on canvas, 90 x 114 in. (228.6 x 289.5 cm), acquired in 2006

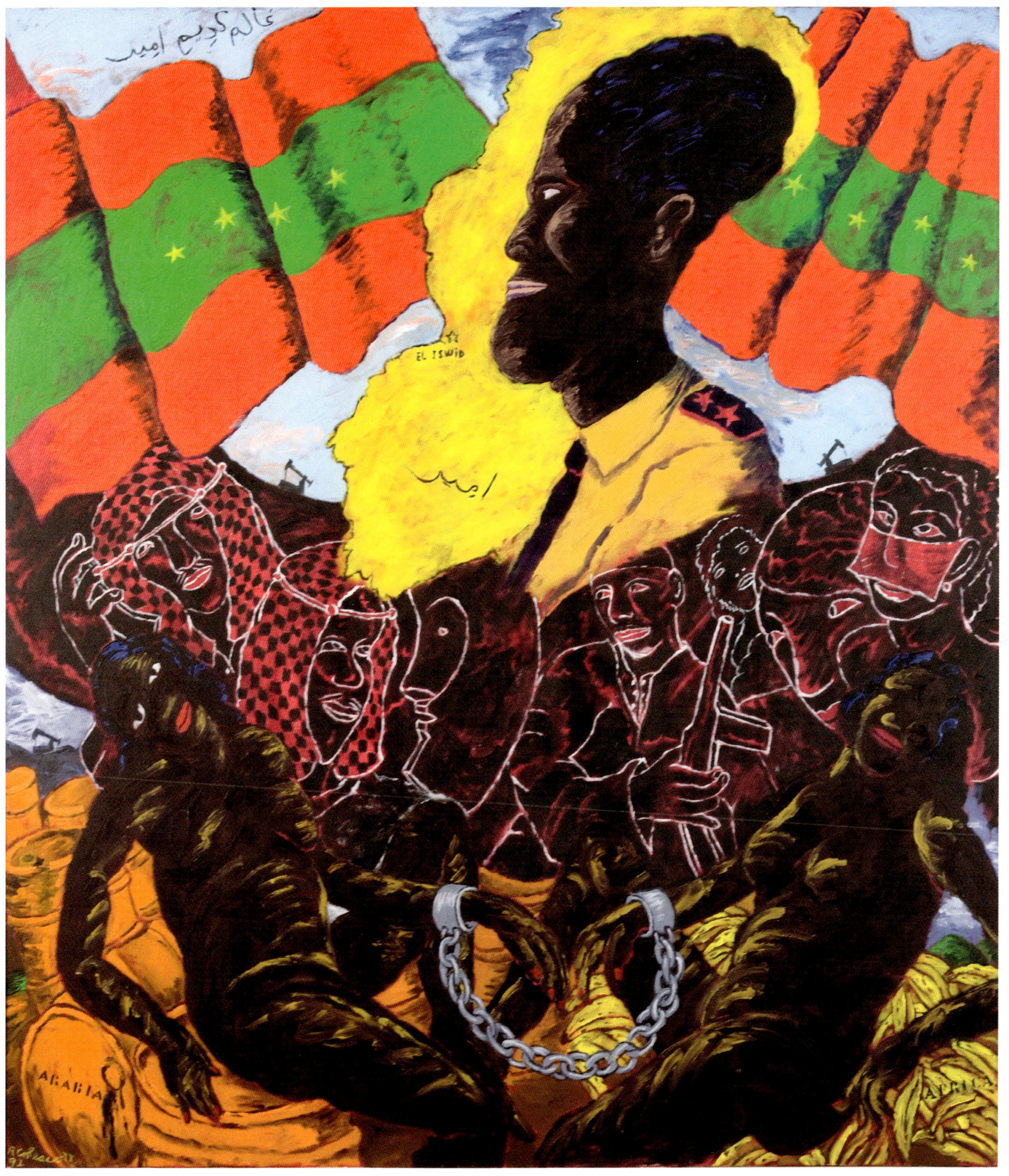

Arabs: The Emir of Iswid (How Wide the Gulf?), 1992, acrylic on canvas, 84 x 72 in. (213.4 x 182.9 cm), acquired in 2006

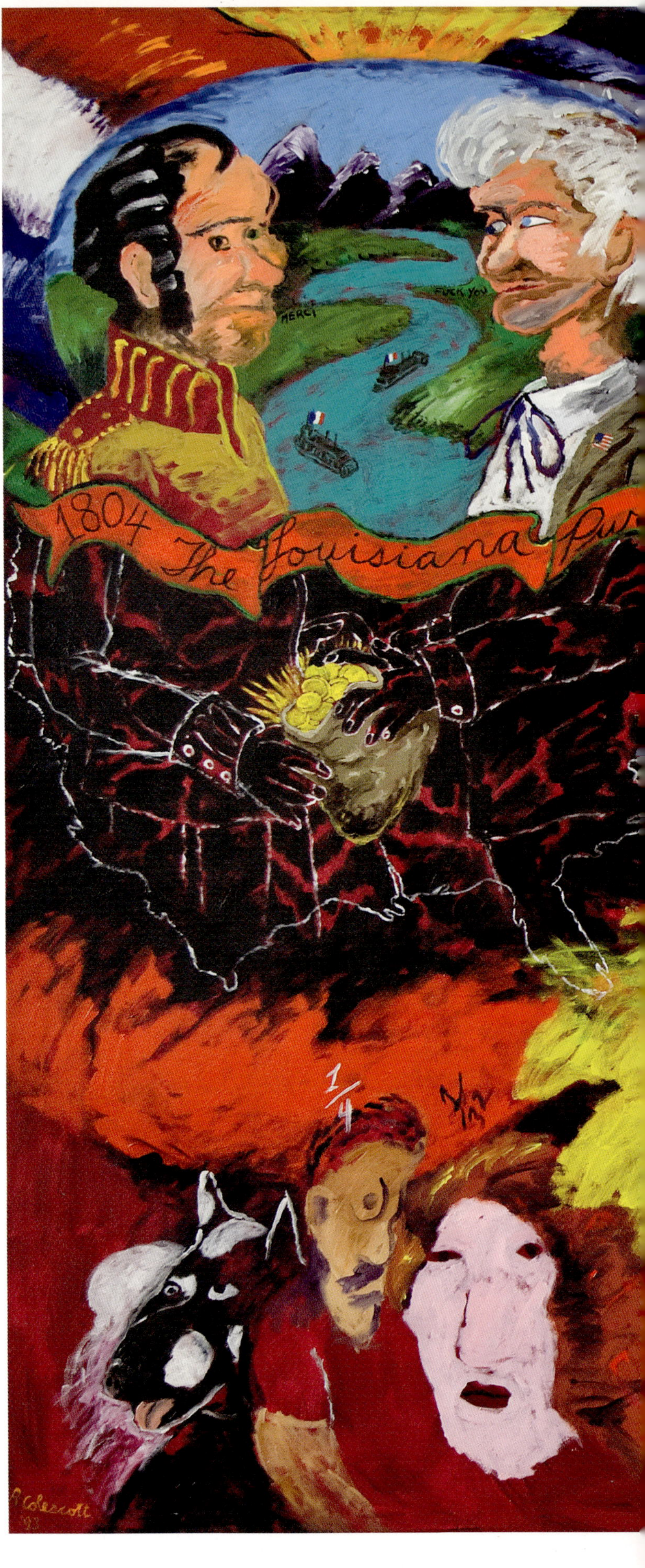

ROBERT COLESCOTT *Sunset on the Bayou,* 1993, acrylic on canvas, 90 x 114 in. (228.6 x 289.5 cm), acquired in 2006

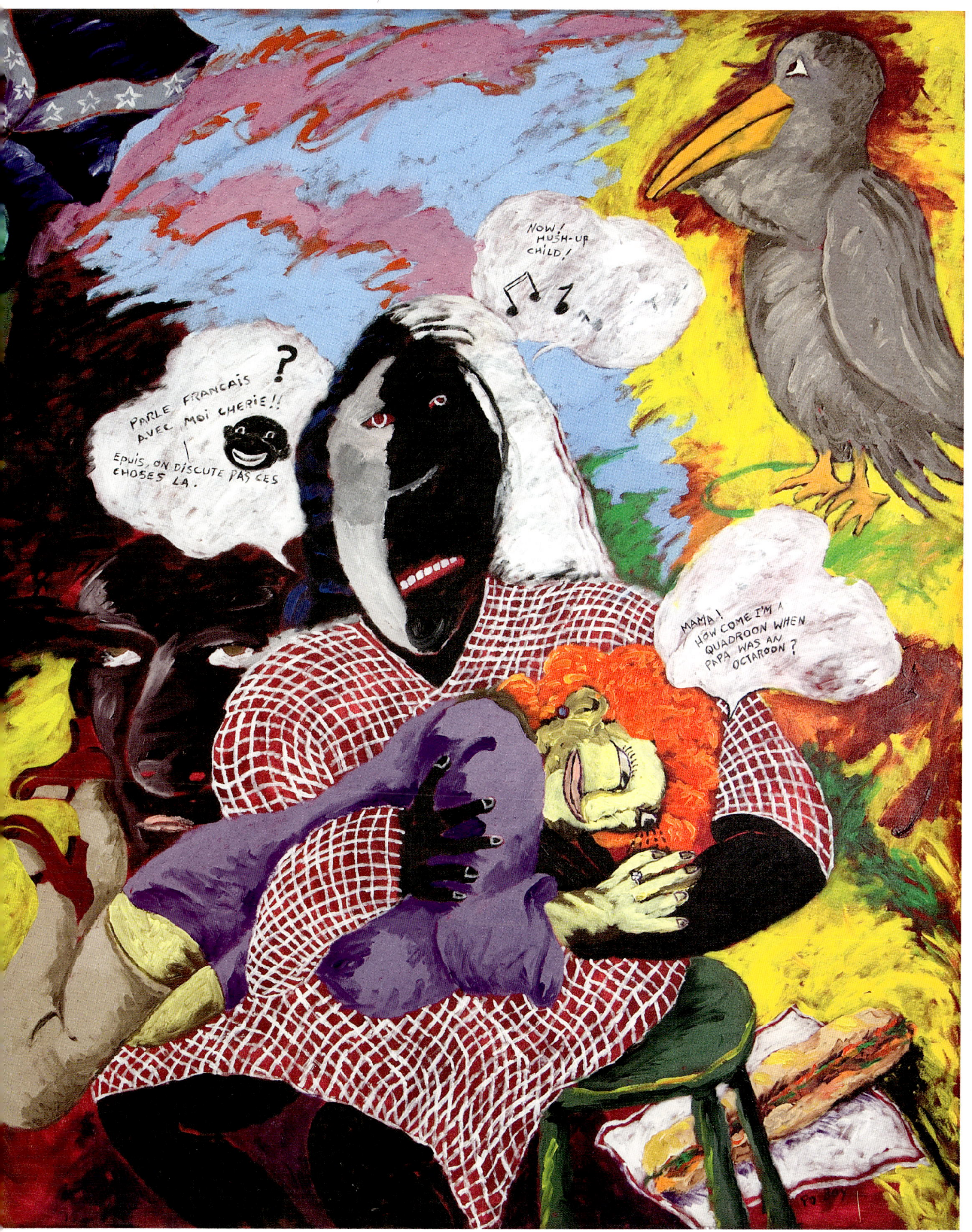
NOW! HUSH-UP CHILD!
PARLE FRANCAIS AVEC MOI CHERIE!!
EPUIS, ON DISCUTE PAS CES CHOSES LA.
MAMA! HOW COME I'M A QUADROON WHEN PAPA WAS AN OCTAROON?

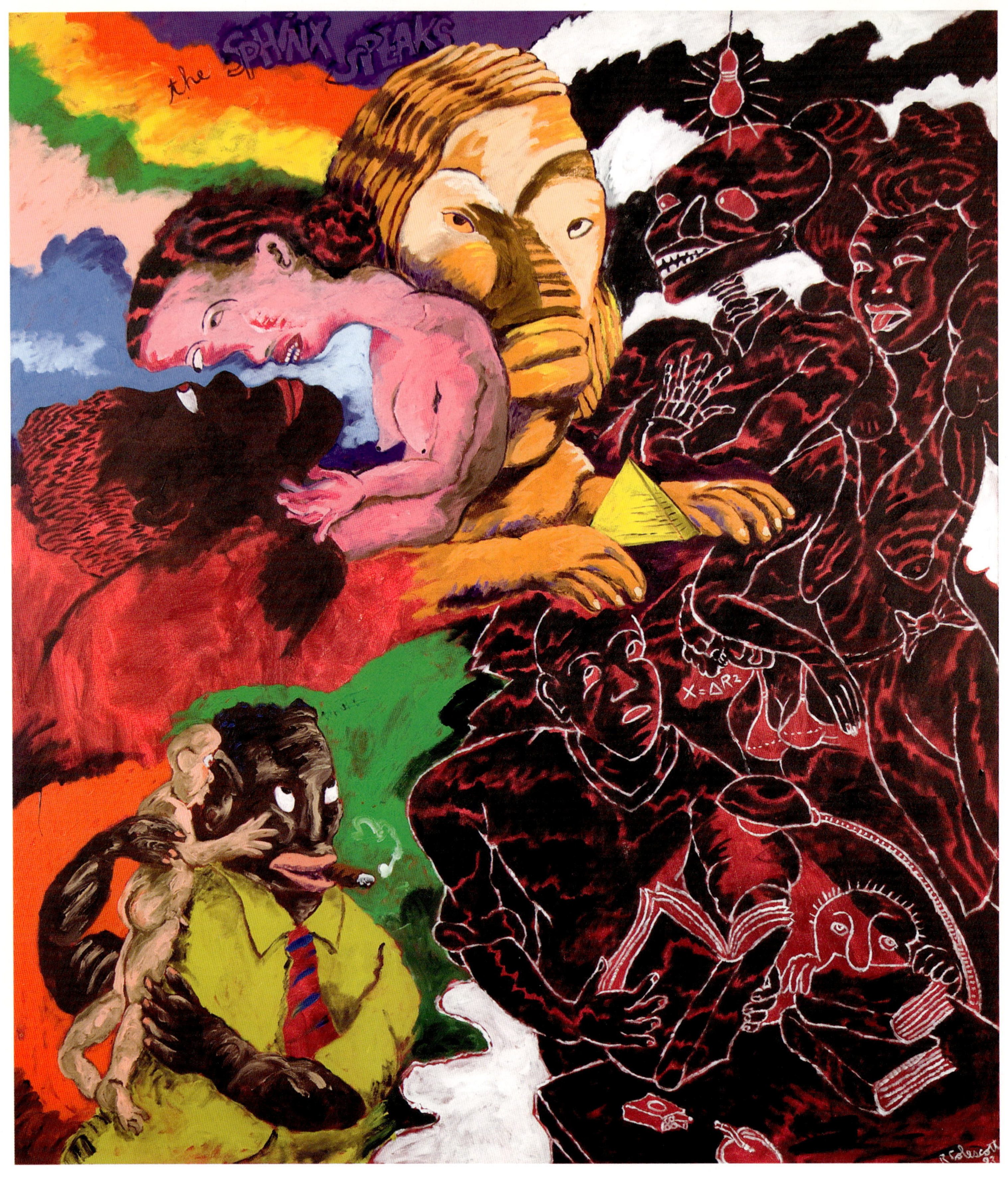

 ROBERT COLESCOTT *The Sphinx Speaks*, 1993, acrylic on canvas, 84 x 72 in. (213.4 x 182.9 cm), acquired in 2006

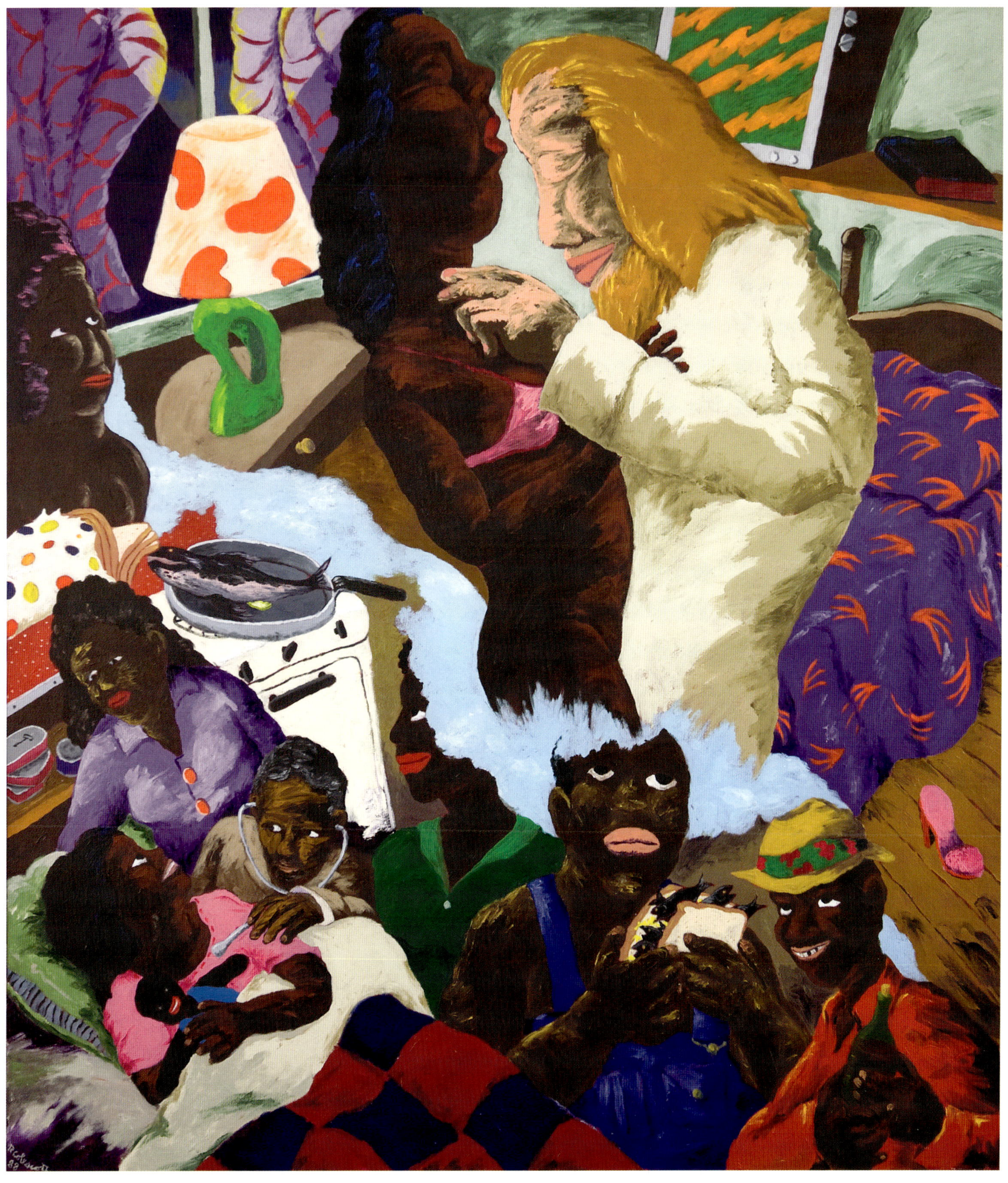

Modern Day Miracles, 1988, acrylic on canvas, 84 x 72 in. (213.4 x 182.9 cm), acquired in 2004

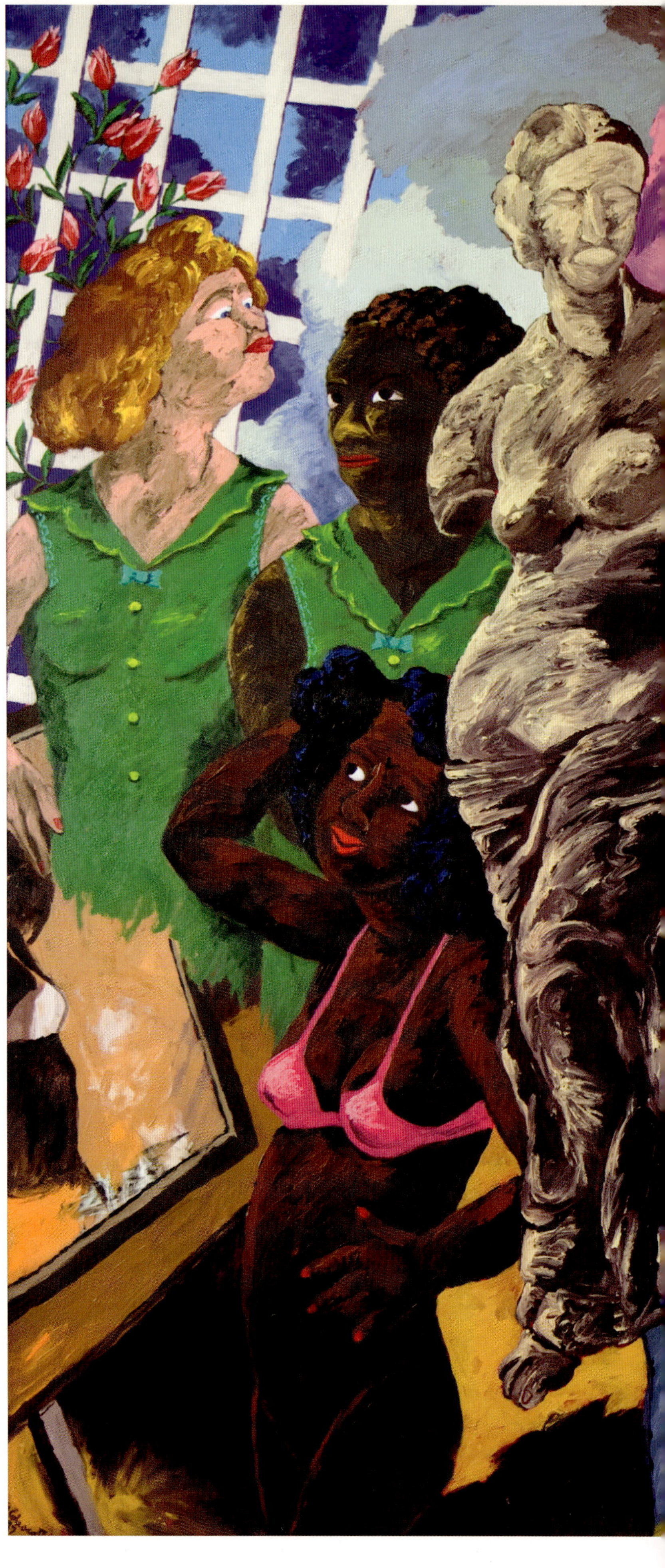

 Pygmalion, 1987, acrylic on canvas, 90 x 114 in. (228.6 x 289.6 cm.), acquired in 2006

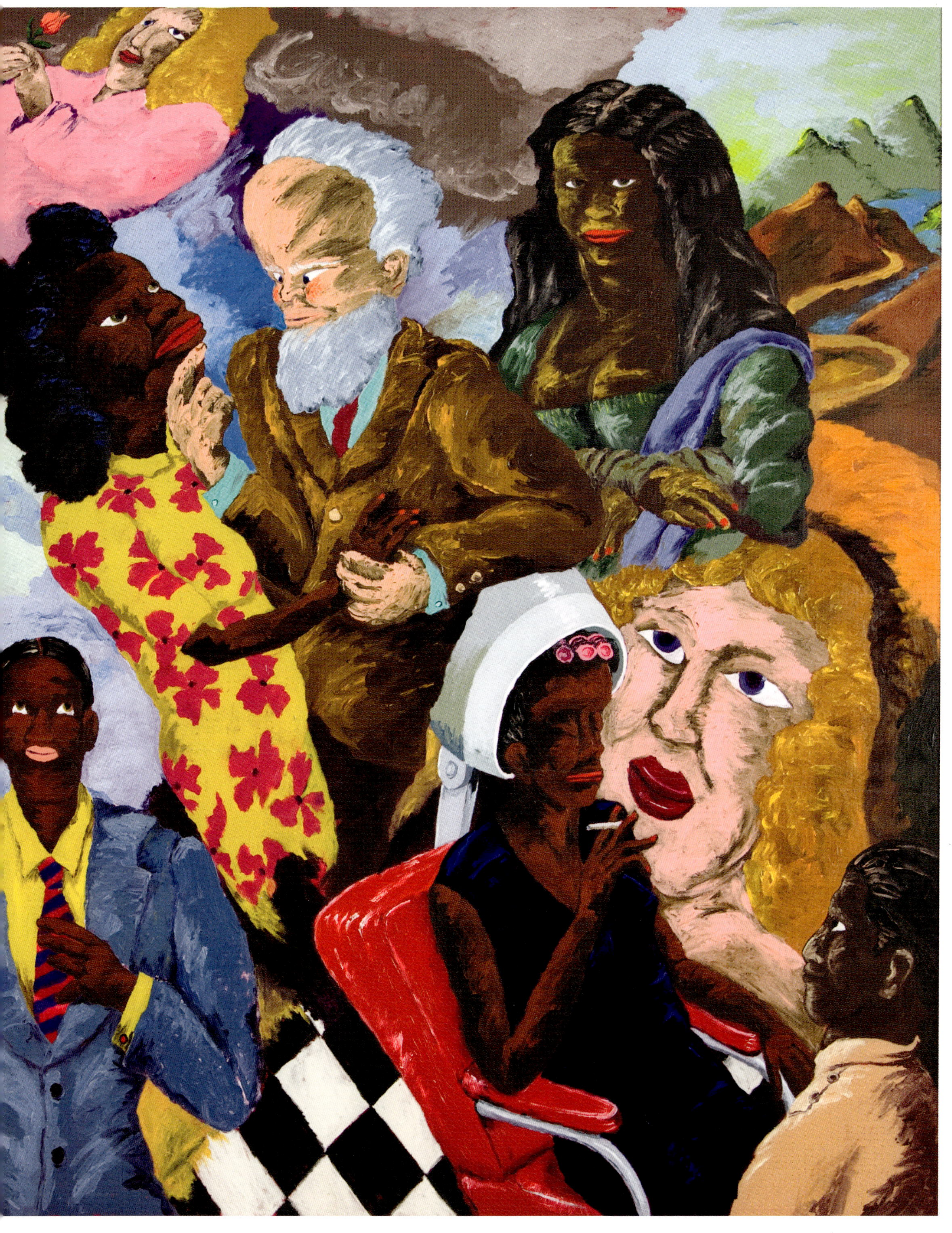

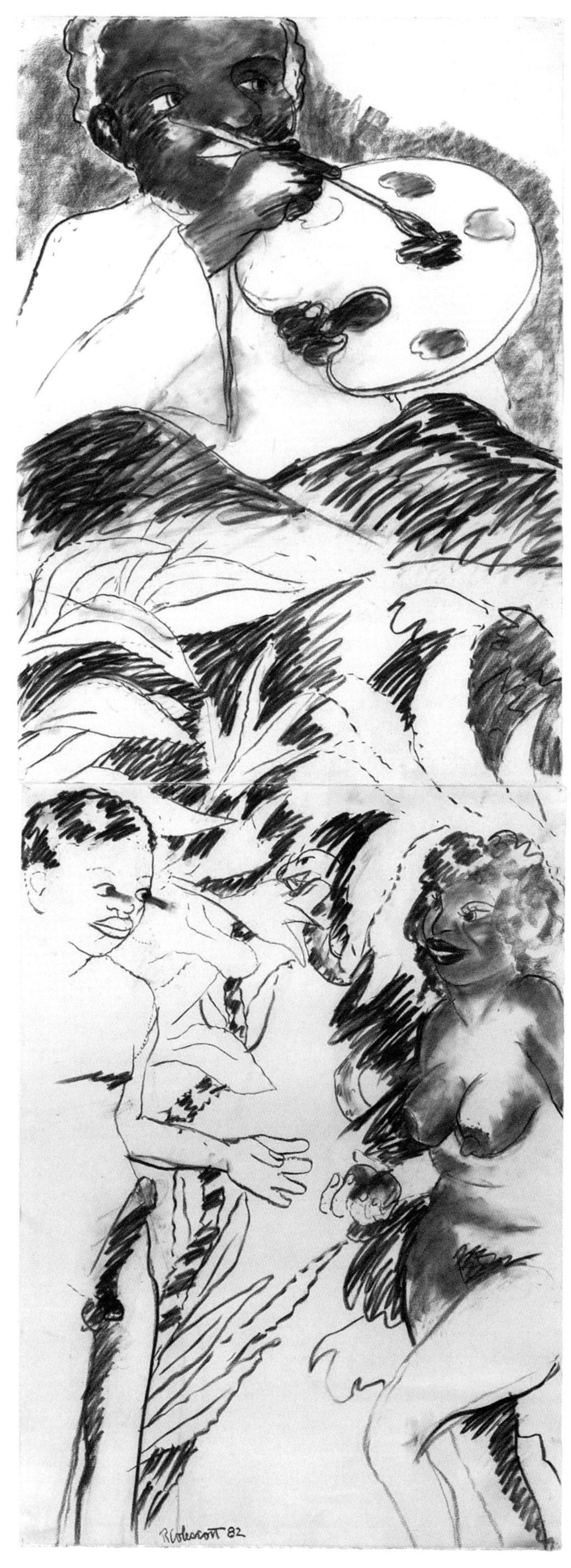

 ROBERT COLESCOTT *Untitled (Adam and Eve)*, 1982, charcoal on paper, 83 1/2 x 29 1/2 in. (212 x 75 cm), acquired in 2006

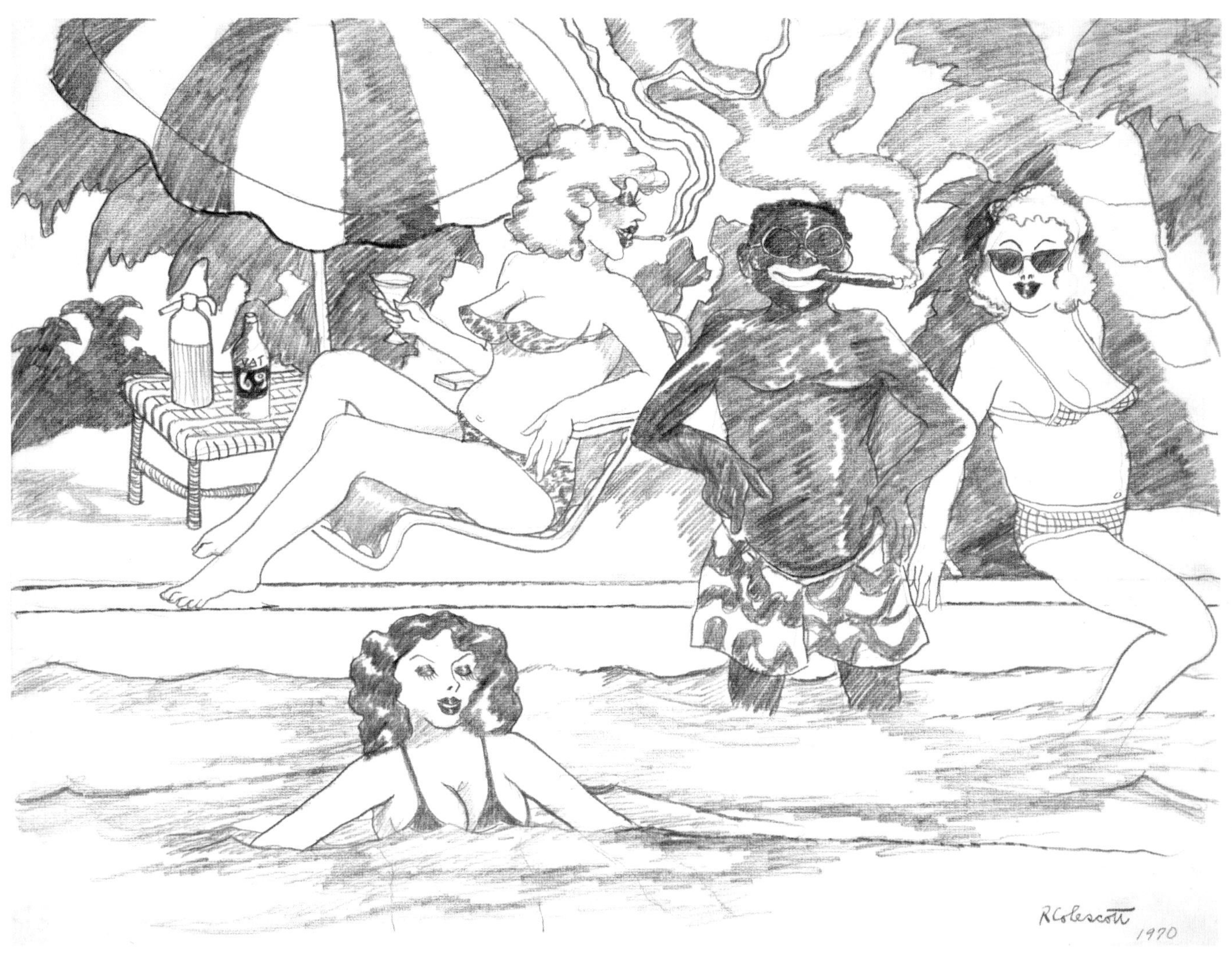

Untitled, 1970, graphite on paper, 19 3/4 x 26 in. (50.2 x 66 cm), acquired in 2006

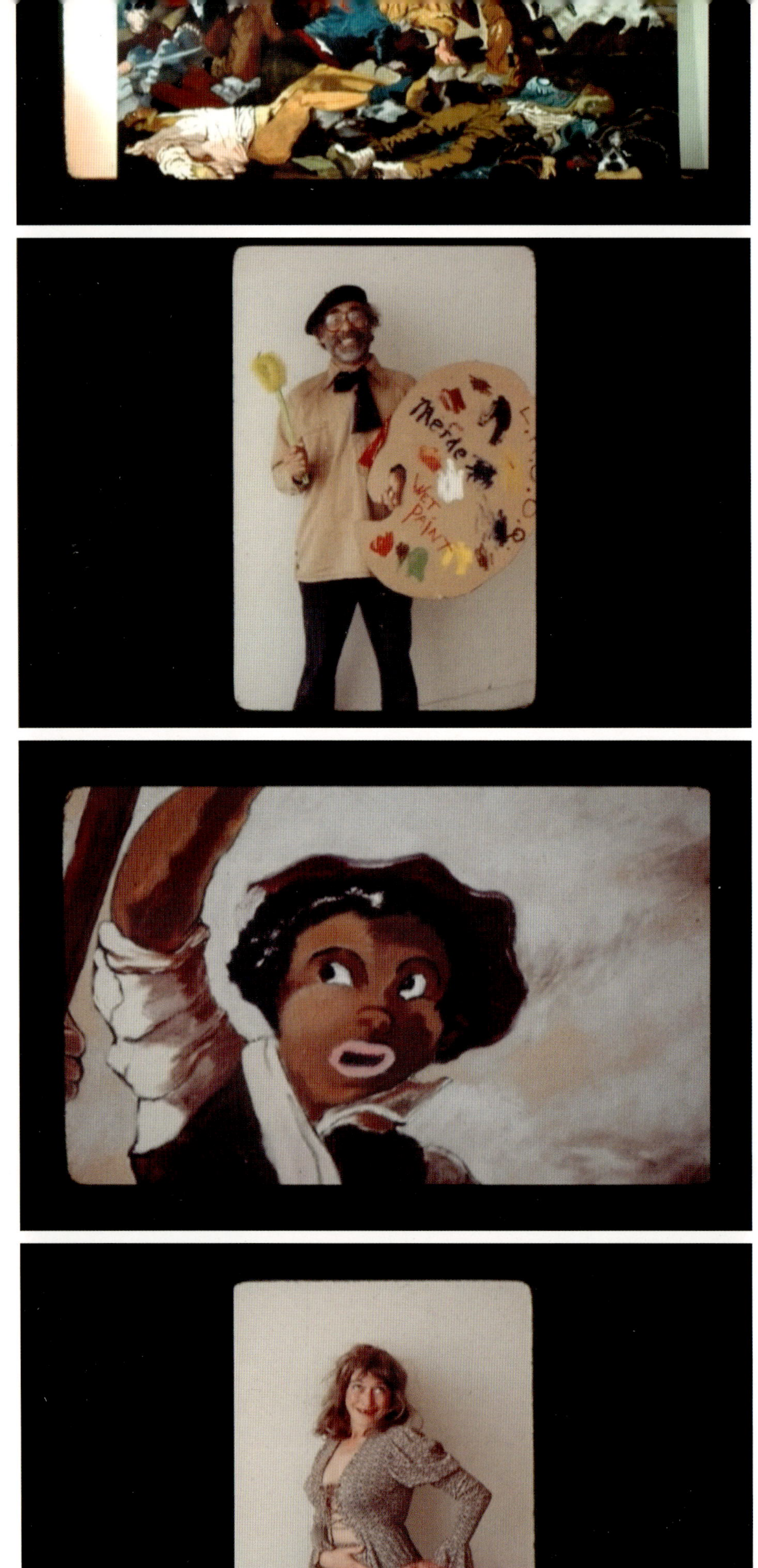

Stills of *Dulacrow's Masterwork: A Mockumentary Film*, 1976, digital video (color, sound), 43 min. 50 sec., ed. 1/10, acquired in 2008

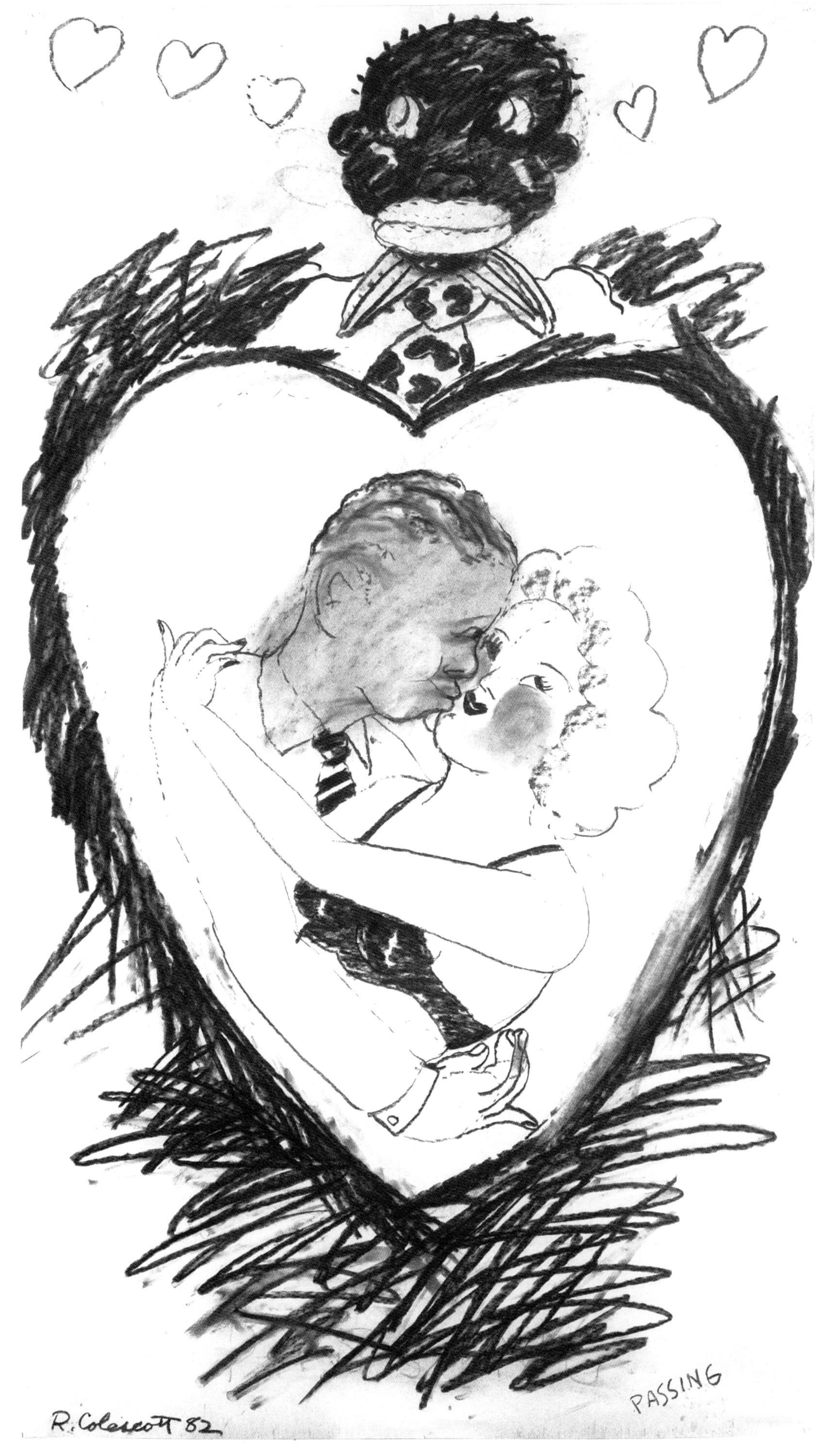

Passing, 1982, charcoal on paper, 60 x 33 in. (152.4 x 83.8 cm), acquired in 2007

The book at hand represents a selection, a small selection of a much larger collection of paintings, sculpture, drawings, and videos in the Rubell Family Collection. Yet, it is a very important selection, presented at this time to represent a body of work of diverse minds that happen to share some cultural traits and thus have some things in common. Their work speaks to each other's artistic output as much as to larger issues in the history of contemporary art.

Yet, to ponder the work in this show as a point of departure for an essay about the art of thirty-one disparate and diverse artists is to consider a proverbial catch-22. On one hand, I can fall in behind the fact that this exhibition's title makes only a small defining note in regard to the art assembled. There is the telling fact that these artists are all considered to be Americans. But, there is no description of the art, no subheading that conveniently gives one a little more to go on. Thus, the title for this essay remains under careful consideration. And, thus, I could not have possibly begun to write with a quote from one of the three thinkers that are so central to this discussion, as that would have been a dead giveaway. (As if it weren't already, by the book in your hand.) Yet, we have to consider, can such a show be useful?

Considering that Thelma Golden's 2001 exhibition "Freestyle"—one of the inspirations for this exhibition—posited the fact that a show of black artists could in fact be post-black in subject matter, this presentation also questions the term and wantonly throws it into flux. The art at hand is wildly different in materials and themes, though it does offer hints to an assembled collection of a cultural consciousness.

Yet it also begs the question, recently posed by the art historian Darby English, "What becomes of black art when black artists stop making it? Without being much remarked as yet, the category's instability now defines it far more clearly than do its supposed contents, as 'black art' has come to have less and less descriptive bearing (which is not to say influence) on the work many black artists actually produce."[1] Thus, it is a fitting title.

1. Darby English, "Beyond Black Representational Space," in *How to See a Work of Art in Total Darkness* (Cambridge and London: The MIT Press, 2007), 27.

Four years after "Freestyle," the curator questioned her own motives, in the catalog essay for the exhibition "Frequency," where she said, "After the tremendous success of 'Freestyle' in 2001, I had both privately and publicly acknowledged that there might no longer be a need for me to organize group shows featuring the works of emerging black artists."

More recently, Hamza Walker, who wrote the signature essay in the "Freestyle" catalog, has said, "Given that an exhibition of all African-American artists no longer passes for one about race, the discourse of race, as it resides in the visual arts in the broadest sense, is a very diffuse affair. Race is no less mercurial and complex as an organizing principle for an exhibition than it is a tricky issue in general."[2]

2. Hamza Walker, "Domino Effect," from the exhibition catalog, *Black Is, Black Ain't* (Chicago: The Renaissance Society, 2008).

Thus, why call attention to it, with a subordinate clause on the end of a title?

Yet, as is suggested in a recent essay by Kobena Mercer, the work in this exhibition also treads upon some contentious ground (as should any collection presentation worth its salt) while delineating between what he sees as a shift in the narrative of African-American art from late modernism to post-modernism. Grouping together the artists Betye Saar, Robert Colescott and David Hammons, he identifies what he considers to be a black avant-garde in the late 1960s and

1970s, which included the three very different artists. Whereas black artists were called upon and many engaged in a practice that was consciously about race before Abstract Expressionism, abstraction freed many artists to pursue an art, at least a little bit more, in the mode of art for art's sake. Mercer's position of a later shift also takes into account a time when all artists were reconsidering the work of art as a conceptual and often political tool. "Black artists opened up a wider range of questions about 'race' and representation as a result of the crisis of modernism that came to a head during this period."[3]

3. Kobena Mercer, "Tropes of the Grotesque in the Black Avant-Garde," in *Pop Art and Vernacular Cultures*, ed. Mercer (Cambridge: The MIT Press; London: Iniva, 2007), 138.

This collection and this show are clearly on the other side of both shifts. Representation is more the mode of thought than abstraction. And, there is no more a crisis between modernism and post-modernism. Sources are multivalent and the vernacular is coded enough to remain in the realm of contemporary art, as we know it. We are dealing with the here and now, and no need to be restrained by the vagaries of modernism versus post-modernism as constricting categories. Jacob Lawrence and Romare Bearden still don't sell. And, don't even think about a woman.

Cluttered by theories, let us turn to thoughts of utility. Sometimes lists tell stories, narratives even. Lists can contain just enough information. Lists of facts provide background. Artists' lists, when given as the primary information concerning an exhibition of contemporary art, provide the most basic information. And, if you add a few more things, other than a name, sometimes, the list is all you need to see the connections between the artists and to understand the thematic of the show.

Because of the many fascinating exhibitions that have played a pivotal role in the presentation of the artists' work, it is tempting to line them up for yourself. *I saw such-and-such with so-and-so at this show*, for instance. Or, *so-and-so talked about such-and-such being an important influence on her work...*

Or, going down the list on a first pass and placing dates for birth is also interesting in the parallel lines drawn or not. The earliest work is from 1970, but percentage-wise, most of the work has been made in the last ten years. There are only two artists born in the '40s, none in the '30s and a lone representative from the '20s. Citing these three artists by name, in order of date of birth, gives an important foundation to the other twenty-eight. Robert Colescott, Purvis Young and David Hammons. One is a mixed-media-based conceptualist (a pioneer of a peculiarly American brand of *arte povera*), one is a representational painter with an expressionist surface tension and the other is a pronounced self-taught painter who works on varied materials. Together they provide a foundation of stylistic tendencies and genres of art making that encompass some of the most prevalent trends in contemporary art since the late '60s. But, they are all black. To some that may be a surprise: that black artists employ all the strategies and styles of contemporary art. Others invariably would take a glance at this list of artists and let out yet another exasperated "WTF?"! Industry rule number 5,080: *Don't show in all colored exhibitions*, someone might say.

But, we have to go there, so let's throw the issue out there, lay it on the table, if you will, because it continues to bend my brain. Basically, I love to see lists like this. It excites me to see the recognition of a gang of artists who can hold their own. And then to have a little historical sense behind it all, to be intergenerational, makes it all the more exciting.

And, it must be noted that these artists in the Rubell Family Collection have been shown before in other focused ways: for example as artists from a specific city in "Red Eye: L.A. Artists from the Rubell Family Collection." The RFC has also focused in on 'painters from Leipzig' and more broadly on artists from Europe. So the presence of thirty-one Americans in one exhibition is right in line with those preceding shows.

Excuses, excuses..., one might say. So, just in case, I haven't tip-tapped on a tightrope enough, and kept my distance while obviously being up in it, we can recognize that this work has not been brought together under the auspices of a non-profit but it was purchased with strong beliefs.

But, if we are counting categories, English's question prefaces this discussion: What happens to black art if black artists stop making it? Or, the similar invocation of Walker's exhibition, "Black Is, Black Ain't," a show that featured a variety of artists of different cultural backgrounds.

Needless to say, we aren't in Kansas anymore.

"The African spirit ... is at its best in abstract decorative forms."
—Alain Locke, The Legacy of the Ancestral, in Alain Locke, ed. *The New Negro*, Athenaeum, New York, 1969 (1925), p. 267.

The artists collected here, for the most part, eschew such antiquated sentiment. It is most obviously seen in one of the cornerstones of the collection in the work of Robert Colescott (b. 1925), playing elder statesman here. Colescott provides an example from the earliest works in the show as the oldest artist in this collection. Born in the same year that Dr. Locke issued his call to gather up the African spirit, Colescott came of a mature age at a time when Abstract Expressionism had come into much question all around. He studied in Paris with Fernand Léger—whose work embodies the early push and pull between abstraction and representation—and turned to the figure much like Philip Guston, in an attempt to reinvigorate representation via expressionism. In the late '50s, like David Park, Richard Diebenkorn, and Elmer Bischoff, Colescott was a second wave progenitor of Bay Area figurative painting. Yet, the turmoil of the '60s and its calls to political action bear a stark mark on the work. With a sense for pushing America's cultural buttons, Colescott found his unique style in addressing age-old stereotypes with a raw and rare disregard for correctness, as in the 1970s drawing shown here, where a bulbous-lipped black man stands in a pool surrounded by scantily-clad white women.

Enough has not been made of this important painter who represented the U.S. at the Venice Biennale in 1997. Though he shares that recent honor with the likes of Felix González-Torres, Fred Wilson, Hans Haacke, and Robert Gober, Colescott has only recently found new prominence via his exhibition two years ago at the Kravets/Wehby Gallery. With a drawing from 1970, his 1976 video *Dulacrow's Masterwork: A Mockumentary Film*, and paintings from the late '80s to the late '90s, this collection of works by Colescott is immensely important. Though he has been collected by major museums such as New York's Museum of Modern Art, and the Hirshhorn, a concentrated view of paintings by Colescott such as this is a rare find. Several younger artists within the collection are evidence of his influence.

Taking cues from Colescott, Nina Chanel Abney (b. 1982) reminds one also of the mask-like faces of Vincent D. Smith's paintings and the eccentric primitivism of William Henry Johnson, though she also shares a penchant for the contemporary grotesque with the work of her near contemporary Dana Schutz. The bodies in her paintings are often contorted like a child's plastic dolls, but menacing—attack of the body snatchers on crack. Henry Taylor (b. 1958), John Bankston (b. 1963),and the exceptionally precocious Noah Davis (b. 1983), all bear a stylistic affinity to the work of Colescott in surface tension and subject matter, which often borders on the absurd and the surreal.

A central figure in the tendency for representational figuration in a realist mode is Barkley L. Hendricks (b. 1945). Hendricks also acts as an elder statesman here; his work often tests the heavily contested boundaries between representation and abstraction. Favoring the former, Hendricks is known for his late Pop Art influences combined with a more up-to-date flavor for the people. A third and chronologically later strain of painterly representation meets conceptualism in the work of Kerry James Marshall (b. 1955). Born in Birmingham, Alabama, and raised in South Central Los Angeles, Marshall's work has always been steeped in a black aesthetic, whether he is referencing El Greco, Bouguereau or his college professor, the artist Charles White. Like Colescott, Marshall has amplified blackness in his figures with charcoal black characters against luscious super-saturated primary colors. As is well represented in the collection, Marshall's practice is multi-dimensional and also includes sculpture, drawing and video. Using all of these tools, Marshall's charge remains to question the way we see black people in the history of art.

Peerless in stature is the work of Jean-Michel Basquiat (1960-1988). Three paintings from Basquiat's early years—*Bird On Money* (1981), *One Million Yen* (1982), and an untitled self-portrait—give a look at one of the most important artists of the last thirty years. *Bird On Money* presents one of Basquiat's most popular subjects in the form of an homage to Charlie "Bird" Parker. Loaded with repeated symbols and arrows, the canvas includes the words *para morir* (for death) in the lower right hand corner.

The influence of these four painters is also felt in the fact that they have been an abundant source of reference for other artists in the exhibition including the young painters Iona Rozeal Brown, Jeff Sonhouse, Mickalene Thomas, Wangechi Mutu and Kehinde Wiley. It is worth noting that as much as these artists, who are all relatively close in age, may agree with the idea of the aforementioned as being influential to their work, there is no disputing the popular place of painting since the late 1990s in our contemporary art. Familiar American artists like John Currin, Elizabeth Peyton, and Lisa Yuskavage have had a profound effect in making a place for the figure in representational painting as a more than viable option for young painters.

Iona Rozeal Brown's (b. 1966) work takes equally and liberally from 19th-century Japanese erotica (*shunga*), early 20th-century American vaudeville, and contemporary hip-hop culture, exaggerating tropes of cultural identification. In an ongoing series of works, she has concentrated on picturing Japanese women in blackface. Also intrigued by gender and ethnicity, Wangechi Mutu's work also has a profound focus on women. Utilizing collage as in *Non je ne regrette rien* (2007), Mutu (b. 1972) uses her medium to evoke a ruptured (and carefully put back together) monstrous exoticism. With more surface tension than the work of Brown or Mutu, Mickalene Thomas's (b. 1971) paintings are often encrusted with rhinestones. Early after graduate school, Thomas completed a series of works of black women in the classic odalisque position, evoking a mix of Manet and '70s black "power girl" pinups.

Jeff Sonhouse (b. 1968) and Kehinde Wiley (b. 1977) question the portrait tradition as it relates to sartorial splendor, decoration and the power of the sitter. Concentrating on black male figures, both artists borrow from an amalgamation of sources including art history and the everyday urban environment. Sonhouse has used various forms of masking in his paintings, via color, texture and sometimes surface ornament, suggesting a twoness: that of the person depicted and that of the true person within, or behind the mask. If Sonhouse's characters—from *Exhibit A: Cardinal Francis Arinze* to the rapper Busta Rhymes—are ambivalent about taking off the proverbial mask, Wiley's subjects pose stridently with confidence from the street into the Baroque poses they assume in his canvases.

While not necessarily conjuring the African spirit as Locke suggests is a possibility via abstraction, a few artists do work in an abstract mode. Embracing the cool, measured pleasure principle of painting embodied by an artist like Agnes Martin or Brice Marden, Mark Bradford (b. 1961) opens up and extends the discourse around abstraction informed by conceptualism—think arte povera via Alighiero e Boetti, who also shared an interest in mapping and for whom the final product was an endnote to a much longer process of negotiation in making art inside and outside the studio. *Whore in the Church House* (2006), is a prime example of Bradford's all-over abstraction, informed as much by Jackson Pollock as by the abstractions of big city urban cartography. The works of Rodney McMillian (b. 1969) and Shinique Smith (b. 1971) both touch upon abstraction in painting strategies while also embracing the three-dimensional mode of sculpture.

David Hammons's (b. 1943) presence here is minimal though remarkably important. Hammons came to prominence in the '70s. His interest in conceptualist strategies including body art has been an important influence on many of the artists within the collection. In Hammons's *Esquire (or John Henry)* (1990), as in certain works by Max Ernst, Joan Miró or Jimmie Durham, the found rock has a special resonance. *Esquire* is one of the rare Hammons portraits of a head defined by the lines and content of a hairdo on a common found object. The ease with which Hammons's piece suggests a portrait of a person is in line with his long and ongoing interest in hair as a purveyor of character and identity. Using the found rock, he would then bring it in to a barber shop for a shave or a lineup, its simple natural surface and lines evocative of so much more.

Carrie Mae Weems (b. 1953), Renée Green (b. 1959), Glenn Ligon (b. 1960), Lorna Simpson (b. 1960), Leonardo Drew (b. 1961), Gary Simmons (b. 1964), and Kara Walker (b. 1969) are all represented by significant works. Simmons's work in particular bears mentioning for its in-depth view of early work in this artist's career. An important early sculpture, *Duck, Duck, Noose* (1992), is joined by several of Simmons's trademark erasure drawings from the same year. *Duck, Duck, Noose* is a great example of Simmons's early sculptures that often took on stereotypes and symbols of racial connotation. In this case, the work comprises nine Ku Klux Klan hoods sitting atop stools (the kind that might be used in a graduate art class). In the middle is a hanging rope tied in a noose ready for the lynching. Equating the childish behavior of a group known for its racial hatred with the setting of learning, Simmons questions the nature of racism: is it learned or is it innate? Ligon is also well-represented with three of his iconic neon text pieces and two of his classic joke paintings.

Three of the most in-depth presentations are reserved for very young artists, evidence of the risk and unabated desire with which this collection has been put together. Kalup Linzy (b. 1977) uses fiction in a narrative sense through his hilarious video works featuring himself. With the heat of a telenovela and the faux drama of soap operas, Linzy's film and video works are scripted and directed by him as he plays a starring role.

No artist is shown as comprehensively as Hank Willis Thomas (b. 1976), with over 80 works in the collection, all since 2003. Thomas's focus, perhaps not surprisingly, has been on found images from advertising. The images that pepper our magazines or are blown up for use on billboards are his stock, his archive. Reimaging many crude or senselessly banal adverts from the 1960s to the present, Thomas puts the attention on the mediated image as a source of understanding, not just a source for selling something. With the designed texts and symbols removed, we concentrate more on the image than the original creator could have ever imagined.

Working in a variety of modes, though trained initially as a photographer, Rashid Johnson (b. 1977) has six large works in the collection, all from his early 2008 exhibition in New York. Featured as a photographer in "Freestyle" seven years ago, Johnson went to graduate school in that time and has steadily explored diverse media ever since. The new work resembles a mad scientist's lair or the meeting grounds of the Mu'tafikah before another raid on a museum (Center for Art Detention). Nick Cave's afrofuturist soundsuits are heavily costumed figures, which look as though they would be right at home.

But, can such a show be useful? Ultimately part of the importance of this collection of work is that it was purchased. In this case, the RFC has recognized, more than any other public institution—except the Studio Museum in Harlem—the importance of this work. That's useful.

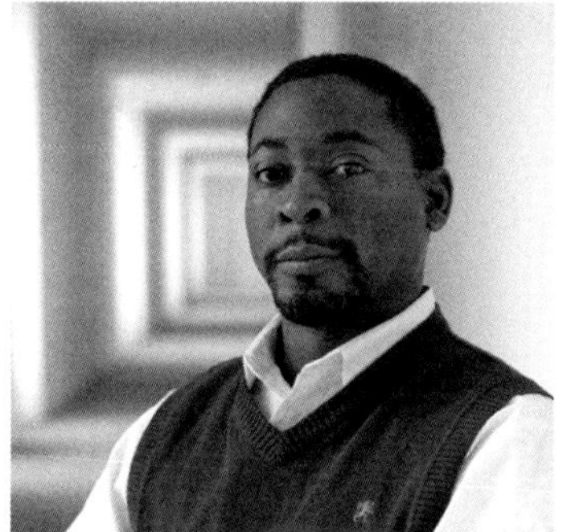

Franklin Sirmans is the director of the Pérez Art Museum Miami (PAMM) since fall of 2015. Prior to his appointment, he was the department head and curator of contemporary art at Los Angeles County Museum of Art from 2010 until 2015. At LACMA Sirmans organized *Toba Khedoori, Noah Purifoy: Junk Dada; Variations: Conversations in and Around Abstract Painting; Futbol: The Beautiful Game, and Ends and Exits: Contemporary Art from the Collections of LACMA and the Broad Art Foundation*. From 2006 to 2010, he was curator of modern and contemporary Art at The Menil Collection in Houston where he organized several exhibitions including *NeoHooDoo: Art for a Forgotten Faith, Maurizio Cattelan: Is Their Life Before Death?* and *Vija Celmins: Television and Disaster, 1964-1966*. He was the artistic director of Prospect.3 New Orleans from 2012-2014. He is the 2007 Driskell Prize winner.

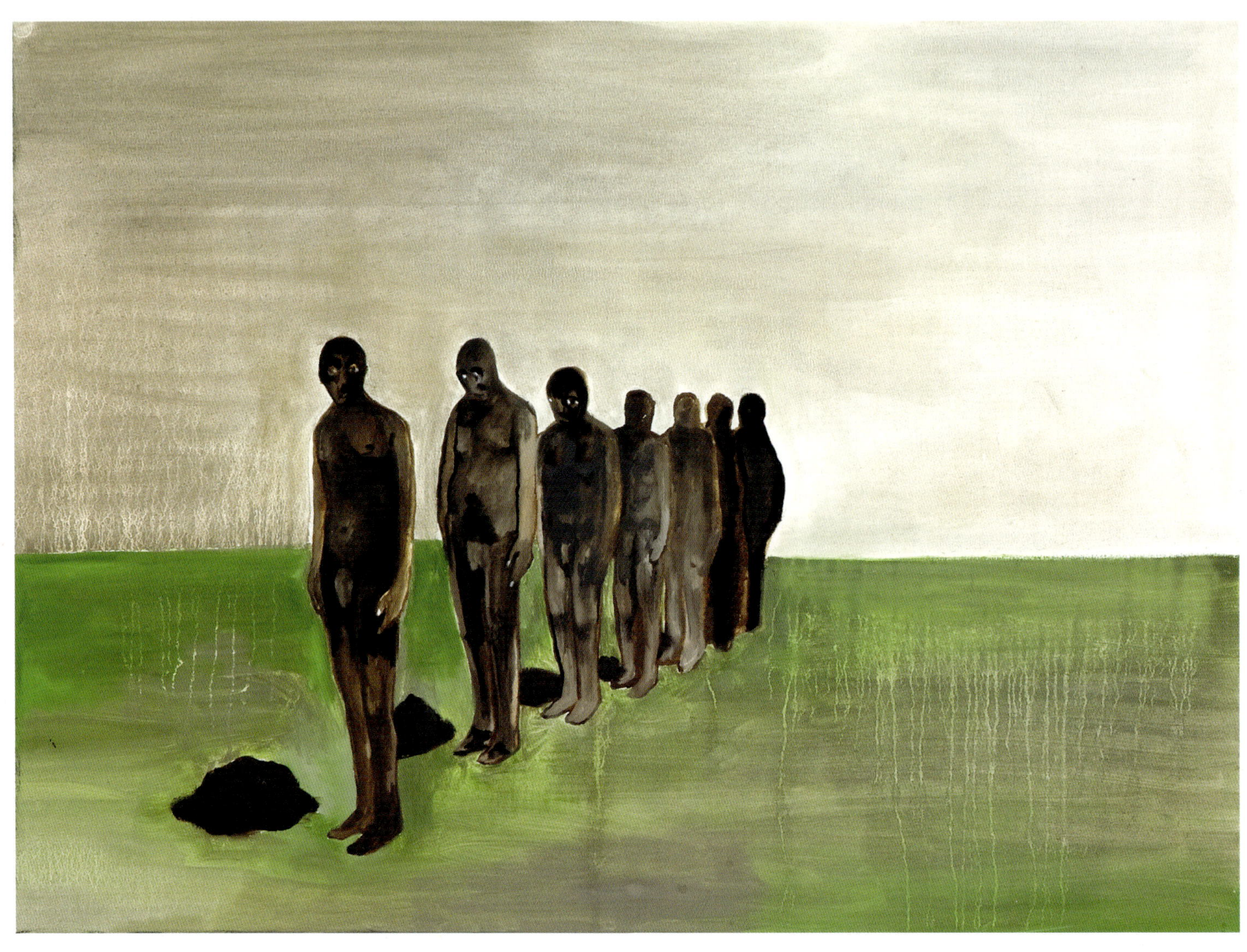

 NOAH DAVIS *The Seven Prisoners of the Abyss*, 2008, oil on canvas, 30 x 40 1/4 in. (76.2 x 102.2 cm), acquired in 2008

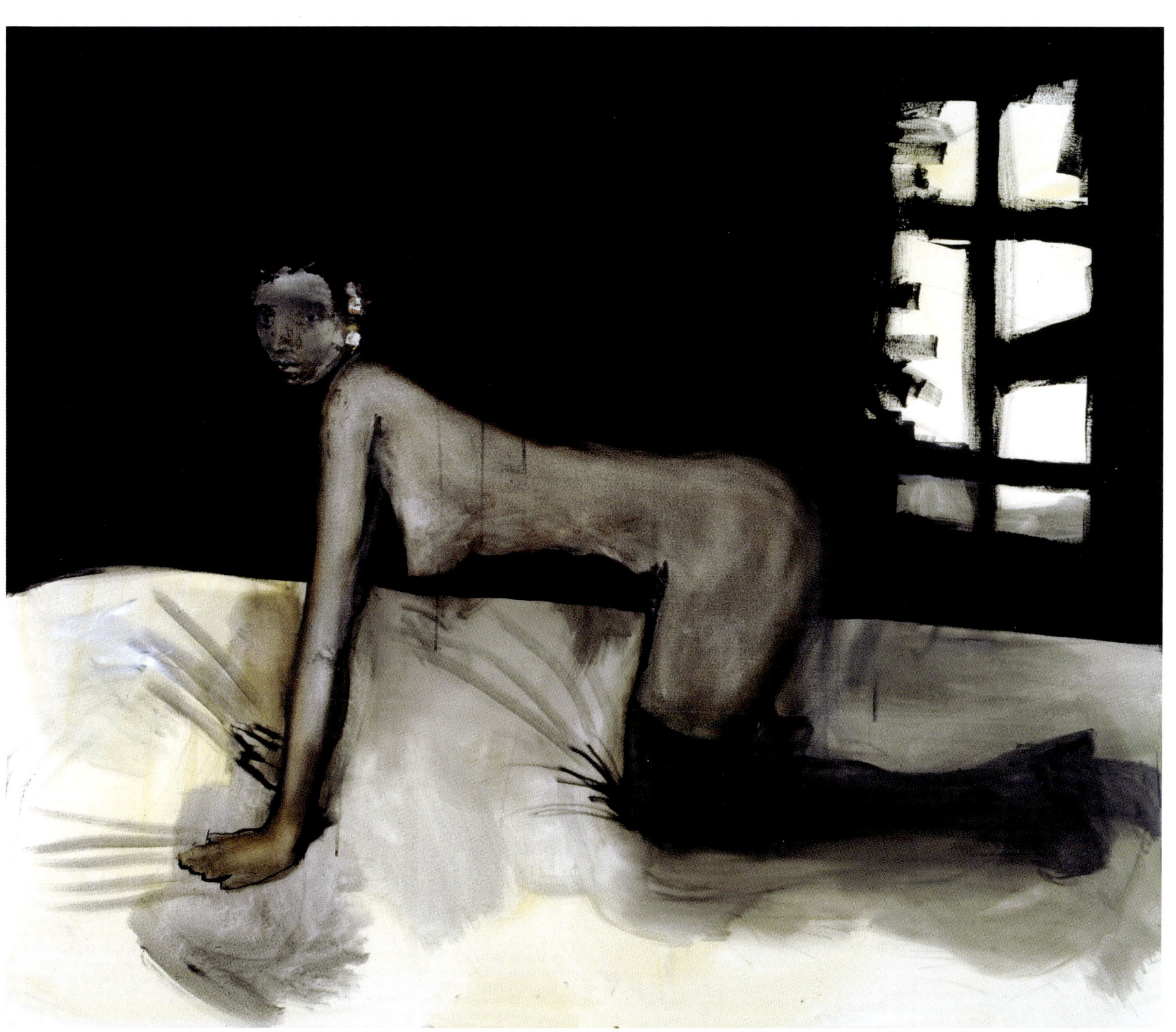

American Sterile, 2008, oil on canvas, 52 x 60 in. (132.1 x 152.4 cm), acquired in 2008

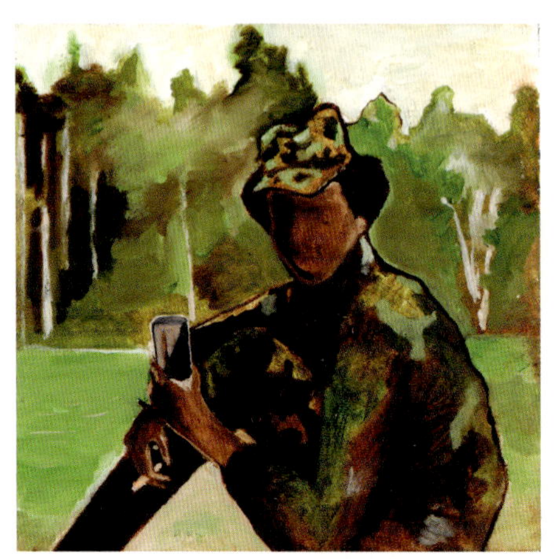

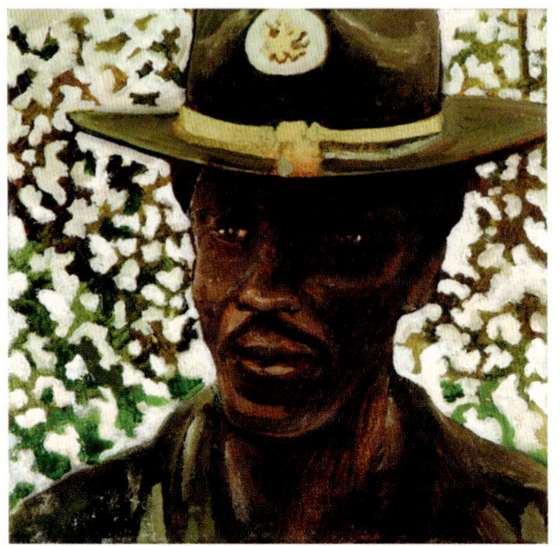

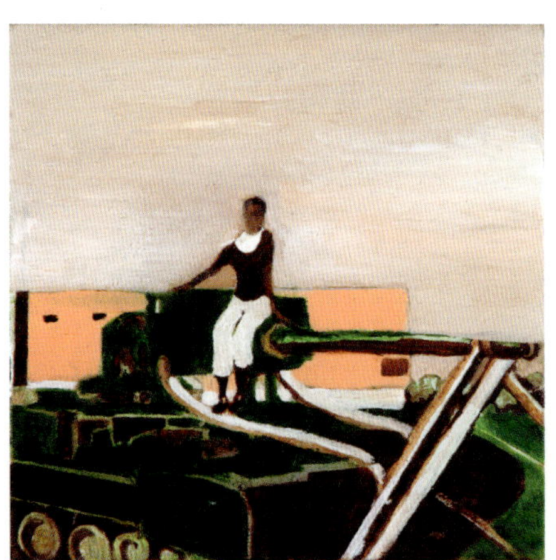

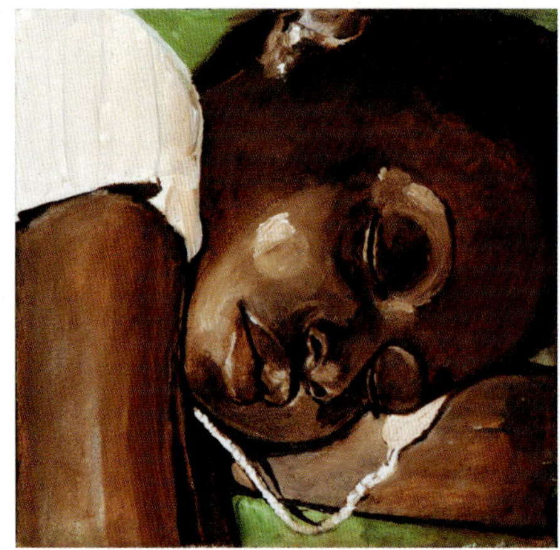

Clockwise from Top left: *Basic Training 1*, 2008; *Basic Training 2*, 2008; *Basic Training 3*, 2008; *Basic Training 4*, 2008, oil and acrylic on canvas, each 10 x 10 in. (25.4 x 25.4 cm), acquired in 2008

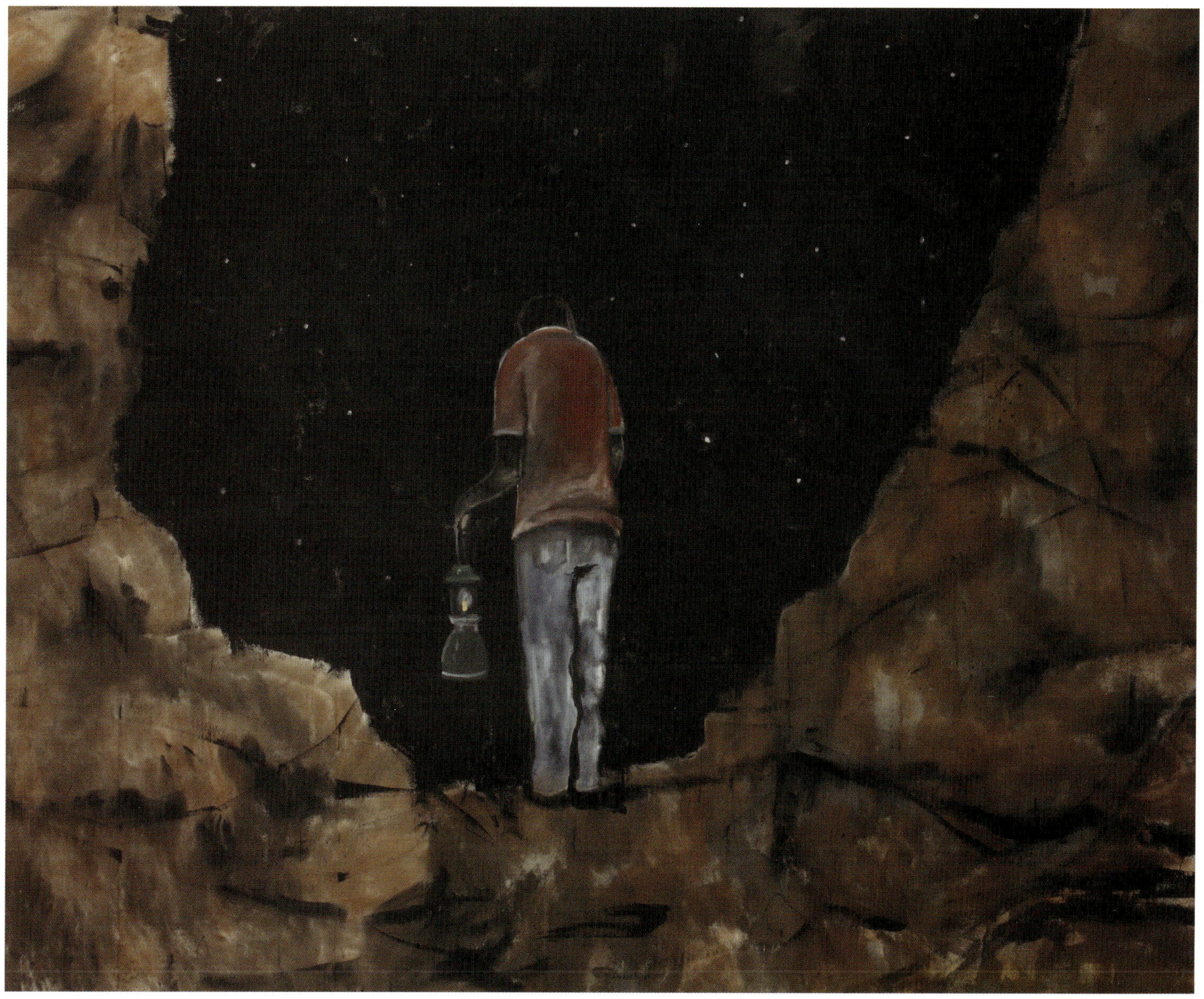

I think, like painting, spirituality makes many people very uncomfortable; spirituality is an interesting word. It is highly underrated in contemporary painting, and I feel it is the driving force behind the practice. Any attempt for me to verbalize the act of painting will ultimately fail. But, it is the spiritual nature of painting that makes it different from any other art form. The practice has a history so vast and forgotten that it can only exist in the land of the spirits.

Ultimately, I want to change the way people view art, the way people buy art, the way they make art. I've always tried to balance the tight rope of making my art accessible to those who are aware of the craft, and those who aren't convinced of art, or more specifically, my artistic objective. I believe that concealing too much in theory is problematic and that art can function in every-day life. I strive for an artistic legacy that not only transcends blackness but confluences and impacts all cultures.

Noah Davis

Painting for My Dad, 2011, oil on canvas, 76 x 91 in. (193 x 231.1 cm), acquired in 2011

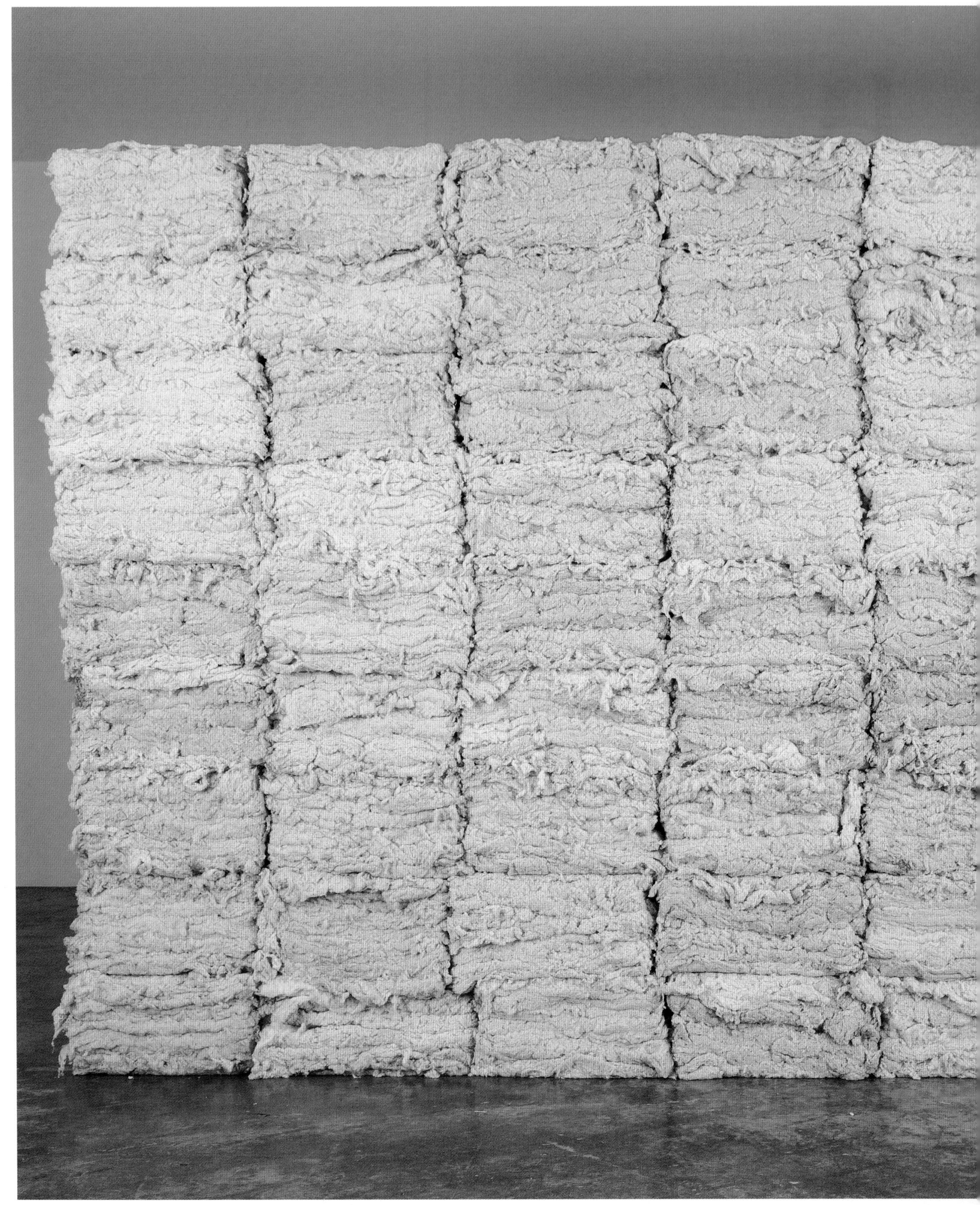

 LEONARDO DREW *Untitled #25*, 1992, cotton and wax, 102 x 158 x 33 in. (259 x 401.3 x 83.8 cm), acquired in 1992

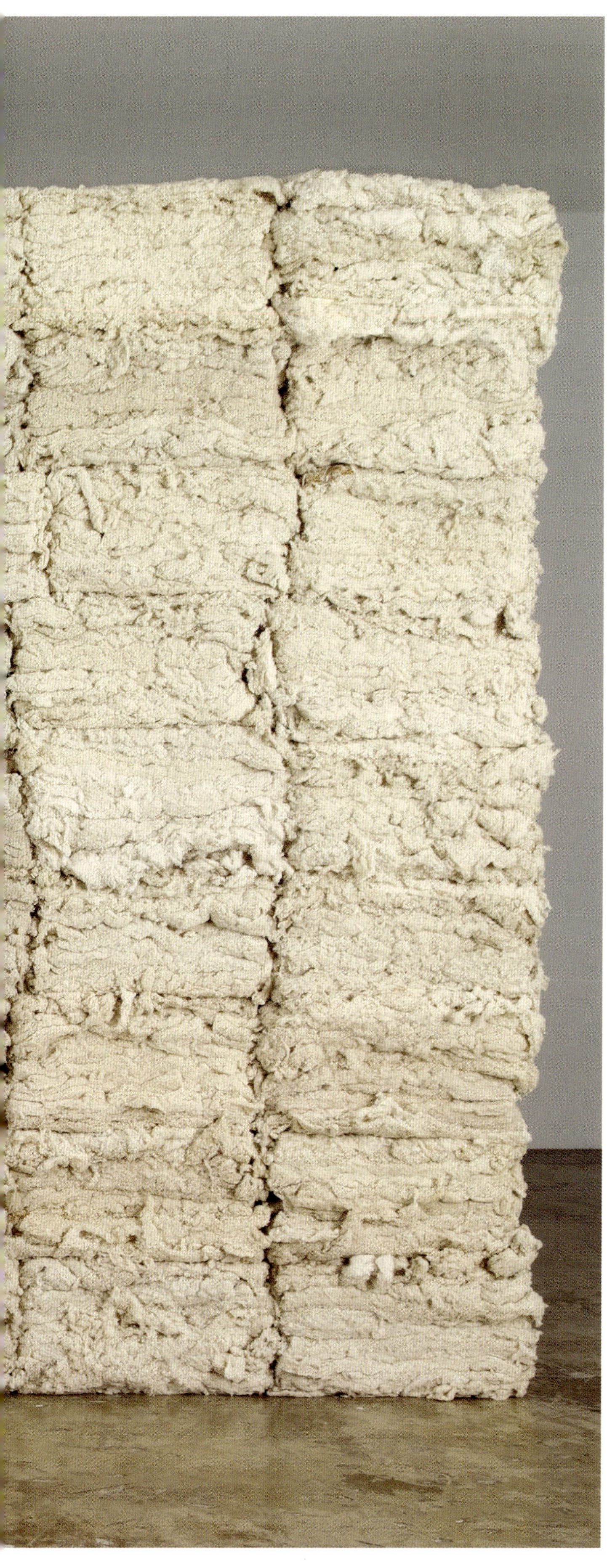

I can only say that creating the wall (*Number 25*) brought the toil and sweat of the old days. Having no vehicle and no driver's license I found myself using a dolly to transport full bails of cotton down the streets of Broadway. But that was only the beginning. The nature of the material only allowed it to be cut with scissors. Through focus, pain and heart, *Number 25* was painstakingly realized. Of course I found in my travels years later that machines in the South are producing the very same walls of cotton…within minutes.

Leonardo Drew

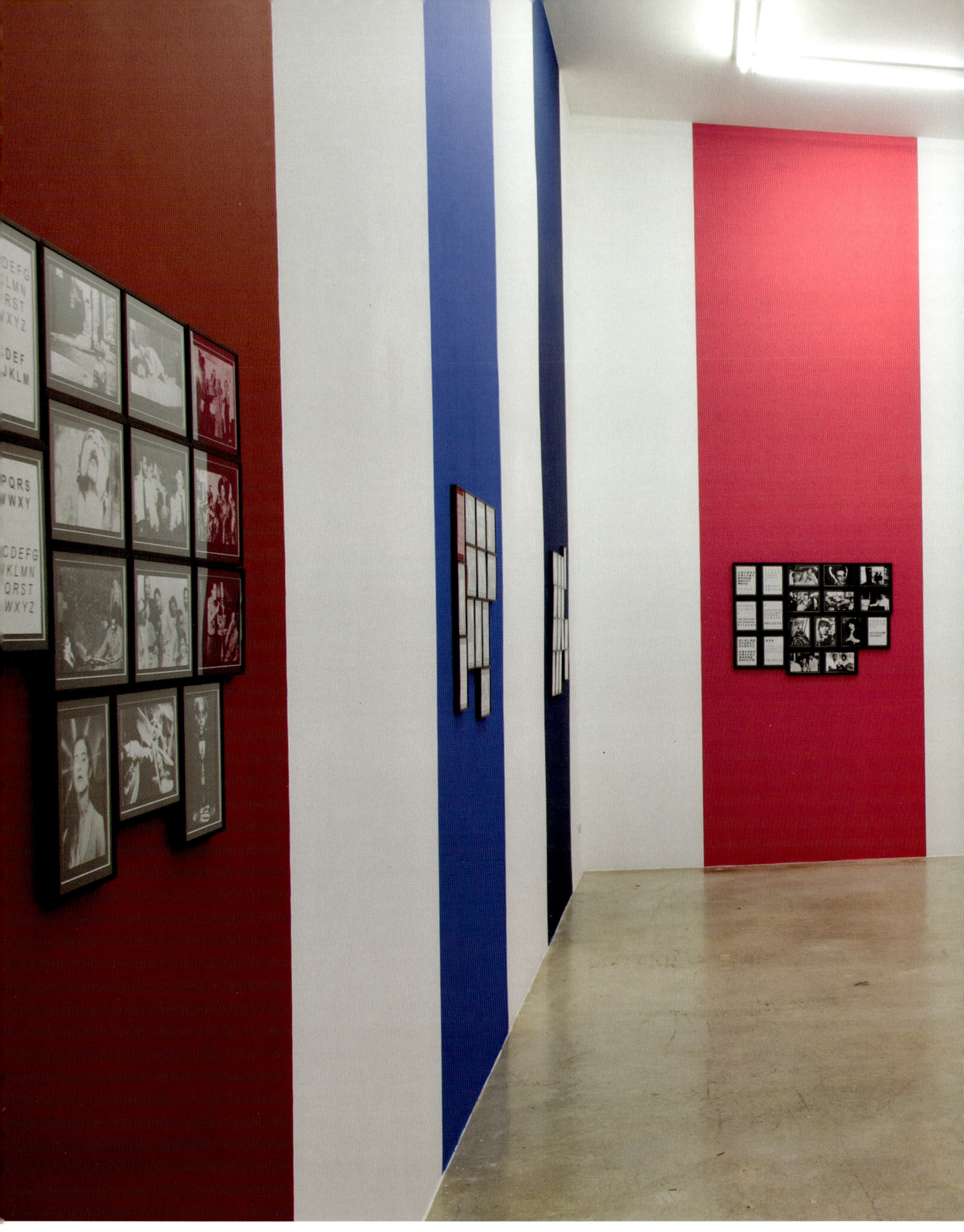

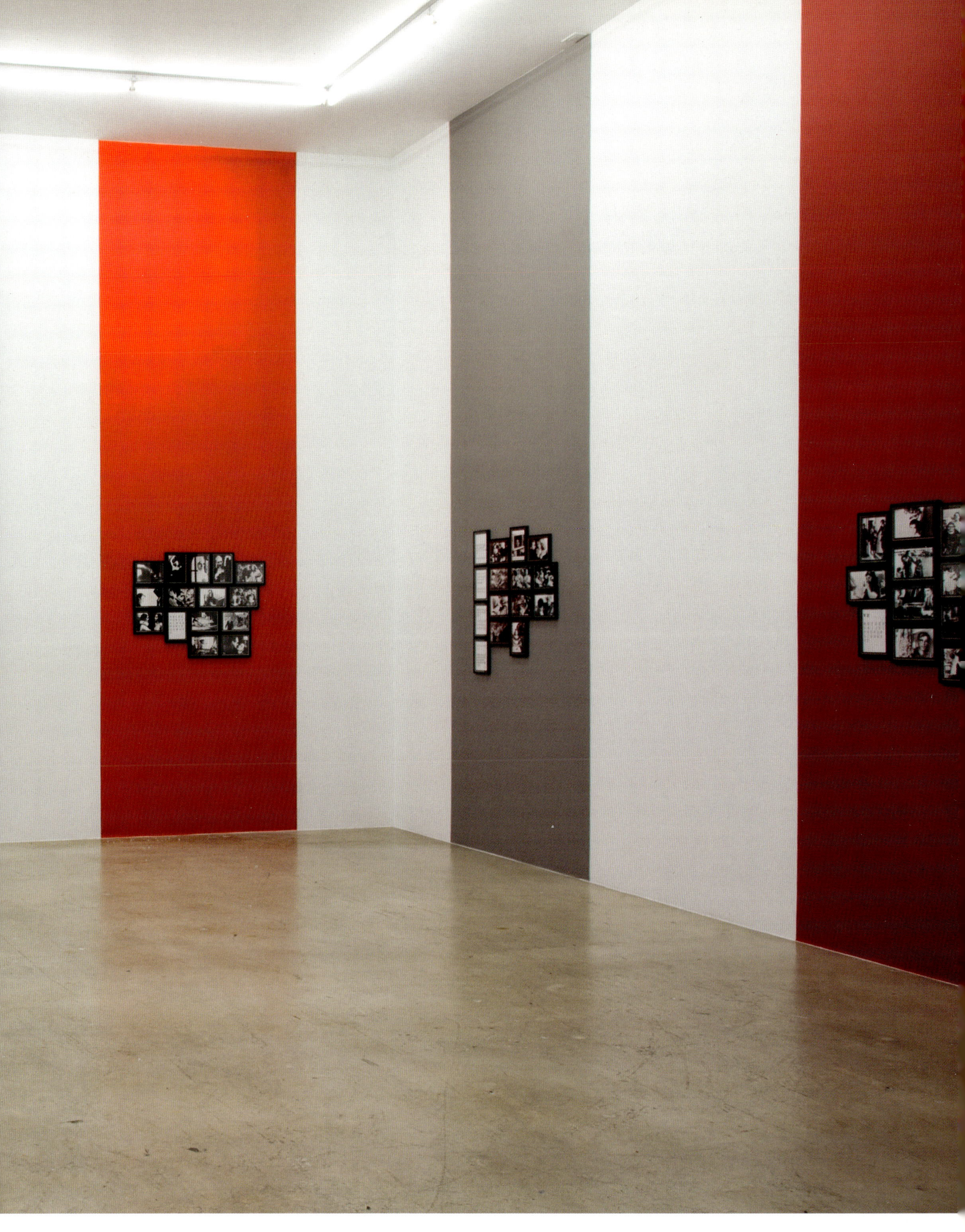

ABCDEFGHI

ABCDEFGHI 123456789

Nine walls; nine colors: one for each. Sets A to I. Alphabetical listing of film stills and film frames from A to Z. Number of sets: nine. Number of sets determined by the number of alphabet sets printed by the Claris program on the Stylewriter printer. Set defined as the number of typefaces printed from A to Z which appear consecutively until there is a break in the A to Z sequence. Sets are organized from A to I in the sequence in which they were printed. Colors determined by the first nine card stock colors, sound, and the graphic art supply store of the Technical University of Vienna. Film stills and film frames determined by the A to Z listings of the three named references. Abridged choices made based on what could fill three rolls of film, time and space limitations, both dependent on expense for labor and exhibition facility. A selection from the infinite cinema. Beyond 26 places. Computer generated. 109 images. Divided to form an average of eleven per set.

*****

The films listed are arranged from A to Z and form a selection taken from the reproductions of film stills and film frames from three alphabetically arranged film references of three different decades with three different emphases. They are:

The Oxford Companion To Film (1976)
The Psychotronic Encyclopedia of Film (1983)
The Women's Companion to International Film (1990)

The question might arise, "Why these three reference books in 1998 when there are such a range of references about film, especially since its 1995 centenary?" One might also wonder, "Why didn't she simply use the Internet, isn't it constantly updated?" One answer is that these books were in the writer's possession. Another is that they were obtained by chance or inexpensively. Yet another is that they fit easily into her suitcase and didn't require using a modem connection to different servers in different cities. Access was more immediate and tactile than she found Internet use to be in different parts of the world. Another answer is that they formed three instances of international film guides, yet expressed extremely different tones. This dissonance was provocative. What, she wondered, would happen if they were combined? What kind of A to Z book might come about? Visually, what might the images look like juxtaposed, with the basis for juxtaposition being an alphabetical category? What variations of response might occur given this arbitrary, but definite demand? How might two such demands (the above-stated demand and a computer-generated alphabet), arbitrary yet definite, appear? Might these appear as "isolated frame[s] taken out of the infinite cinema" in the location referred to as the "metahistory of cinema," which Hollis Frampton described? Why not test some of Sol LeWitt's Sentences on Conceptual Art, manually and with a computer? She wonders what he thinks of these sentences now, nearly thirty years later.

PREFATORY ADMONITION: This index is not comprehensive. Further information can be found in the aforementioned references. Speculative desires and the act of passing time spurred its making.

Renée Green

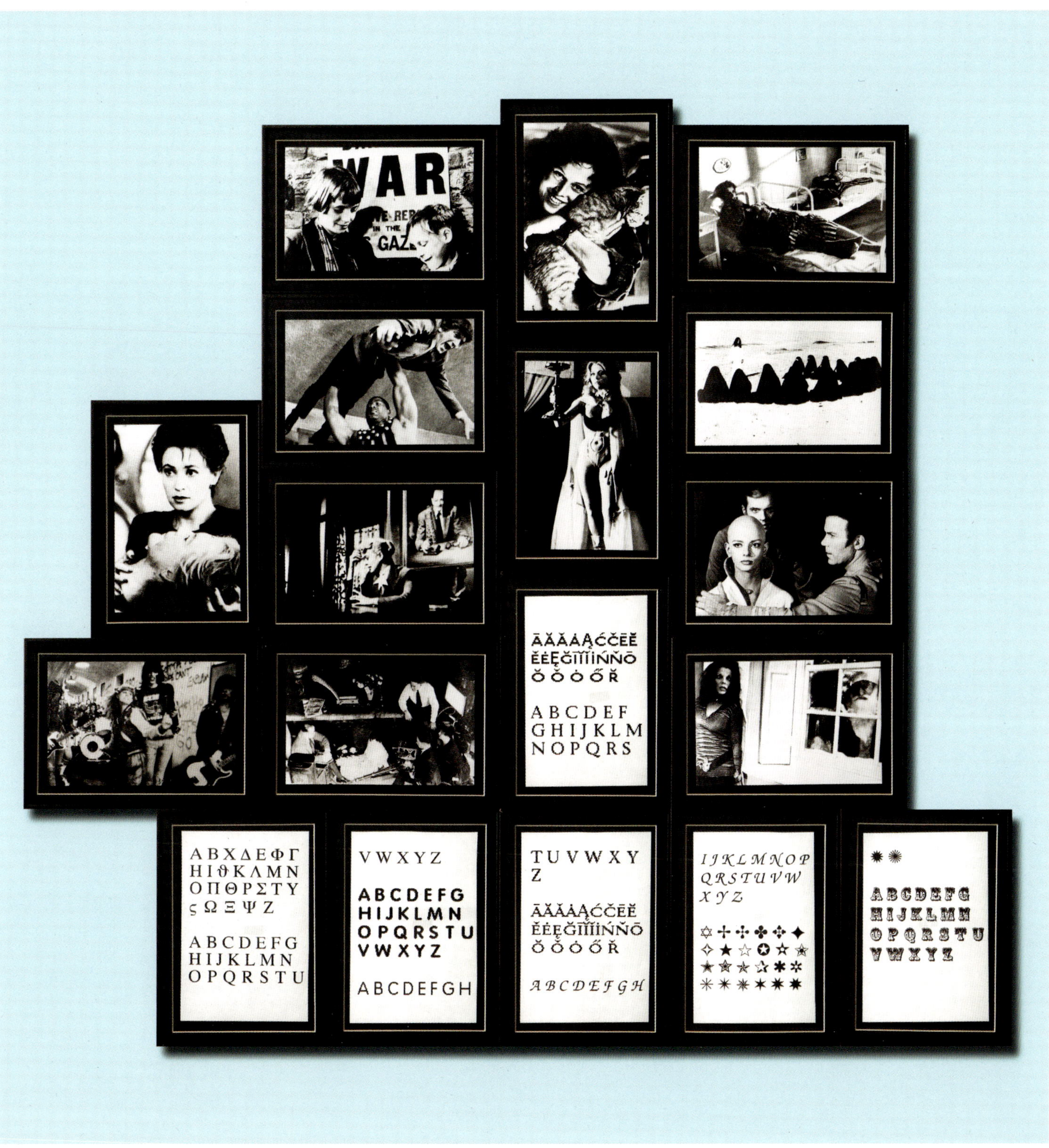

Detail of *Between and Including, Set H (Rock 'N' Roll Highschool to Things to Come)*, 1998, black and white framed photographs, framed texts and painted wall, height variable; painted wall 55 in. (140 cm), acquired in 2008

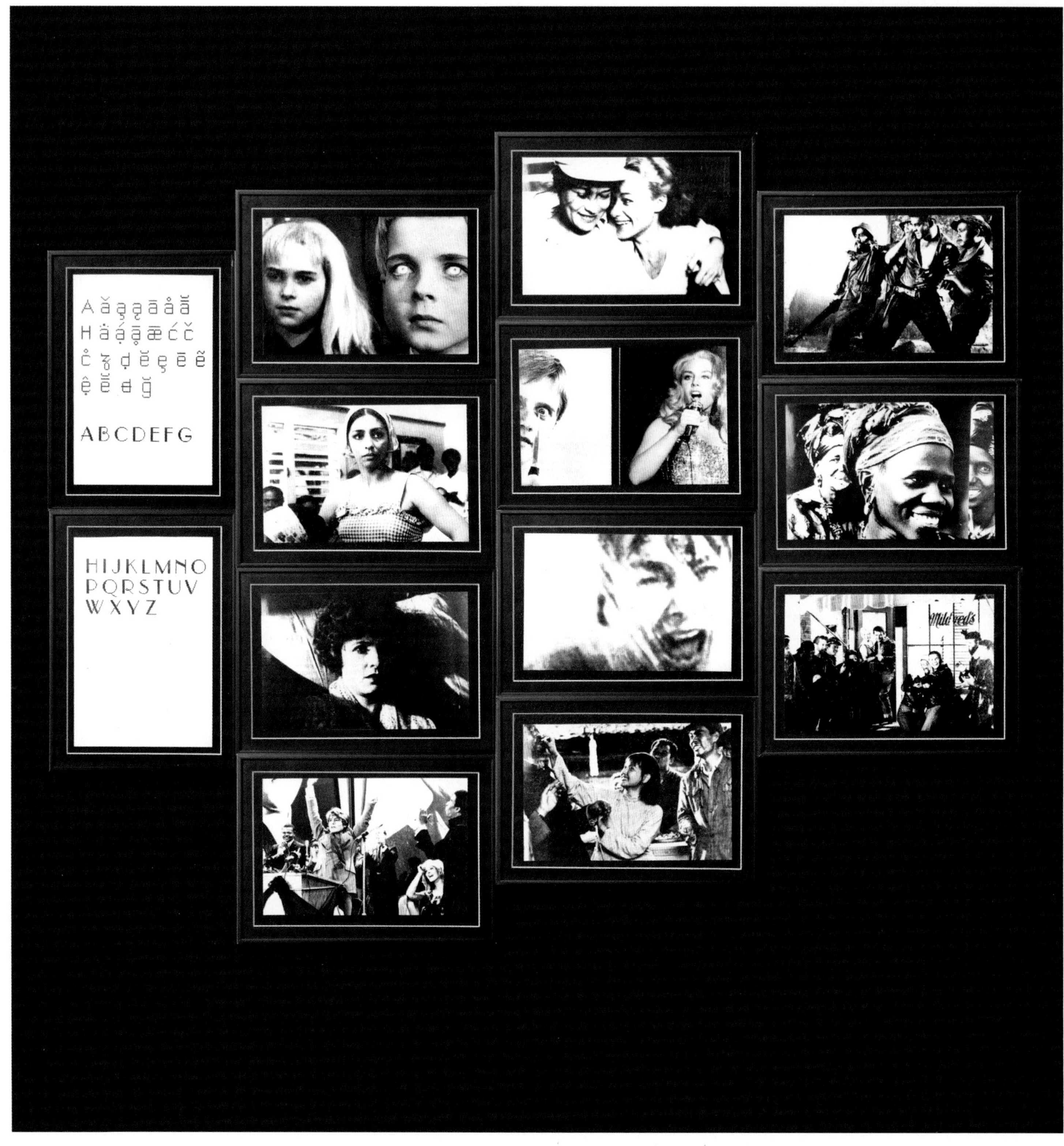

RENÉE GREEN

Detail of *Between and Including, Set I (Trinth T.Min-Ha to Xie Jin)*, 1998, black-and-white framed photographs, framed texts and painted wall, height variable; painted wall 55 in. (140 cm), acquired in 2008

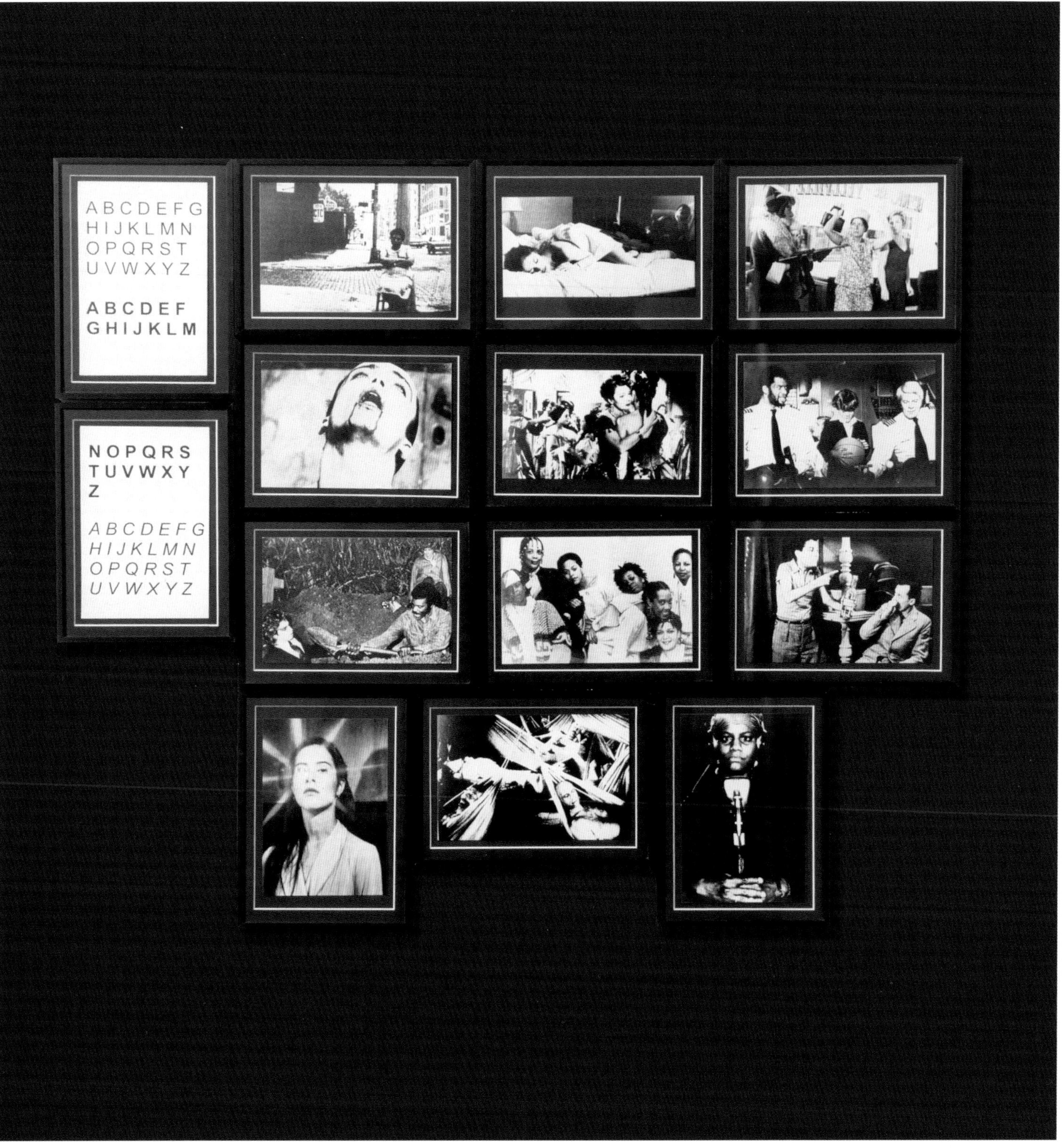

Detail of *Between and Including, Set E (Marion Haensel to Invisible Invaders)*, 1998, black-and-white framed photographs, framed texts and painted wall, height variable; painted wall 55 in. (140 cm), acquired in 2008

DAVID HAMMONS

Esquire (or John Henry), 1990, steel, rock, human hair and tin, 45 x 9 x 5 in. (114.3 x 22 x 13 cm), acquired in 1991

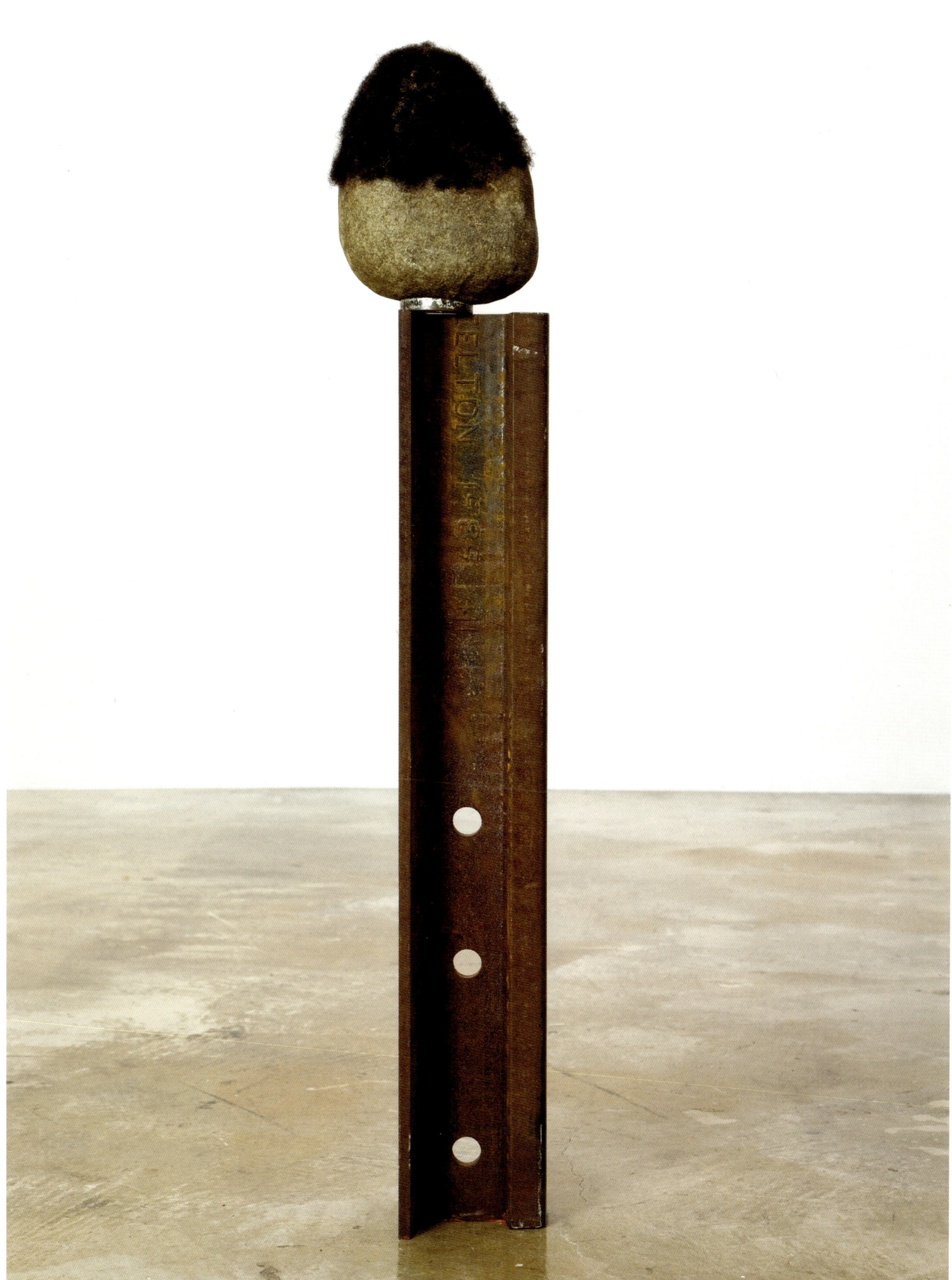

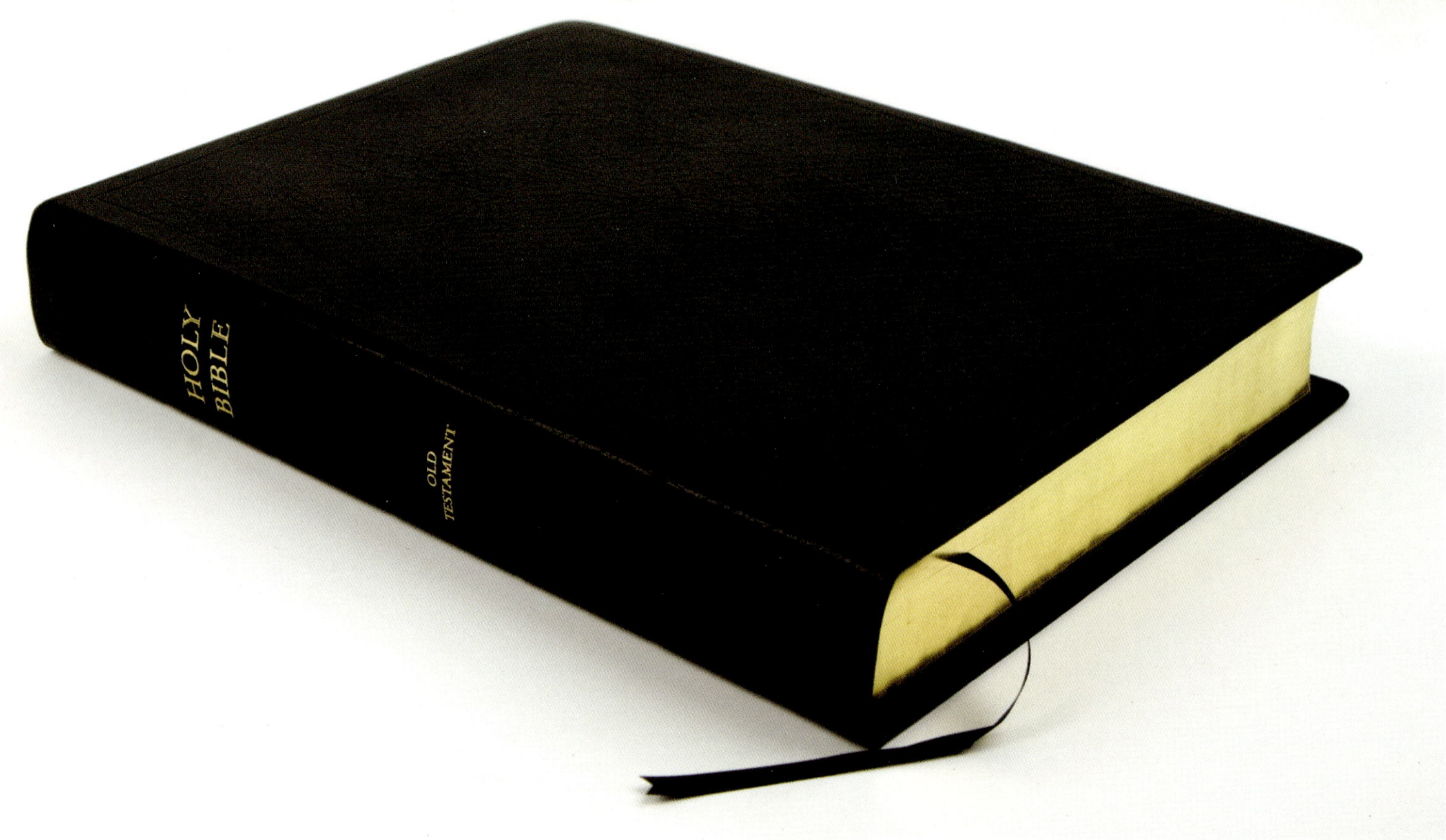

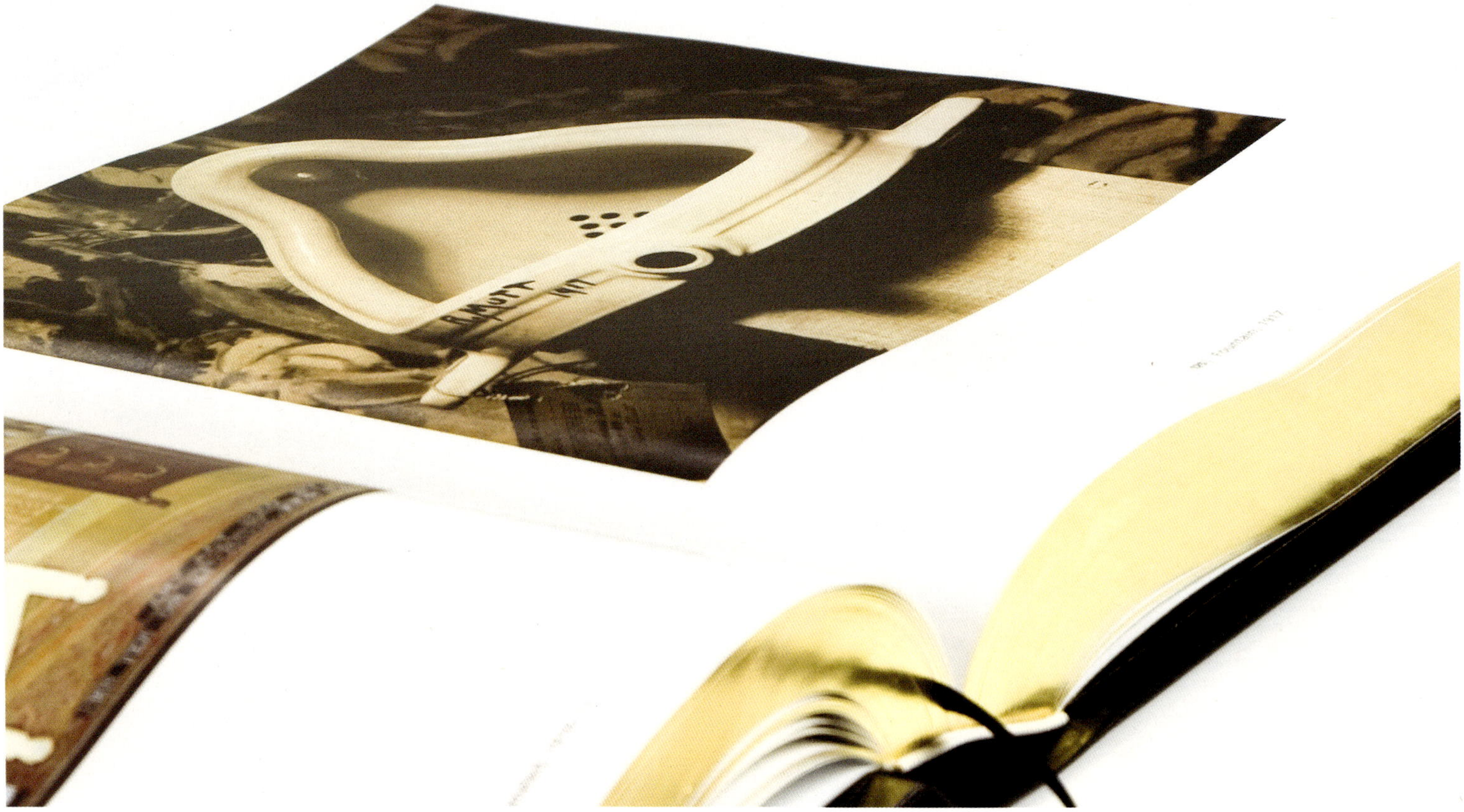

DAVID HAMMONS

The Holy Bible, Old Testament, 2002, 1,002 page artist's book, 225 color plates, leather-bound, softcover, gilt edged, gold tooling, and slipcase, ed. 116/165, 13 1/2 x 10 1/2 x 2 1/2 in. (34.3 x 26.7 x 6.4 cm), acquired in 2008

THE COMPLETE WORKS OF

Marcel Duchamp

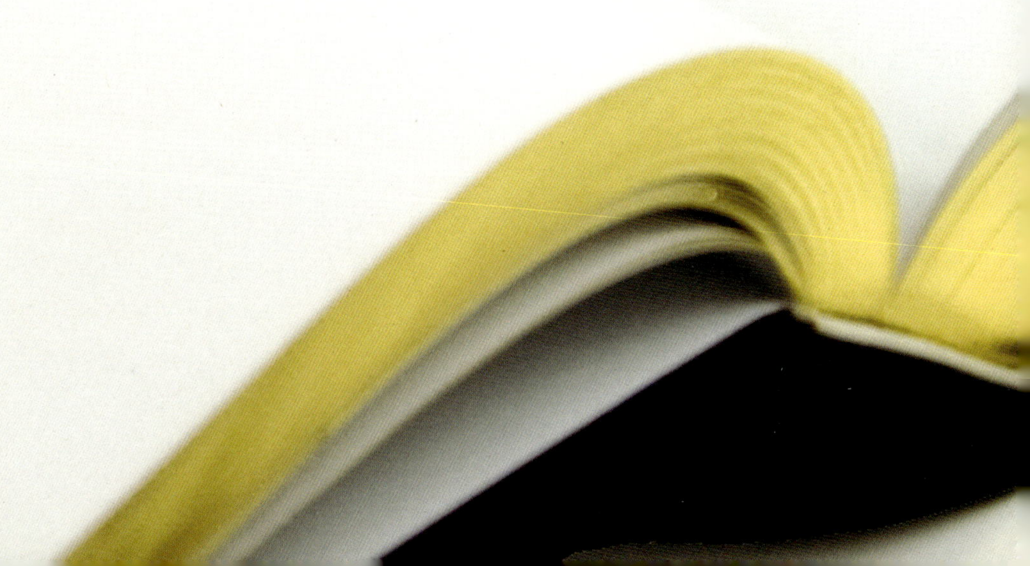

When I was in Paris, France, in 1978, there was a bevy of long, leansuited French- African men on the streets of Pigalle wearing graceful, tailored, high-vented "vines" (a colloquial name for suits from my Philadelphia neighborhood).

Noir was the one of two portraits I crafted from photographs I took. The other painting is in the collection of the Yale University Art Gallery. It is a double portrait titled *APB's (Afro-Parisian Brothers). APB's* featured one of the male subjects (also the solo subject of *Noir*) in a plain fabric garment. This work, *Noir*, shows that same suited man in a blue pinstripe suit. All I can say is that the pinstriped pattern took a lot out of me. I avoided painting pinstripes for many years after.

Barkley L. Hendricks

 Noir, 1978, oil and acrylic on canvas, 72 x 48 in. (182.9 x 121.9 cm), acquired in 2008

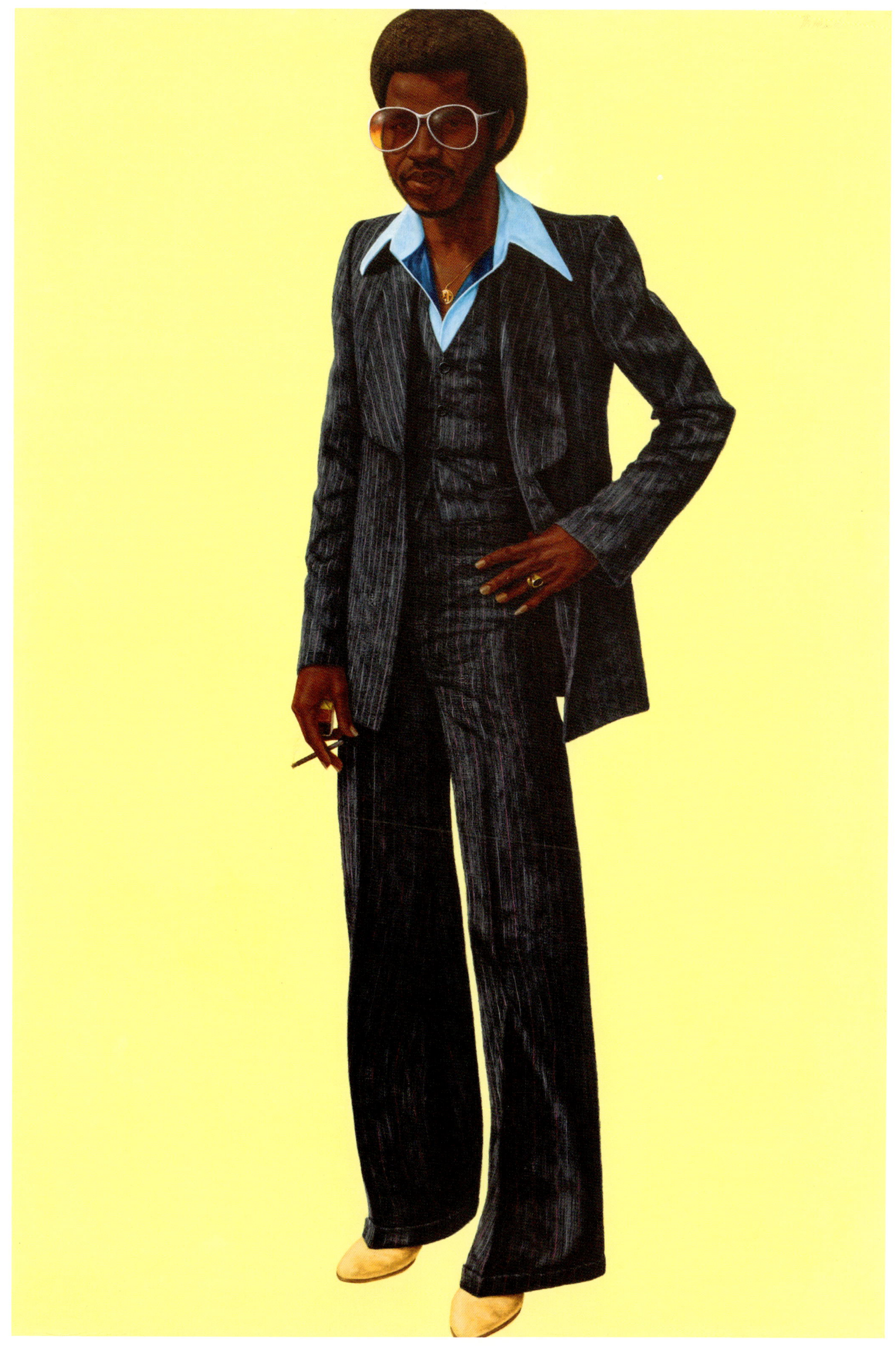

When I first met Eddie, he was a model for local art classes and arts organizations. Upon hiring him, I learned he was a jack-of-alltrades in addition to being a Connecticut state relay champion. I'm not sure this fact was known by the group of young men he was drinking and smoking with one Saturday evening. They challenged him to a race after their testosterone and booze made them push Eddie's buttons. The summer sun was giving off its last light of the day when they squared off at the starting line in the valley of the long dirt drive. When "Go!" was shouted, the four racers could be heard making their way up the dusty road. One of the racers fell midway through the sprint and was left in a cloud of dust as the remaining three made their way to the finish line at the top of the hill. Eddie was well out in front and very much over the finish line when James and Bobbie finally crossed the line. Eddie was there waiting and laughing at them when they staggered to the end. Bobbie didn't take losing well, whereupon, calling Eddie a "jive niggah," Eddie's retort was "I may be a jive niggah but I can beat you slow motherfuckers any day of the week and twice on Sundays!"

Barkley L. Hendricks

 BARKLEY L. HENDRICKS *Fast Eddie Jive Niggah*, 1975, oil and acrylic on linen, 48 1/2 x 36 1/2 in. (123.2 x 92.7 cm), acquired in 2008

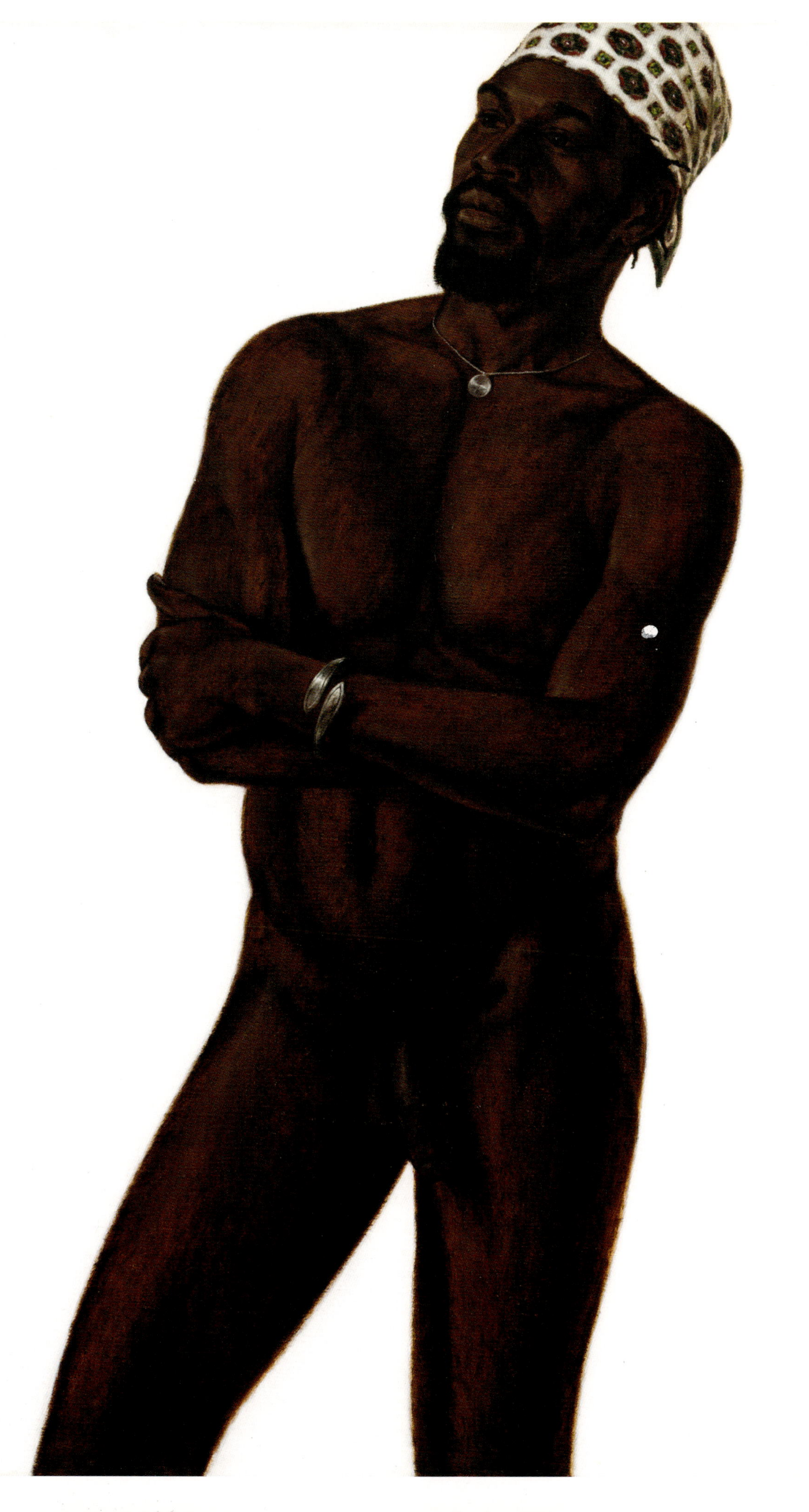

Thee Big Guy, meaning the Lord, is chock full of symbolic objects, some obvious, some personal—for instance, the red rubber Christ mold and the self-portrait in the blade of the straight razor. The hands and majorette boots are connections to past ill-fated romances. Still lifes allowed me to scatter objects about for the desired visual inside jokes inspired by where my head was at the time of its construction. To say one painting could lead to another would be an understatement. The final statement could be "read 'em or weep, or laugh," depending on the story I want to tell. So, go figure – I'm not telling...

Barkley L. Hendricks

 Thee Big Guy, 1983, oil, acrylic and gold leaf on canvas, 43 1/2 x 43 1/2 in. (110.5 x 110.5 cm), acquired in 2008

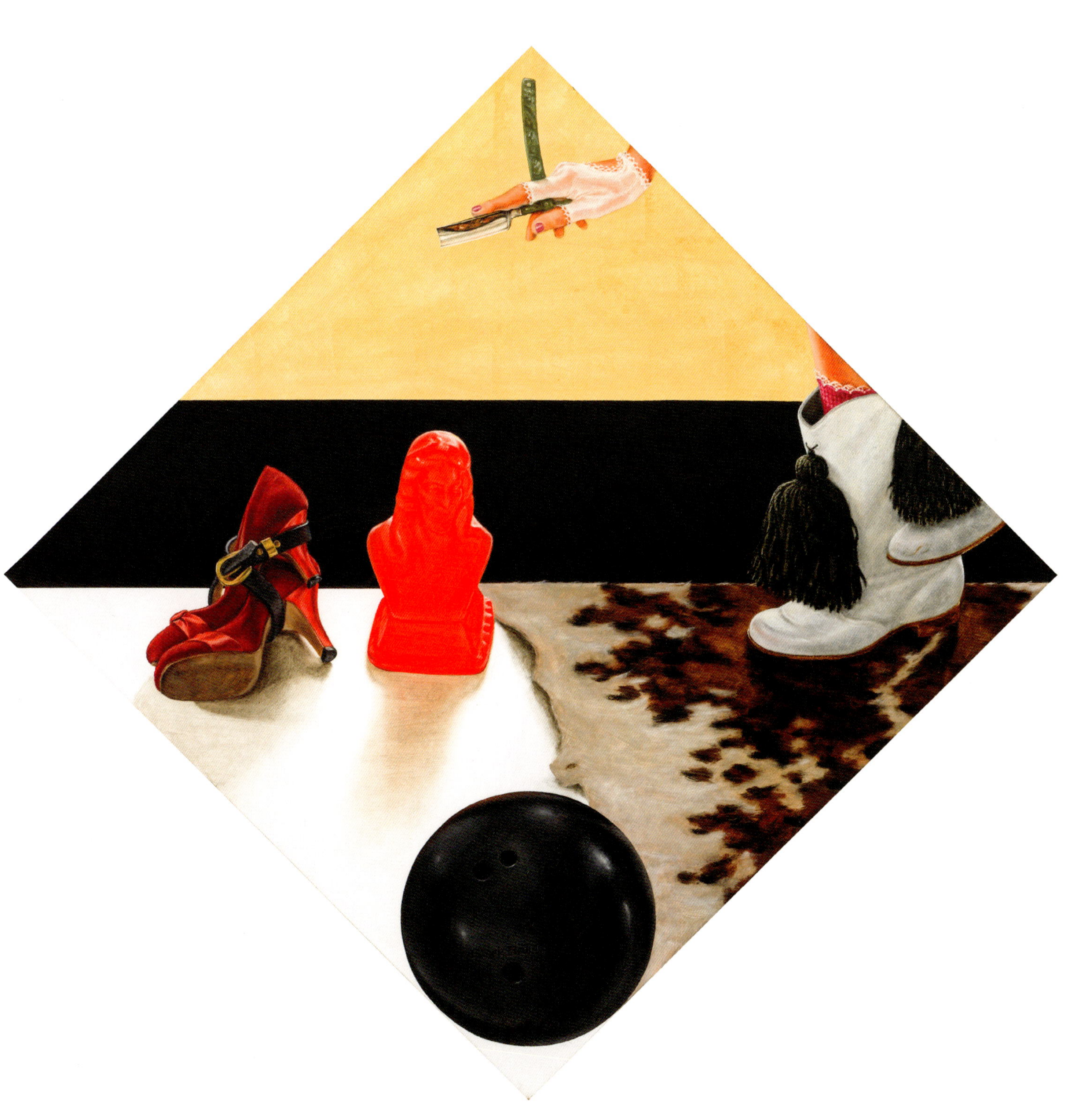

Young American artist seeks audience to enjoy poly-conscious attempts at post-medium condition production.

Must enjoy race mongering, disparate disconnected thoughts and sunsets (really). Familiarity with the work of Sun Ra, Joseph Beuys, Rosalind Krauss, Richard Pryor, Hans Haacke, Carl Andre and interest in spelunking in the death of identity a plus. I'm looking for an audience with a good attention span that is willing to stay with me through the good and the bad. I enjoy creating movies, producing sculptures, painting and making photographs. My interests are costuming, Sam Greenlee novels, Godard films and masturbation. Ability to hold conversation using only rap lyrics, and a sense of humor a must.

Rashid Johnson

The New Negro Escapist Social and Athletic Club (Thurgood), 2008, Lambda print, ed. 2/5, 69 x 55 1/2 in. (175.3 x 141 cm), acquired in 2008

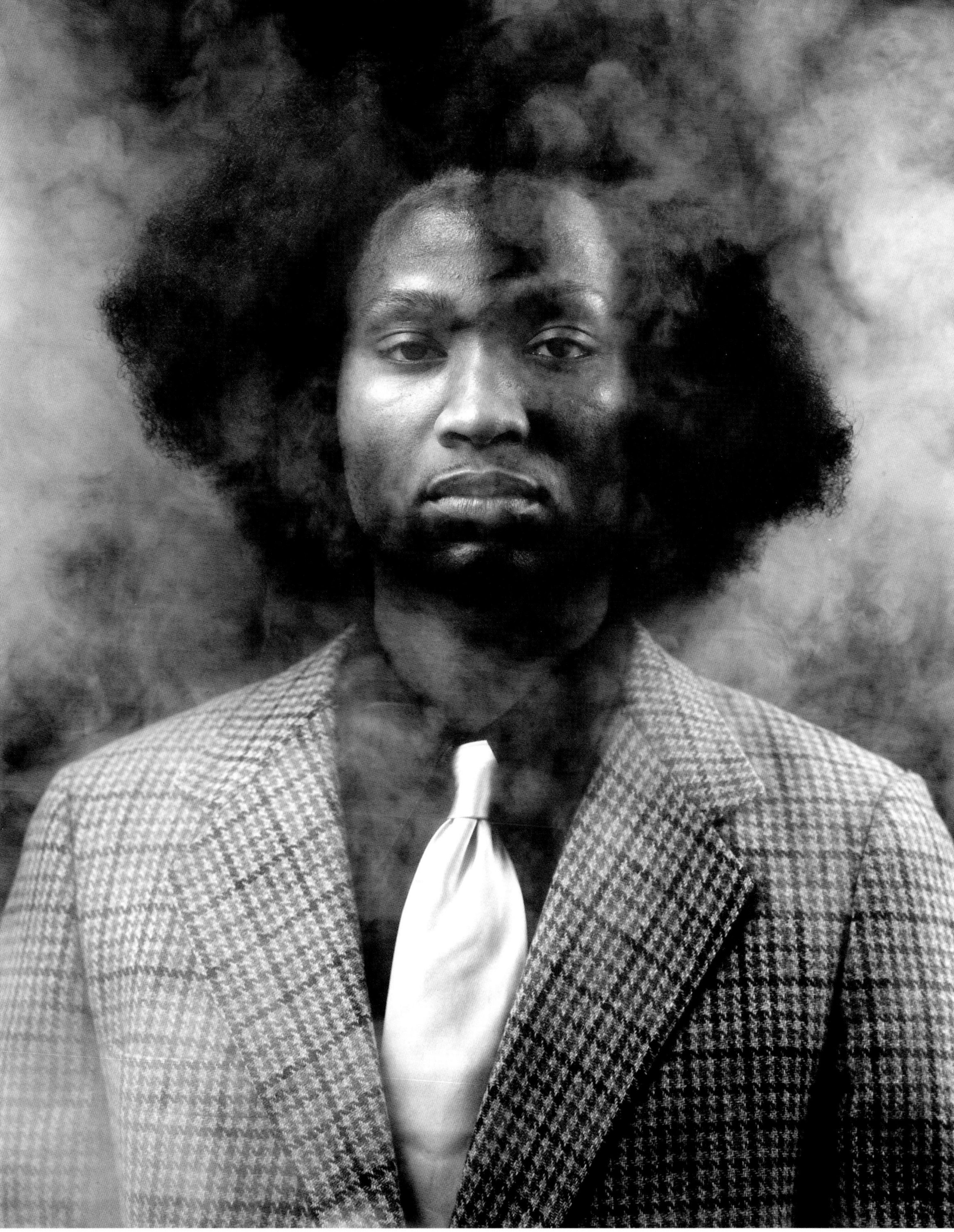

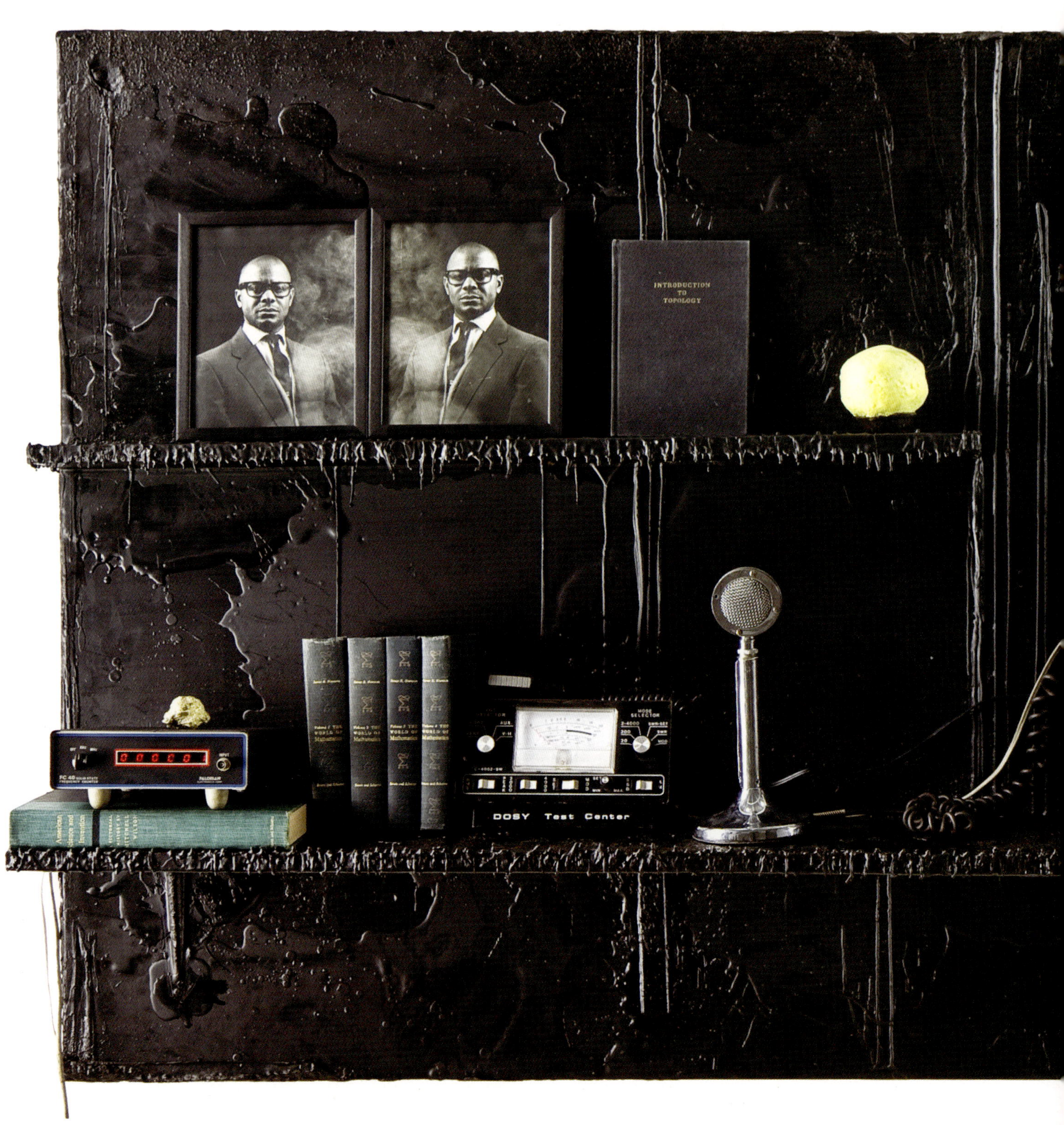

Citizen Band (Explorations in Topology), 2008, wax, soap, shea butter, framed photographs and mixed media on fiberboard, 48 x 96 x 12 in. (121.9 x 243.8 x 30.5 cm), acquired in 2008

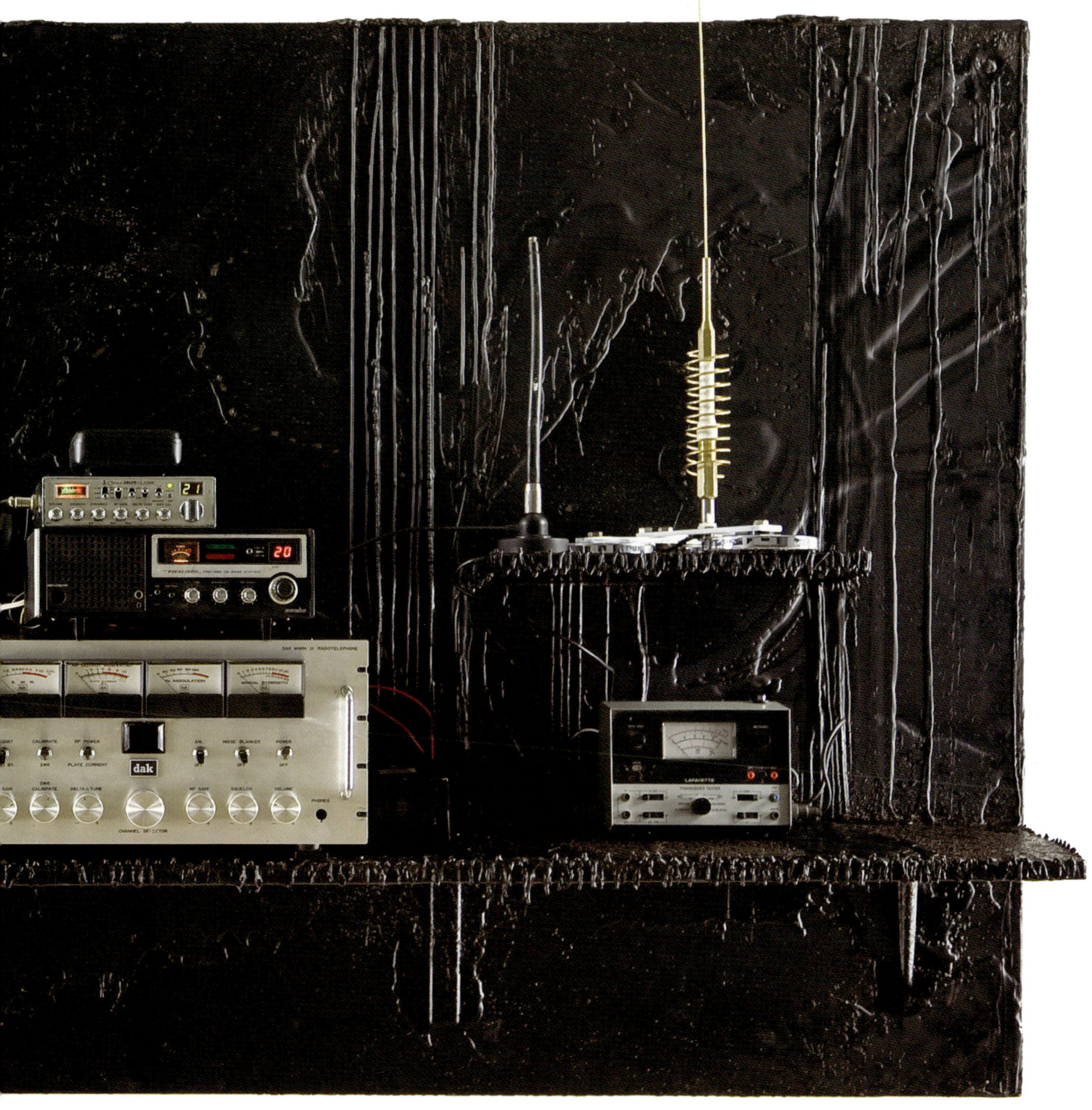
21
20
DAK MARK III RADIOTELEPHONE
CALIBRATE
RF POWER
ANL
NOISE BLANKER
POWER
SWR
PLATE CURRENT
OFF
dak
CALIBRATE
DELTA TUNE
RF GAIN
SQUELCH
VOLUME
PHONES
CHANNEL SELECTOR
LAFAYETTE

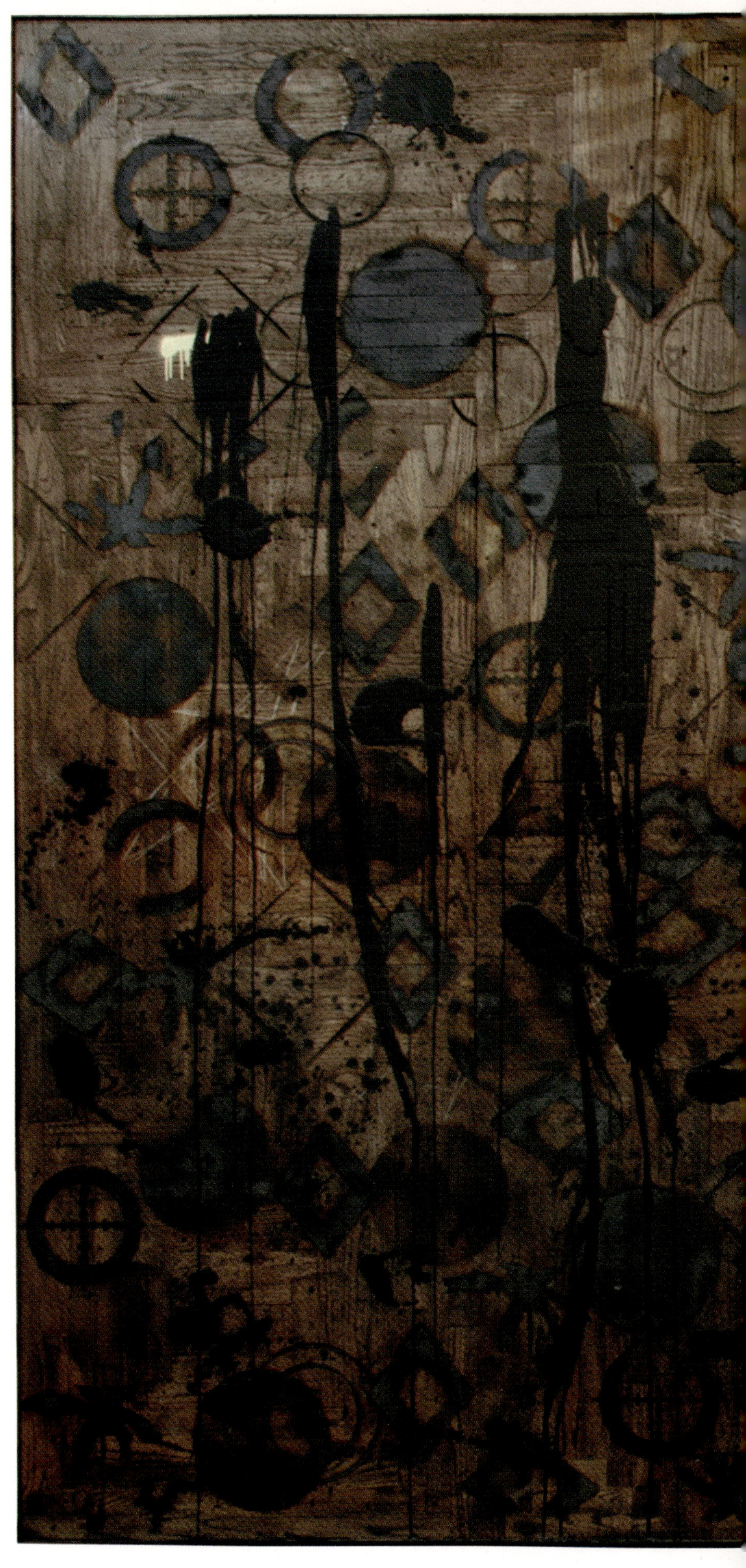

After Medium, 2011, branded red oak flooring, black soap, wax and paint, 132 x 168 x 2 3/4 in. (335.3 x 426.7 x 7 cm), acquired in 2011

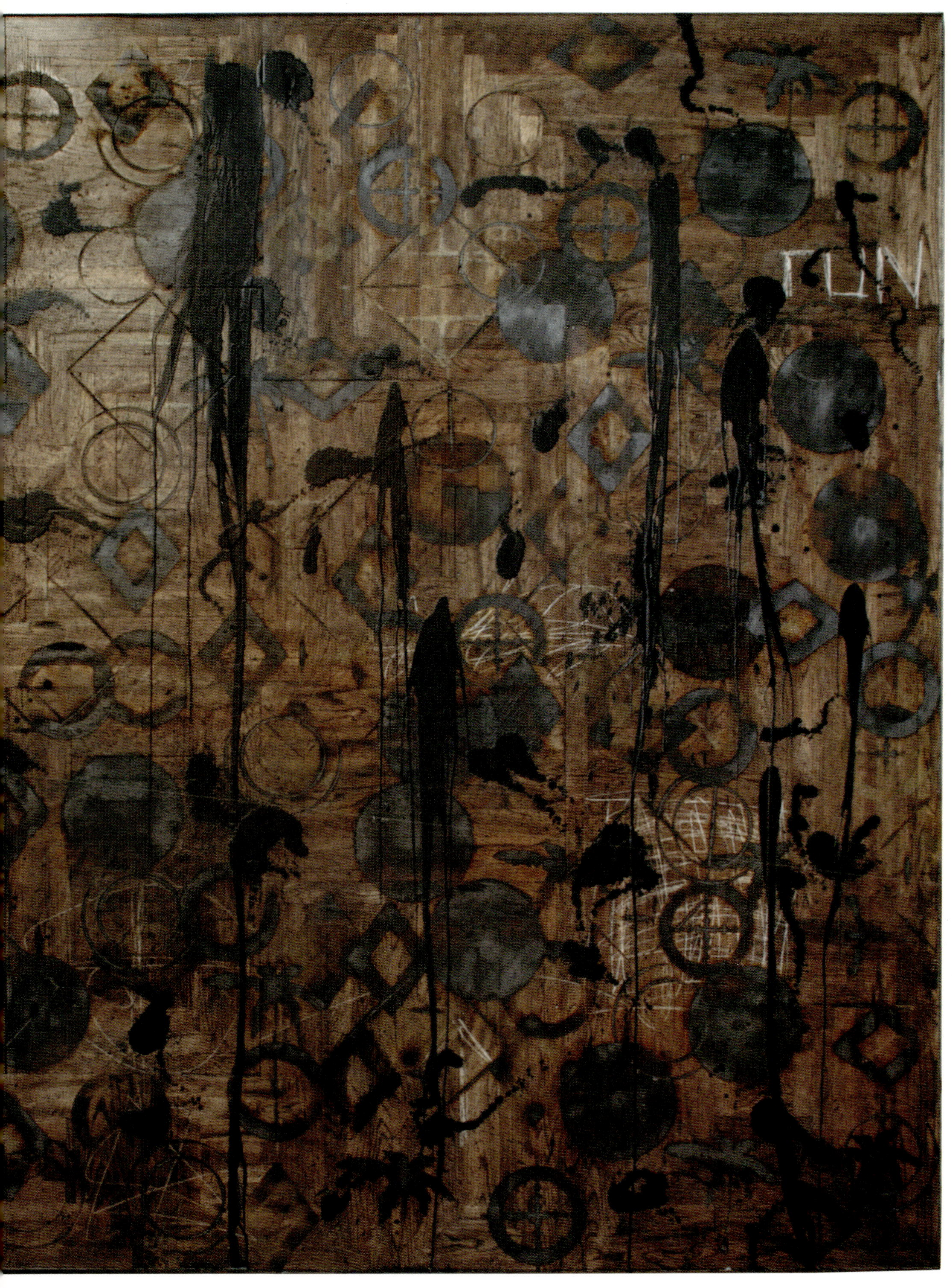

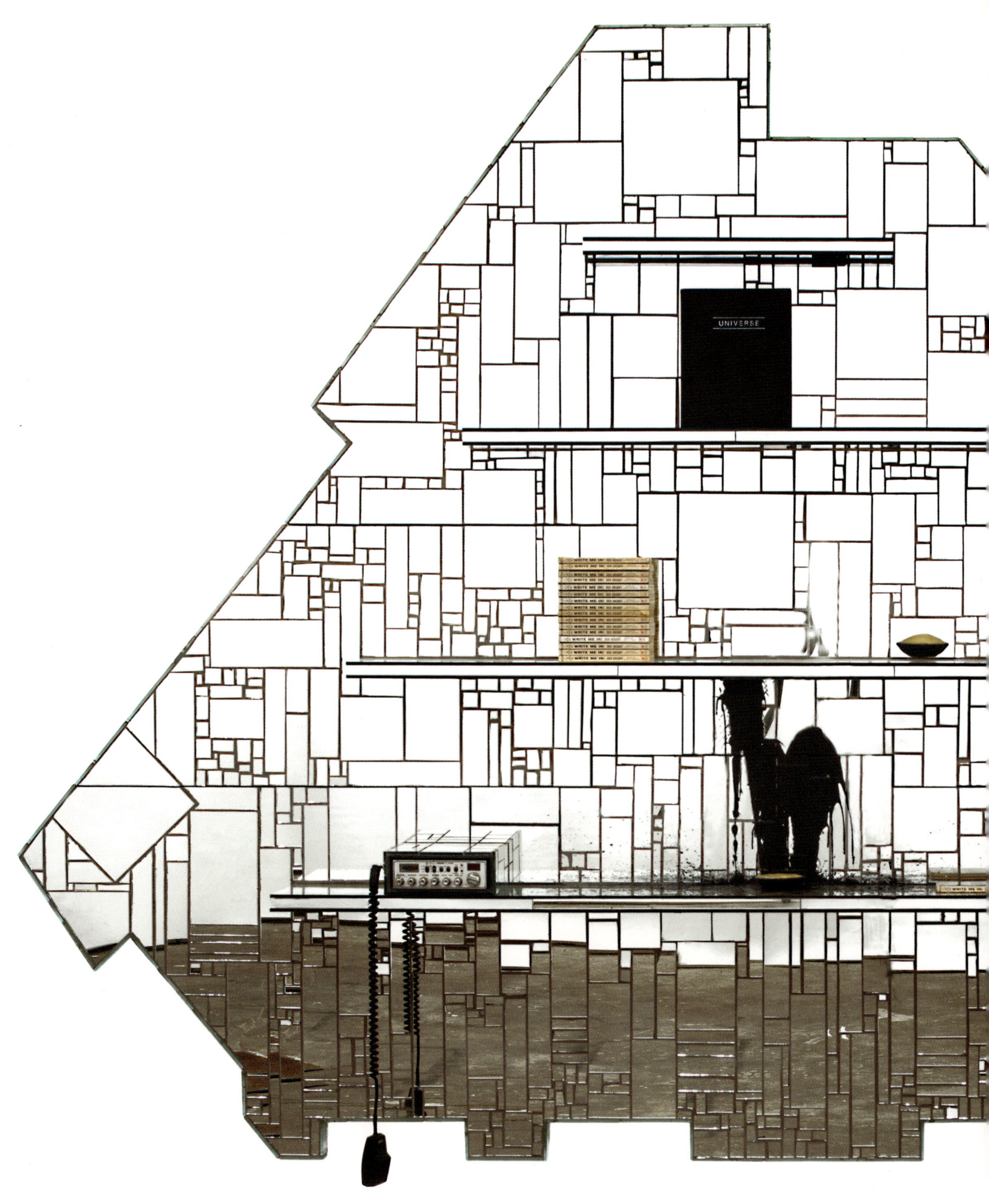

 RASHID JOHNSON

The Shuttle, 2011, mirrored tile, black soap, wax, books, shea butter, oyster shells, plant and cb radio, 96 1/2 x 125 x 11 3/4 in. (245.1 x 317.5 x 29.8 cm), acquired in 2011

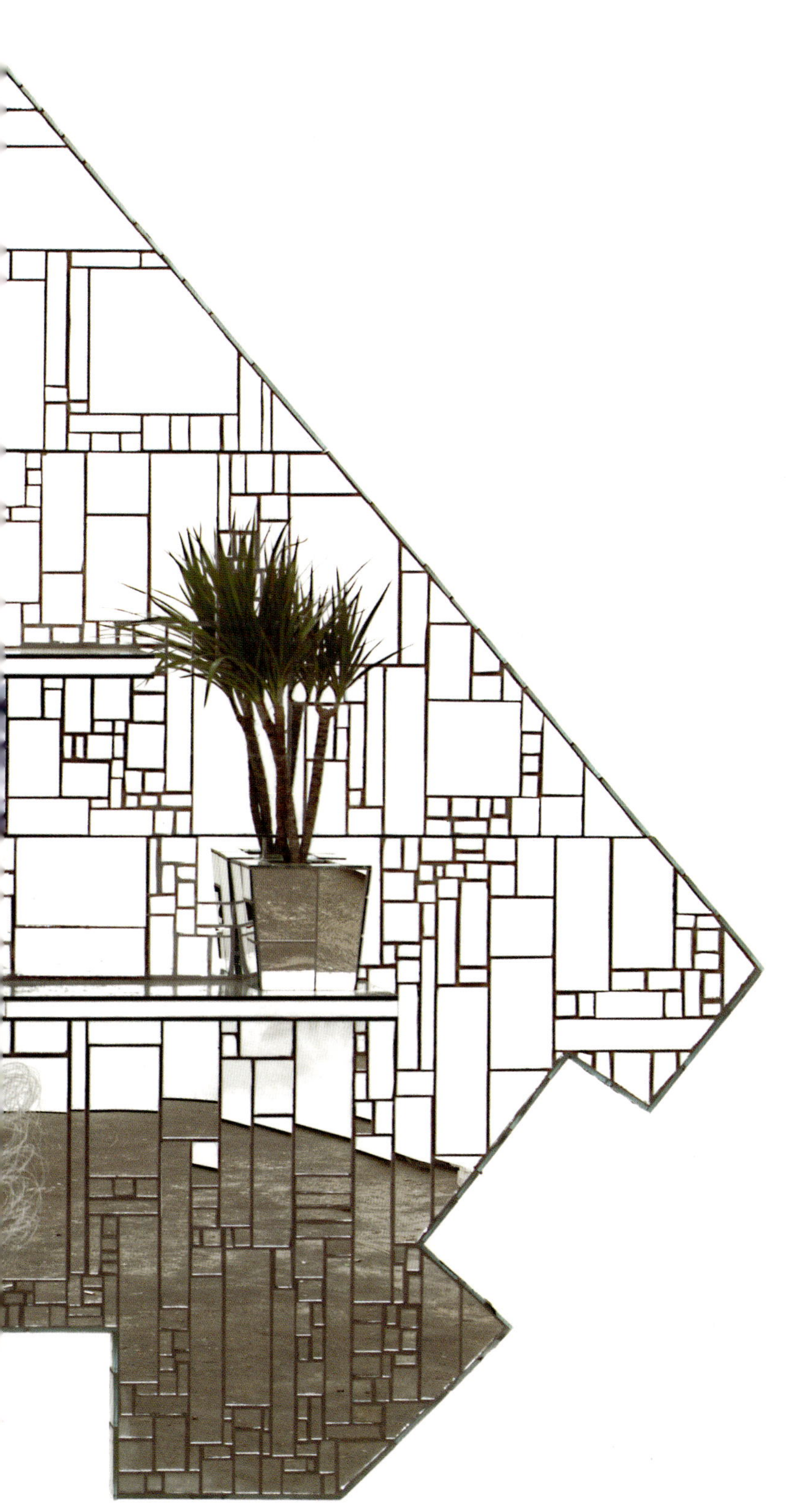

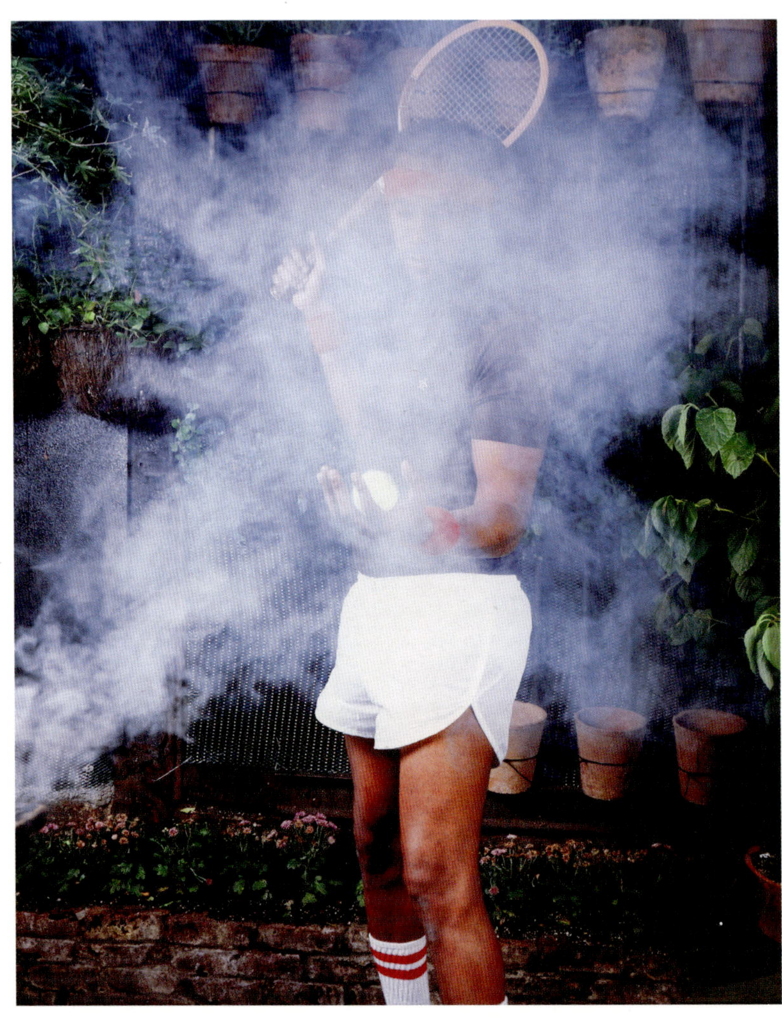

 RASHID JOHNSON *Self-portrait as the black Jimmy Connors in the finals of the New Negro Escapist Social and Athletic Club Summer Tennis Tournament*, 2008, Lambda print on dibond with stained wood frame, 60 x 48 in. (152.4 x 121.92 cm), acquired in 2008

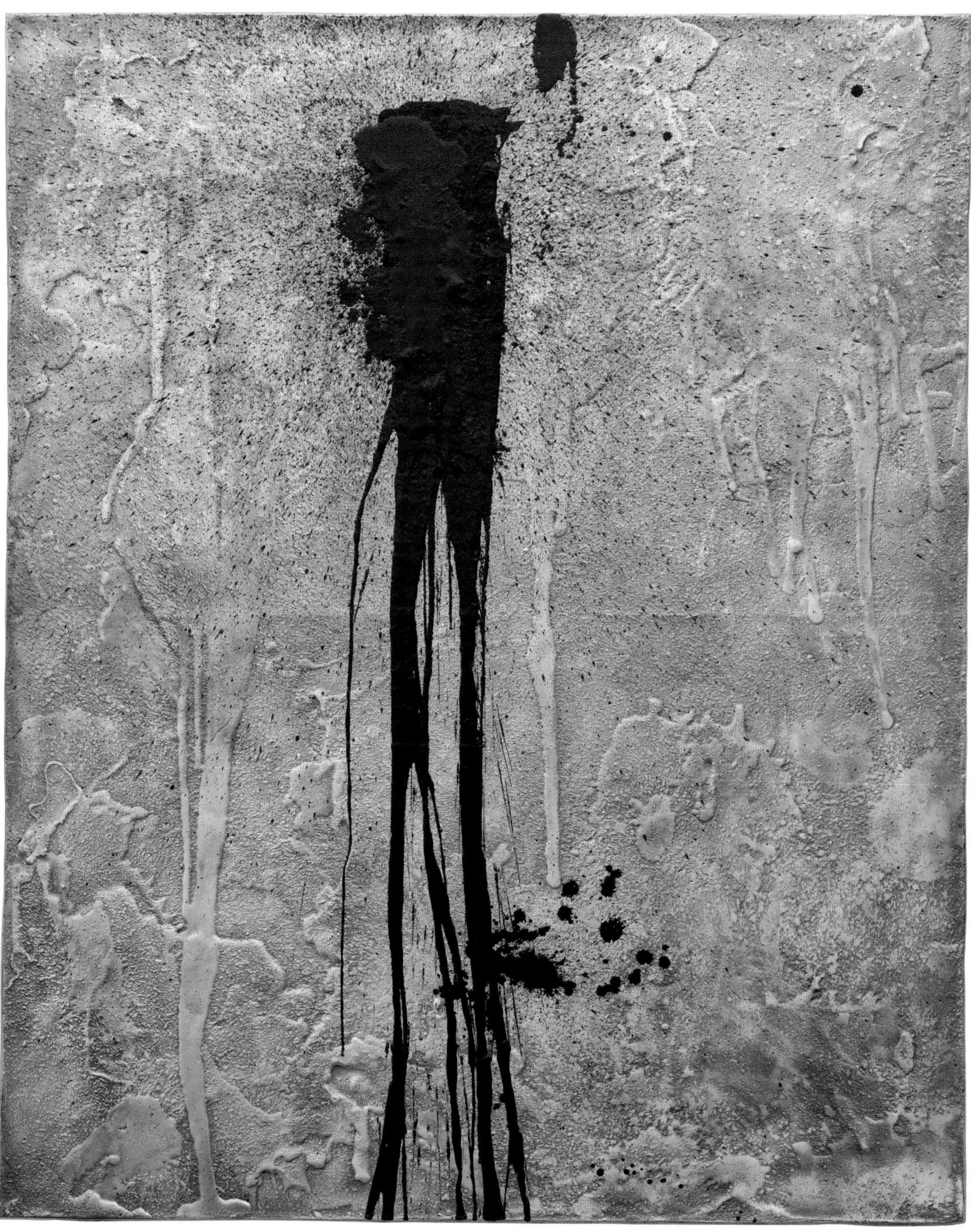

Barnburner, 2011, cast bronze, black soap and wax, 49 x 39 x 1 in. (124.5 x 99 x 2.54 cm), acquired in 2012

A IS FOR AFROPESSIMISM

A dyspeptic variation on Afrocentrism, Afrofuturism, Afronauts and various other "Afro" words.

B IS FOR BLACK

A child of the civil rights movement, my mother believed that as black people we would use our natural talents and abilities to rise above adversity. Paradoxically, she also believed that blackness consisted of habits, not nature, and most of those that she associated with it were negative. In response to the "grown acting" of my childhood years she used to say, "Roll your eyes at me again and I will knock the black off you." For years I imagined that blackness was like the shell of a hard-boiled egg, which, if tapped frequently and methodically, could be peeled away; or that blackness could be scraped off like the surface of burnt toast.

C IS FOR COCOROSIE

My mother attributed some of my bad habits to "following what white people do," which only added to my general confusion about racial identity. Nowadays, following white people's behavior is not an option because there is so little of it left to emulate. The breadth of this scarcity was made clear to me when I read a recent article in *The New York Times* about the band CocoRosie ("Twisted Sisters," July 6, 2008). Bianca, one of the sisters who make up the group, explained that their mom was ashamed of the looks she had inherited from her Syrian Orthodox mother and Native American father. "Our mom's a seriously beautiful woman; she looks like Cher after the surgery, but growing up, she was ashamed of who she was," Bianca said. "Nowadays, who would want to be white? But back then, in farm country, anything other than button-nosed blonde didn't fly."

While I applaud the sentiment behind this white flight, I note that it occurs at a moment of increasing black misery and hopelessness. It would seem that not all forms of disappearance are created equal.

D IS FOR DISNEY

A more radical instance of *dis*identification was Sun Ra's retreat from the category of "human." After all, better to be from Saturn than to be from pre-civil-rights-era Birmingham. What Ra did not give up, ironically, was his love of Disney. Ra's 1989 album, *Second Star to the Right,* is composed of freewheeling versions of Disney classics such as "Some Day My Prince Will Come" and "Zip-a-Dee-Doo-Dah." While some jazz musicians have been drawn to popular music in general, Ra—with his sense of self-invention and the fantastic—perhaps found a particular resonance in the *gesamtkunstwerk* that Walt Disney created at his theme parks.

E IS FOR ELMO

And better to be an alien than unemployed. Actors such as Michael Dorn and Tim Russ as Worf and Tuvok in *Star Trek,* Joe Morton as the

Brother in *Brother from Another Planet*, Ahmed Best as the voice of Jar Jar Binks, James Earl Jones as the voice of Darth Vader, and Kevin Clash as Elmo have excelled in giving voice to the non-human.

F IS FOR "I BELIEVE I CAN FLY"

Rising above the confines of the terrestrial reminded me of another act of levitation I witnessed at the opening of "Frequency," an exhibition at the Studio Museum in Harlem in 2005. Standing in front of Rodney McMillian's *Untitled* (2004), an abject piece of canvas with strokes of latex paint and charcoal that started on the floor and traveled eight feet up the wall, I thought, 'The children believe they can fly.' This is not to say that I haven't flown too, but the effortless, Michael Jordan-like virtuosity of the piece and its dialogue with the work of artists such as Marcel Duchamp and David Hammons left me speechless.

G IS FOR GREEN

Richard Green burst into seventh grade French class to ask what *Voulez-vous coucher avec moi ce soir?* meant. Richard was what my Uncle Tossy called "a complicated Negro." Streetwise yet slightly 'country,' athletic, yet bookish, Richard was an anomaly in the overly liberal, predominantly white private high school we attended. My more wicked classmates would sing Kermit the Frog's theme song, "It's Not Easy Bein' Green," whenever he walked into the student lounge. Richard's outburst in French class became legendary, although I knew he was simply asking about lyrics from the Labelle song "Lady Marmalade." Embarrassed for him and for my people, I told my classmates that I didn't know what all that mess was about.

H IS FOR HAPPENS TO BE BLACK

Obama, it is said, is a presidential candidate that "happens to be black." This is despite the fact that he is biracial and chose to call himself an African American. I happens to be black too, though I don't know how it happened. Because I never felt I was in a position to choose my racial identity, it never occurred to me that blackness was something that could happen to you, like being mugged, or winning the lottery. I thought one was just black and that was that.

I IS FOR INVISIBLE MAN

I first read Ellison's novel in high school. The density of the text mirrored what I thought about black people: that we were a deep people. It was reading that book that made me think I wanted to be a writer, although when it was first published not everyone was happy with its depiction of black life. One critic claimed, black people "need Ralph Ellison's *Invisible Man* like we need a hole in the head or a stab in the neck." Still, that novel was a crucial catalyst for the use of text in my paintings.

J IS FOR JERRY LEWIS

Every Labor Day I would watch his muscular dystrophy telethon. I wondered what it would be like to have someone raise money for *my* cause. What that cause would be, I wasn't sure. Brooding Negro Syndrome, perhaps?

K IS FOR KRAZY KAT

I, too, used to mistake bricks for love.

L IS FOR LIGON!

My mother worked as a therapist's aide at Bronx Psychiatric Center, a large mental health facility in the Northeast Bronx. Sometimes, after school, I would meet her at work to go to the lunch counter at Woolworth's for grilled cheese sandwiches and ice cream sundaes. Since the hospital was an outpatient facility, half of the people we ran into on the walk to Woolworth's were being treated at the hospital. I would play a game with my mother called "Patient or Employee," the object of which was to guess whether the person who shouted "Ligon!" at my mother as we passed on the street was a mental patient or a co-worker. I was never very good at this game.

M IS FOR THE MANY THINGS SHE GAVE ME

International Children's Day, a United Nations-sponsored holiday celebrating the rights of children, was a holiday that my brother and I took very seriously. Every year on Children's Day I would ask my mother what presents she had bought for me. "When you are a parent, every day is Children's Day," she would reply, rolling her eyes.

N IS FOR NEGRO SUNSHINE

"Rose Johnson and Melanctha Herbert had been friends now for some years. Rose had lately married Sam Johnson, a decent, honest kindly fellow, a deck hand on a coasting steamer.

Melanctha Herbert had not yet been really married.

Rose Johnson was a real black, tall, well built, sullen, stupid, childlike, good looking negress. She laughed when she was happy and grumbled and was sullen with everything that troubled.

Rose Johnson was a real black negress but she had been brought up quite like their own child by white folks.

Rose laughed when she was happy but she had not the wide, abandoned laughter that makes the warm broad glow of negro sunshine. Rose was never joyous with the earth-born, boundless joy of negroes. Hers was just ordinary, any sort of woman laughter."

Three Lives, Gertrude Stein

O IS FOR OPRAH

Oprah Winfrey believed her ancestors were Zulus, but they turned out to be from Liberia. "Oprah, of course, wants to be Zulu. She's announced to the world she's Zulu," said scholar Henry Louis Gates, who helped her trace her lineage. "Oprah is not Zulu. None of us are Zulu. There is no African American who comes from the Zulu people."

("Fascinating look into history, race and DNA," *Oakland Tribune*, January 31, 2006)

P IS FOR PROUD

James Brown's "Say it Loud" was released in 1968. When it came on the radio I could sing the "Say it Loud" part but I could only whisper, "I'm black and I'm proud."

Q IS FOR QUESTIONS AND ANSWERS

I gave a lecture at Princeton where, as an aside during a lull in the question-and-answer period, I said that black people were going to disappear. Afterwards at the wine and cheese reception, an elderly woman came up to me to thank me for the talk. "When you said you thought black people were going to disappear I knew exactly what you mean," she said, her face full of sympathy. "I mean you're just not interesting to us any more. Now there are Chinese people and Mexicans..."

R IS FOR RACE

Childhood crushes: Race Bannon on *Jonny Quest,* and Racer X on *Speed Racer.* Every Saturday morning I would wake up at 6 a.m. to wait for my cartoon paramours to appear in black-and-white on the old console TV we had in the living room of our apartment.

S IS FOR SHADOWS

I first saw Warhol's *Shadow* paintings at the Heiner Friedrich Gallery in 1979. I remember thinking that it was an awfully big room in which to show paintings of nothing. Although I never met Andy Warhol I saw him once on the street in SoHo. He was thin, ghostly, and almost transparent. To make a career out of being fascinated with one's own disappearance is quite a feat. I realized that if disappearance could be a subject matter, I could be an artist.

T IS FOR TYRONE

My brother Tyrone was a year older than I and although we didn't look alike, people would often ask if we were twins. When we were in elementary school, my mother used to give me his secondhand clothes to wear. She stopped doing that when I told her that wearing hand-me-downs made me feel like "I was not myself."

U IS THE UNITED STATES OF AFRICA

The U.S.A. is where Uhura, the communications officer on *Star Trek*, was from. Recently I read that Nichelle Nichols, the actress that played Uhura, wanted to quit the show after the first season but Martin Luther King Jr., persuaded her to stay on because she was a "role model." Although I was proud to see a black person on TV, Uhura annoyed me. In the future, couldn't black people do more than just operate the switchboard?

V IS FOR VULCAN

A planet where they had learnt to suppress emotions. I was obsessed with Vulcans and when I went to *Star Trek* conventions as a teenager I bought all the Vulcan paraphernalia I could find. I tried to imagine being a Vulcan, although I knew it meant that I would have to give up my Richard Pryor and Parliament-Funkadelic LPs and that was too much of a sacrifice. Also, there wasn't a black Vulcan until 1995 when the character Tuvok was introduced on *Star Trek: Voyager*; by that time I had moved on to wanting to be Jeff Koons.

W IS FOR WHITE

Q. You've seen the evolution from Negro to black to African-American? What is the best thing for blacks to call themselves?

A. White.

Sociologist Kenneth B. Clark being interviewed for *The New York Times*. ("An Integrationist to This Day, Believing All Else Has Failed," May 7, 1995)

X IS FOR X

When I was in my twenties, I met a member of the Nation of Islam who told me that since black people took the last names of their masters, we all had slave names. That was why, he explained, Malcolm Little had changed his name to Malcolm X. I considered changing my last name to *X* for a week or so, but decided that it would involve too much paperwork and it would upset my mom.

Y IS FOR "YOU FEEL ME?"

You feel me?

Z IS FOR ZULUS

I remember when being called a "Zulu" was an insult. When I was very young, black people didn't want anything to do with Africa. Ironically, this was after a period earlier in the century when black people organized themselves around leaving America and going back to Africa. In the late sixties, black people rediscovered Africa again, although it was still a mythologized Africa, an Africa where everyone knew our name. Nowadays everybody wants to be a Zulu, though we don't necessarily want to live in Africa. Being a descendant of a Zulu is enough. Zulu is beautiful. Now *that's* change you can believe in.

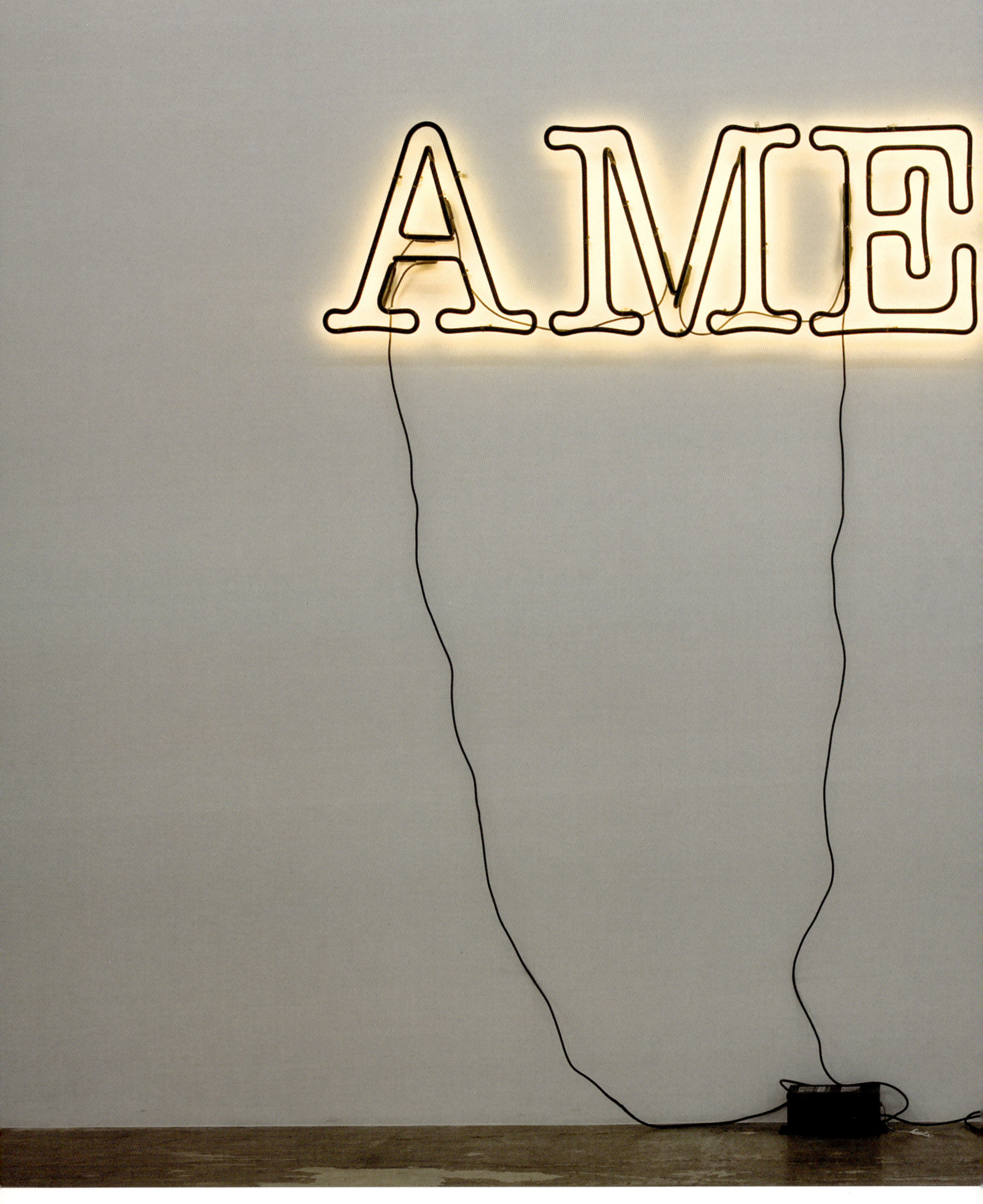

 GLENN LIGON *America*, 2008, neon and paint, ed.of 1 plus AP, 24 x 168 in. (61 x 426.7 cm), acquired in 2008

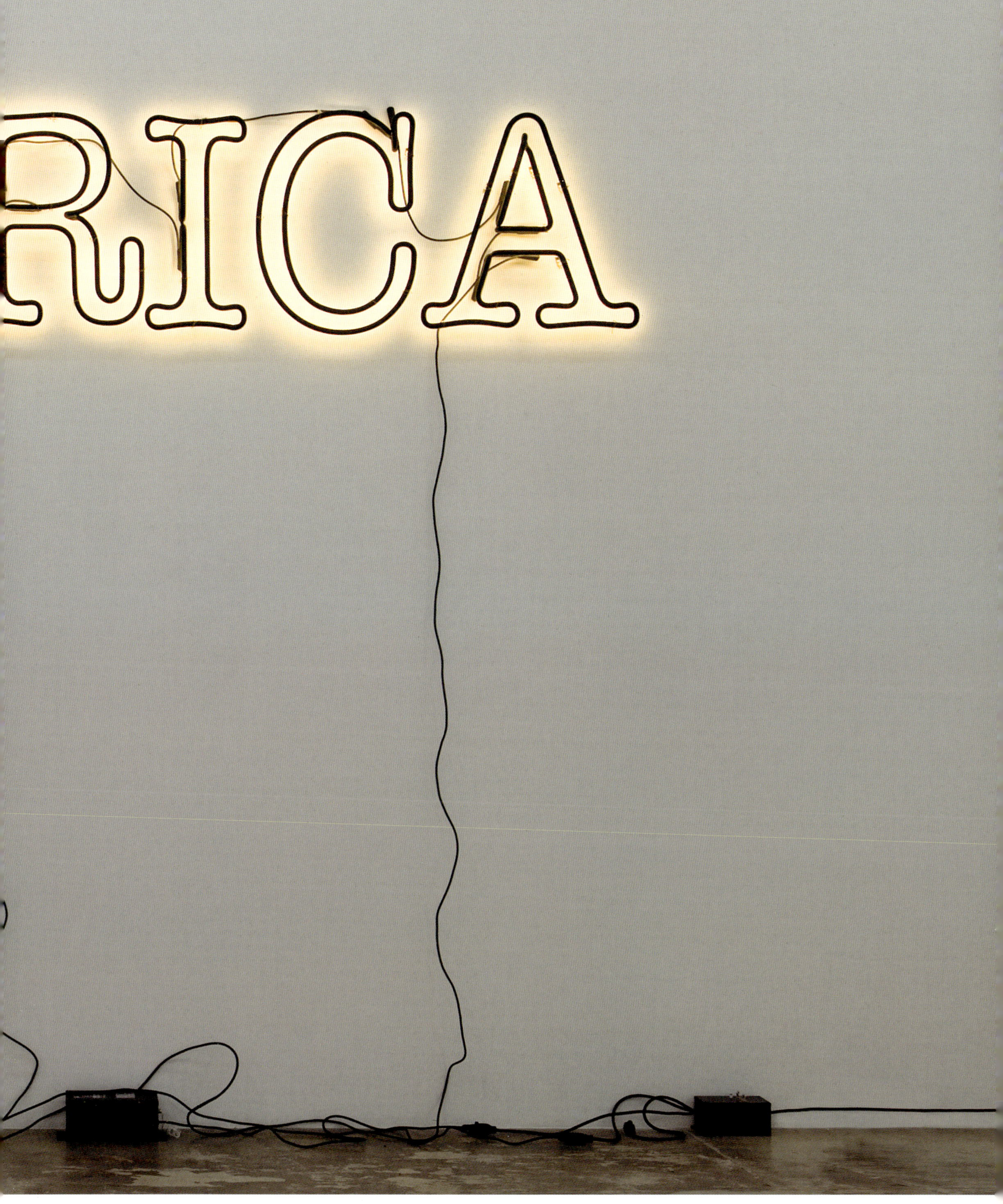
RICA

GLENN LIGON

Untitled (Malcolm X), 2008, acrylic, vinyl-based paint and graphite on paper mounted on fiberboard, 132 x 107 in. (335.3 x 271.8 cm), acquired in 2008

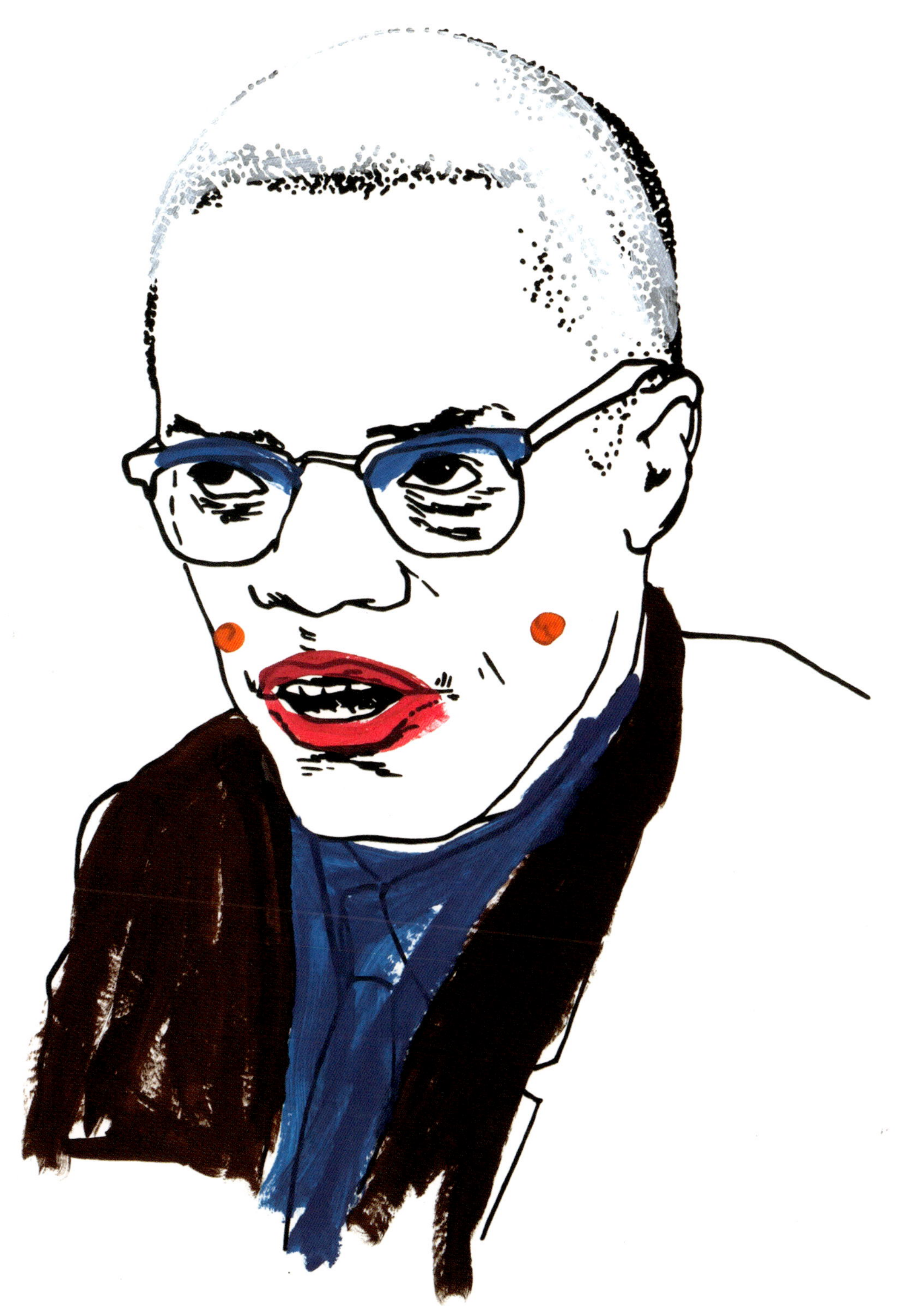

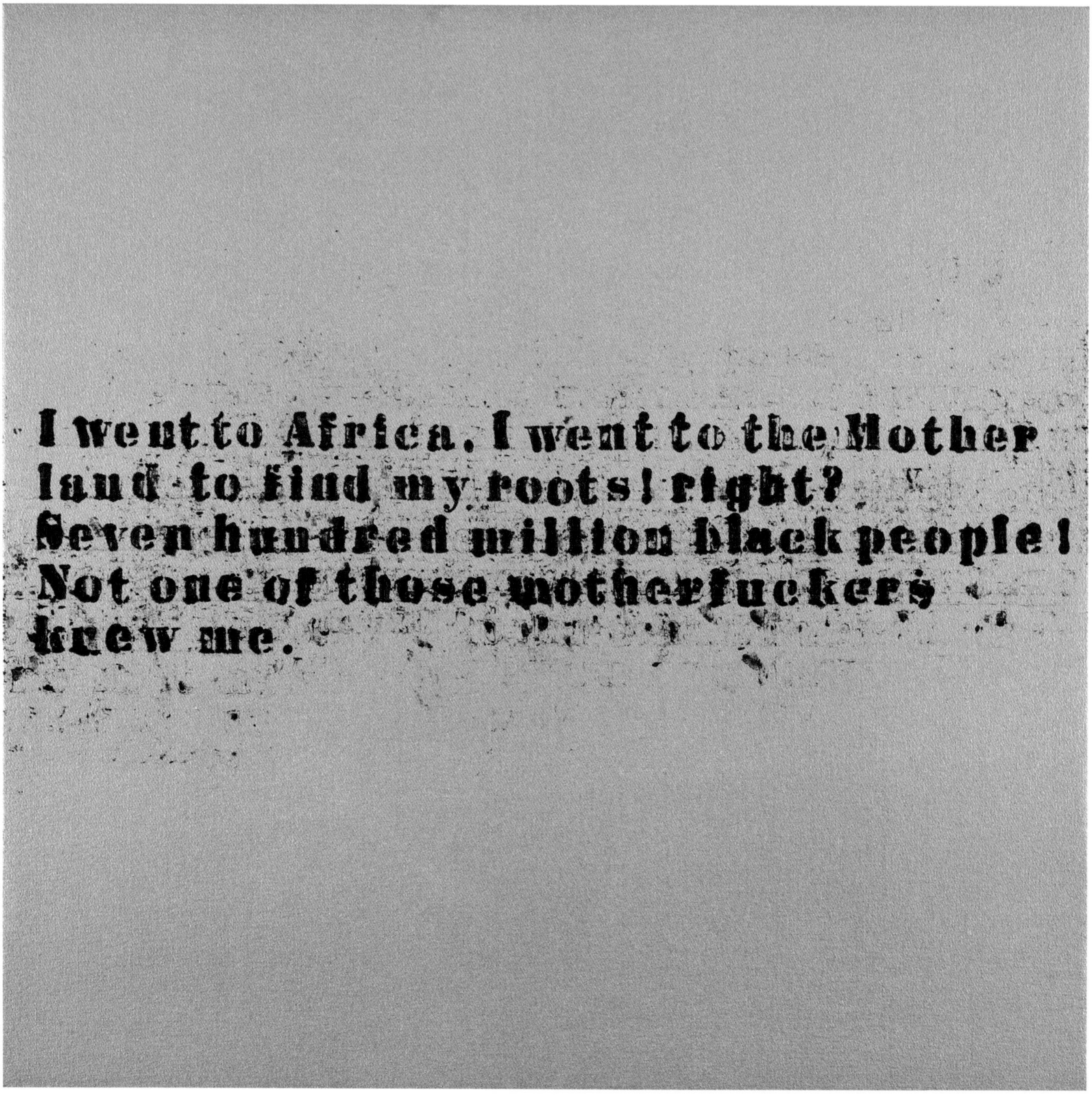

I went to Africa. I went to the Mother
land to find my roots! right?
Seven hundred million black people!
Not one of those motherfuckers
knew me.

 Gold Nobody Knew Me #1, 2007, acrylic and oil stick on canvas, 32 x 32 in. (81.3 x 81.3 cm), acquired in 2008

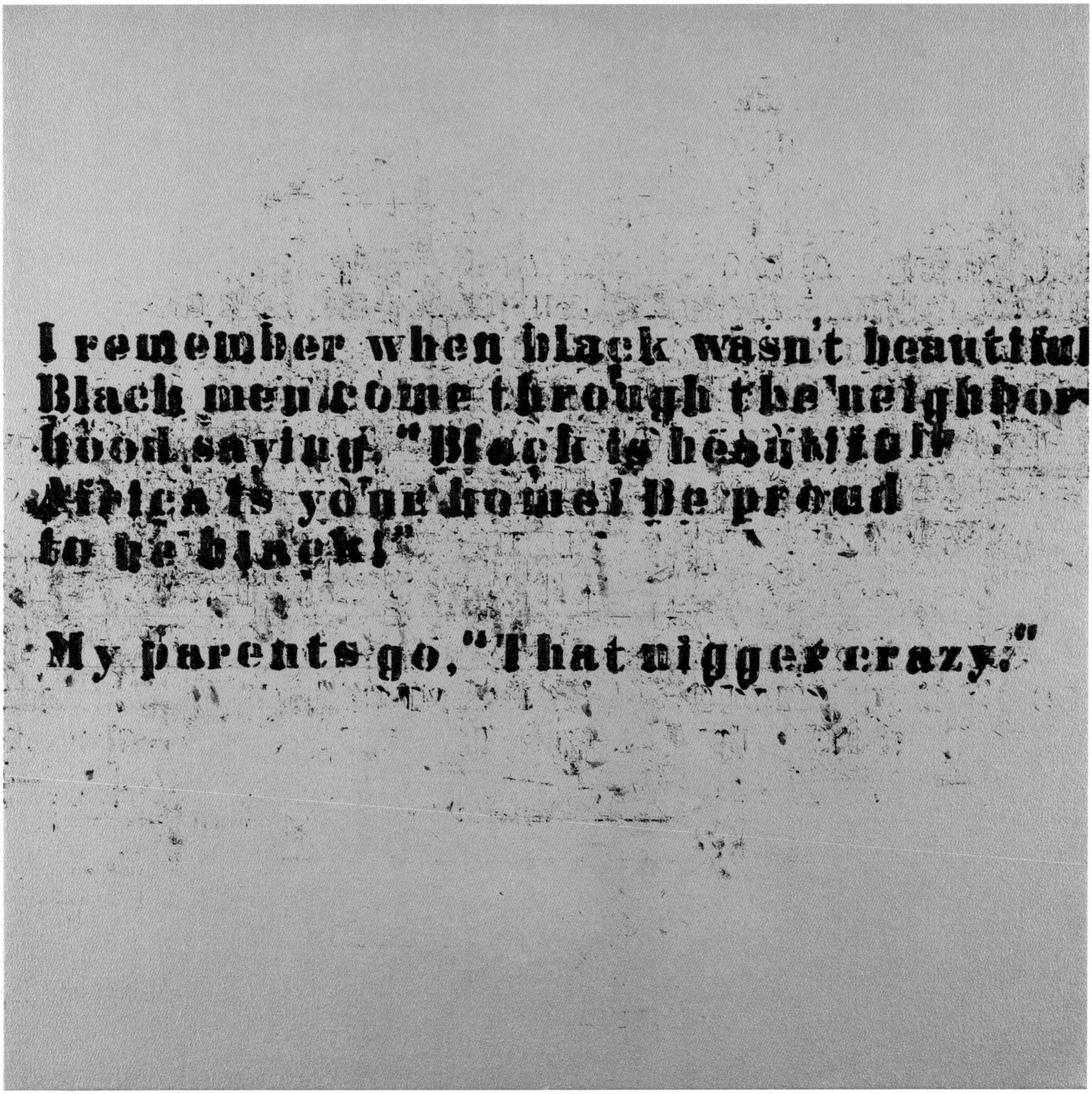

Gold When Black Wasn't Beautiful #1, 2007, acrylic and oil stick on canvas, 32 x 32 in. (81.3 x 81.3 cm), acquired in 2008

GLENN LIGON

Stranger #21, 2005, acrylic, coal dust, screen print, gesso and oil stick on canvas, 96 x 72 in. (243.8 x 182.9 cm), acquired in 2007

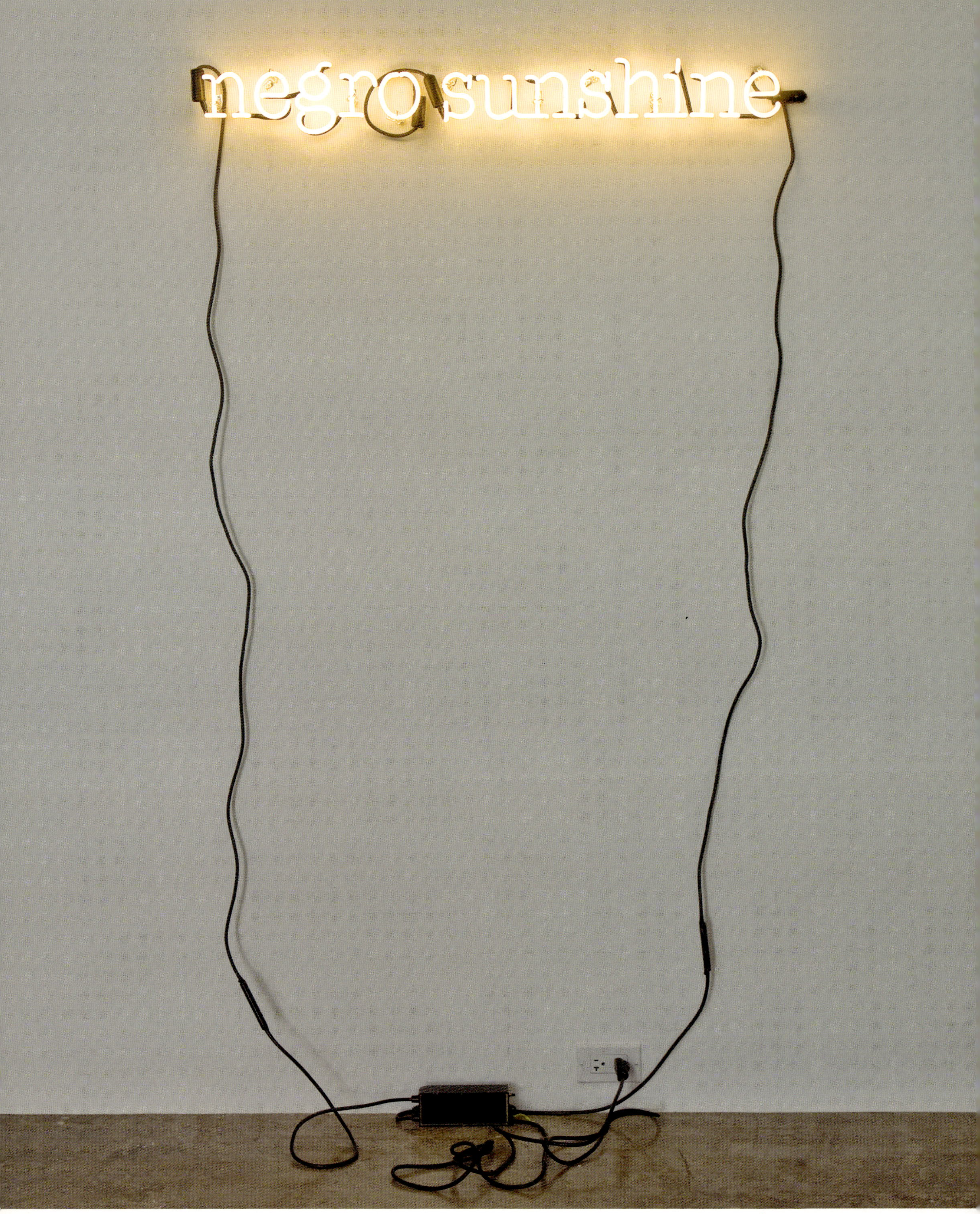

 GLENN LIGON *Untitled (Negro Sunshine)*, 2006, neon, ed. 3/7, 4 x 48 in. (10.1 x 121.9 cm), acquired in 2006

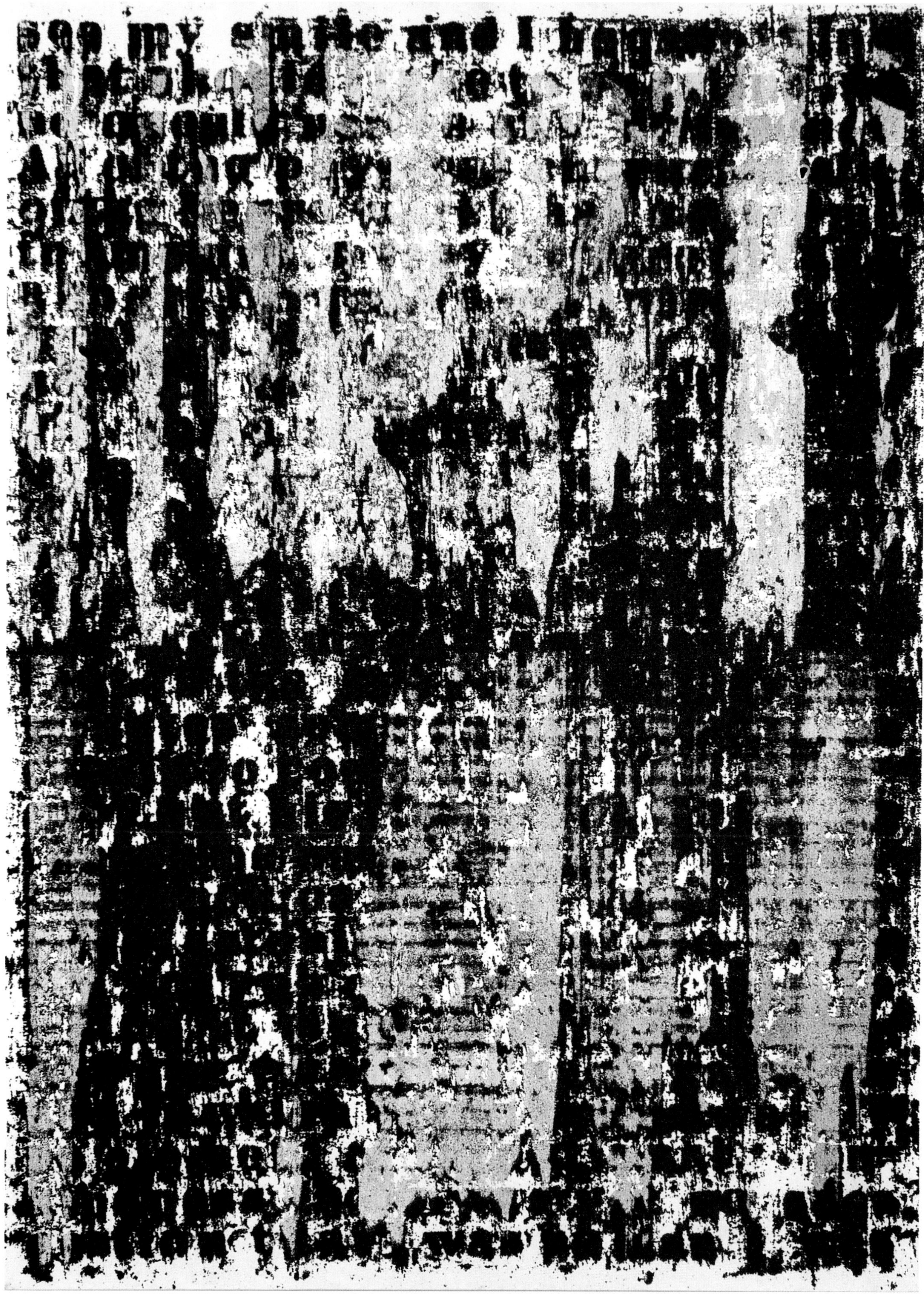

Mirror #7, 2006, acrylic, coal dust, screen print, gesso and oil stick on canvas, 84 x 60 in. (213.4 x 152.4 cm), acquired in 2006

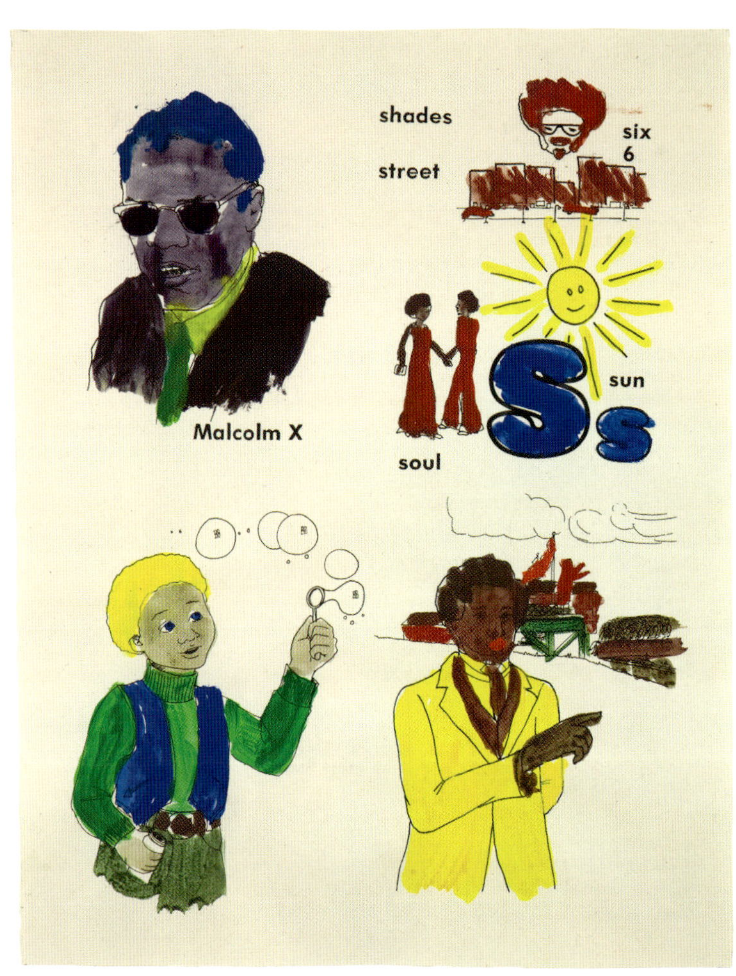

 GLENN LIGON *Malcom X, Sun, Frederick Douglass, Boy with Bubbles # 3 (version 2)*, 2001, vinyl-based paint and silkscreen on paper, 23 x 16 1/2 in. (58.5 x 42 cm), acquired in 2008

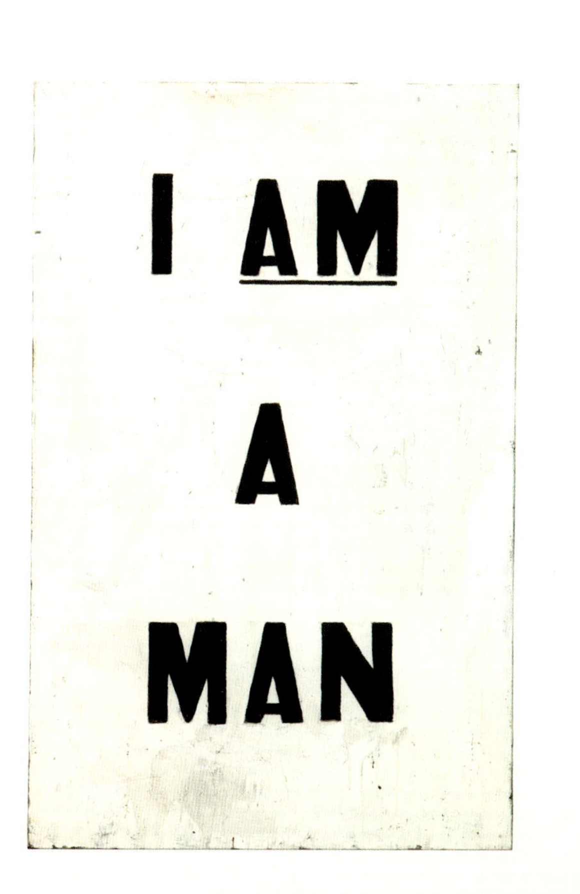

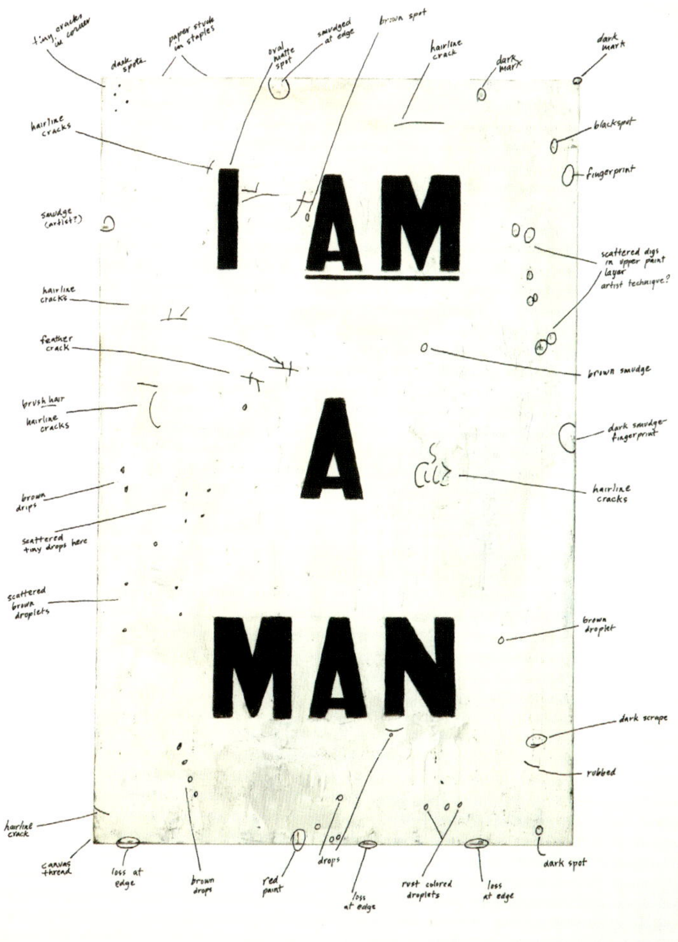

Condition Report D, 2000, iris print and iris print with serigraph, ed. 18/20, diptych, each 35 x 26 in. (88.9 x 66 cm), acquired in 2008

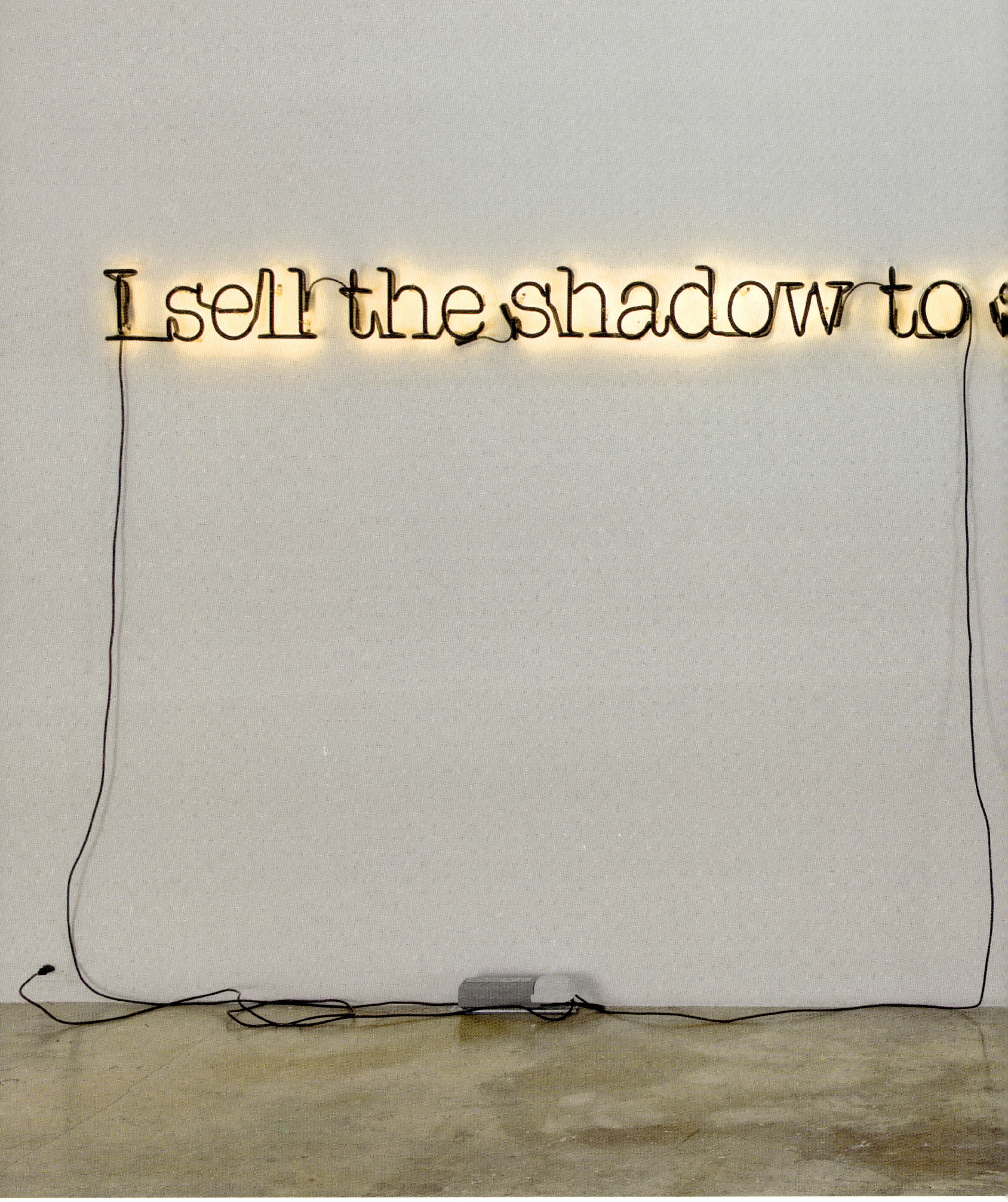

 GLENN LIGON *Untitled (I Sell the Shadow to Sustain the Substance)*, 2006, neon and paint, ed. 3/3, 7 1/2 x 192 1/2 in. (19 x 489 cm), acquired in 2006

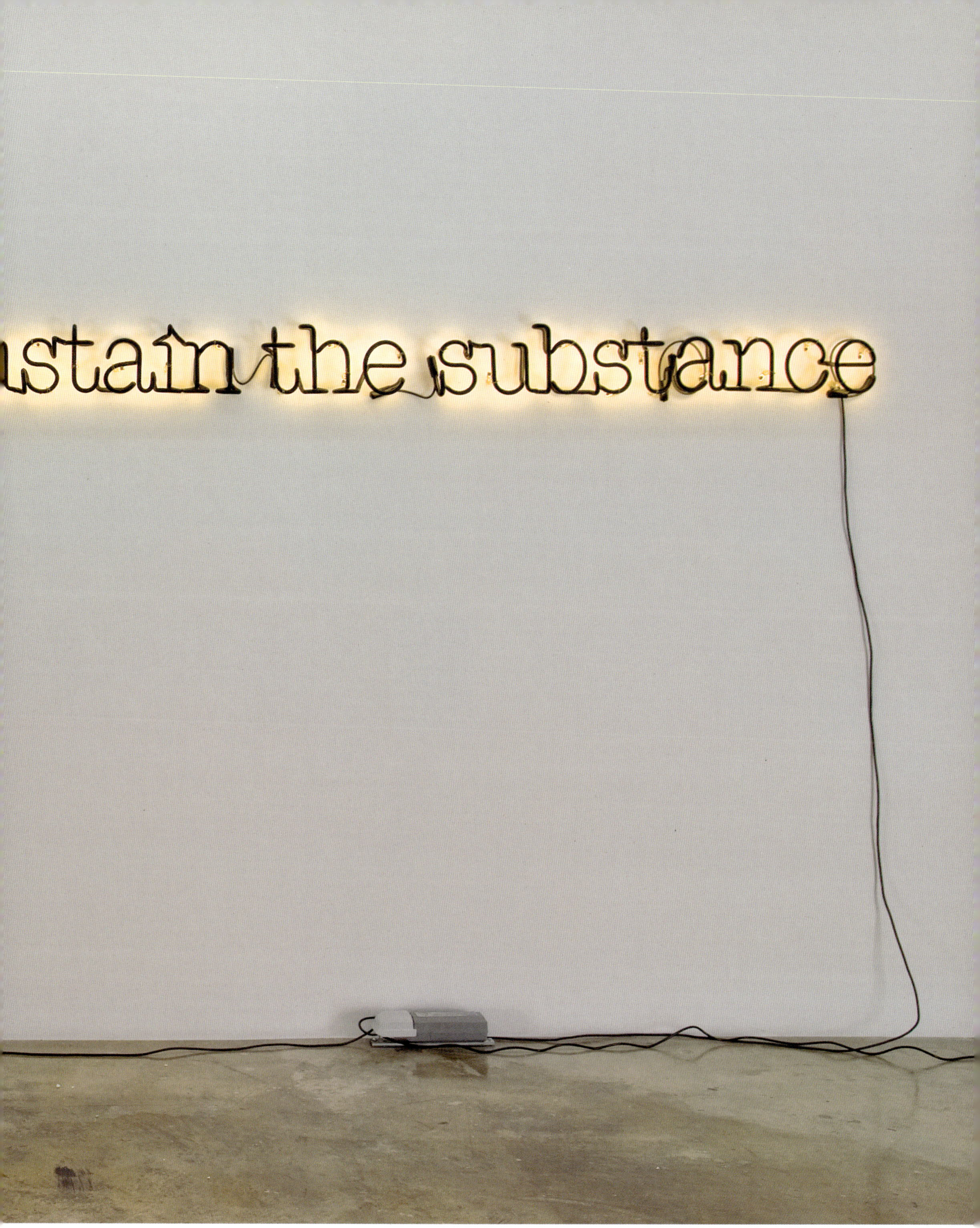

stain the substance

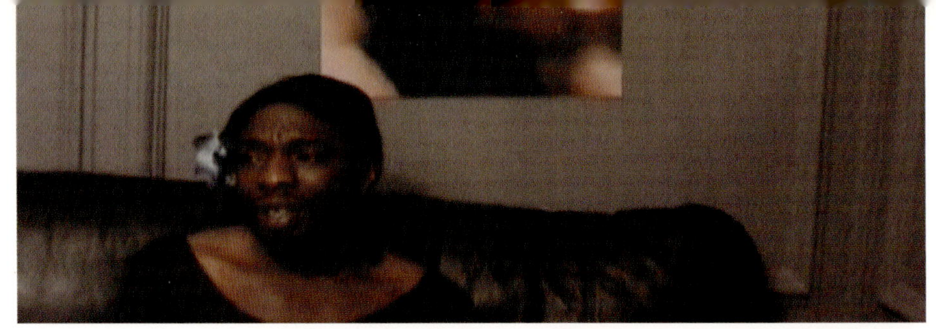

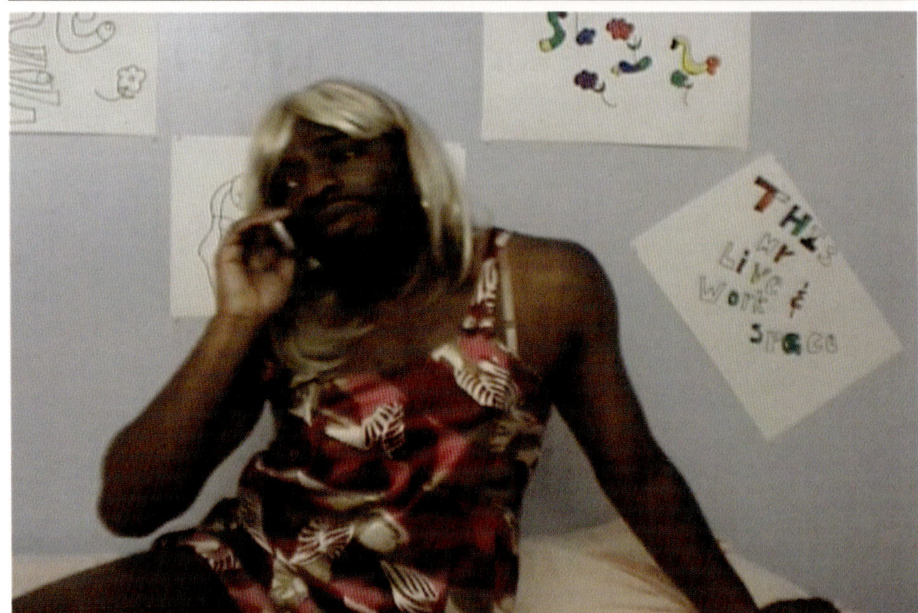

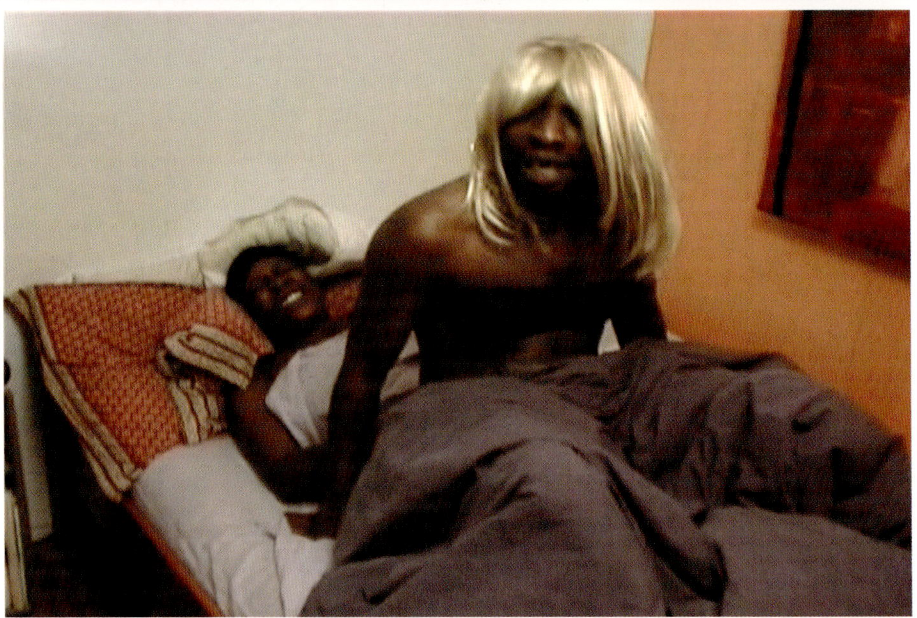

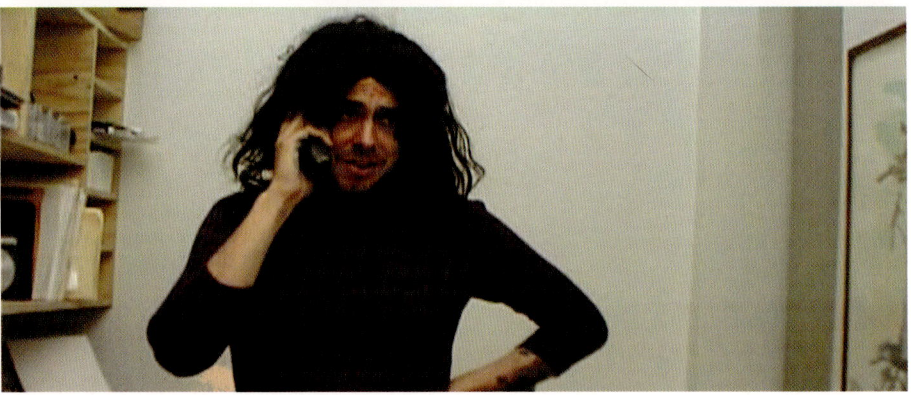

 KALUP LINZY

Stills from *Conversations wit de Churen IV: Play wit de Churen*, 2005, digital video (color, sound), 15 min. 49 sec., ed. 1/5, acquired in 2006

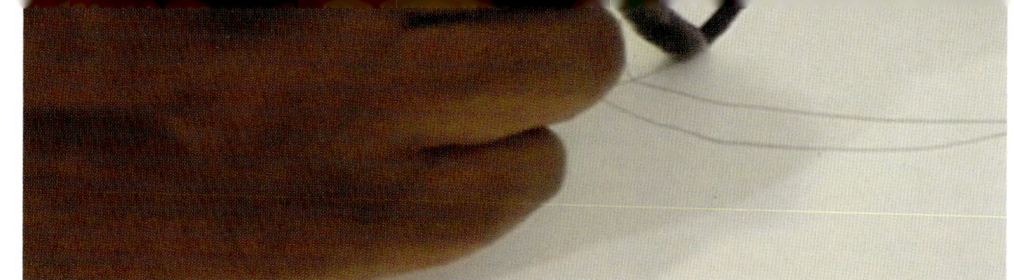

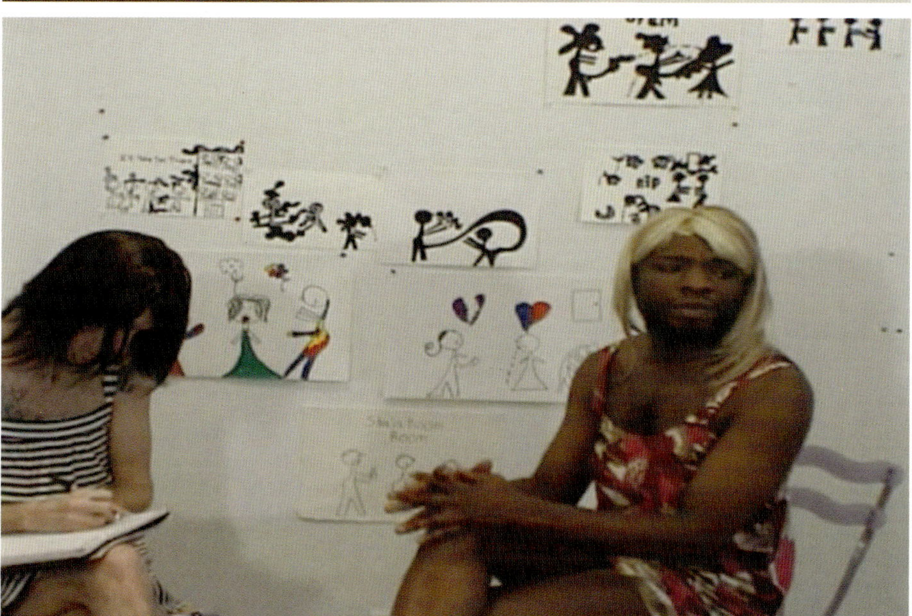

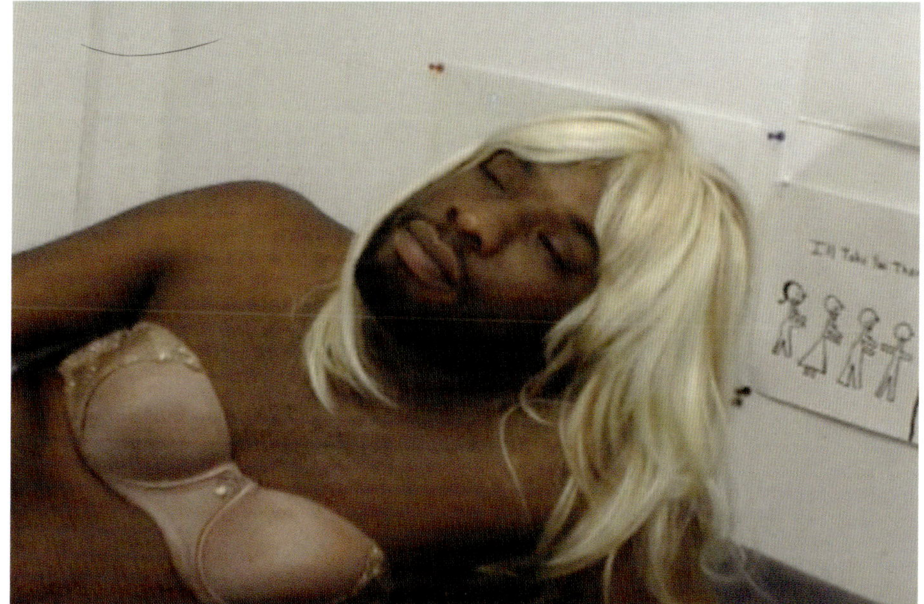

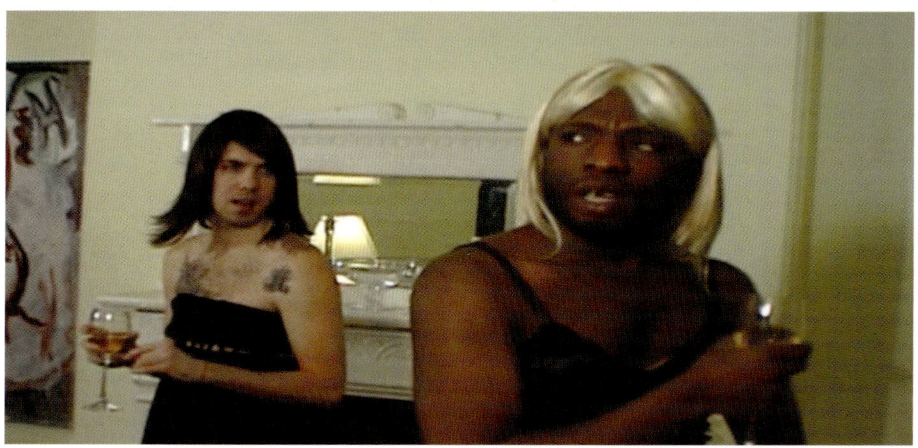

Stills from *Conversations with de Churen V: As da Art World Might Turn*, 2006, digital video (color, sound), 11 min. 15 sec., ed. 2/5, acquired in 2006

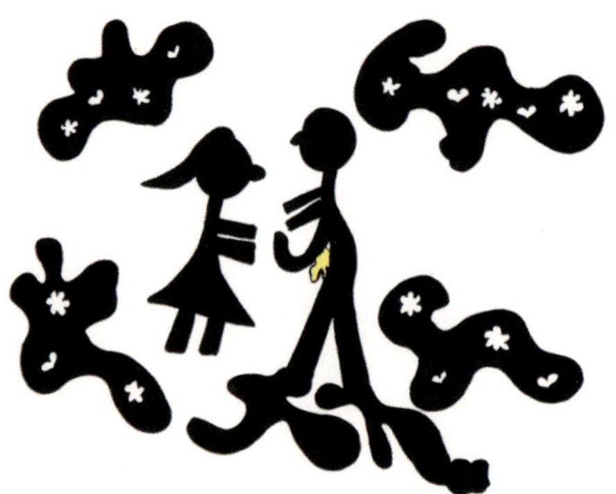

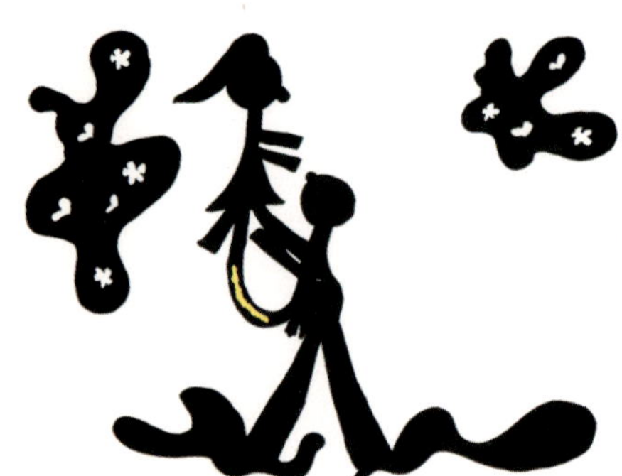

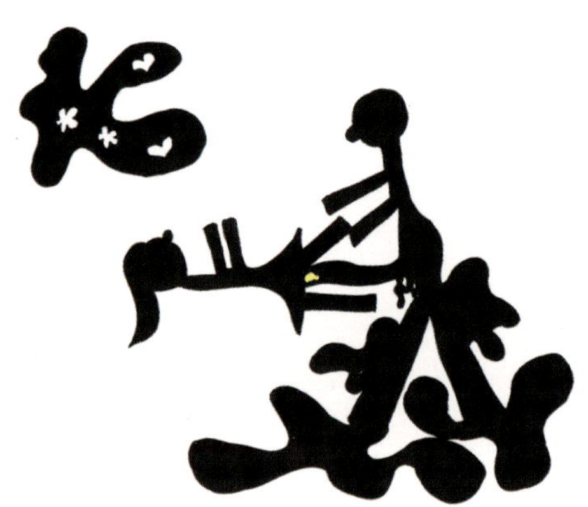

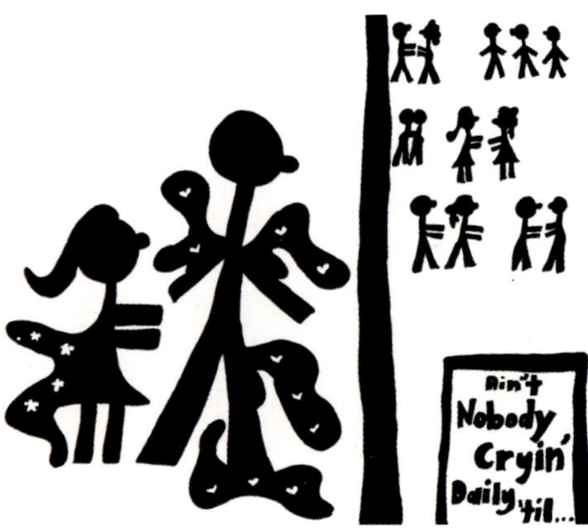

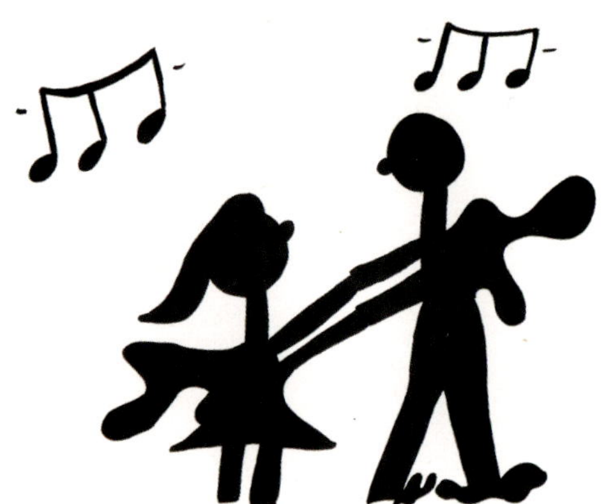

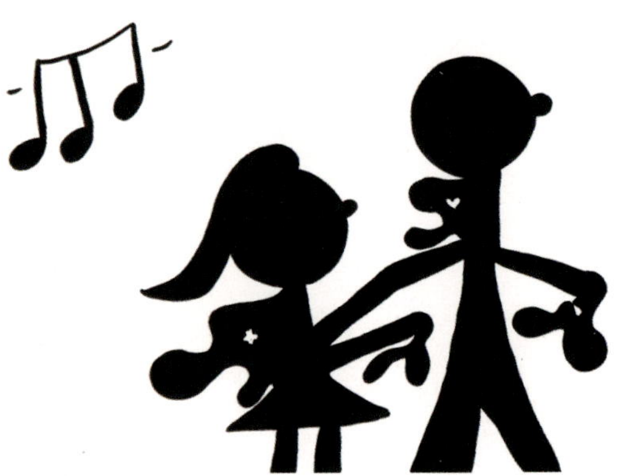

Top row, left to right: *Untitled (Golden No. 1)*, 2006; *Untitled (Golden No. 2)*, 2006
Middle row, left to right: *Untitled (Golden No. 3)*, 2006; *Untitled (I'll Take You There No. 1)*, 2006
Bottom row, left to right: *Untitled (I'll Take You There No. 3)*, 2006; *Untitled (I'll Take You There No. 4)*, 2006
gouache on paper, each 12 x 16 in. (38.1 x 40.6 cm), acquired in 2006

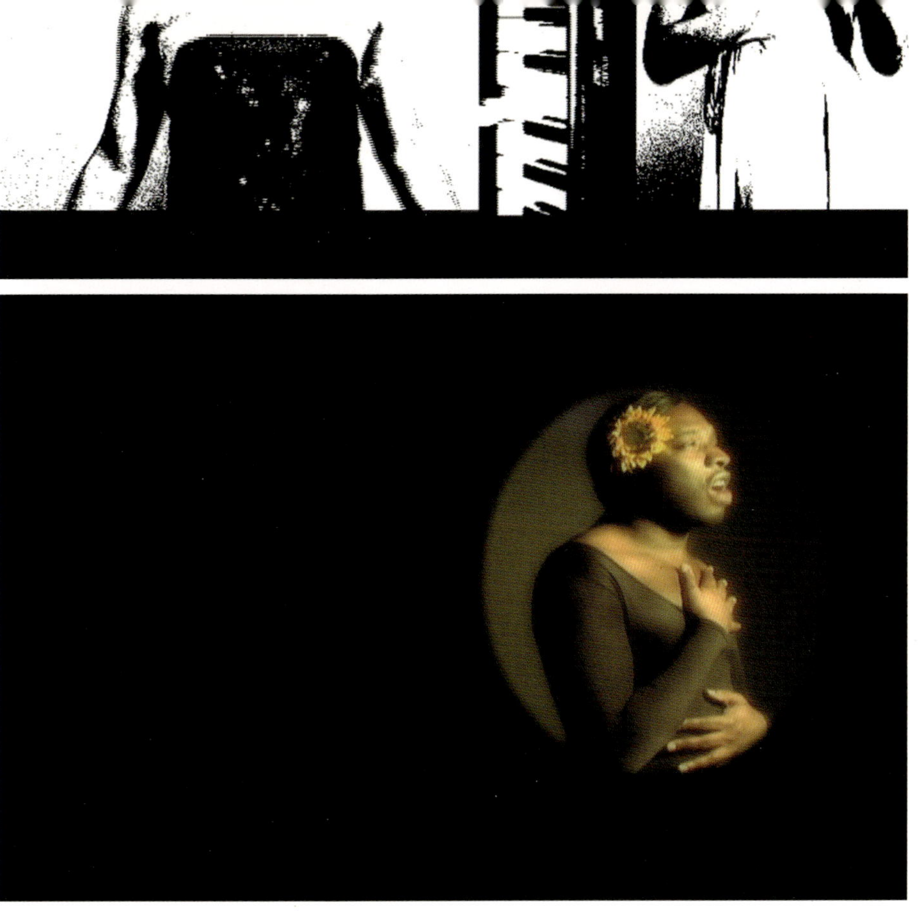

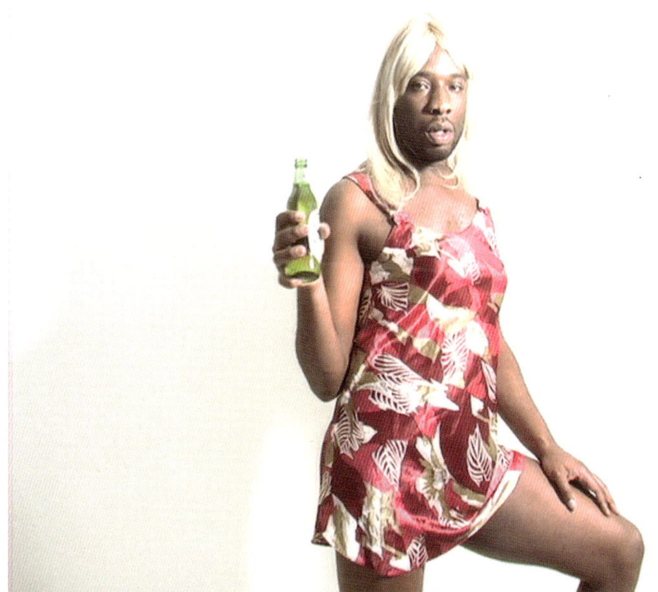

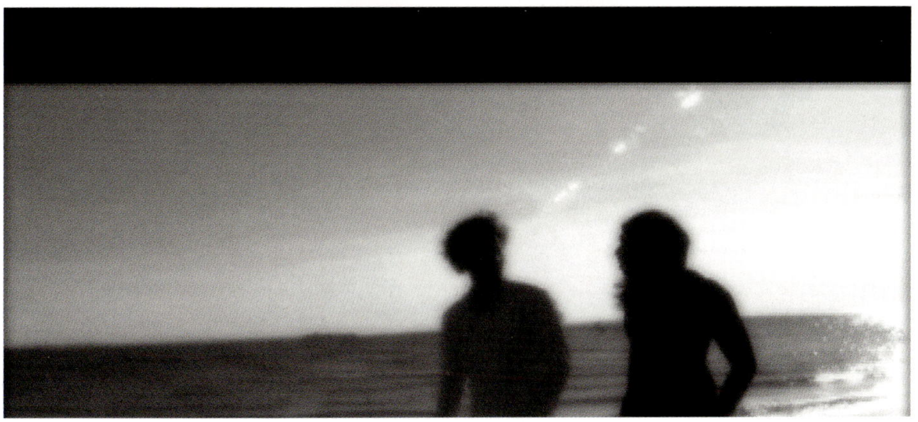

Stills from *SweetBerry Sonnet*, 2008, digital video (color, sound), 37 min. 54 sec., ed. 1/5., acquired in 2008

Presence is a prelude to power.

Everything I do is meant to foreground the image and the idea of Black people in the narrative of painting as a conversation about art history. Figure representation is crucial to my goal because a critical mass of multinational and multiracial images in museums and art history, produced by artists of color, can correct an imbalance that suggests only white artists produce important, and meaningful, work. It also demonstrates that black bodies can be representative for broadly aesthetic considerations.

Kerry James Marshall

Souvenir: Composition in Three Parts, 1998-2000, plastic, glass, paper, wood, steel and framed video still, 98 x 32 x 22 in. (248.9 x 81.3 x 55.9 cm), acquired in 2002

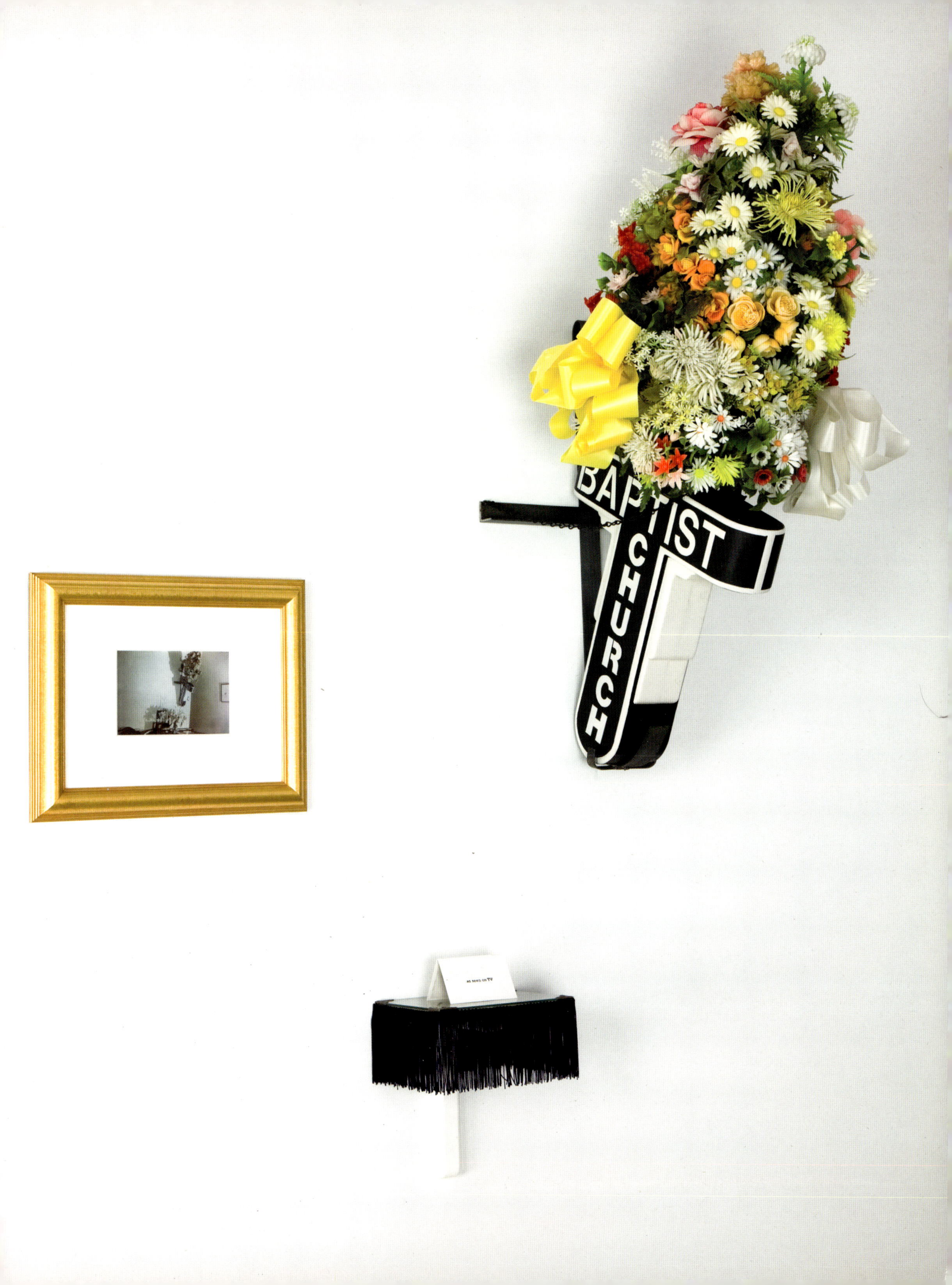

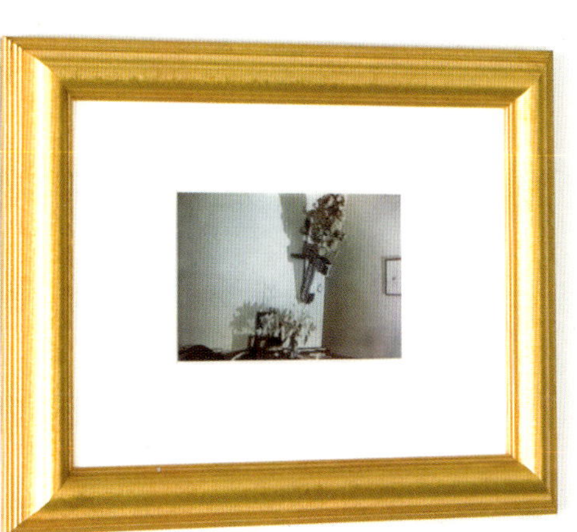

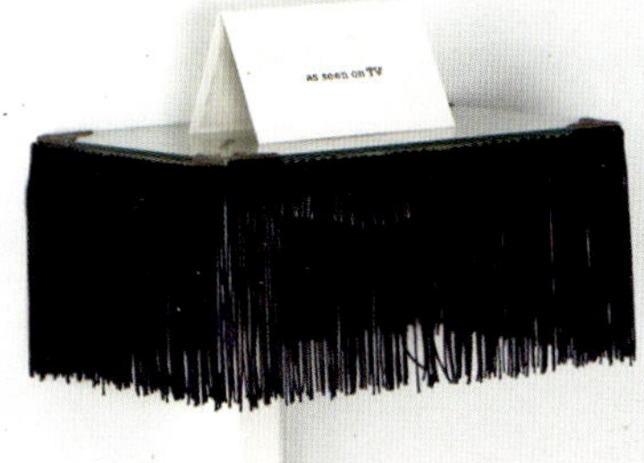
as seen on TV

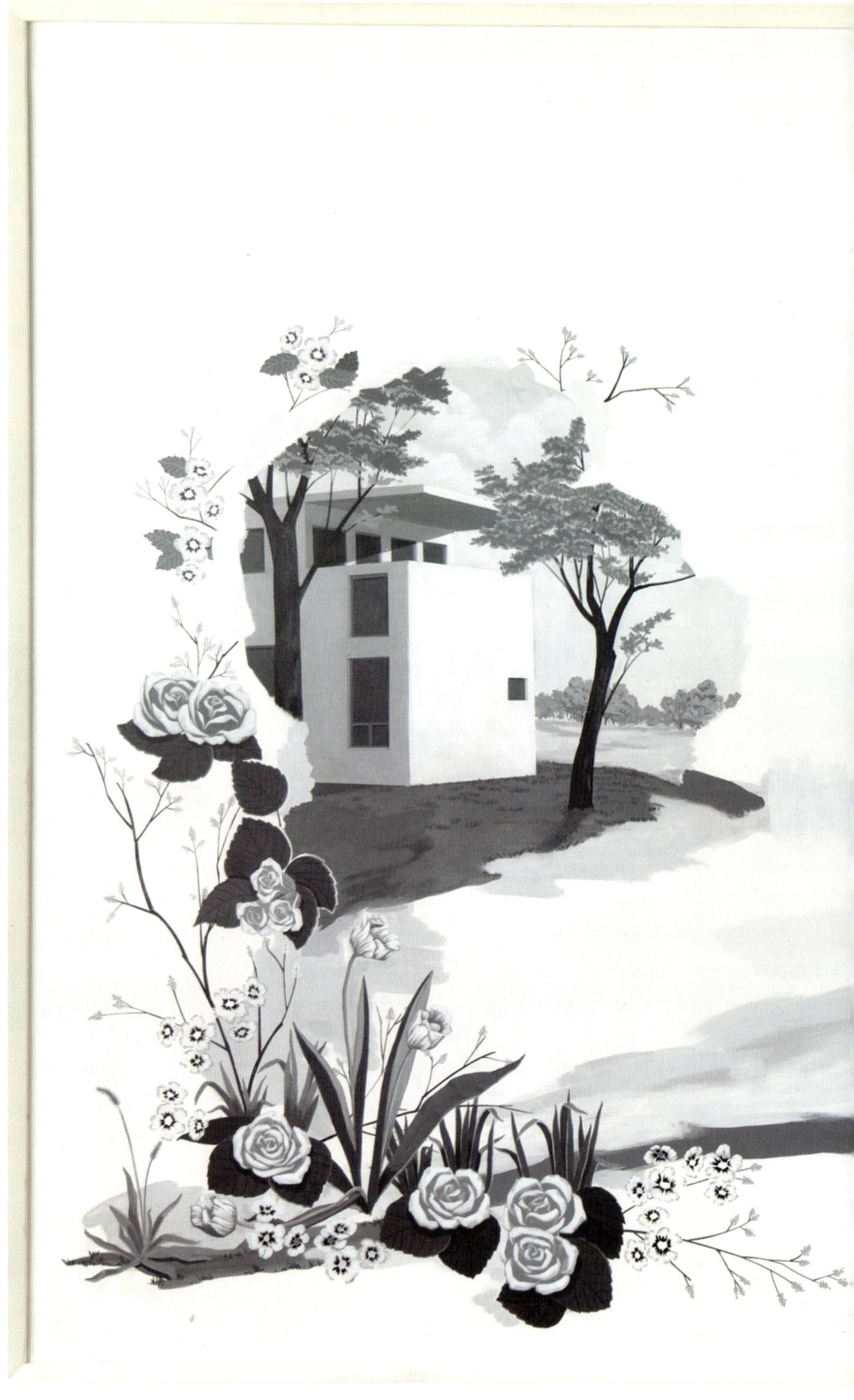

Vignette #10, 2007, acrylic on fiberglass, 74 x 110 in. (188 x 279.4 cm), acquired in 2007

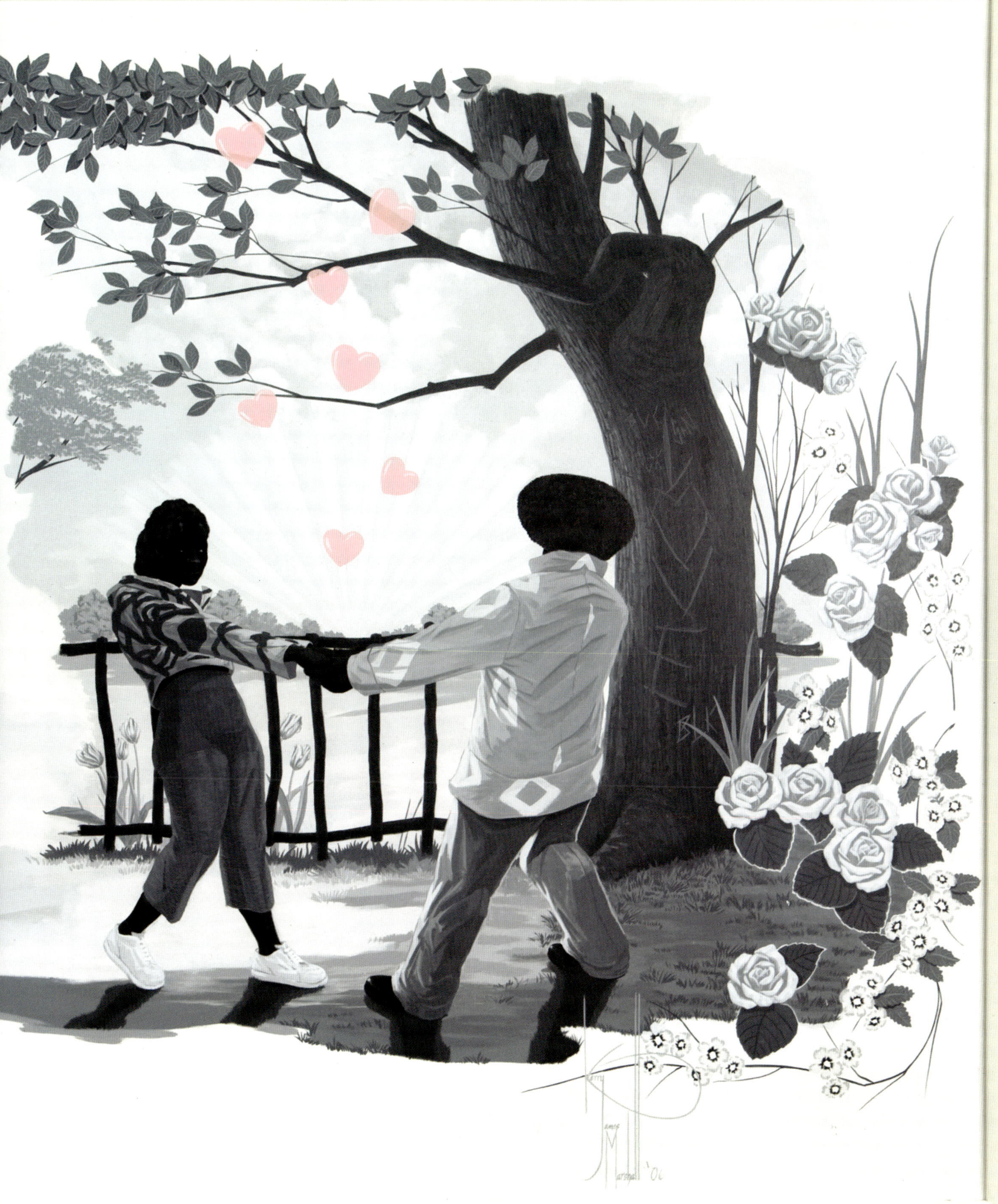

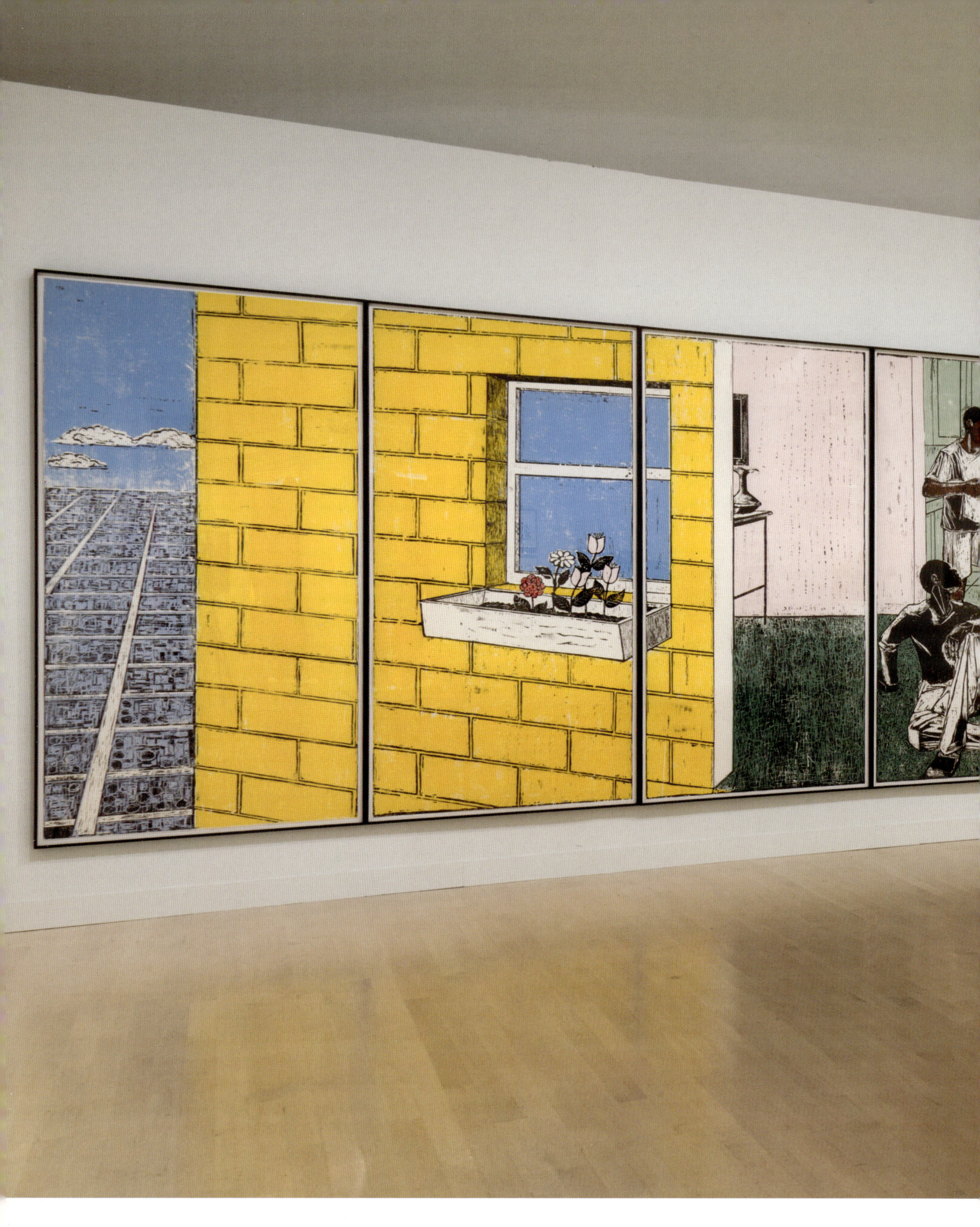

 KERRY JAMES MARSHALL

Untitled, 1998-1999, 8-color unique woodcut, ed. 1/4, 12 panels, overall 98 1/2 x 608 1/2 in. (250 x 1545.6 cm), acquired in 1999, installation view, Milwaukee Art Museum, Milwaukee

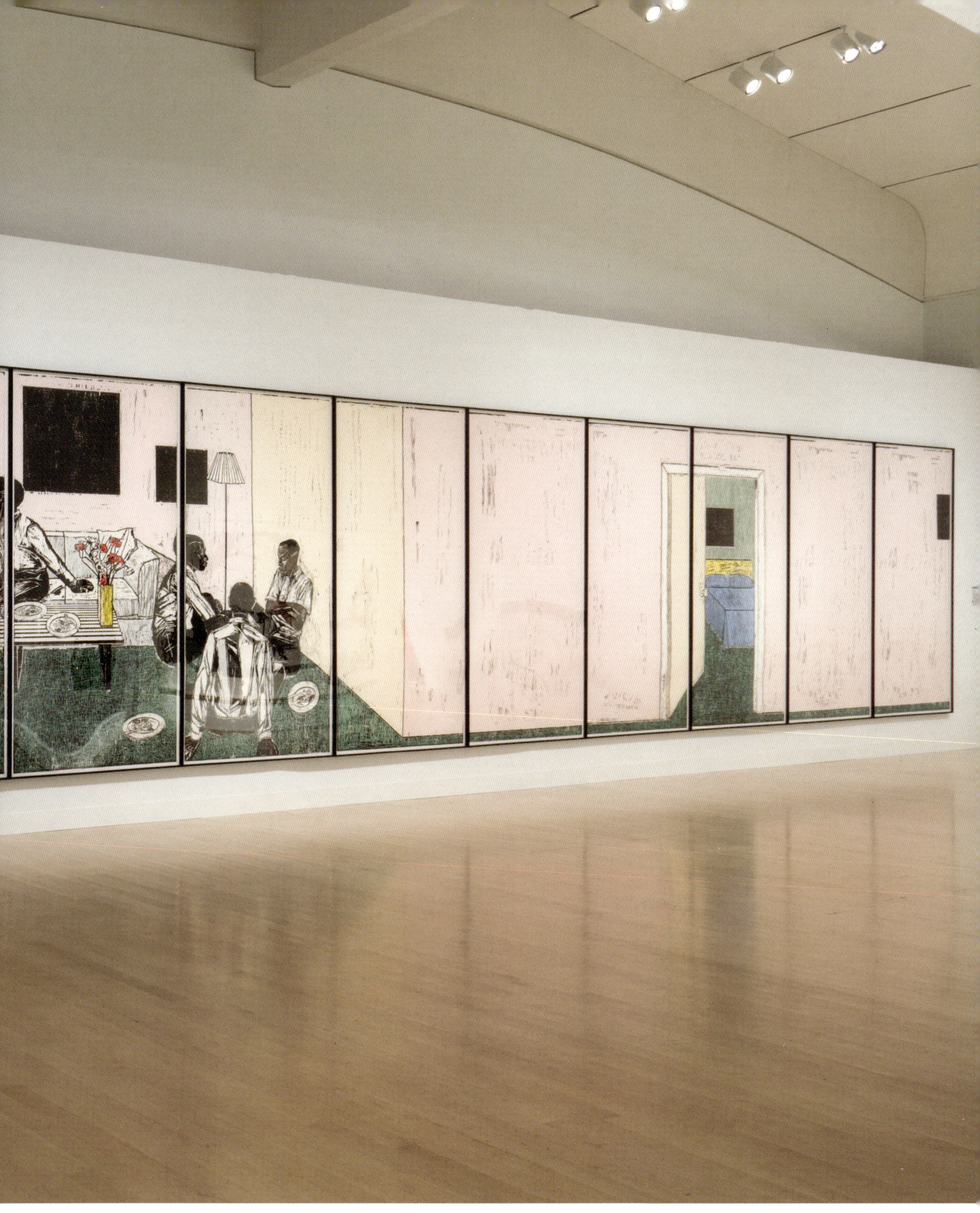

I use historical tropes to challenge indoctrinated narratives and myths, and to acknowledge the gaps in history: the many nameless and faceless individuals who are active participants in society but who are not often recorded or recognized. In my practice I have been concerned with the individuals who seem to hover outside the mythology of the American Dream. I have often felt invisible, and I do not believe I am alone in this understanding.

The post-consumer objects (the carpet paintings and chairs, etc.) are examples of work that tackle those notions. The objects are lowgrade home furnishings, stained and tattered from use. They bear the traces of their owners, which suggests that the objects were used beyond the condition that a more financially secure individual would choose to endure. These objects point to disparages in class. They embody the residue of personal histories, which also speak to absences: the absent bodies that serve as metaphors for the owners whose living conditions and work are not usually represented in historical documents and texts.

When I made *Untitled (black vinyl)* (2008) [following page], I was interested in the absurd; the absurdity of how we project onto bodies, how those projections inform cultural structures and fears and sometimes personal narratives. It was important that it was all hand-sewn because many of these structures and narratives are constructed stitch-by-stitch. The work needed to be larger than the viewer, a monumentality to compete with the volume that can exist inside of a mind. It was made specifically for the Whitney Museum, an institution like most mainstream museums that often normalize a White cultural identity.

As for the material, vinyl is a synthetic material produced from oil products—it's a domestic and commercial material that can also be sexy depending upon how it's used or contextualized. I intended the work to provide a bit of humor, kink, and to be a reflection upon effort. It takes quite a lot of effort, whether consciously or unconsciously, to form and maintain entrenched structures and narratives that shape our identity—even when those structures appear to be seamless.

Rodney McMillian

 Untitled, 2005, carpet, 139 x 178 x 114 in. (353 x 452 x 289.6 cm), acquired in 2008

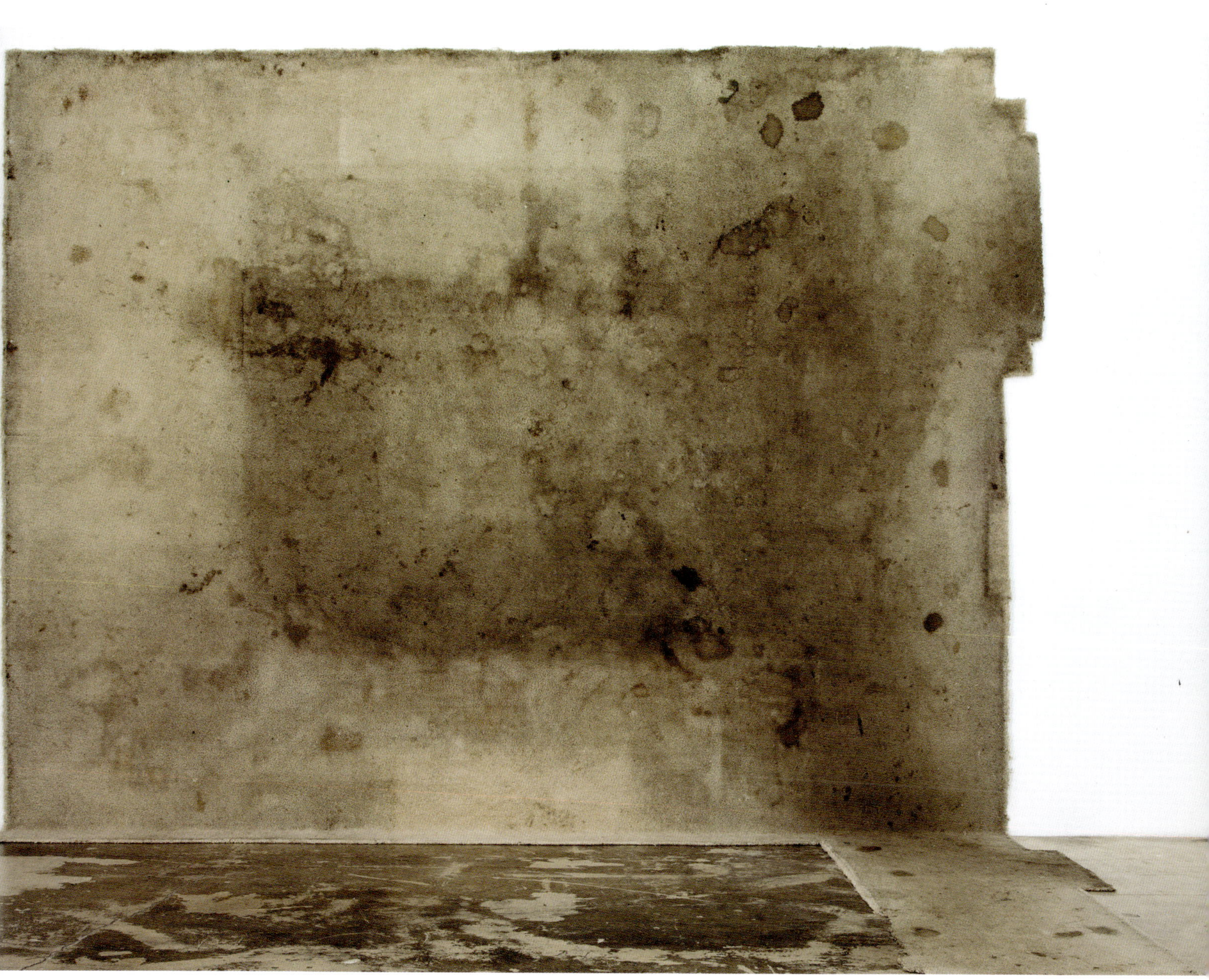

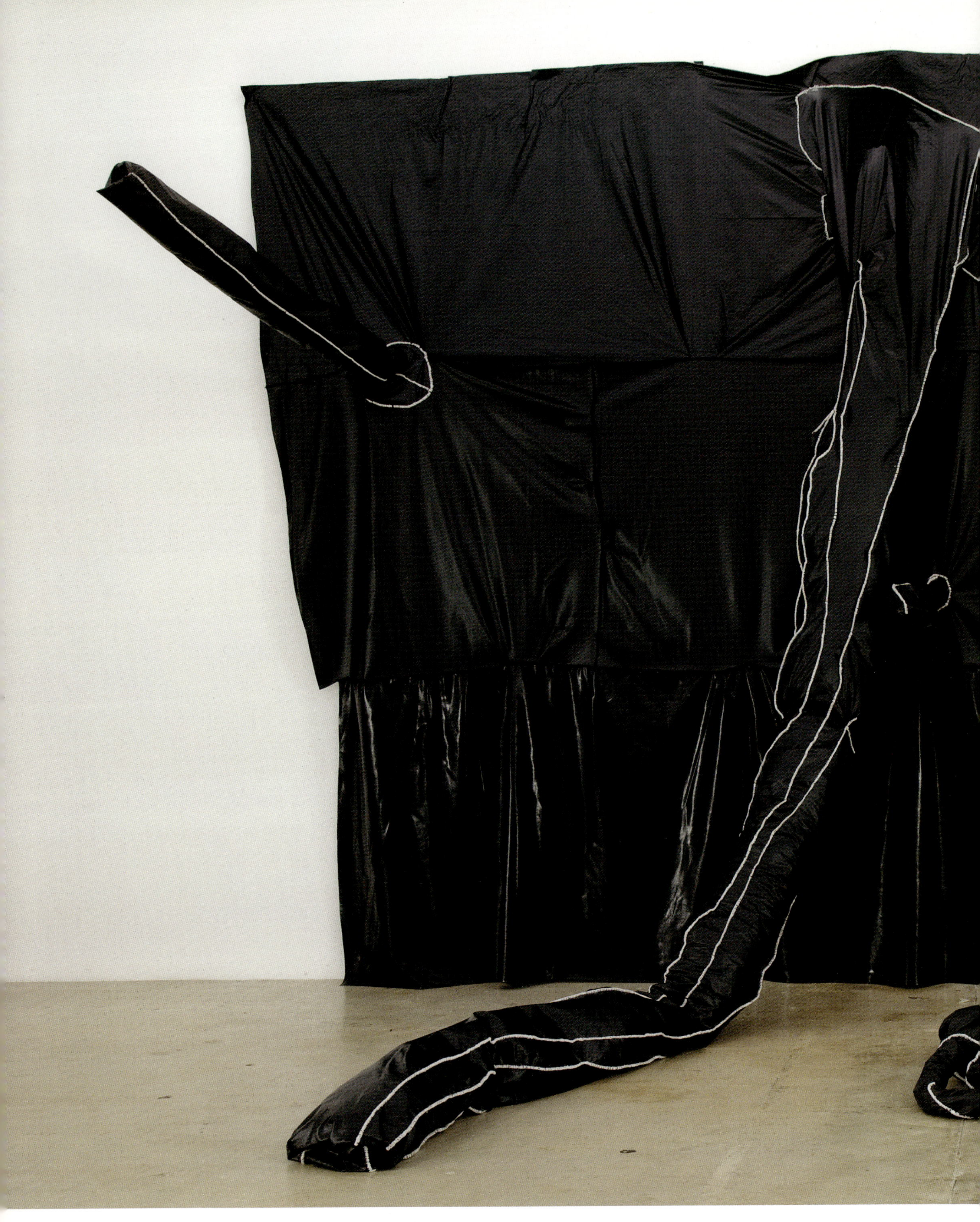

 RODNEY MCMILLIAN *Untitled*, 2007/2008, vinyl, thread, wood, metal and styrofoam, 162 x 264 x 96 in. (411.5 x 670.6 x 243.8 cm), acquired in 2008

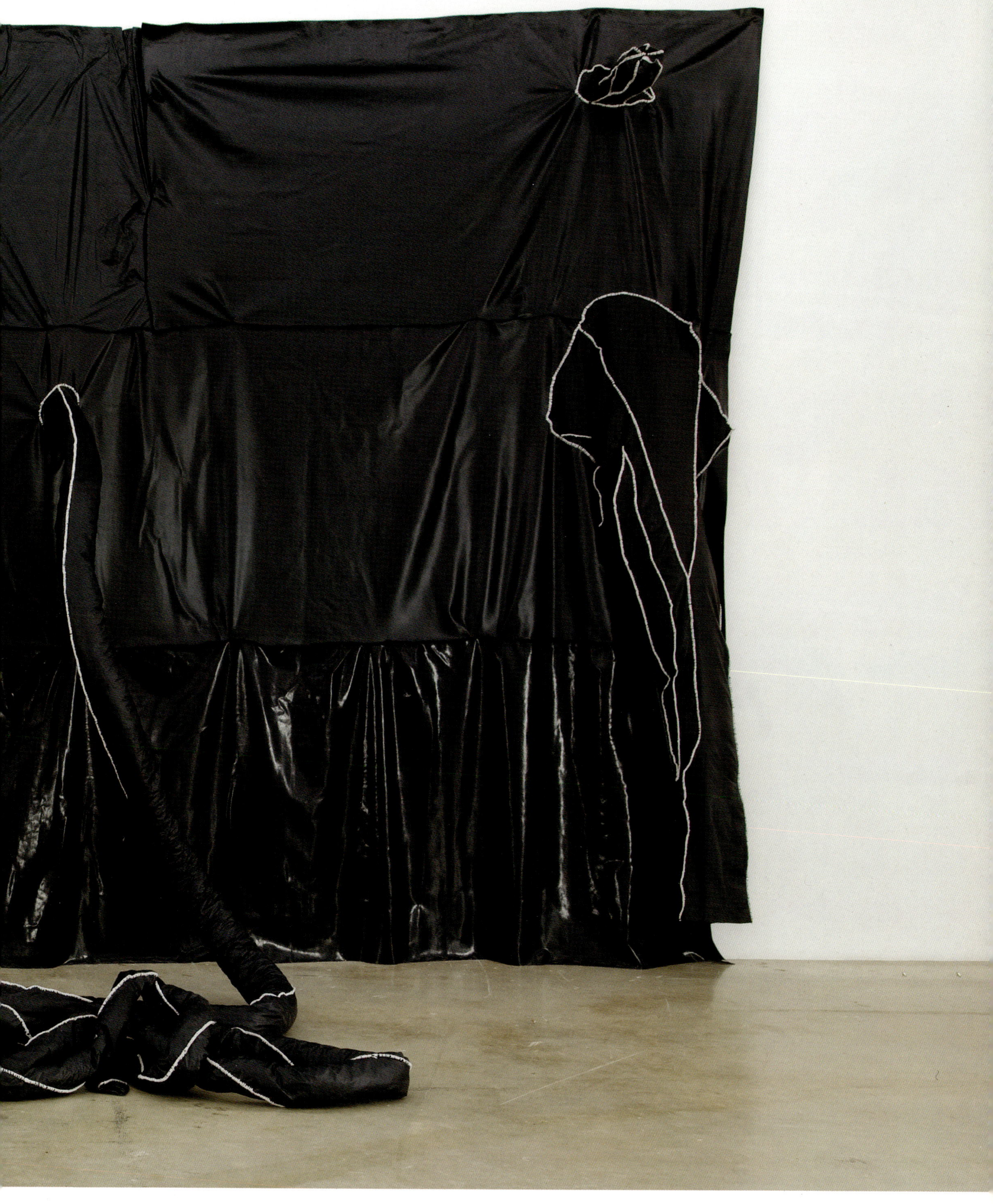

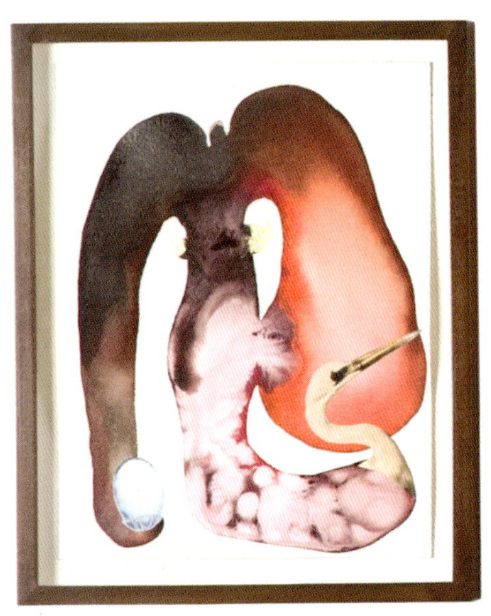

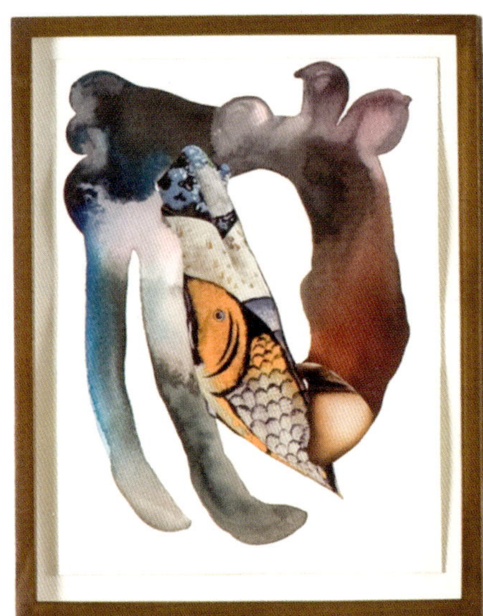

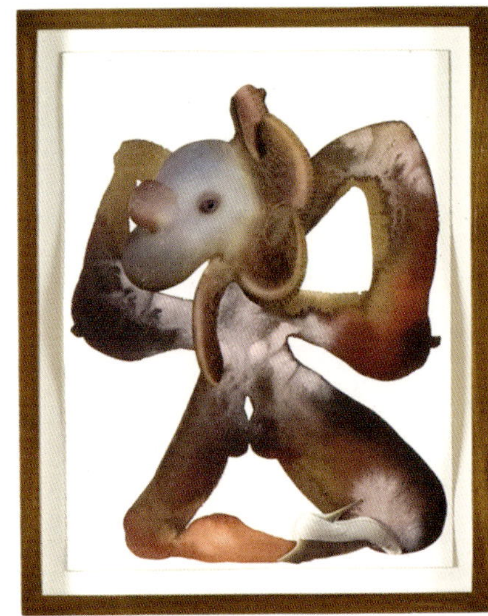

The Evolution of Mud Mama from Beginning to Start, 2008, watercolor, gold leaf and collage on paper, 6 panels, overall 19 1/2 x 75 in. (49.5 x 190.5 cm), acquired in 2008

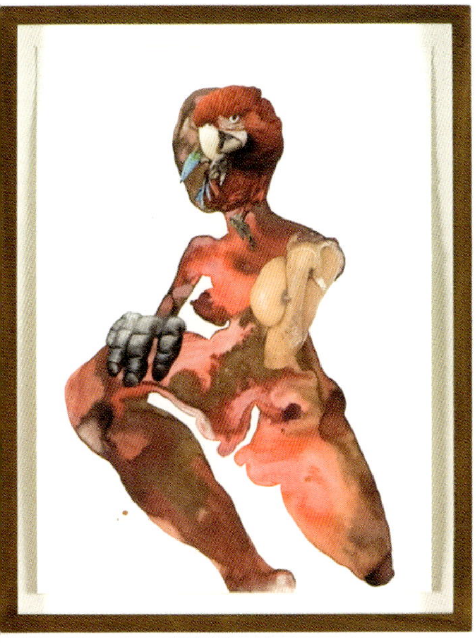
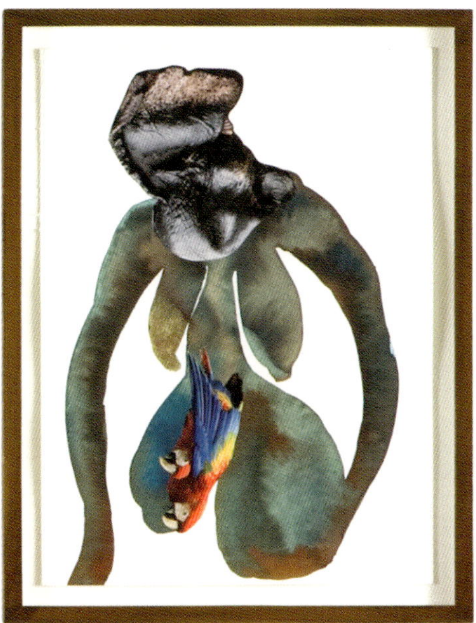
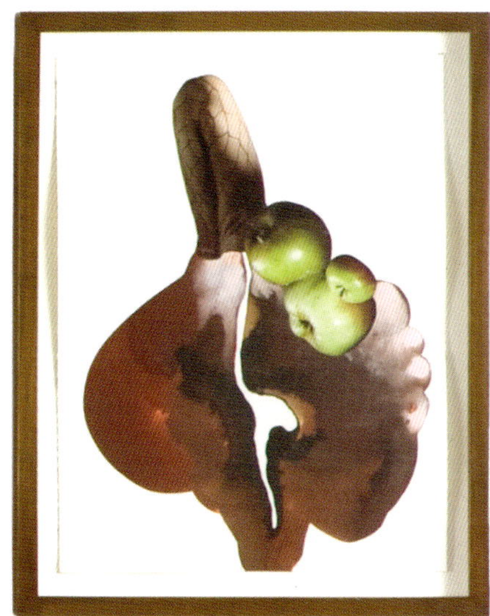

The entire body of work I was making at that point was of these characters suspended inbetween dimensions, between reality and dreams, between being specimens and spirits. The femaleness of the figure is apparent, but it's not clear what in Heaven's name any of these figures are. That includes other works that I did for that particular exhibition; my first show at Victoria Miro was called "Yo.n.I" or "Yoni." This figure is bent over in this very acrobatic, balletic position. It's almost an impossible, painful position for the body. I think, to be quite honest, the work was being done when I had these issues—immigration and travel problems. One of the things I was expressing, either overtly or not, was that I have no regrets, everything is fine, that I'm able to make work, and that even though I couldn't be at my show in London, it didn't take anything away from the experience of creating these creatures and collages.

There's a lot of serpents. There's dragons, and vaginas, and foliage. There's a lot of references to the exotic impression, the aftertaste of Josephine Baker in visual culture. But really I think the title specifically for this piece is more about that I don't regret coming this far, I don't regret leaving home when I was young to go pursue my dreams because that's what I'm doing.

Wangechi Mutu

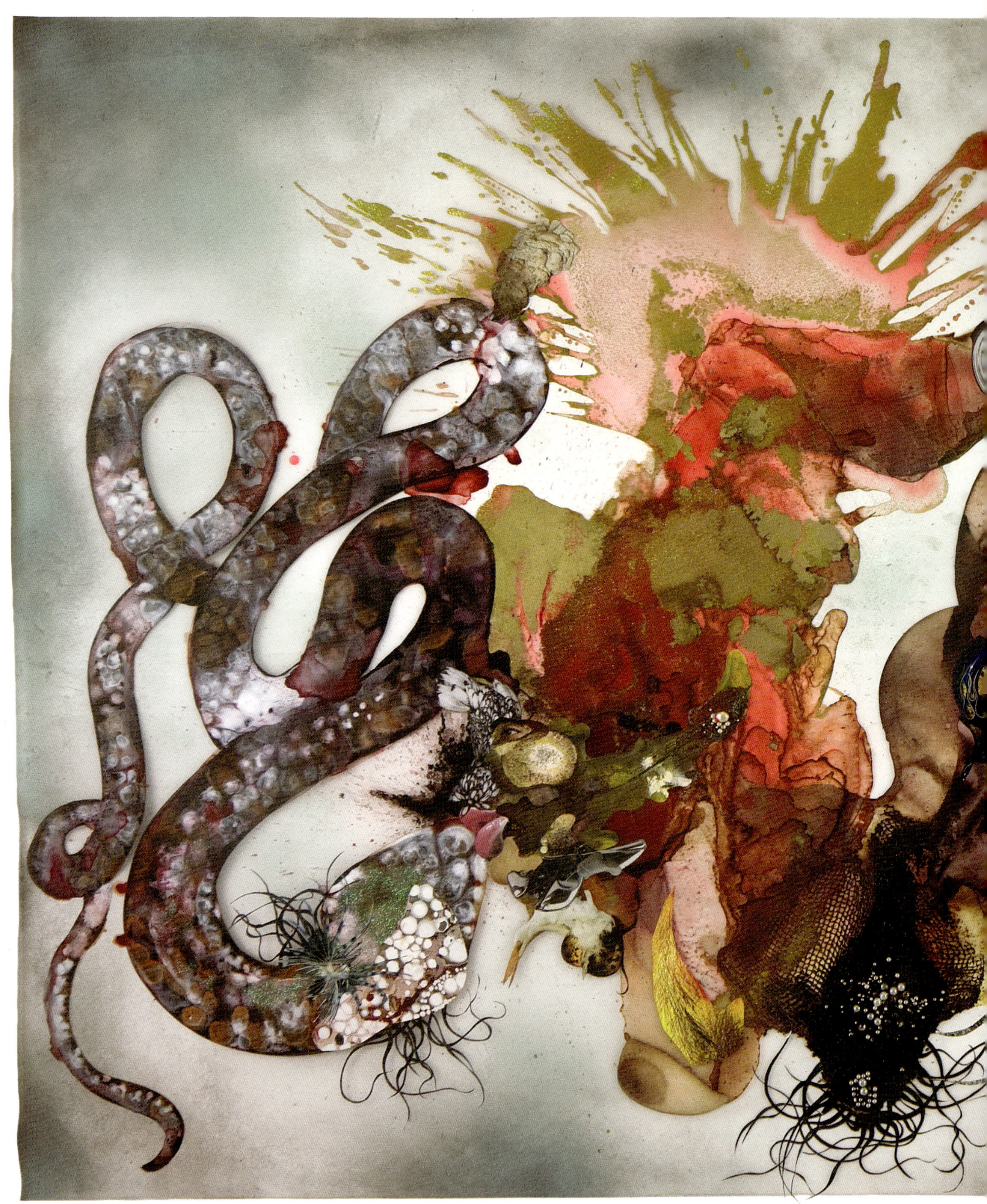

 WANGECHI MUTU *Non je ne regrette rien*, 2007, ink, acrylic, glitter, cloth, paper collage, plastic, plant material and mixed media on Mylar, 54 1/2 x 92 1/2 in. (138.4 x 233.7 cm), acquired in 2008

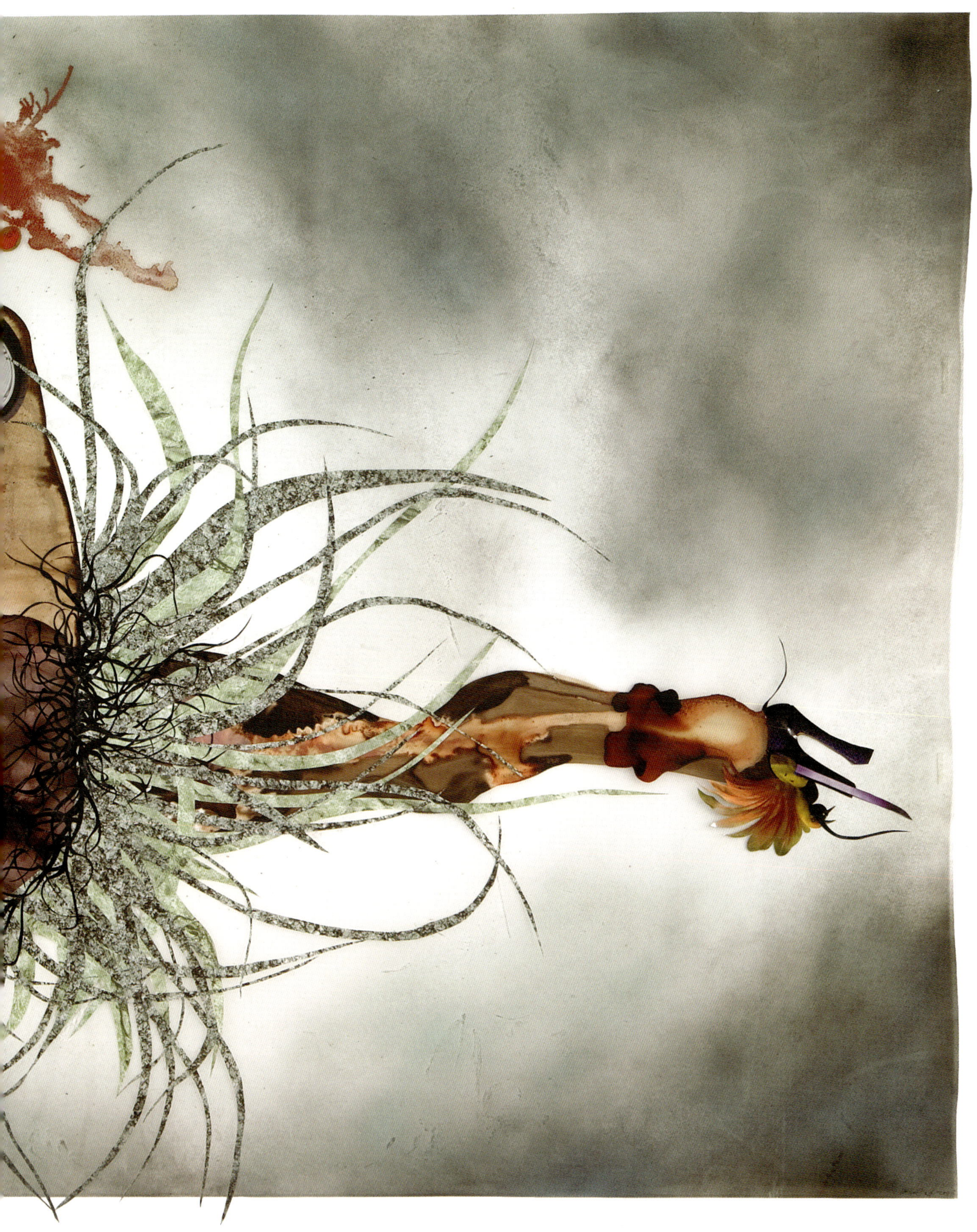

Your country? How came it yours?
Before the Pilgrims landed, we were here.[1]

Immediately following the Senate confirmation hearings preliminary to Clarence Thomas's appointment to the United States Supreme Court, and Anita Hill's public accusations of sexual harassment, I was in full preparation for a conference. The poster announcing the conference juxtaposed images of Clarence Thomas and Anita Hill; it immediately became a collector's item. It was so hot, in fact, that the Studio Museum in Harlem, which hosted the opening night, banned it from being shown on 125th Street.[2] The conference "Black Popular Culture" brought together the most prominent black intellectuals, scholars and critics ever seen in one place at the same time.[3] The event was sponsored by Dia Art Foundation at their SoHo location—a neighborhood that had not yet become the sleek designer mall it is today—as the next in their series, "Discussions in Contemporary Culture," all of which had resulted in important books.[4] At that time, Dia was the acme of white, male, conceptual artists, some of whom the institution had collected and maintained on generous stipends over the years. To the degree that black visual artists had ever been recognized, they were still seen as both marginal to the art world and, evidently, to the beating heart of black authenticity.

The stellar speakers had not flown in from the four corners of the earth at Dia's expense to talk about the art scene. We black folks had real problems to talk about—a blossoming AIDS crisis, increasing rates of crack addiction, teenage pregnancy, homelessness, rampaging homophobia, unemployment and incarceration, not to mention regressing racism and anti-affirmative action on the political and financial fronts. Although such noteworthy filmmakers as Isaac Julien and Arthur Jafa were included in the line-up, they had not been selected for their contribution to visual culture, but rather in spite of it. From the outset there was an intrinsic misunderstanding in the notion of "Black Popular Culture" as it was presented at the conference, one I felt helpless to correct as the event progressed for three sleepless days and nights. Although I participated in the selection of speakers, in many cases my judgments were overruled and I ended up having little control over what actually happened.

"Black Popular Culture" drew equally and in combination on the trend toward mechanized and commercialized mass culture as well as toward a notion of cultural production, which was expected to exhibit a greater "honesty" and appeal to a larger, more roughly hewn audience. On one hand, *popular* was intended to cater to the masses (black or otherwise), or to "the folk furthest down" (as Zora Neale Hurston would call them), but on the other hand, it also meant capable of reproduction and dissemination at a rapid rate owing to the increasing cheapness and availability of technological modes of reproduction. Then, as now, hip-hop epitomized the nexus of mechanical reproduction and the possibility for artistic genius. Despite these two qualities—convenience and popularity—which might easily have contributed in a previous century to the perception that the resulting art was less than fine, in the case of "Black Popular

1. From W.E.B. Du Bois, "Of the Sorrow Songs," in *The Souls of Black Folk* (Chicago: A.C. McClurg & Co.; Cambridge: University Press John Wilson and Son, 1903).

2. 125th Street in New York City's borough of Manhattan is a major thoroughfare and shopping district and often considered the "heart" of Harlem.

3. The conference, titled *Black Popular Culture, A Project by Michele Wallace*, had in attendance: Houston Baker, Jr., Jacqueline Bobo, Hazel Carby, Angela Davis, Manthia Diawara, Coco Fusco, Henry Louis Gates, Jr., Paul Gilroy, Ada Gay Griffin, Stuart Hall, Thomas Allen Harris, bell hooks, Arthur Jafa, Isaac Julien, Julianne Malveaux, Manning Marable, Marlon T. Riggs, Tricia Rose, Valerie Smith, Greg Tate, Cornel West, Sherley Anne Williams, Margo Jefferson and Judith Wilson; and was followed the next year by the publication of the book *Black Popular Culture, A Project by Michele Wallace,* ed. Gina Dent (Seattle: Bay Press and Dia Center for the Arts, 1992).

4. Titles included *Discussions in Contemporary Culture,* edited by Hal Foster; *The Work of Andy Warhol,* edited by Gary Garrels; *Remaking History,* edited by Barbara Kruger and Philomena Mariani; *Democracy,* edited by Brian Wallis; *If You Lived Here: The City in Art, Theory and Social Activism,* edited by Martha Rosler and Brian Wallis; and *Constructing Masculinity,* edited by Maurice Berger, Brian Wallis and Simon Watson.

Culture," excellence of a high order was still considered possible and even likely.

What generated the excitement in the air throughout "Black Popular Culture" was precisely this new atmosphere of what some might call "the black postmodern," in which a primal appeal could be forged with the highest level of technological apparatus.[5] It also appeared as though the cultural byproducts of the African diaspora were the particular focus of this postmodern twist. Deeply relevant to this amalgamation of the folk and the postmodern were such internationally famous musical performers as Fela Kuti, Bob Marley, Otis Redding, Sam Cooke, Aretha Franklin, John Coltrane, Charlie Parker, Dinah Washington, Sarah Vaughan and Nina Simone, and the list could go on and on.[6] Thus many of the speakers at "Black Popular Culture" didn't go any deeper than the music.

5. Thelma Golden, *Black Male: Representations of Masculinity in Contemporary American Art*, (New York: Whitney Museum of American Art, 1994).

6. Linda Nochlin, "Why Have There Been No Great Women Artists?" *Art News* 69 (January 1971); reprinted in Nochlin, *Women, Art, and Power and Other Essays*, (New York: Harper & Row, 1988), 145-78.

In my experience, the discussion of black popular culture has been limited to music and sports. Yet my hesitation went beyond the question of what we should have done because I knew, firsthand, that most of the participants had not given a thought to issues of visual culture in any sense. Moreover, most of them had never considered the possibility that visual culture could be a productive participating factor in "Black Popular Culture." If anything, the visual would have been cited as a negative component of popular culture in the sense that the visual is most commonly associated with the problem of negative stereotypes and mistaken impressions of race. At that time visual culture still wasn't part of the lives of most blacks, even bourgeois blacks, perhaps because of this old unpleasant link between visual stereotypes and American popular culture and illustration. Much of this history has even been deliberately suppressed from public view. Taking into account that most museum exhibitions are subject to corporate sponsorship, it's evident why this work is never seen despite the abundance residing in the storehouses of major American museums, archives, and libraries.[7]

7. Wallace, "De-Facing History," *Art in America* (October 1991).

I was disappointed by the pointed lack of reference to African-American visual artists, apart from my own closing remarks concerning the lack of "great" black artists as the canon of art history was then constructed, and the address of Judith Wilson on the use of pornographic images in the collages of Romare Bearden. It seemed to me that black artists were not being given their dues by the canon of world art history. In 2008, this may still be partly true but I think that art-historical judgment matters less, and/or simply takes a backseat to market trends in relation to contemporary art, while the designation *great* no longer carries with it its once presumably timeless and inviolable aura. All inequality hasn't been corrected or addressed but it's obvious that African-American contemporary artists have begun to make a dent in the bottom line of the marketplace, and further, that the marketplace may trump the museum in the end.

Thankfully, the art world is no longer quite as color*blind* and color*stupid* as it once was. Today, a broad range of art by living African-American artists is being collected, displayed, and exhibited in public and private museums and galleries throughout the world, not to the degree that it could ever make up for the prior neglect, but in a manner that is nonetheless interesting to study and notice. How contemporary art will transit into the contested terrain of the museums of the future is difficult to fathom but it seems to me that many black artists will stand a pretty good chance of surviving the fray at least as well as many of their white contemporaries.

In the conference "Black Popular Culture," I asked, "Why are there no great black artists?"[8] I was paraphrasing Linda Nochlin's important essay "Why Have There Been No Great Women Artists?" (1971), as well as drawing attention to how Nochlin invokes simultaneously the idea that there were no great black artists for much the same reason: the achievements of both women and blacks had been suppressed because of bigotry and suppression. I used the Nochlin piece to emphasize the erasure of black visual artists in our black popular culture conference. Today I feel comfortable in the assumption that not only is there a wide range of wonderful black artists, but that, increasingly, their contribution to the world language of the visual arts has been and will continue to be recognized and understood. Moreover, I question the indistinguishable *great*ness of an artist or any other cultural achievement, along with the notion that important objects are more important than individual lives. Life, which cannot be objectified, is more important than things, which can be counted but never really endowed with spiritual qualities.

8. Wallace, "Afterword: Why Are There No Great Black Artists? The Problem of Visuality in African-American Culture," in *Black Popular Culture, A Project by Michele Wallace.*

With museums and research libraries attracting megacrowds to their websites, and with 500 television channels broadcasting everything from avant-garde silent films to vulgar dreck, not to mention the information and entertainment coming our way via computers, iPhones, and Blackberries, the distinctions between elite and mass culture have ceased to carry their former importance. Each of us is invited by the Internet to carve out his or her own individual culture from the endless resources of a growing electronic archive of information and images. Barack Obama has been nominated as the Democratic candidate for the office of President of the United States by unanimous acclamation, something that has never happened to an African-American in the history of the United States. (Indeed, by the time this essay is published he may be president.) Today, even as I have been keeping my eye on the elections, I've been watching on and off a documentary summary of the Lyndon Baines Johnson audiotapes, the last volume of which is devoted to the FBI conspiracy against Martin Luther King and leading up to the murders of JFK (1963), RFK and King (1968). When events overtake me, I like to situate myself in history. Johnson was not only the person who screwed up in Vietnam; he was also the president who provided this country with its first national legislative racial landmarks after Reconstruction with the passage of the civil rights bills of 1964 and 1965, making it possible for black men and women to vote in large enough blocks to throw local, state, and even national elections. Such possibilities were a ticking time bomb as far as southern segregationists like J. Edgar Hoover were concerned. The more one becomes a humble student of history, the more one realizes that not much happens either suddenly or completely by accident.

The situation is nowhere near the ideal of racial or gender equality many of us long to see, but the fame and financial heat of the international art world was never designed to be fair. Nor can we really discuss equality between the races until we can broach the subject of reparations—whatever that might mean—for the lasting damage of centuries of African slavery.[9] And who should pay since both culprits and victims are long in their graves? And it's evident that the descendants of both groups still find it impossible to occupy the world peacefully together, or so the high rate of incarceration of black men would seem to suggest.

9. I have begun collecting cultural references to reparations. My favorite thus far is Cassandra Wilson's song devoted to the topic, "Justice," from *Belly of the Sun*, Blue Note Records, 2002.

Thirty years or so ago, Mera and Don Rubell began collecting art according to their passions. In the course of this activity, they amassed a prescient and substantial collection of art by African-Americans. "30 Americans" at the Rubell Family Collection in Miami displays works by many of these artists throughout the twenty-seven galleries of the former DEA warehouse that is now this museum.

A number of these works immediately set me contemplating the African *sublime*, which I think of as the generations of pain and suffering of our black ancestors, now transformed into the beautiful, poetic, and lyrical by the emotional and spiritual patina of experience. I felt closest to the photographs of Lorna Simpson and Carrie Mae Weems, which take me back to the exhibition "Harlem on My Mind"[10] at the Metropolitan Museum of Art in 1969. This was the first time that I saw the photographs of the great James VanDerZee. It still makes me weep when I search the Metropolitan Museum's art history timeline on the web for VanDerZee, to find no trace of him or "Harlem on My Mind"!

10. Allon Schoener, ed. *Harlem on My Mind: Cultural Capital of Black America, 1900-1968* (New York: New Press, 2007).

One must take into account the perpetual scandal of the image of the black (male or female) in Western civilization in order to comprehend the ongoing problem of inadequate recognition and contextualization for black artists. Nonetheless, the exquisite flair that VanDerZee exhibited over a lifetime as a Harlem photographer, persistent in his desire to document every strand of contemporary African-American culture—right up to a portrait of Jean-Michel Basquiat—is well represented by the meticulous sensitivity of Lorna Simpson's photographs. In the twenty-two precisely executed images of false hairpieces that comprise *Wigs (Portfolio)*, Simpson wrestles with the philosophical and feminist issues of representation and subjectivity in the context of the black body. The rigor of her work engages in the same kind of imaginative anchoring of black culture and consciousness as Carrie Mae Weems's re-stating of the intersections of European anthropological methodologies with American slavery as evidenced by Louis Agassiz's photographic studies of four slaves in the late antebellum period, in her series *From Here I Saw What Happened and I Cried (Descending the Throne)* (1995-1996). Hank Willis Thomas's sly and subversive photo-montages present compositions of advertising images denuded of their logos and banal consumerist messages, revealing the vulgar and graceless racial manipulations in which these photographs were initially conceived.

Other conceptual artists in this exhibition—David Hammons, Glenn Ligon and Renée Green—are all represented by some of their best work. For Hammons, it is *Esquire (or John Henry)* (1990), a rock set on a shoe-polish lid, atop a plinth made from a section of rusted railroad track. The crown of the "rock head" is covered with nappy hair gathered from a local barbershop and adhered with the sweat of the human hand. John Henry is one of Afro-America's favorite legends: a steel-driving man, the most powerful in the land, who, in a match of strength against the steam-powered hammer, beat the machine only to die from exhaustion. Renée Green examines tropes of race and gender in her selection of representative film stills throughout history. In *Untitled (I Sell the Shadow to Sustain the Substance)* (2005), Glenn Ligon uses glowing white neon to convey a message taken from a daguerreotype of the former slave and vocal black feminist abolitionist leader, Sojourner Truth, drawing comparison between Truth's relationship to public discourse as a nineteenth-century black female, and his own as a black male artist living in the twenty-first century. His is one of the many references to the enslavement of African-Americans throughout the works in "30 Americans." By drawing upon the less well-known aspects of American history and culture related to the African-American experience, these artists are at once testing and training their still predominantly white audiences.

Years before "Black Popular Culture," New York's Museum of Modern Art staged their infamous exhibition "Primitivism in Twentieth-Century Art: Affinity of the Tribal and the Modern," curated by William Rubin, which attempted to map the relationship between modernist art and "primitive" art from Africa, the indigenous cultures of North America, and the Pacific Islands. The copiously illustrated, double-volume catalog for the exhibition immediately set the standard for the incorporation of the visual cultures of people of color into the narrative of modernism. At the time, the participation of contemporary African-American artists was not even imagined by anyone other than themselves, and yet by 1984 there were and had been for some time key African-American artists participating meaningfully in the unfolding of the American art scene—William Johnson, Norman Lewis, Jacob Lawrence, Romare Bearden, Alma Thomas, Barbara Chase-Riboud, and Faith Ringgold, just to name a very few. But the extensive and heated debate at the time over the exhibition and the catalog centered on whether or not the museum's narrative had diminished the importance of the modernist debt to Native American, Pacific Islander, and African cultures by insisting upon referring to them as *affinities* rather than *influences.* On the face of it, their argument versus mine would seem a minor, even moot, distinction.

Yet what was really at stake in this linguistic squabble—between one side that seemed to have all the right of way and the other that was inhabited ideally by the subject position of people of color who had produced these highly influential works of primitive art—was the theft and appropriation of cultural legacies whose importance and intelligence had been dismissed and denied ad infinitum. If this work wasn't pivotal, then why so much discussion about it? Why, indeed, couldn't modernist art legitimately admit to influences from outside of European cultural conventions? And why was this position so emphatically stated in precisely the country in which the pressure of racial and cultural differences had always been so intensely manifested in a variety of noxious forms, from blackface minstrelsy to spectacle lynchings, to the explosive rage of the Civil War?

Rubin wrote in his introduction to the exhibition:

> Only since World War II has the discipline of art history turned its attention to this material, however, graduate level programs in Primitive Art are still comparatively rare, and few of their students are also involved in modern studies. It should come as no surprise, therefore, that much of what historians of twentieth-century art have said about the intervention of tribal art in the unfolding of modernism is wrong. Not familiar with the chronology of the arrival and diffusion of Primitive objects in the West, they have characteristically made unwarranted assumptions of influence.[11]

11. William Rubin, ed., *Primitivism in Twentieth-Century Art: Affinity of the Tribal and the Modern*, 2 vols. (New York: The Museum of Modern Art, 1984).

In unconscious justification of the Western ownership of some of the most prized and magnificent objects of "Primitive Art," he willed himself to forget entirely the millions of African bodies lying at the bottom of the ocean and those that helped to populate and generate the modern cultures of the New World. Such works as those of Jean-Michel Basquiat included in this exhibition, *Bird on Money* (1981), *One Million Yen* (1982) and *Untitled (Self-Portrait)* (1982-83), might have persuaded him of the folly of making such projections regarding the exchanges between the primitivism harvested from the Pacific, the Americas and Africa, and the consequences for the most revered artists of European and American modernism of the twentieth century. Rubin's claims involved an over-simplification of a complex series of cultural and historical events across continents and language groups. Suffice it to say that art-making simply doesn't work as Rubin would have it. It is neither predictable nor definable. His very use of the category *art* has a specific and finite history whereas the objects drawn upon in making art are virtually unlimited.

In considering questions of primitivism, I think rather of the struggle over the classification of the *Outsider* in today's art world, and how this term has been applied to explain the extraordinary and profoundly moving presence of African-American visual art in communities that were assumed to have no visual life—yet another manifestation of the invisibility Ralph Ellison so accurately diagnosed in his masterpiece, *Invisible Man*. All African-American artists have been considered outsiders both to African-American culture and European-American culture for a very long time. If outsider isn't stamped on the life or lifestyle of the black artist, it is surely somewhere in his or her use of form, design, color, and/or materials.

In this exhibition the outsider is everywhere. Take the over three thousand paintings on found objects and materials by Purvis Young, made between 1985 and 1999, as well as the film *Purvis of Overtown*, and the illustrations in the second volume of *Souls Grown Deep*.[12] Young is not the product of the New York art scene, nor is he the product of a prominent art school, and yet his work reflects as surely as Basquiat's the prototypical tragedy of African-American life, that of the saga of the African diaspora via the Middle Passage, slavery, Jim Crow and racism—a saga that gave rise to a very particular type of

12. William Arnett and Paul Arnett, eds., *Souls Grown Deep: African American Vernacular Art*, vol. 2, (Atlanta: Tinwood Books, 2001); *Purvis of Overtown*, DVD, directed by David Raccuglia and Shaun Conrad (Atlanta: Tinwood, 2005). The work of Purvis Young is featured on the cover of *Souls Grown Deep*, vol. 2.

compulsion to create, regardless of the visible lack of education, and despite poverty and deprivation.

Kara Walker's *Camptown Ladies* (1998), comprises a series of inscrutable silhouettes, with urine and semen squirting through the air and a mountain of feces concluding the tale. It seems the Middle Passage is never far from her creative process. Walker's fascination with its dynamics was most apparent in her recent exhibition "Kara Walker at the Met: After the Deluge" at New York's Metropolitan Museum of Art in 2006.[13] Together with her own drawings, silhouettes, and paintings, Walker drew upon the art of John Singleton Copley, John Carlin, Winslow Homer and Joseph Turner—nineteenth-century painters who reflected on the consequences of slavery and American racism—together with silhouettes by Auguste Edouart, William Henry Brown and John Warner Barber,[14] and some African sculptures, in order to recall the poignant collective histories of floods and water in intersection with narratives of race. In *Camptown Ladies,* she continues to manifest her singular path as a commentator on the African-American condition, the title referring to a song written by Stephen Foster and made popular in the late nineteenth century by blackface minstrelsy. In Walker's characteristic appropriation of blackface and the pretense of submission, there is a mocking of the simplicity, naiveté, and roughness of the so-called American primitive. Here the primitive is no longer African or even tribal or ancestral but rather it refers to the animalistic or psychologically primal. The Enlightenment gradually offered a scientific and biological notion of inferiority to substitute and supplement the cultural one, since the cultural definition of inferiority would become less reliable as the technologies of visual reproduction, travel and communication advanced, and made imaginative speculation about the other less conclusively seductive.[15]

13. Kara Walker, *Kara Walker: After the Deluge* (New York: Rizzoli, 2007).

14. Ibid.

15. Interestingly, in the eighteenth century there was a former slave named Moses Williams who worked as a silhouette maker in the museum of his owner, the famous American painter Charles Willson Peale. Cutting silhouettes was considered a lesser art form, more appropriate to William's status as a former slave in antebellum Philadelphia society.

Robert Colescott pursues a different manifestation of the primitive in his compelling charcoal drawing *Passing* (1982), in which a white female and a light-skinned black male kiss inside a heart, at the top of which is a man who exhibits the exaggerated features of a stereotypical cartoon of a black man. In an untitled unique woodcut in twelve panels, Kerry James Marshall depicts a set of average African-American lives. Moving across a brick wall, a window, a living room, an expanse of pink interior wall, and finally a bedroom—obviously in an apartment or tenement building—the viewer's gaze scans the life of a group of African-Americans relaxing in a circle of conviviality and conversation. The subtle focus of this image of people captured inadvertently in their lives is compelling, as is his innovative use of the traditional woodcut. In her cross-cultural emulations of historical Japanese woodcuts, Iona Rozeal Brown combines African and Japanese signs—black skin, decorative fingernails, Japanese textiles, and hairstyles—into ornately detailed paintings. Fascinated by a Japanese sub-culture that devotes itself to imitating African-American hip-hop culture, Brown renders blackface, perhaps more palatably, upon a grid of Japanese cultural and visual signs.

"30 Americans" contains a near-comprehensive repertoire of the tropes of black postmodernism and the African-American sublime, in which the negativities of slavery, Jim Crow, blackface minstrelsy, racism, sexism and sexual slavery are constantly invoked and interrogated for the rich, dark spaces and designs that their still-warm undersides may reveal. Every African-American artist I can think of whose work I admire finds some way to signal his or her existential *outsiderness*. In a dominant visual culture in which blackness is often viewed as a negation of both culture and worth, the outside holds as much interest and cachet as the inside. We black people always want to know, regardless of our education and family background: What relation does your work have to the outside where most black people continue to be found everywhere you can look?

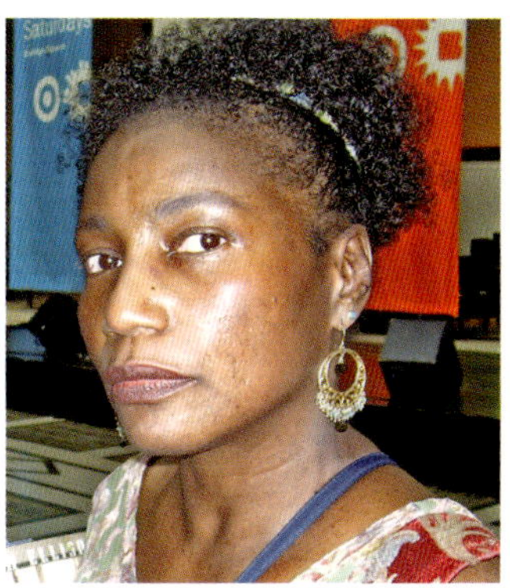

Michele Wallace is a professor of English, Women's Studies and Cinema Studies at the City College of New York and The City University of New York Graduate Center. Since her 1979 influential work, *Black Macho and the Myth of the Superwoman* (New York: The Dial Press, 1978), Wallace has continued to contribute significantly to the field of visual culture as it relates to gender and race with books such as *Invisibility Blues: From Pop to Theory* (New York: Verso, 1990) and *Dark Designs and Visual Culture* (Durham: Duke University Press, 2004). In 1991, she organized a groundbreaking conference at the Studio Museum in Harlem entitled "Black Popular Culture." In the subsequent book by the same name, she contributed an afterword titled "Why Are There No Great Black Artists? The Problem of Visuality in African-American Culture."

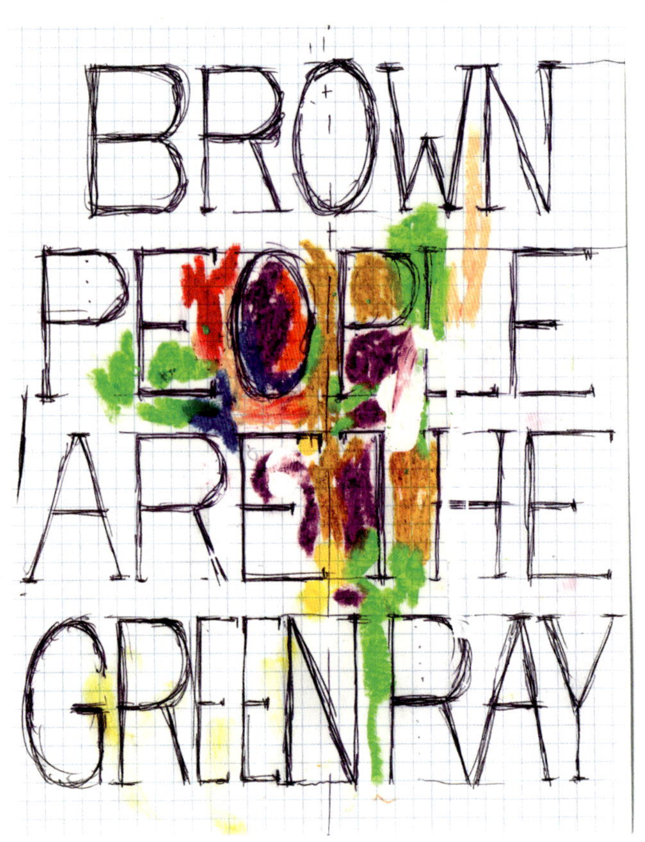

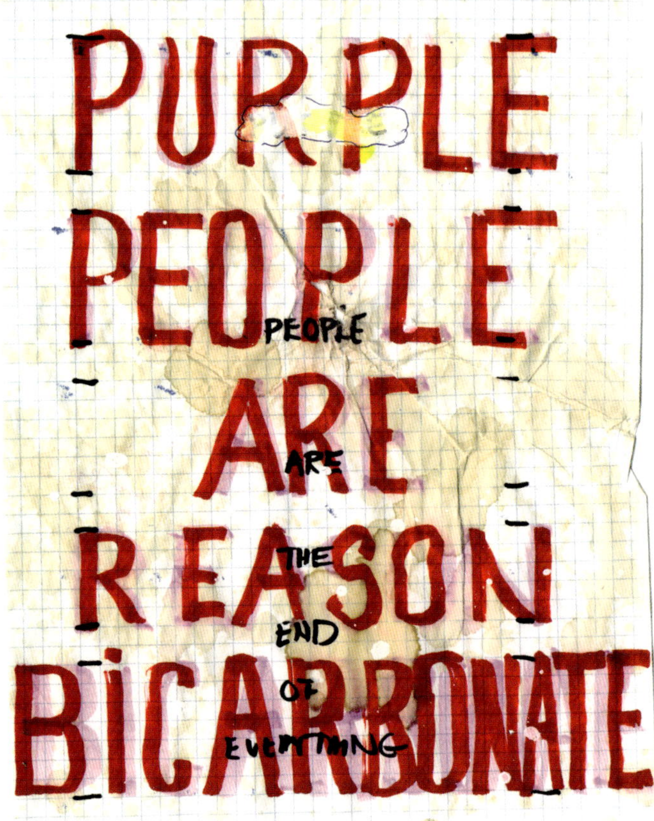

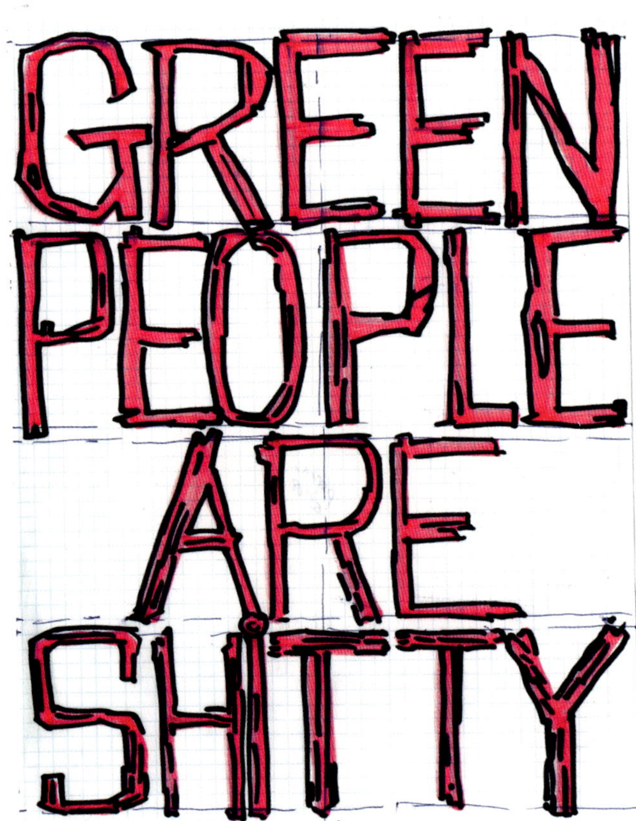

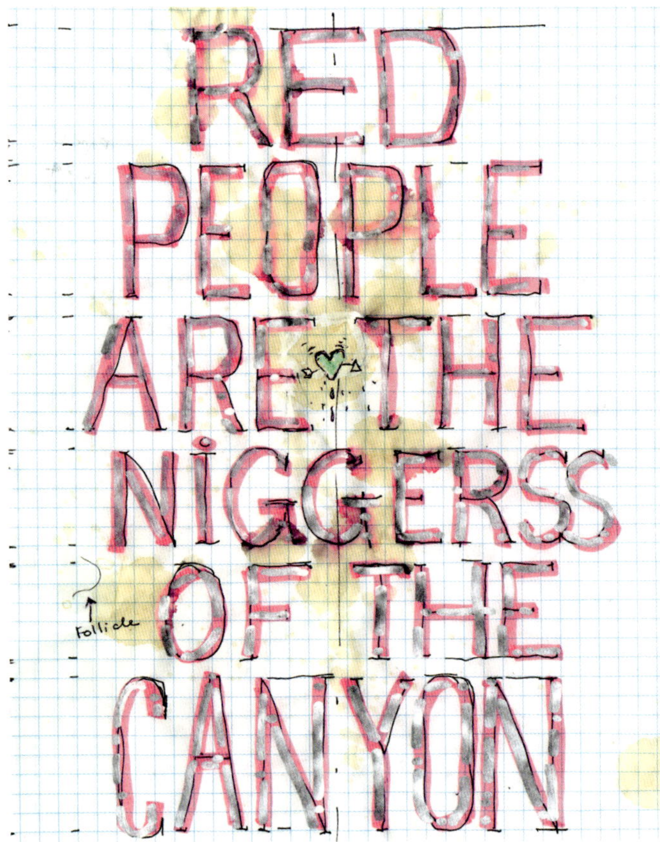

Clockwise from top left: *Skin Set: Brown People Are the Green Ray*, 2008, Cray-Pas, acrylic and ink on paper, 8 1/2 x 11 in. (21.6 x 28 cm), acquired in 2008; *Skin Set: Purple People Are Reason Bicarbonate*, 2006-2007, ink, Wite-Out and coffee on paper, 8 1/2 x 11 in. (21.6 x 28 cm), acquired in 2008; *Skin Set: Red People Are the Niggerss of the Canyon*, 2004, ink, Wite-Out, coffee and hair on paper, 8 1/2 x 11 in. (21.6 x 28 cm), acquired in 2008; *Skin Set: Green People Are Shitty*, 2008, ink on paper, 8 1/2 x 11 in. (21.6 x 28 cm), acquired in 2008

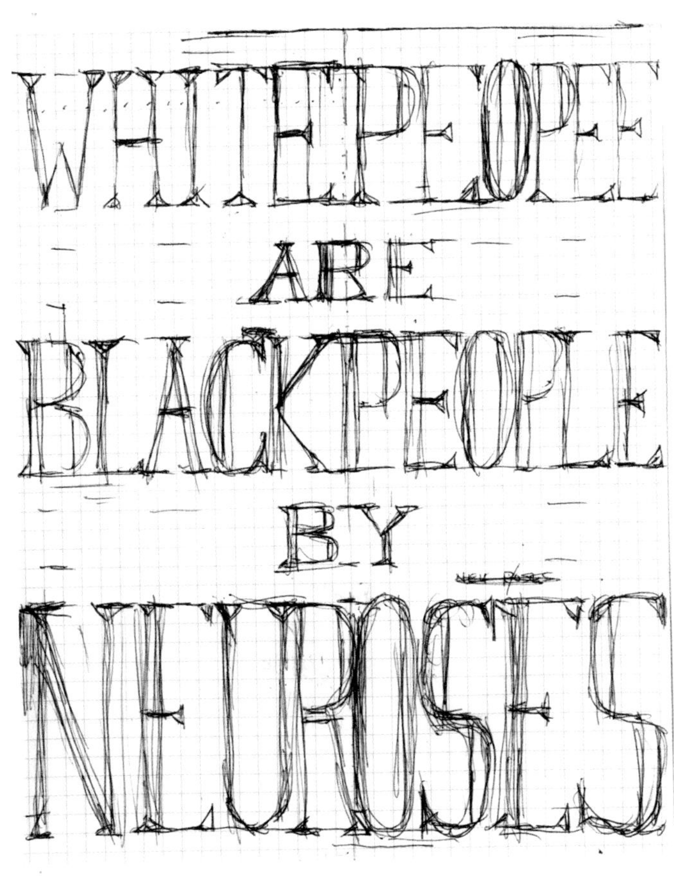

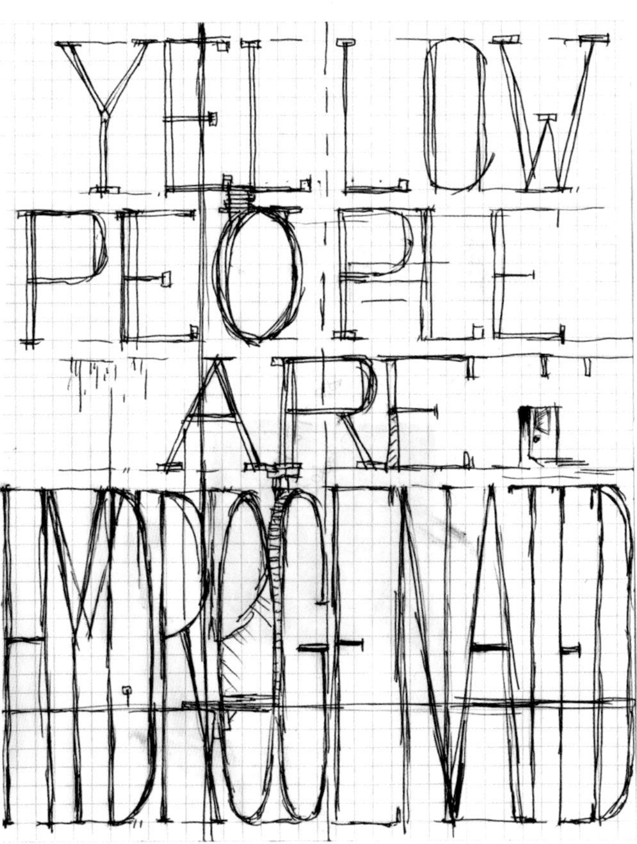

Drawing is a way of performing a problem or a situation. Drawing is a way of navigating historic, geographic and psychological time. *Skin Set* is an ongoing drawing project which, upon completion, will contain 3,500 drawings. I have created 850 so far. As the project develops, I re-think it. Initially the project circumscribed two families of drawings: black and white. Later, I added red and yellow and then green and brown. Most recently I introduced blue and am currently experimenting with purple and orange.

Skin Set results from my interest in several activities: writing as performance, philosophy of language, concrete poetry, set theory and race. So, regarding race, what more can you say about it? So much has been said. What else can be said? Nothing. And nothing is the fullness within which *Skin Set* operates. The project is a kind of visual mumbling, an incantatory graphology, a kind of speaking that is more about speaking than fulfilling. After all, what does it mean to speak? It means to be. So what does it mean to speak again? It means to survive. Scheherazade knew this. Rodney King believed this and look what happened to him. Freedom of speech is overrated. There are some things that can only be defined by endlessness. So, if black people are lice then white people are mice then orange people are bright then yellow people are rice then blue people are brion gysin.

William Pope.L

Top: *Skin Set: White People Are Black People by Neuroses*, 2008, ink on paper, 8 1/2 x 11 in. (21.6 x 28 cm), acquired in 2008
Bottom: *Skin Set: Yellow People Are Hydrogenated*, 2008, ink on paper, 8 1/2 x 11 in. (21.6 x 28 cm), acquired in 2008

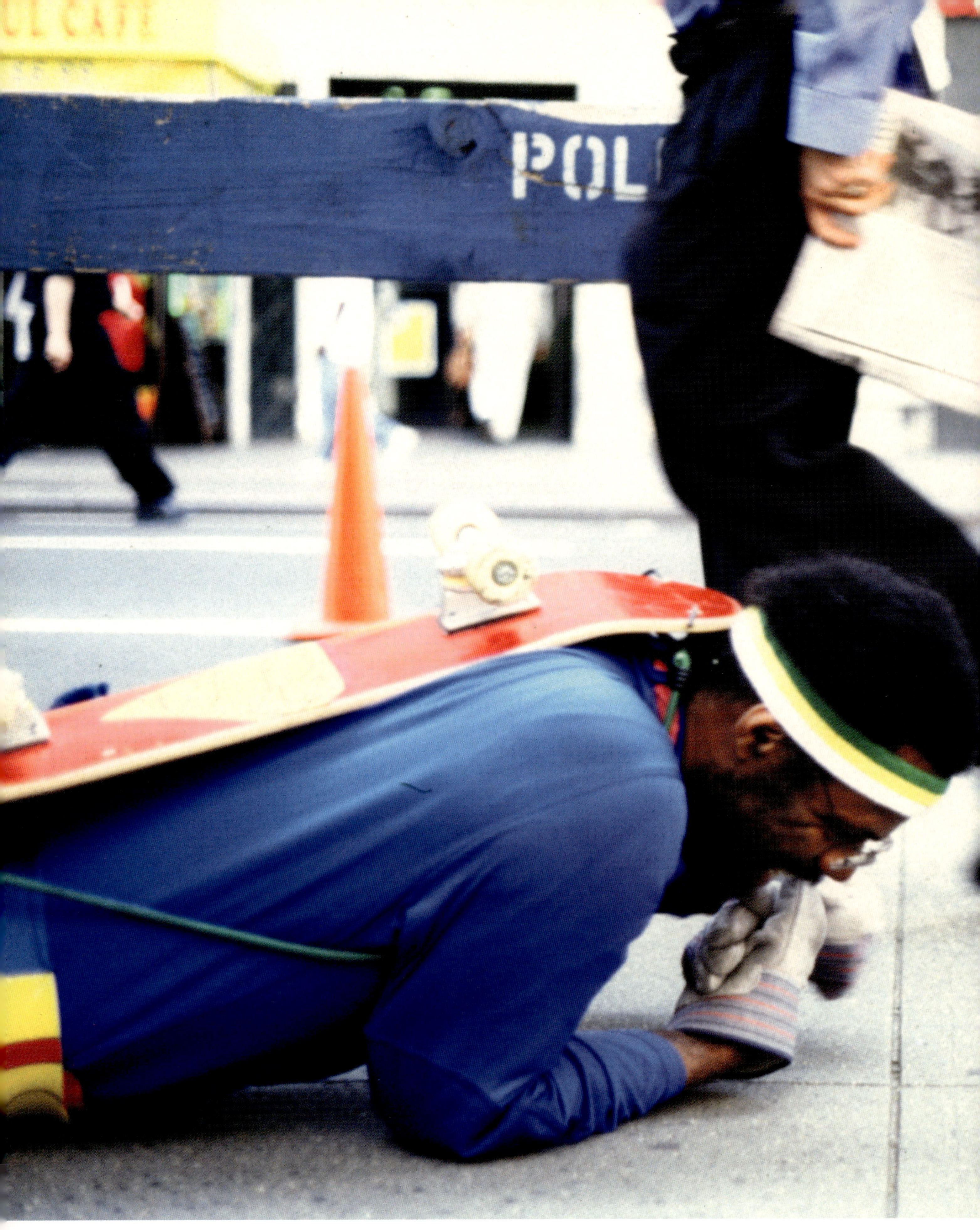

WILLIAM POPE.L *The Great White Way, 22 miles, 9 years, 1 street,* 2001-2002, digital video (color, sound), 5 min., ed. 1/5, acquired in 2008

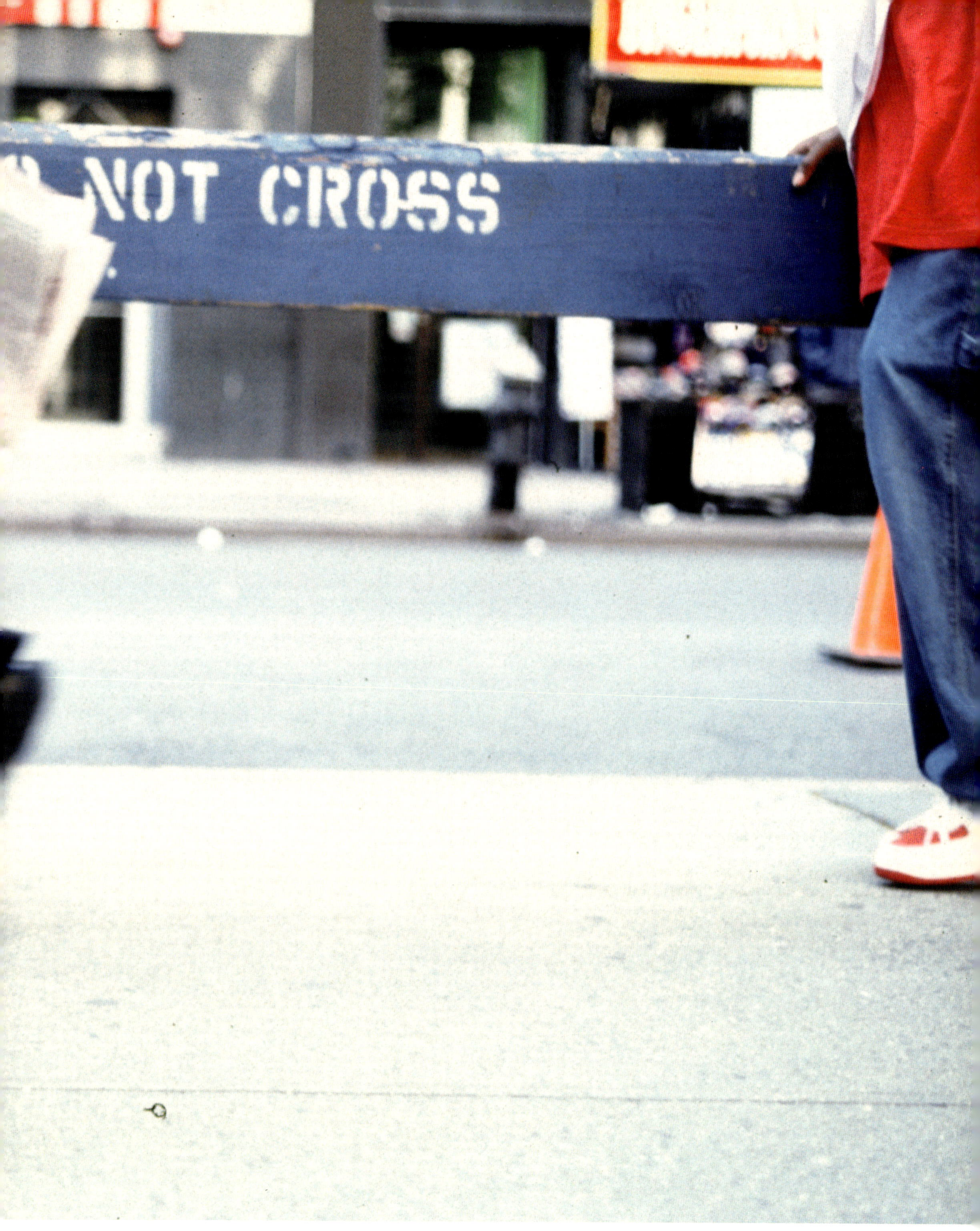

NOT CROSS

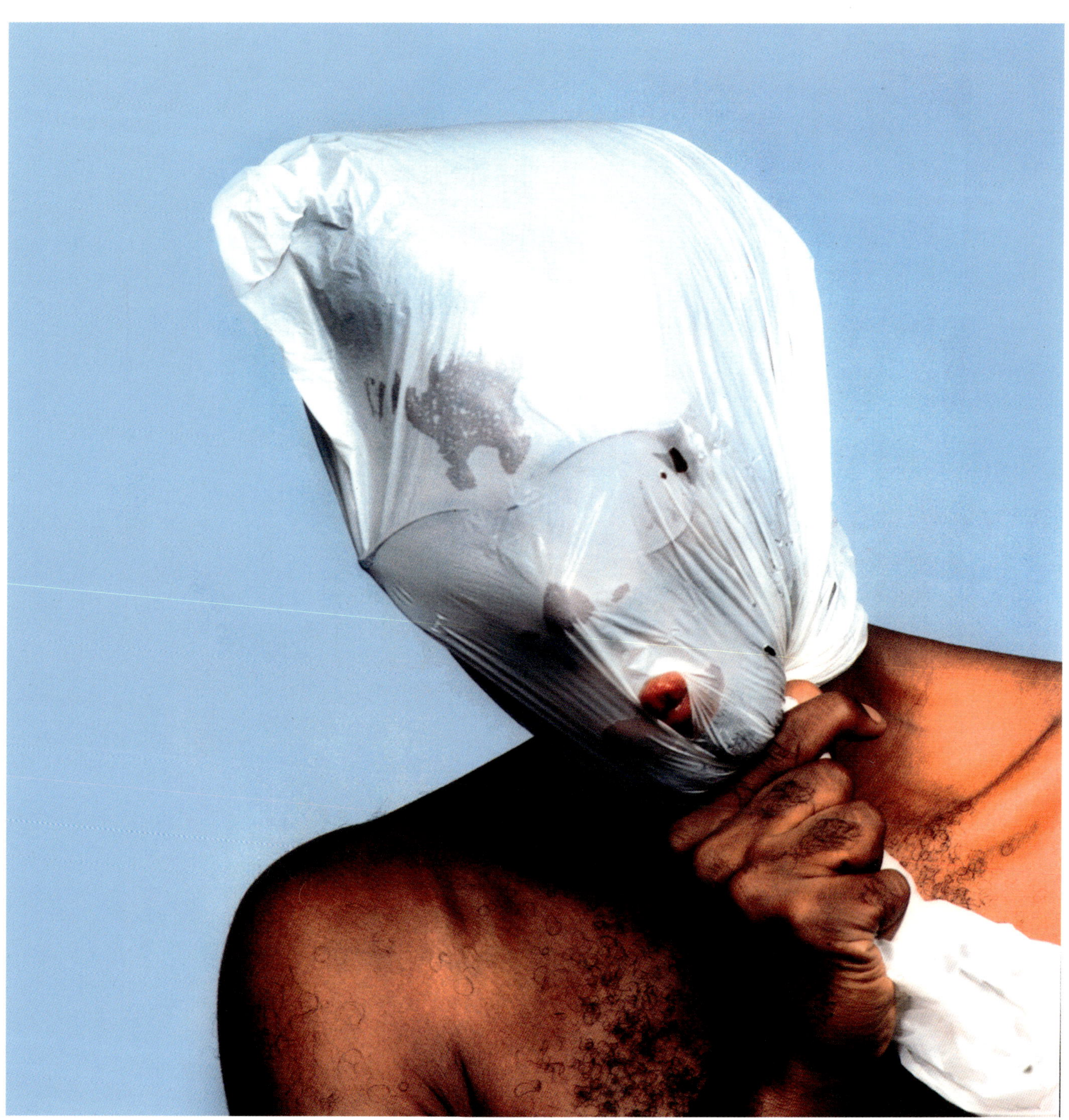

Foraging (asphixia version), 2008, digital chromogenic print, ed. 1/5, 23 1/8 x 24 in. (58.8 x 61 cm), acquired in 2008

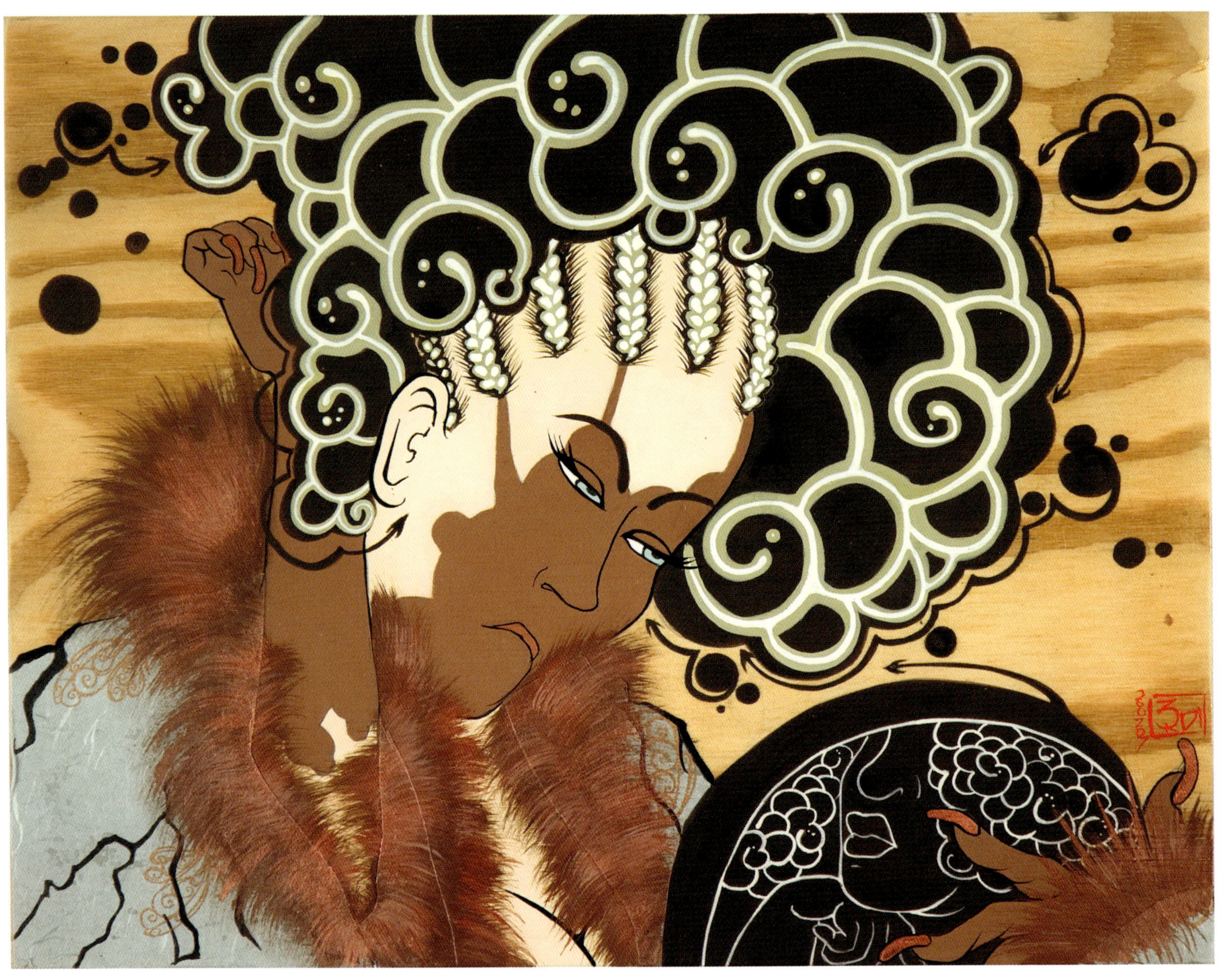

The piece *after Kikugawa Eizan's Furyu nana komachi* is one of the last pieces that i did in the *a3 blackface* series. it still has elements of the earlier type of masking but includes collage and some hint of white line drawings that i had been doing at the time.

Sacrifice #2 [opposite page] is a more current direction, including more full-figured characters. this piece reflects a commonality of which i had been aware for some time. along with looking at woodblock prints, i viewed photos of geisha napping, with their heads propped up by their own arms. what i enjoyed about these images was how similar this method of sleeping was to the way black women can sleep after coming home from the beauty parlor. i have done so myself; having a fresh perm/relaxer in my hair, not wanting it to lose it's "bone straightness."

Rozeal

Top: *Untitled (after Kikugawa Eizan's "Furyu nana komachi" [The Modern Seven Komashi])*, 2007, acrylic and paper on panel, 12 x 14 5/8 in. (30.5 x 37.1 cm), acquired in 2007
Right: *Sacrifice #2: It Has to Last (after Yoshitoshi's "Drowsy: the appearance of a harlot of the Meiji era")*, 2007, enamel, acrylic and paper on panel, 52 x 38 in. (132 x 96.5 cm), acquired in 2007

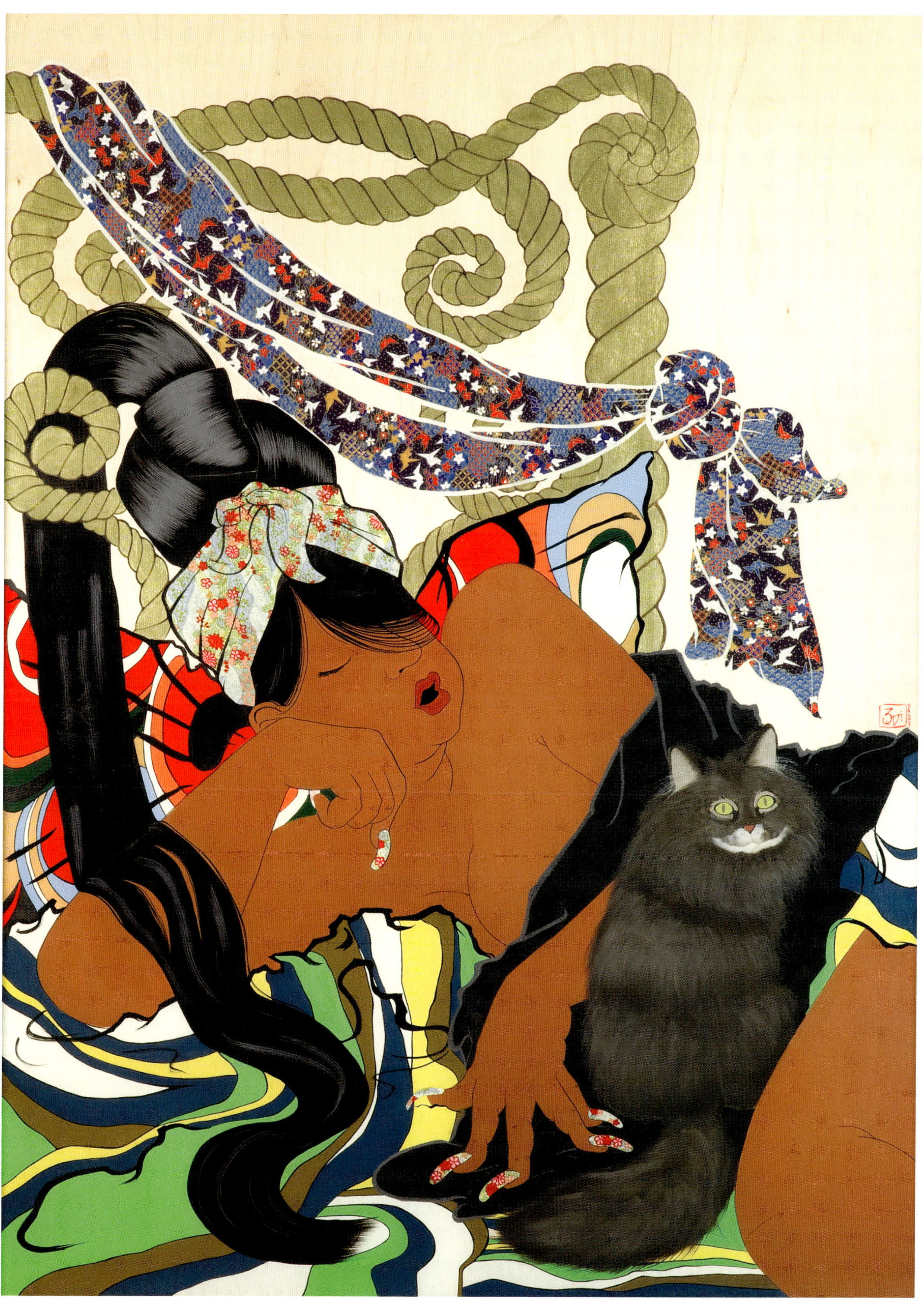

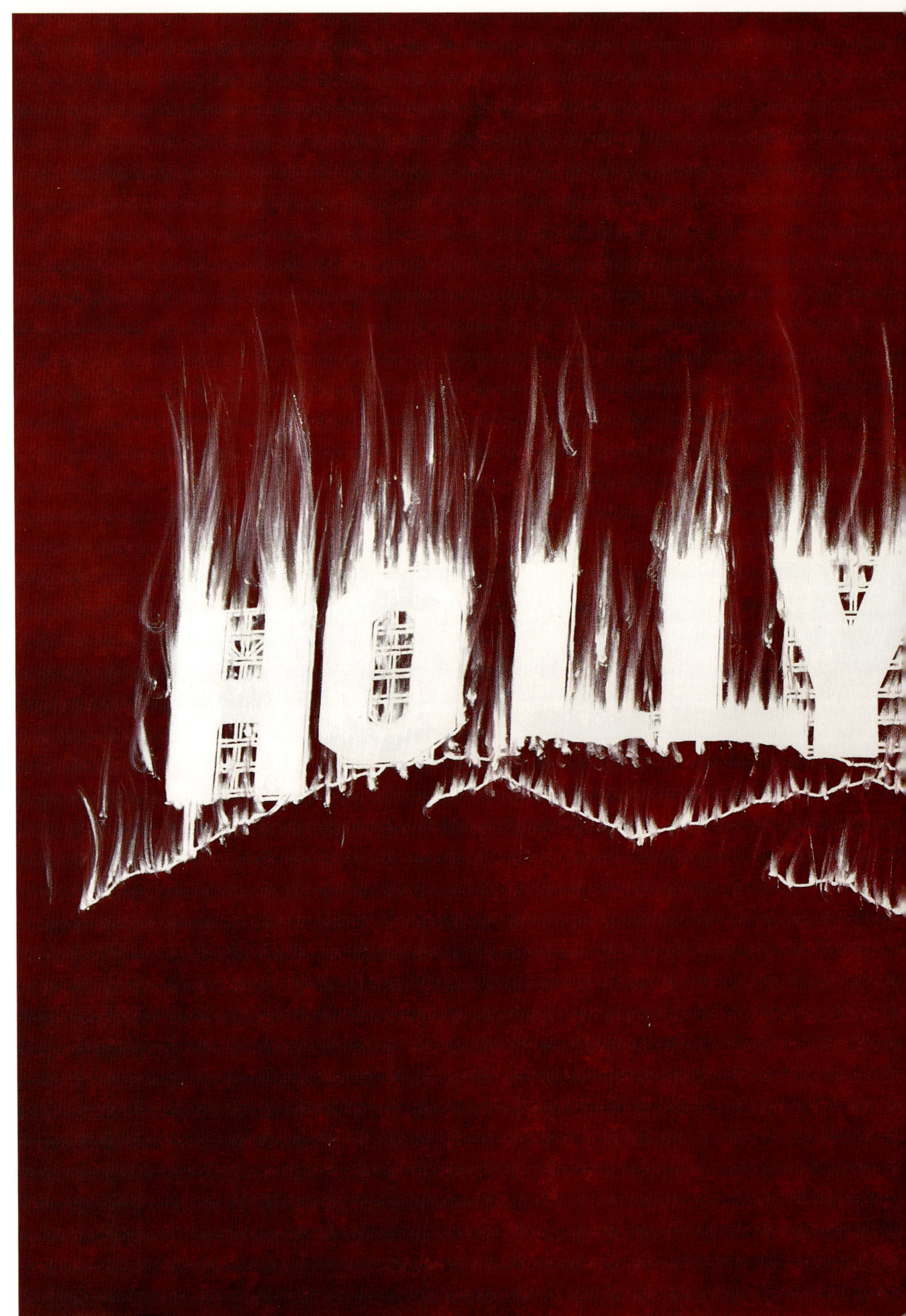

 GARY SIMMONS *Hollywood*, 2008, pigment, oil and cold wax on canvas, 84 x 120 in. (213.4 x 304.8 cm), acquired in 2008

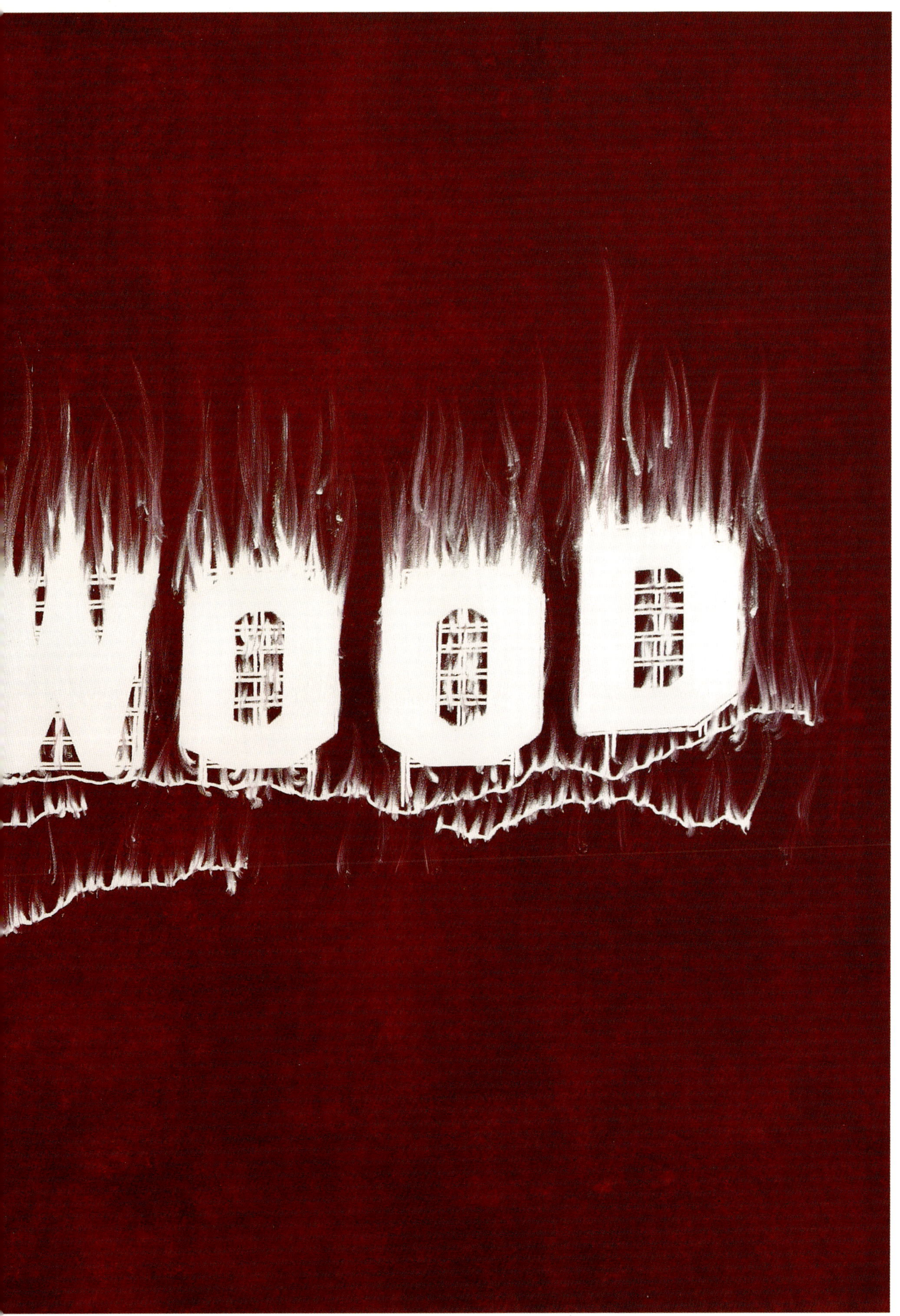
WOOD

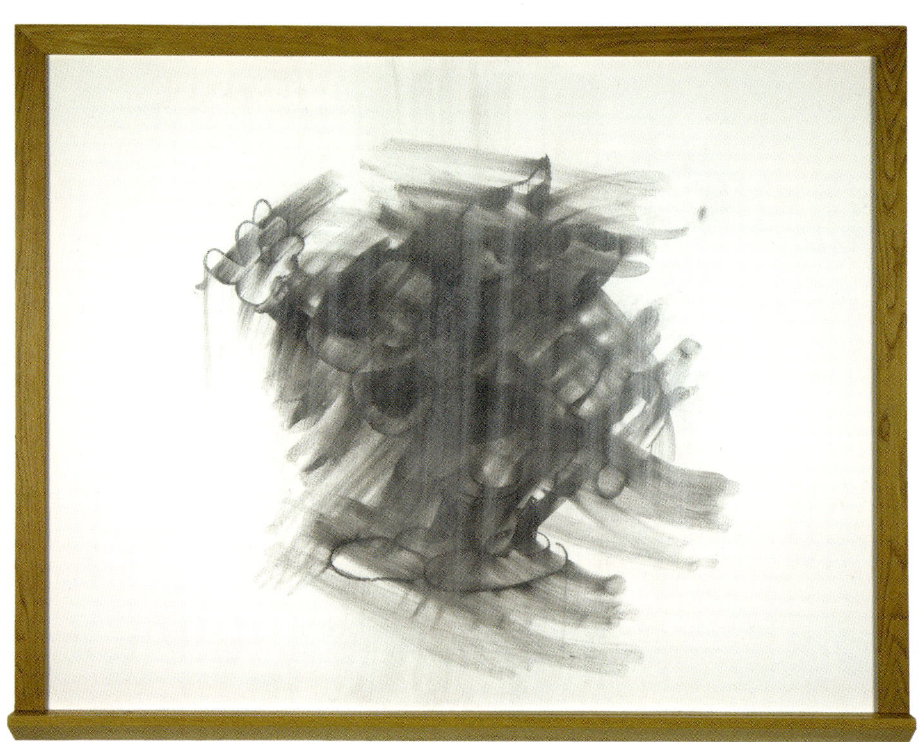

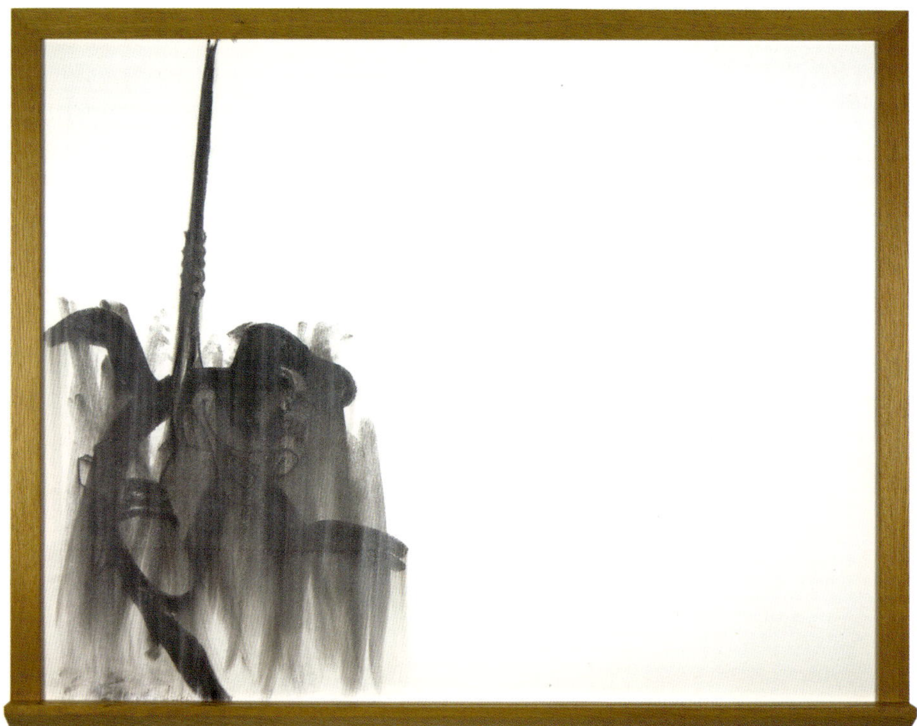

Top to bottom: *Chalkboard Drawing #1*, 1992; *Chalkboard Drawing #3*, 1992, acrylic and charcoal on chalkboard, each 47 x 60 in. (119.4 x 152.4 cm), acquired in 1992

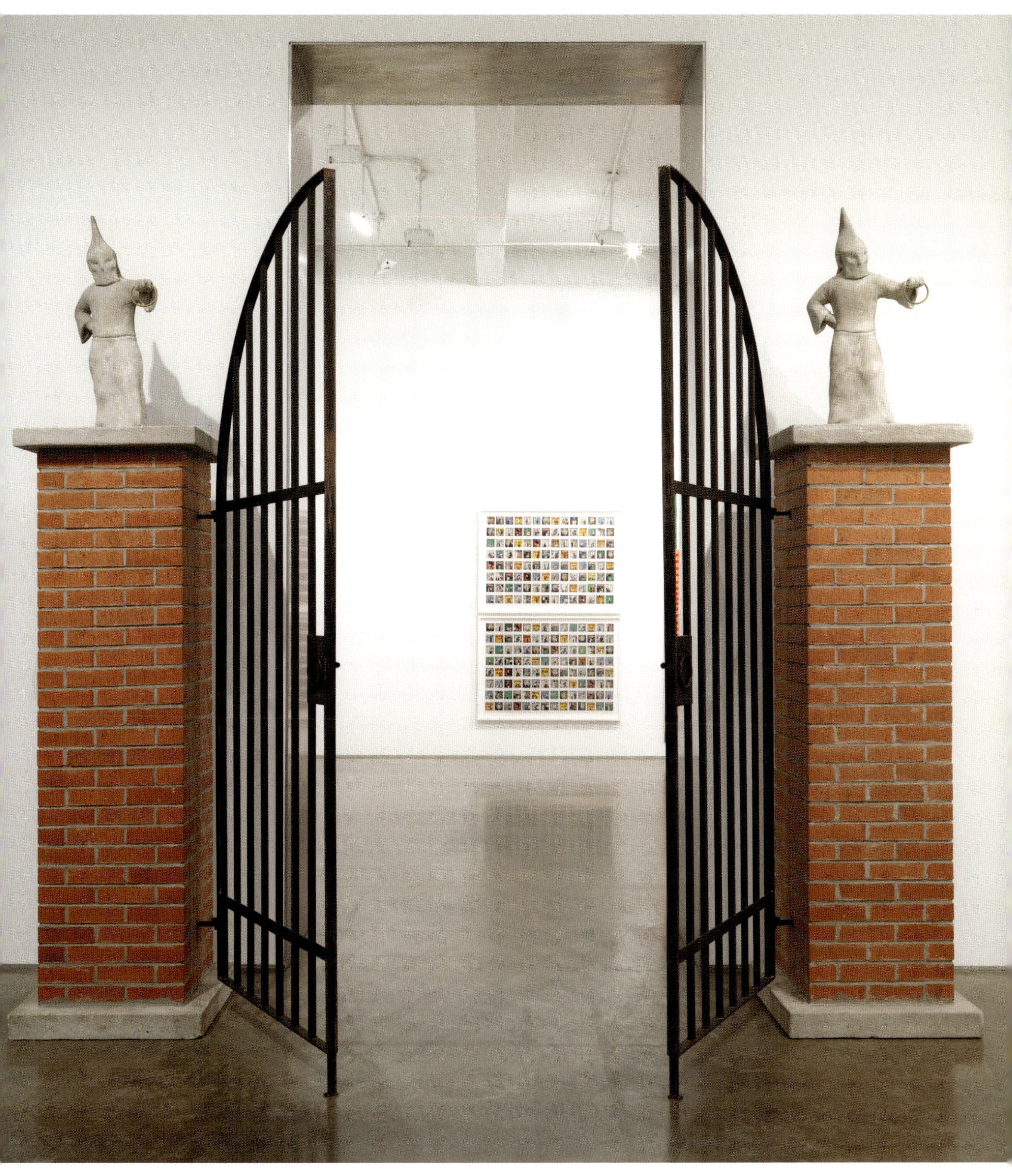

Klan Gate, 1992, cast concrete, wood , brick and steel, 120 x 114 x 25.5 in. (305 x 290 x 64.8 cm), acquired in 1992, installation view, Metro Pictures, New York

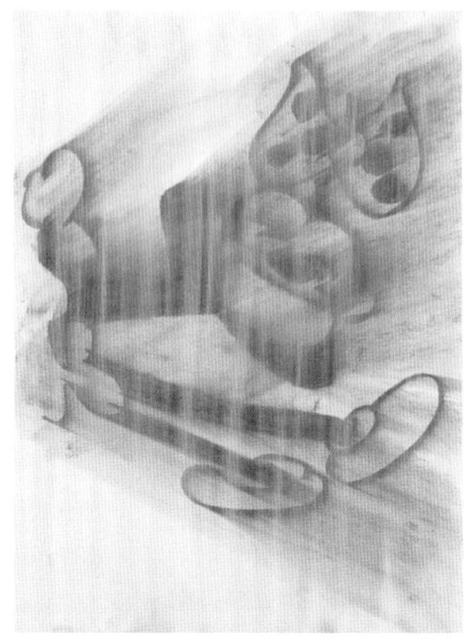

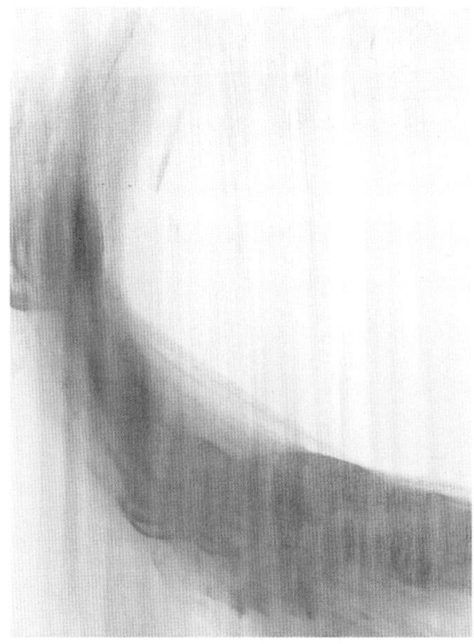

Clockwise from top left: *Erasure Series (White Washed Drawings) #2*, 1992; *Erasure Series (White Washed Drawings) #8*, 1992; *Erasure Series (White Washed Drawings) #9*, 1992; *Erasure Series (White Washed Drawings) #11*, 1992, each: acrylic and charcoal on paper, 30 x 22 1/4 in. (76.2 x 56.5 cm), acquired in 1992

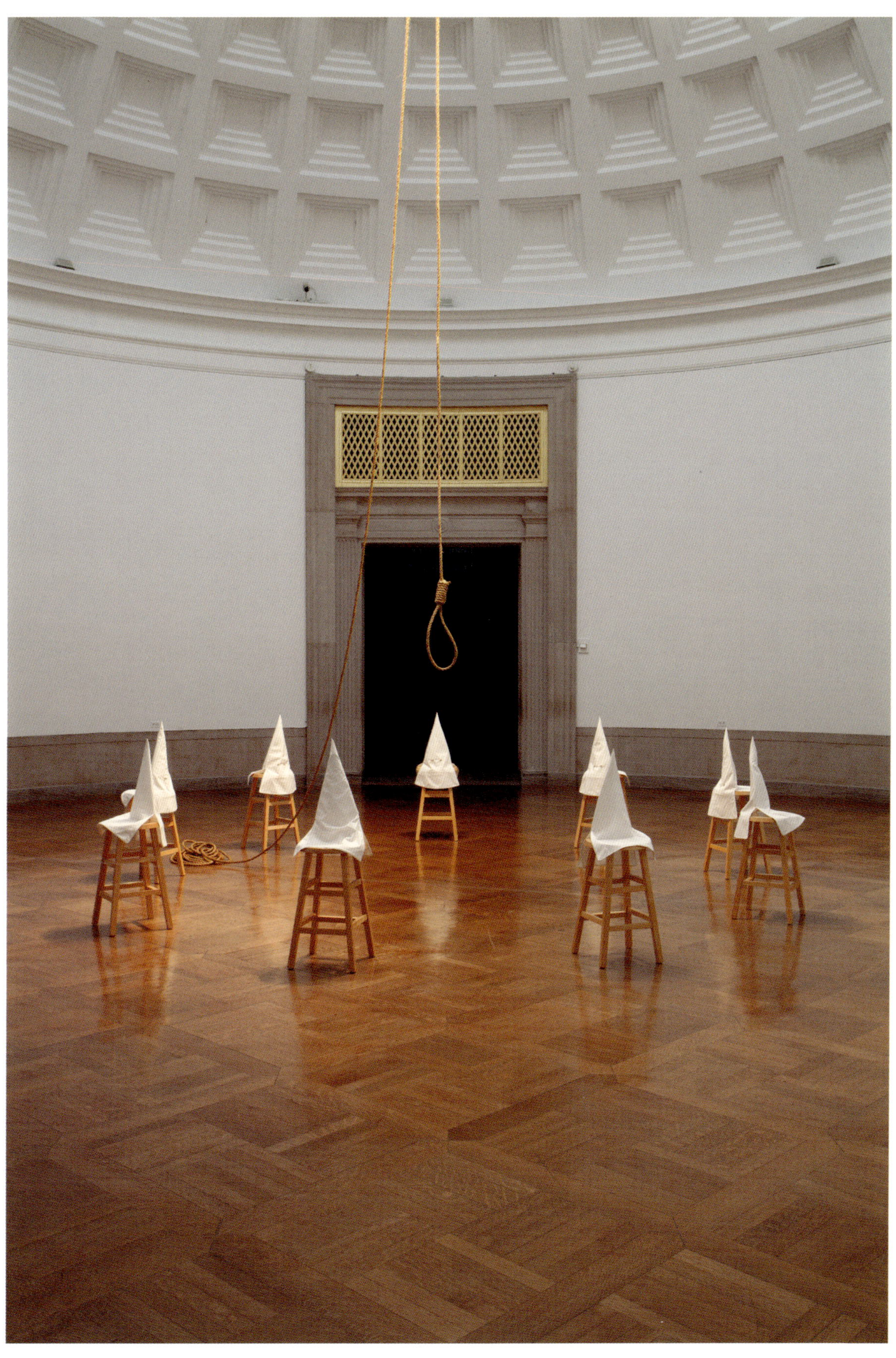

Duck, Duck, Noose, 1992, wood, cloth, metal and hemp, dimensions variable, acquired in 1992, installation view, Corcoran Gallery of Art, Washington, D.C.

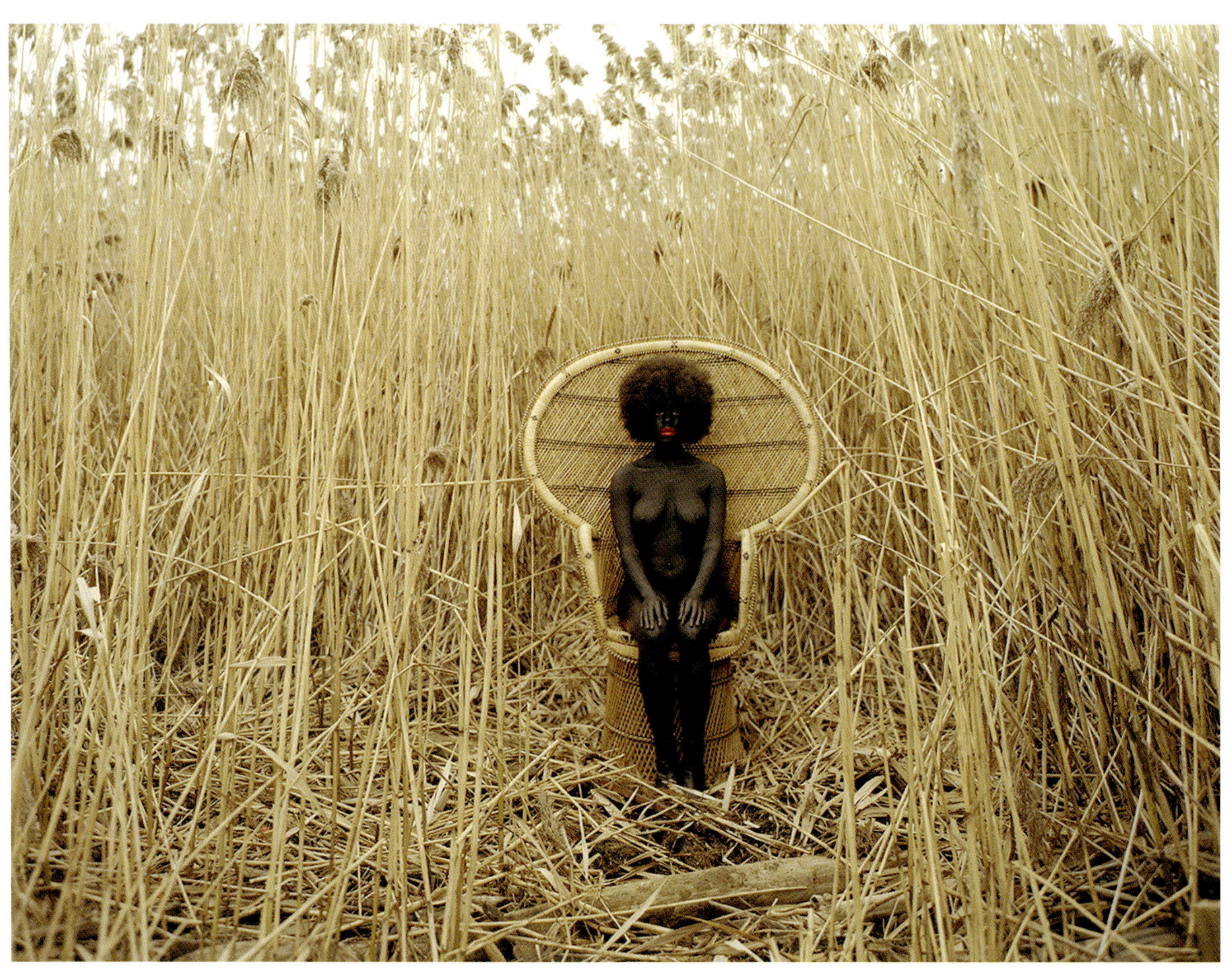

 XAVIERA SIMMONS *One Day and Back Then (Seated)*, 2007, color photograph, ed. 3/7, 30 x 40 in. (76.2 x 101.6 cm), acquired in 2008

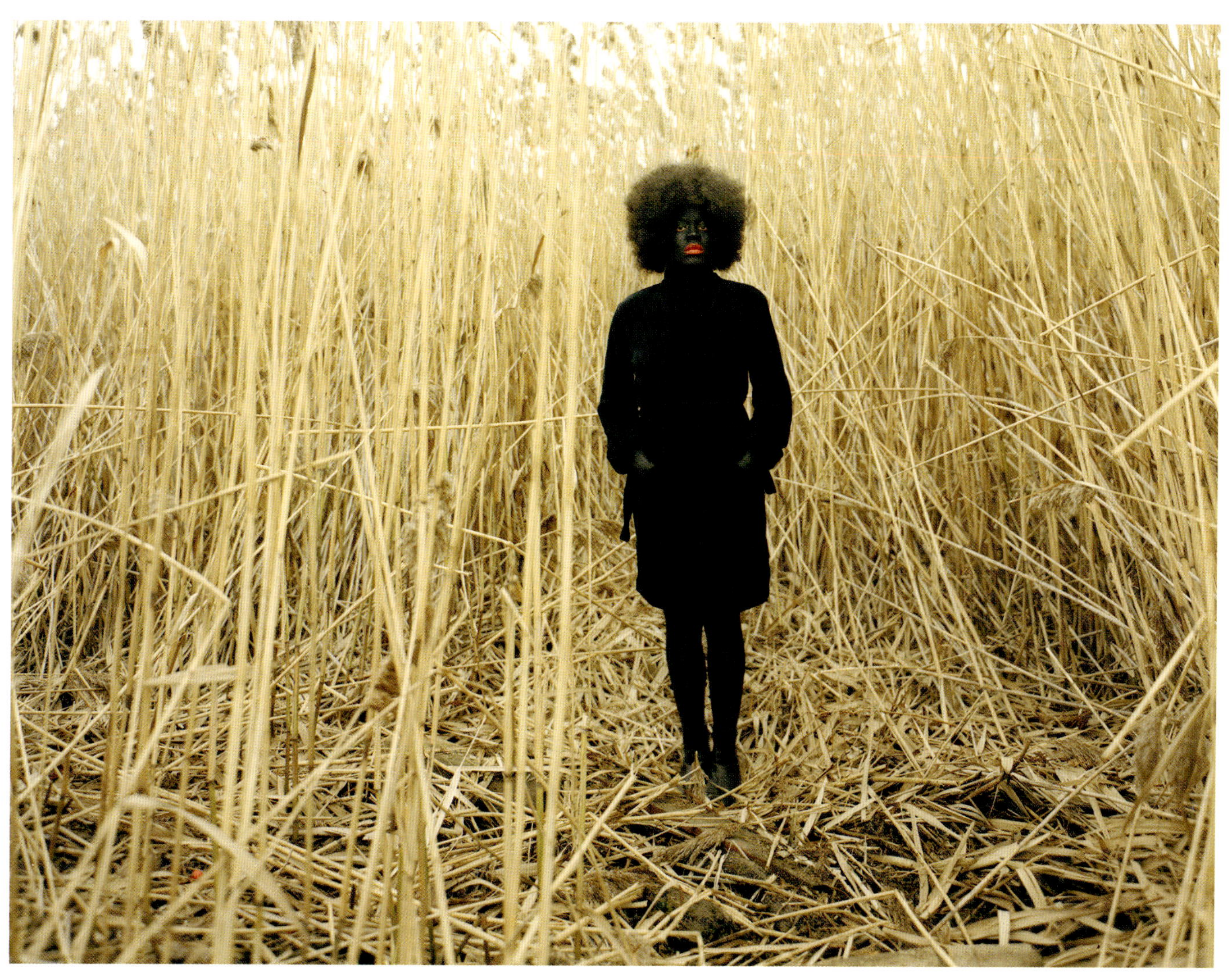

One Day and Back Then (Standing), 2007, color photograph, ed. 2/5, 30 x 40 in. (76.2 x 101.6 cm), acquired in 2008

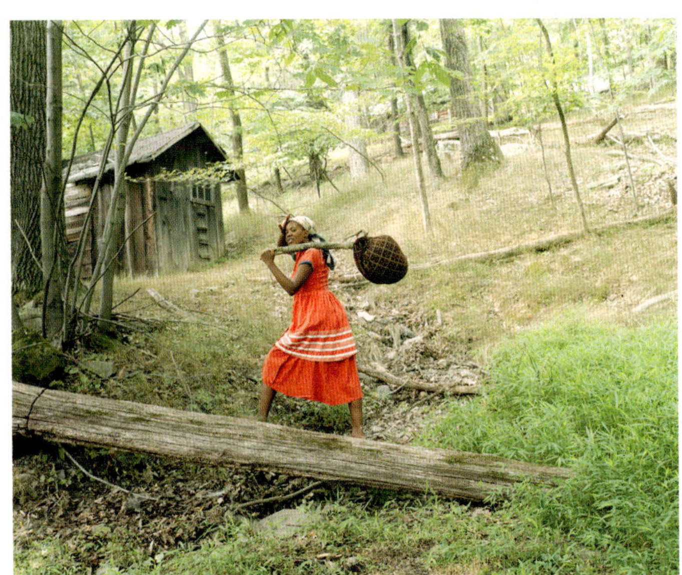

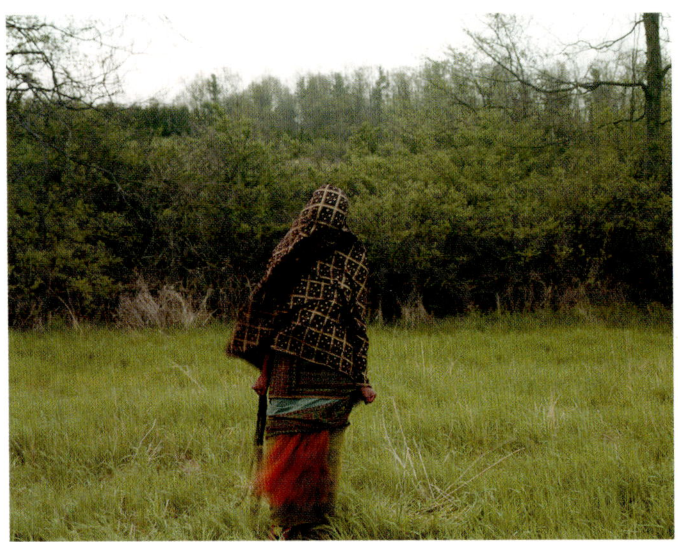

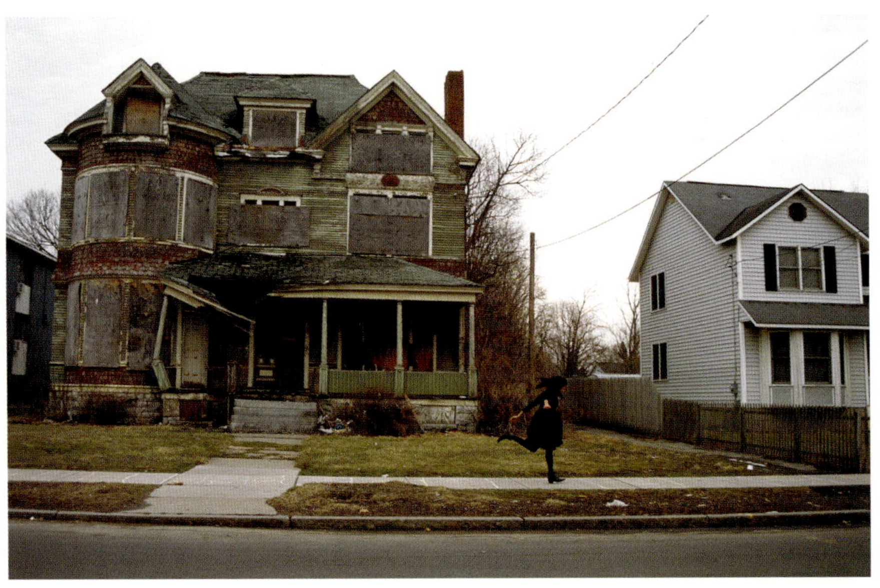

Top to bottom: *American Book Covers*, 2007, color photograph, ed. 1/5, 30 x 40 in. (76.2 x 101.6 cm), acquired in 2008; *Make the Fist*, 2004, color photograph, ed. 1/5, 30 x 40 in. (76.2 x 101.6 cm),acquired in 2008; *Appear, Appease, Applaud (Also, Perhaps, Maybe)*, 2008, chromira print, ed. 1/5, 30 x 40 in. (76.2 x 101.6 cm), acquired in 2008

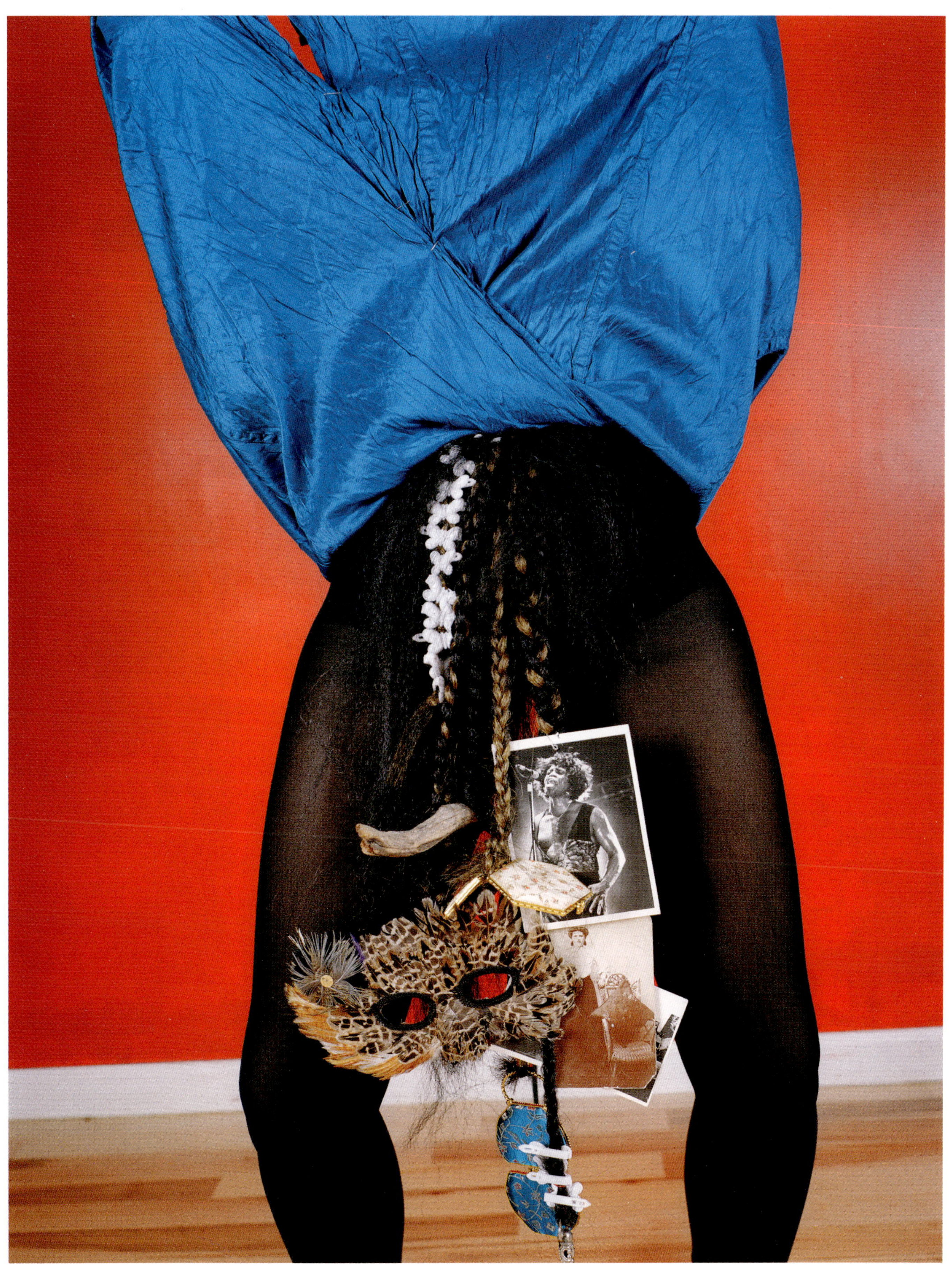

Beyond the Canon of Landscape (For Orhan. P, Zadie. S, Nia and Naima. M), 2008, chromira print, ed. 1/5, 40 x 30 in. (101.6 x 76.2 cm), acquired in 2008

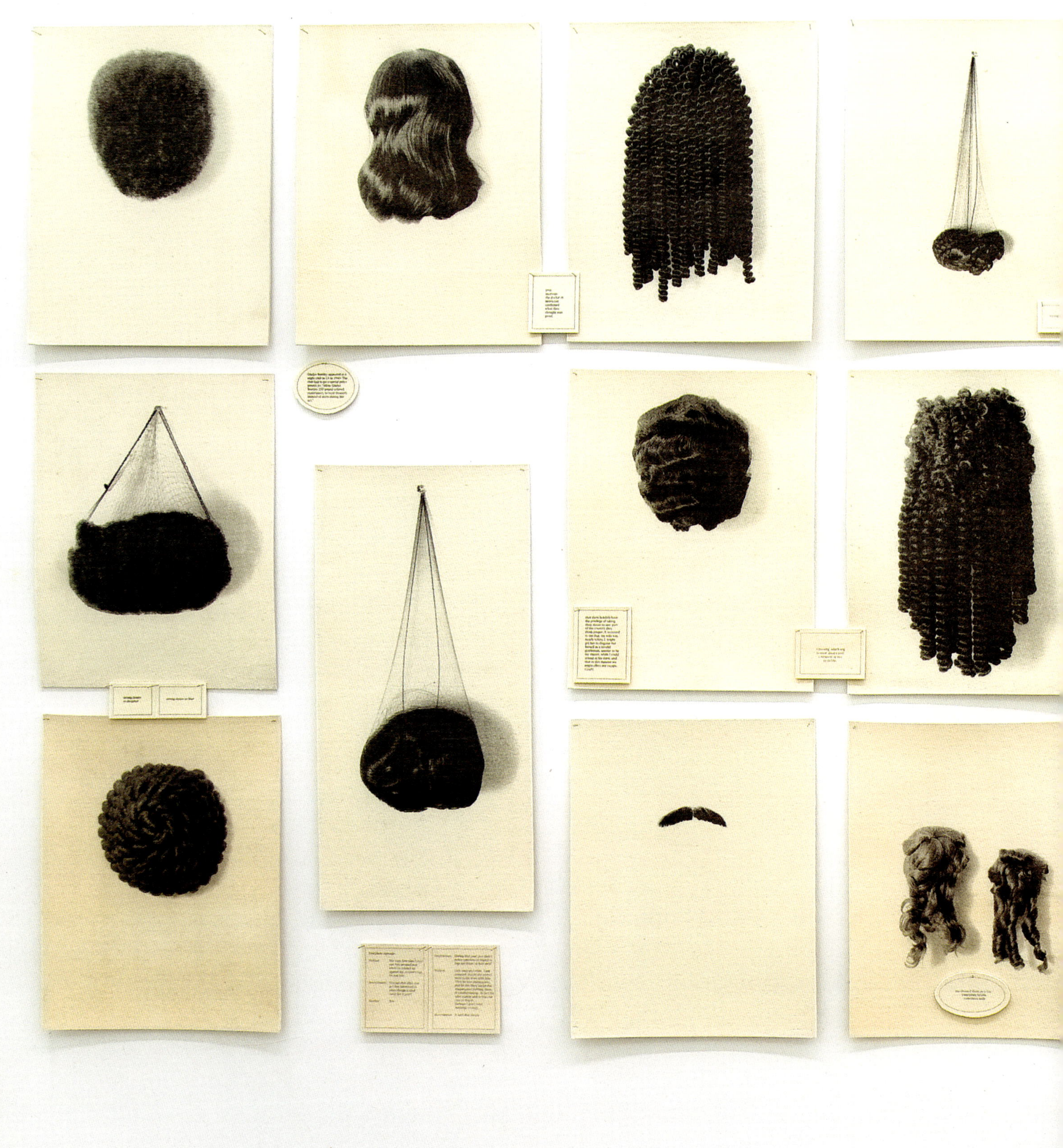

 LORNA SIMPSON *Wigs (Portfolio)*, 1994, waterless lithograph and felt, 38 panels, overall 72 x 162 1/2 in. (182.9 x 412.8 cm), acquired in 2008

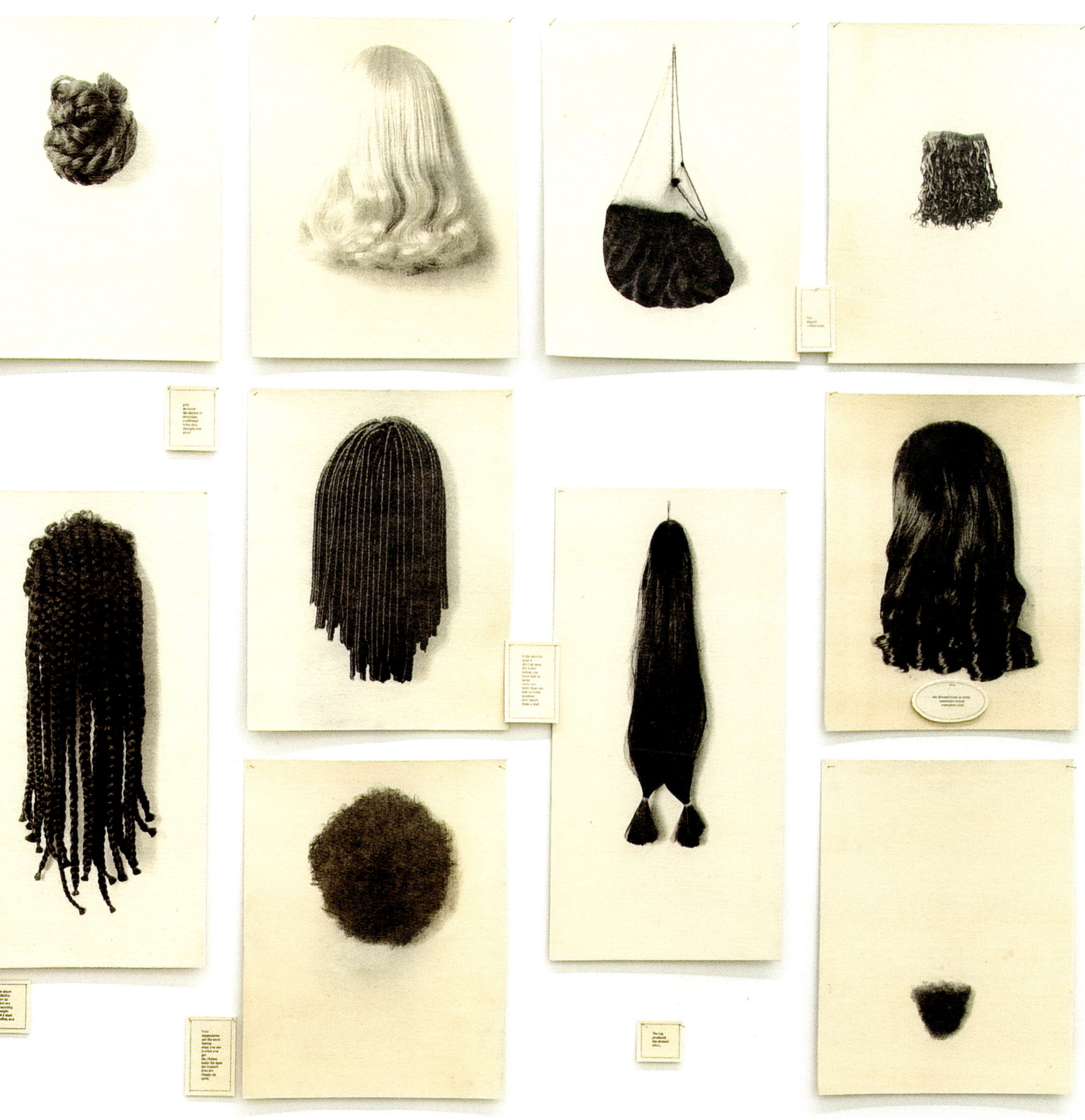

a bull, a rose, a tempest began the collection of items for a larger sculptural "requiem" of sorts. I had been contemplating the memorabilia surrounding celebrities who passed away since I've been alive. I began with Tupac, a prince to the music industry, a renegade and, in a more personal context, an artist whom I knew as a teenager when we attended high school together. The title comes from a line in Borges' short story "The Circular Ruins" – a tale of birth, death, love and loneliness that bends perceptions of reality and dream.

Menagerie [following page] is the first within a new series of mixed media paintings that allow me to indulge in my desire to fill an entire space – a menagerie of marks, fabrics ... a combination of chaos and restraint.

Crone-huntress [following page] is a Goddess. This piece conjures references to mythologies of magical women. "Cast-offs" were used to build an idol of sorts: my homage to warrior women, to the wise "crone." It references mythological figures like Diana (the huntress), Artemis (the "collector of souls") and Kali (goddess of time and change). As the Crone, in pagan circles, represents the third phase of a woman's life filled with wisdom and experience, she is a protector, a giver and taker of life. For me, this form is the perfect vehicle for expressing the consumption and transformation of used materials and of my own attraction to these myths.

Shinique Smith

 a bull, a rose, a tempest, 2007, fabric and found objects, 43 x 29 x 26 in. (109 x 73.6 x 66 cm), acquired in 2007

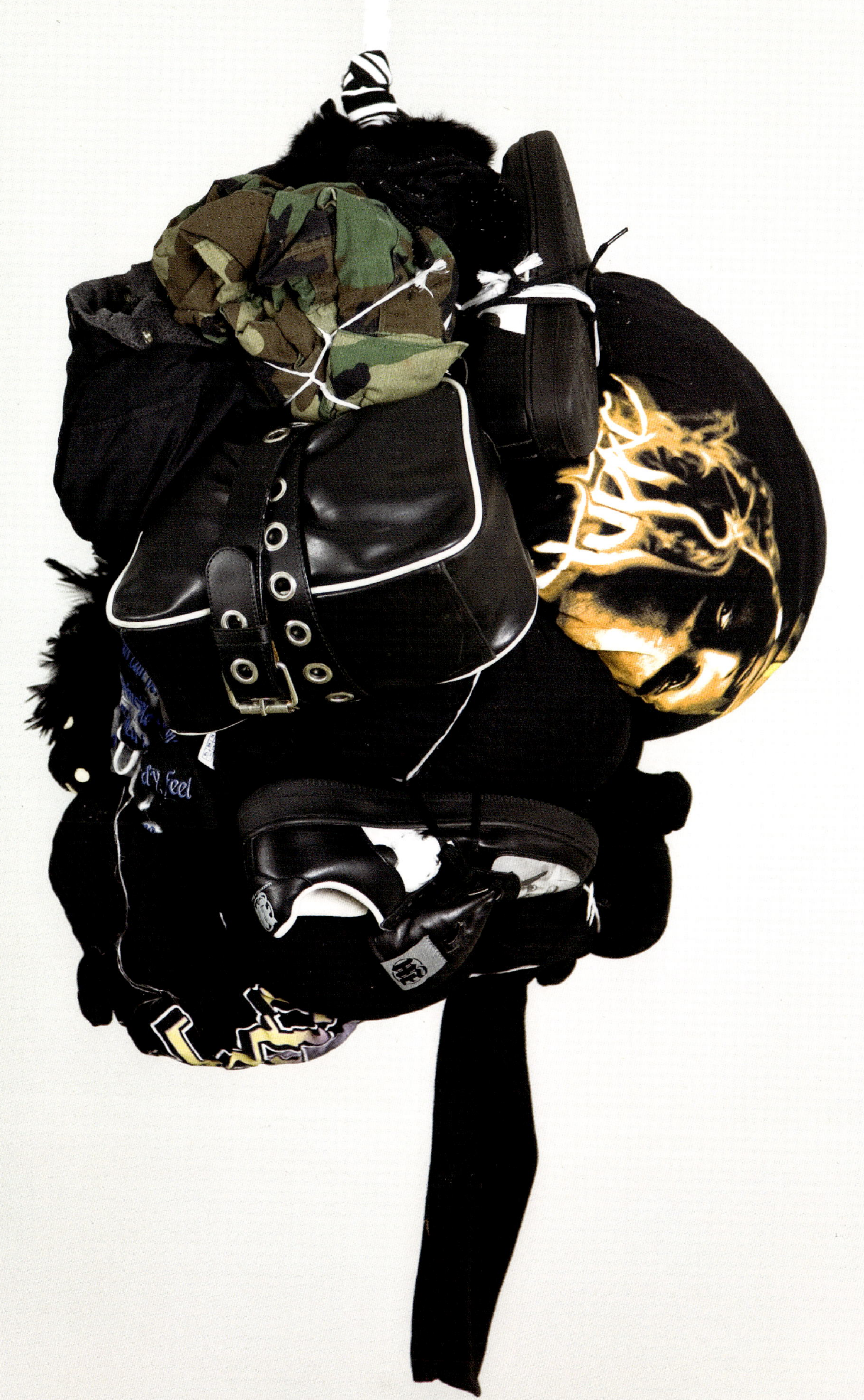

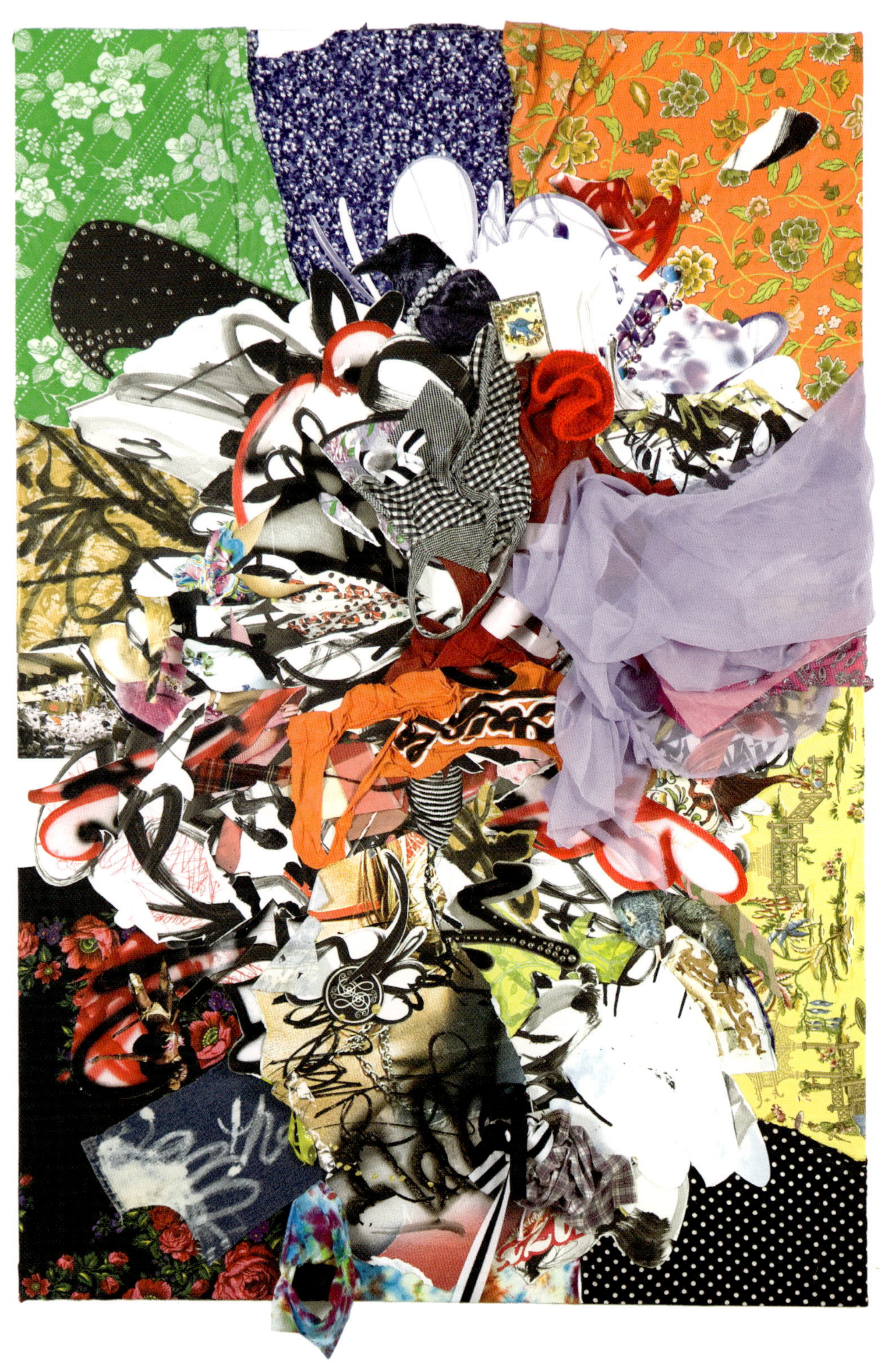

 SHINIQUE SMITH

Menagerie, 2007, mixed media on canvas, 72 x 48 in. (183 x 122 cm), acquired in 2007
Crone-Huntress, 2007, wool, fabric and mixed media, 75 x 100 x 70 in. (190.5 x 254 x 177.8 cm), acquired in 2007

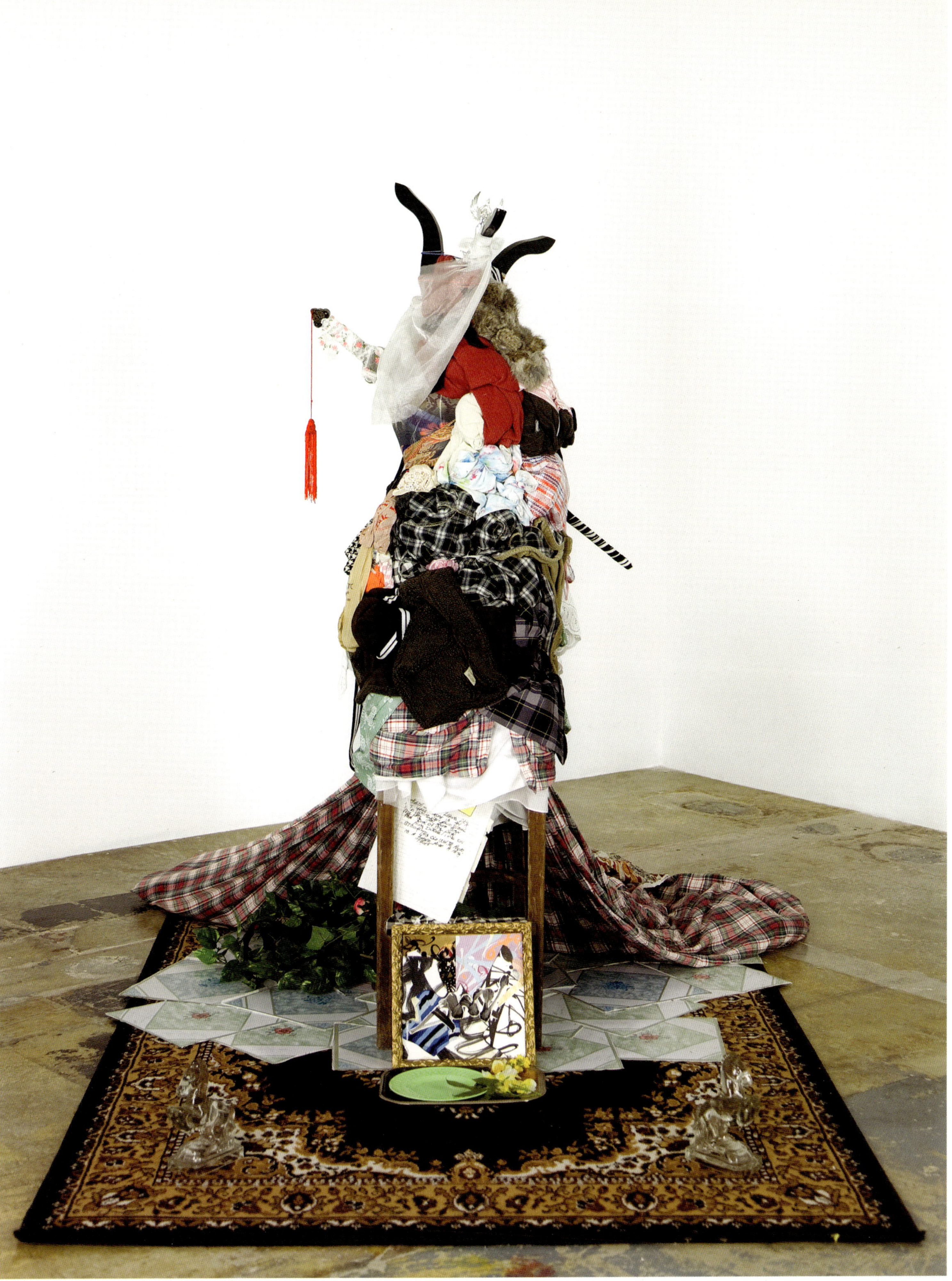

I became aware of Cardinal Francis Arinze during the Catholic Church's process to replace then-deceased Pope John Paul II in 2005. Although the cardinal lacked the credentials of a handful of his contemporaries, the coverage he received from mainstream media outlets would lead one to think he was born for the position.

The skepticism that arose in their overzealous reporting made him an attractive figure for a painting. Visualizing him as the First Black Pope, along with the papacy being a subject of contention for the great artists Diego Velázquez and Francis Bacon, had emboldened me to take the dubious cynicism I sensed permeating the subjects to compose a portrait of Cardinal Arinze as pope.

To assist me I employed charcoal briquettes, matches, and other non-traditional painting materials I sensed had the symbolic strength to dictate my representation of a Black Nigerian Pope. This however was not enough to deflect the observer's attention from what seemed a larcenist act I'd committed against the aforementioned artists.

Eliminating Francis Bacon, who became a father figure of sorts, in the conception of the painting proved to be more of a challenge than just removing my fingerprints; but in an attempt to do so I believe the beholder would see the painting *Exhibit A: Cardinal Arinze* in a richer context.

Mainstream media outlets capitalized in the spinning of the cardinal's image and so did I with their assistance. In so doing I discovered while using unorthodox materials as accomplices in my painting process that I was narrowing the gap between painting and sculpture, and creating distance from what I've learned to accept in art history as the norm. What WE THE PUBLIC learned last year with the election of His Holiness, Pope Francis, was that Cardinal Francis Arinze was no nearer to the position of pope than he was eight years ago.

Jeff Sonhouse

 Exhibit A: Cardinal Francis Arinze, 2005, oil and mixed media on panel, 78 x 61 in. (198.1 x 154.9 cm), acquired in 2006

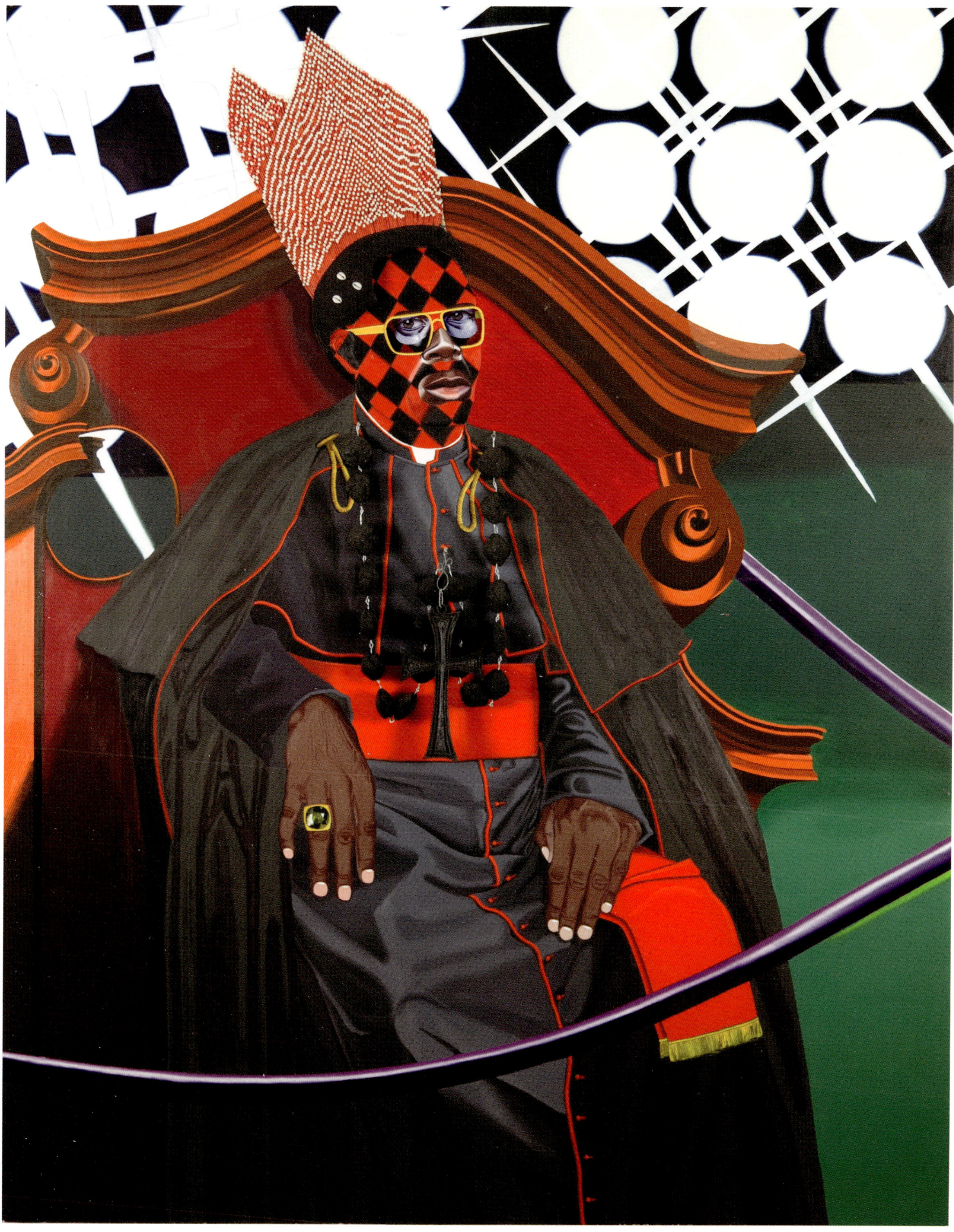

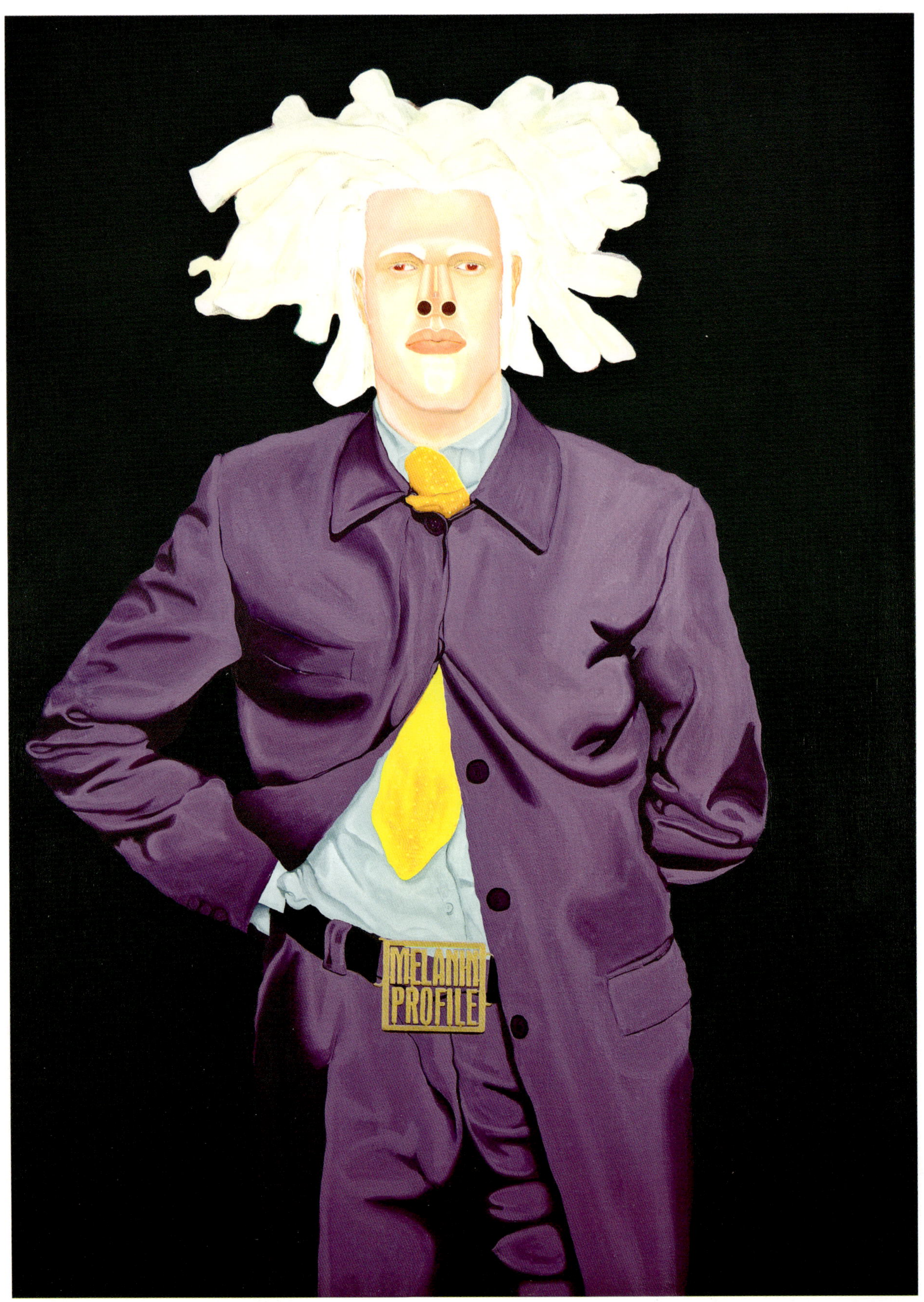

 JEFF SONHOUSE *Yellow is Mellow*, 2001, oil on canvas, 59 1/2 x 42 in. (151.1 x 106.7 cm), acquired in 2008

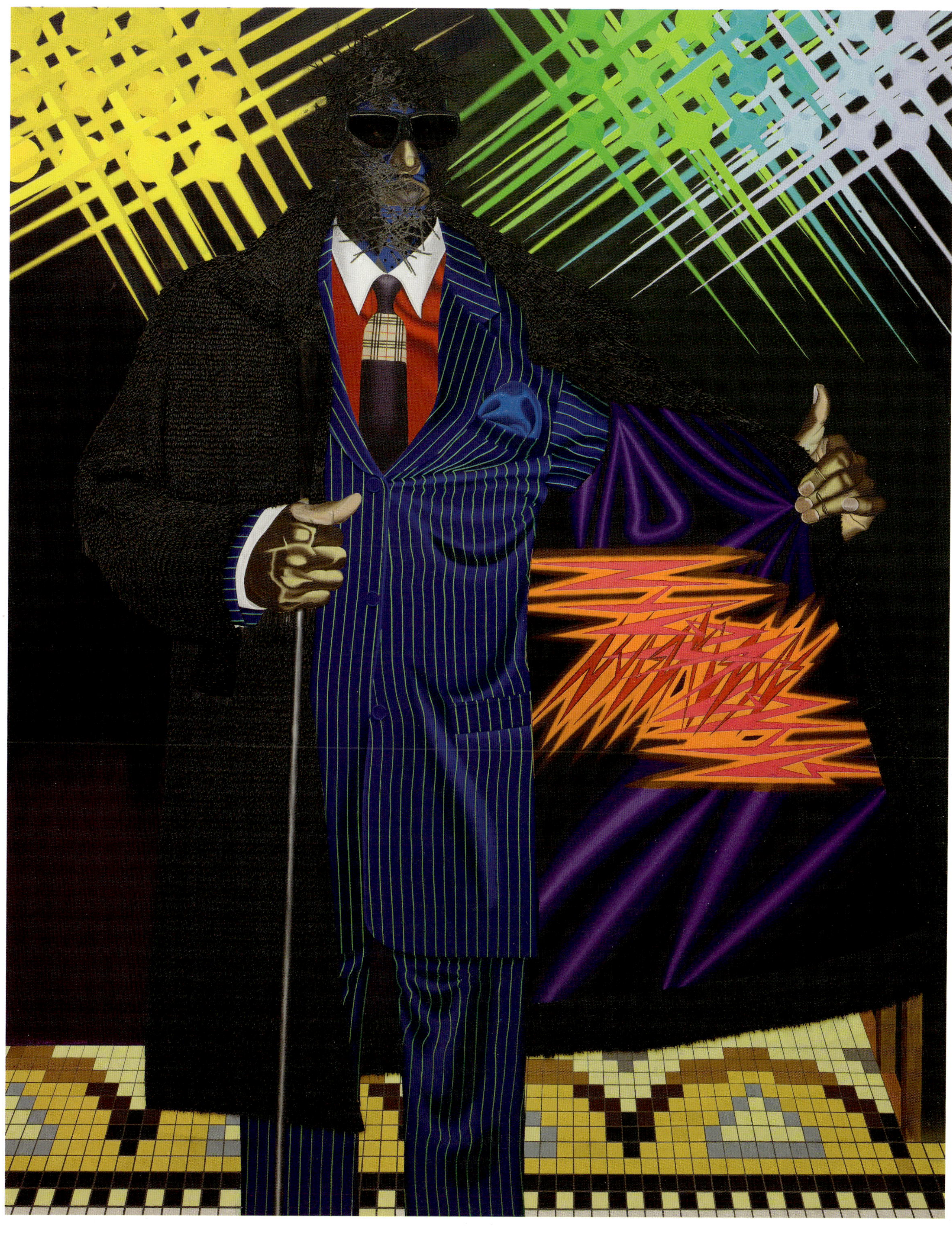

Visually Impaired, 2008, oil on canvas, 78 x 61 in. (198.1 x 154.9 cm), acquired in 2008

Ontology . . . does not permit us to understand the being of the black man. For not only must the black man be black; he must be black in relation to the white man. . . . The black man has no ontological resistance in the eyes of the white man. Overnight the Negro has been given two frames of reference within which he has had to place himself. His metaphysics, or, less pretentiously, his customs and the sources on which they were based, were wiped out because they were in conflict with a civilization that he did not know and that imposed itself on him. . . .

Frantz Fanon, *Black Skin, White Masks*, 1967

The fact is "black" has never been just there either. It has always been an unstable identity, psychically, culturally and politically. It, too, is a narrative, a story, a history. Something constructed, told, spoken, not simply found. People now speak of the society I come from in totally unrecognizable ways. Of course Jamaica is a black society, they say. In reality it is a society of black and brown people who lived for three or four hundred years without ever being able to speak of themselves as "black". Black is an identity which had to be learned and could only be learned in a certain moment.

Stuart Hall, "Minimal Selves," 1984

The ways in which [white mainstream] artists—and the society that bred them—transferred internal conflicts to a "blank darkness," to conveniently bound and violently silenced black bodies, is a major theme in American literature. . . .

Toni Morrison, *Playing in the Dark: Whiteness and the Literary Imagination*, 1992

For a while now, scholars of race and whiteness have understood that the construction of white culture as the invisible norm is one of the most, if not *the* most pernicious, constructions of whiteness in the post-civil rights era. . . . [W]hite identity seemed cultureless because white cultural practices were taken for granted, naturalized, and, thus, not reflected on and defined.

Pamela Perry, "White Means Never Having to Say You're Ethnic: White Youth and the Construction of 'Cultureless' Identities," *Journal of Contemporary Ethnography,* 2001

A portrait in black by Kehinde Wiley.
We are the canvas. Genius. Original.
Breathtaking. A style our own, never
Before seen, ground breaking. You see
Us, admire us and when you reach out
to touch us, we are gone, leaving art,
impressions and influence in our
passing to be admired, studied and
imitated in black.

Nissan Ad, 2004

In 2008 Hank Willis Thomas scanned the Nissan ad (referenced above) before digitally erasing its text to reveal the image's latent meaning. The completed photo-based work, which he calls *We are the Canvas 2004/2008* (after the ad's second sentence), is one of two images representing the year 2004 in his extended series entitled *Unbranded Reflections in Black by Corporate America 1968-2008* (2005-2008). This series, in which all language has been digitally excised, focuses on advertising images from the late 1960s to 2008, found in such popular and widely disseminated African-American magazines as *Essence* and *Ebony.* An artist with an M.F.A. in photography and an M.A. in visual criticism, Thomas is intrigued with corporate ads that target black audiences by first

1. Hank Willis Thomas, interview with author, New York, 2008.

selling them provocative and timely images of themselves in order to instill a desire for their products.[1] Working in concert with ads intended for middle-class black audiences, Thomas's *Unbranded* series begins appropriately with 1968, a very conflicted time in American politics. Just four years after the Civil Rights Act was passed, guaranteeing equal employment opportunities for all Americans regardless of their race, color, religion, sex, or national origin, Martin Luther King Jr. was assassinated, the Fair Housing Act was enacted, Robert F. Kennedy was killed, and in the summer of that same fateful year race riots broke out in hundreds of cities across the United States.

Before initiating this group of works, Thomas had been involved with his *B®anded* series. In a few of these works he Photoshopped Nike's distinctive swoosh logo directly on the bodies of black figures and implicitly contrasted this company's emphasis on speed with the incarcerating marks that in the nineteenth century had sometimes been branded on the bodies of recalcitrant slaves or left there as telltale marks of brutal whips. Thomas stopped this series, however, when he decided that its overall premises were too subjective and idiosyncratic; he decided that he wanted his art to rise above the personal in order to reveal the ideological filters of corporate advertising that, in the interests of selling products, projects its images of desire on the bodies and lives of African-Americans in both blatant and subtle ways.

To appreciate the impact of these ideological filters, it helps to look at both the manifest and latent meanings incorporated in the 2004 Nissan ad (cited above) that features the cutting-edge young painter Kehinde Wiley seated in the foreground mixing paint. Printed in white, the first line of the ad's text, which reads "A portrait in black by Kehinde Wiley," involves a highly sophisticated intertextuality, connecting it formally with the 1966-67 series known as *The First Investigation, Titled (Art as Idea as Idea)*, created by white conceptual artist Joseph Kosuth. Kosuth presented this series—informally known as Definitions—to the public in the form of Photostats, enlarged exhibition copies of cut-out dictionary definitions affixed to index cards, which more directly documented the specific concepts with which he was working. Thus, through its implied connection with Kosuth's Definitions, this ad has the net effect of making the reference to Wiley's portrait conceptual and ephemeral.

Following this first line in white is the rest of Nissan's text, printed in gray, which begins with the statement "We are the canvas." Appearing in a magazine geared to a black readership, the Nissan ad's gray-and-white text appears to extol the brilliant protean spirit of contemporary African-Americans alluded to in the text, even as it celebrates its own product's ability to transcend, through the open road, the material conditions encumbering them. Supposedly working in tandem with this Japanese automobile is an evanescent spirit so irrepressible and creative that it cannot even be captured by the important representational conceptual work of Kehinde Wiley, who is known for contrasting such traditional images of power as aristocratic European portraits with blacks in contemporary hip-hop dress. According to the text in this Nissan ad, Wiley will paint portraits in which the exuberant spirit of African-American Nissan owners can "be admired, studied and imitated in black."

This ad's very smart allusions to the extraordinary benefits accruing to its prospective customers enable us to see how mass-media culture can appropriate and even co-opt aspects of high art with dry wit and sure intelligence, making its products highly competitive inversions of Pop Art. In consideration of this Nissan ad's complex form of address, we need to ask exactly what Thomas accomplishes when he excises its entire text in order to create his work. My answer is that he needs to remove this message because it is directed to the specific goal of generating desire for an innovative lifestyle of consummate freedom that, according to this ad's implications, can only be attained with a new Nissan. When Thomas erases this complex sales pitch, he moves the canvas referred to in the text away from Nissan in the direction of African-Americans, and he also encourages viewers of this work to enact their own reflective judgments for ascertaining the work's meaning. When he erases Nissan's message, Thomas also breaks down the implied conjunction between the product's use and Wiley's painting to reveal another message superintending both of them, and this communiqué concerns the clean blank slate of black identity, which is synecdochically represented by the now empty black void at the center of this work. Excising Nissan's text but not its carefully constructed latent image, Thomas is able to underscore the paramount role that corporate America assumes in its attempts to incite and manage blacks' desire by restaging, redirecting, and naturalizing, through capitalist means, the racial relations involved in such an effort.

While the Nissan ad employs the extraordinarily subtle verbal and visual incentives of diversity as a means for encouraging its African-American readers to break away from monolithic definitions of blackness while also recruiting or interpellating them as its prospective customers, we need to remember that prior to the full passage of civil rights legislation in the United States, racial relations rarely involved such gentle and positive means of persuasion. Despite Nissan's subtle approach, the subject of race continues to be a conflicted topic. In this essay I intend to present some of the dynamics of race in the past and in the present. These involve the relentless efforts of the white dominant culture to set a racial agenda for blacks; the resistance of African-Americans in the early and mid-twentieth century who redirected race in terms of unique and distinctly humanist sensibilities that were championed during the Harlem Renaissance and the Black Power period; and the current generation of black artists, well versed in French poststructuralist theory, who understand the profound effects of social and political constructions that frame their views and sensibilities. Rather than obviate these constructions and return to an earlier humanism centered on individual subjects, they use these frames as the basis for work that reflects back on these conditions, particularly on the largely hidden racial agenda known in sociological circles as "white blindness." In addition, they readily acknowledge the polysemic nature of the postmodern self with its allegiances to numerous sign systems that in turn convey it. A sub-theme of this essay will be my rereading of the French theorist Louis Althusser's idea of recruitment that has been misunderstood as one of art's effects. I will demonstrate that this approach is inconsistent with Althusser's view that ideology is only reflected in art, thus enabling it (ideology) to be revealed as a grand invention, and then will show how his idea operates in tandem with the cutting-edge work of many artists in "30 Americans."

The overall insidious history of race relations in the United States is predicated on the disturbing fact that ongoing discriminatory acts against African-Americans have created distinct and differential hierarchies that have left whites in dominant positions, while projecting racism on the bodies and desires of blacks, making it appear to be their fault and destiny. By naturalizing the highly artificial situation of racism, thereby transforming it into an efficient and effective ideology, whites have largely camouflaged the preeminent roles they have assumed in producing and directing it. In order to appreciate more fully the perniciousness of racism and its very material effects on both blacks and whites, it helps to review a number of substantially different and often destructive ideological racial constructions that have their origins in slavery.

In his important study of miscegenation in American culture entitled *Amalgamation! Race, Sex, and Rhetoric in the Nineteenth-Century American Novel*, James Kinney outlines five types of racism operative in the United States, beginning in the antebellum period and continuing through the end of the nineteenth century. His first category, *formal racism*, depends on pseudo-scientific beliefs regarding blacks' presumed sub-humanity and natural servility as rationales for perpetuating slavery, which was then transformed into the white race's so-called benevolent, custodial duty.[2] This specious reasoning that sets whites over blacks as their legitimate caretakers, however, did not prevent whites from transgressing this role as they encouraged the reproduction of increasingly greater numbers of slaves in order to sell them to owners of newly developed plantations in the frontier slave states of Alabama, Mississippi, and Louisiana during the 1850s. In fact, rather than shielding blacks from harm, whites were responsible during this decade for a 66.9 percent increase in mulatto slavery; and owners of plantations in Virginia and Kentucky—worn out from planting too much tobacco yet still rich in slaves—"sold down the river" the majority of new workers for this market.[3] At the end of the Civil War, one records office in Vicksburg, Mississippi, calculated that almost forty percent of the more than 9,000 slaves that it registered were mulattoes, who could trace their ancestry to white parents and great-grandparents.[4]

2. James Kinney, *Amalgamation! Race, Sex, and Rhetoric in the Nineteenth-Century American Novel*, Contributions in Afro-American and African Studies, 90 (Westport and London: Greenwood Press, 1985), 151.

3. Joel Williamson, *New People: Miscegenation and Mulattoes in the United States* (New York: Free Press, 1980), 63.

4. Kinney, 7-8.

Slaves fortunate enough to escape from the South before the war, sometimes received educations and affiliated themselves with white northerners intent on ending slavery, but their changed circumstances did not rule out prejudice. Their fellow abolitionists tended to regard them under the seemingly benevolent guise of *romantic racialism* by focusing, according to Kinney, on the "natural Christianity that made blacks innocent, good natured, and docile."[5] This sentimental view of blacks as God's children became a *paternalistic form of racism* in the 1880s and then morphed into the particularly *vicious racism* that was initiated in the 1890s when entire sectors of American society started subscribing not only to social Darwinism's characterization of capitalism's leaders as strong Anglo-Saxons, but also its concomitant reproach of immigrants and people of color, occupying society's lower rungs, as weak and morally degenerate.

5. Ibid., 152.

A limited *differential segregation* had been tentatively established soon after the Civil War by William G. Brownlow, governor of Tennessee, who advocated singling out good and docile blacks, who would be permitted to live and work among whites, and then barring from mainstream society those deemed intractable. Trying to decide which blacks to integrate and which to exclude no longer presented a problem for whites after the 1896 Supreme Court decision in the Plessy v. Ferguson case that upheld the "separate but equal doctrine," which led to segregation as a revived form of social slavery throughout the South. Although the preeminent author and orator Booker T. Washington counseled African-Americans to accept the humiliating constraints of segregation and work slowly for acceptance, his younger archrival W.E.B. Du Bois railed against such a compromising policy, charging that blacks were in danger of becoming slaves of ideology because they were "bound by all sorts of customs that have come down as second-hand soul clothes of white patrons."[6]

6. W.E.B. Du Bois, "Criteria of Negro Art," *The Crisis* 32 (October 1926), http://www.webdubois.org/dbCriteriaNArt.html, consulted 8/18/08.

In his famous 1897 *Atlanta Monthly* essay entitled "Strivings of the Negro People," Du Bois outlined his still prescient concept of "double consciousness." This theory is predicated on the basic idea that white stereotypical views have been projected on the bodies and lives of black people to the point that they knowingly misrepresent themselves. Du Bois concluded that this concatenation of competing worldviews distanced blacks from mainstream society, and he was convinced the internalized split personality resulted from an ongoing awareness of being both black and American at the same time. Instead of considering this two-fold view of the world as a strength, Du Bois regarded it as threat. He characterized "double consciousness" as a never-ending internalized battle and implied, but did not spell out, the omnipresent danger of self-sabotage:

> [t]he Negro is a sort of seventh son, born with a veil, and gifted with second-sight in this American world, —a world which yields him no true self-consciousness, but only lets him see himself through the revelation of the other world. It is a peculiar sensation, this double-consciousness, this sense of always looking at one's self through the eyes of others, of measuring one's soul by the tape of a world that looks on in amused contempt and pity. One ever feels his two-ness,— an American, a Negro; two souls, two thoughts, two unreconciled strivings; two warring ideals in one dark body, whose dogged strength alone keeps it from being torn asunder. [7]

7. W.E.B. Du Bois, "Of Our Spiritual Strivings," Chapter 1 in *The Souls of Black Folk* (Chicago: AC McClury and Co., 1903, rpt. New York: Barteby.com, 1999, http://www.barteby.com/114/1.html, consulted 8/30/08.

Considered in terms of the symbolist rhetoric typical of the times in which he was writing, Du Bois's protracted battle between warring souls can be viewed as a tragic ontological situation because it does not permit blacks direct and easy access to their most profound selves.

Despite its stately period prose, Du Bois's amazingly prescient theory permits us to leapfrog over the modern essentializing currents of twentieth-century African-American art and identity following in its wake, and see how his view prefigures a constructive postmodern understanding of socially and politically constructed selves, understood in terms of the benefits to be accrued from multiple subject positions.

Before following this line of thought, however, we need to consider briefly the intellectual lenses that blacks have established for themselves and their culture in the decades following Du Bois's analysis. During this period African-American artists and writers became involved in such defensive and essentialist moves as empowering the Harlem Renaissance's New Negro (1917-28) and characterizing, in the 1960s and '70s, the Black Arts Movement (BAM) and its emphasis on black pride and group solidarity, which were outgrowths of Black Power's social and cultural activism. Both of these basically modernist positions put positive spins on black identity by developing fundamental reaction formations against ongoing racist relations that art historian Darby English has termed "black representational space" and differentiated as "an effect of a politics of representation raging ever since 'blackness' could be proposed as the starting point of a certain mode or type of artistic depiction." [8] In this situation a reified black identity taking the form of "black consciousness" is misconstrued as coming before segregation and is not viewed as a rationalization of its effects. So persuasive was this ideology of black distinction and self-assumed segregation in the twentieth century that it recruited blacks by turning racism on its head, making difference a badge of honor and not a pariah's mark. In the mid-twentieth century black artists also began affiliating themselves with the modern stylistic traits they discerned in West African art, and this attitude gained more adherents during the years of BAM's hegemony. According to African-American art specialist Richard J. Powell, even such innovators as David Hammons "inadvertently joined his more conservative black colleagues [like members of the AFRICOBRA] in their quest to recreate an African sensibility in American art."[9]

8. Darby English, *How to See a Work of Art in Total Darkness* (Cambridge and London: MIT Press, 2007), 9 and 29.

9. Richard J. Powell, *Black Art: A Cultural History* (London: Thames & Hudson, 1997, rpt. 2002), 154.

Although the literary scholar Henry Louis Gates Jr. ostensibly joined forces with this pan-African current by finding antecedents for black vernacular culture in West African prototypes, he managed to theorize a distinct language game called "signifyin(g)," (or, more simply, "signifying" without the vernacular twist) that updated and redirected Du Bois's "double consciousness" in a postmodern direction. This linguistic strategy constituted an innovative means for positing a sine qua non for African-American culture at the same time that it reconceived Du Bois's "double [or black] consciousness" in terms of a

> homonymic pun of the profoundest sort, thereby marking its sense of difference from the rest of the English community of speakers. Their [African-Americans'] complex act of language Signifies upon both formal language use and its conventions . . . established by middle-class white people.[10]

10. Henry Louis Gates Jr., *The Signifying Monkey: A Theory of Afro-American Literary Criticism* (Oxford: Oxford University Press, 1988), 47.

More than just a word game, signifying is intended to enlist its practitioners in a special empowered subculture that re-encodes the mainstream by both parodying it and diverging from it at the same time it continues to participate in it. The theory is important for highlighting ways that language can be rearticulated and stratified to connote radically different meanings to accord with multiple and different semantic positions.

At this point in our discussion it is tempting to continue with Gates's signifying by demonstrating how it provides blacks with a privileged set of positions, but this situation of creating multiple perspectives through a racially designated underclass's doubly encoded signs is also reflective of a number of different types of subcultures needing to disaffiliate themselves from the mainstream while remaining dependent on it. Most notably, political subgroups including those based on ethnicity, as well as teenagers belong to this larger group because they are also adept at re-interpreting mainstream codes as insider communiqués and jokes that empower, cohere, and partially insulate them from the mainstream. When considered in relation to such situations, Gates's parallels between African-American signifying and the Yoruba-Fon myths of the trickster Esu-Elegbara are insightful concrete historical examples of a far vaster, ongoing double-voiced articulation found in many cultures. Considered in this manner, signifying bears a remarkable resemblance to the oscillating dialogism of double-voice references, advanced by the early twentieth-century Russian literary specialist Mikhail Bakhtin. This theorist defines dialogism in terms of conflicting literary representations predicated on differences between the view of the speaking character or narrator in a piece of fiction and the author's intention. Visual analogies to these essentially linguistic strategies that privilege and denominate African-Americans by transforming segregation into a more socially acceptable and authoritative form of self-isolation, of course, are plentiful, and they come both before and after Gates's landmark study.

Because art usually incorporates a number of ongoing tensions, understood in terms of different subject positions that can be construed as mainstream and outsider at the same time, signifying has become an established strategy for multiplying and stratifying different meanings to the same terms, and as an artistic tool it is capable of generating often brilliant and highly revealing works. Starting with the stock African-American examples of signifying whereby "cool" means "hot" and "bad" means "good," African-American artists can move into the realm whereby they play off entire artistic genres so that mainstream and black meanings are doubly articulated. Examples in "30 Americans" abound, beginning with Robert Colescott's and Xaviera Simmons's acts of signifying on the minstrel tradition by presenting blacks who have assumed the additional mask of impersonating whites who are making fun of blacks. A similar layering of identities and meanings is at work in Kalup Linzy's art that signifies on race, gender, and sex through the various roles he assumes in his television soap-opera spoof, *All My Churen* (2003).

A number of artists in the exhibition signify on stereotypes of black males as athletes by finding ways to attach new and relevant meanings to clichéd ideas. Notable in this area is the Miami-based outsider artist Purvis Young, who creates images of black basketball players that are also images of self-transcendence.

Signifying in a far different manner than these two artists, David Hammons provides substantially different subject positions for looking at his *Esquire (or John Henry)* (1990). His work takes a wary view of African-American culture and its connections to Egyptian art that is identifiable through his modern-day Ka, or spiritual double, assuming the form of a smooth head-shaped stone, that he found abandoned in Harlem. Collecting discarded hair from a barbershop in Harlem, Hammons glued it to his sculpture and then asked the barber, who provided him with this hair, to give the sculpture a haircut. The title of this work plays off white and black identities since *esquire* is a British term originally employed to designate Anglo-Saxon social status, and John Henry was a mid-nineteenth-century slave hired out to a railway company as a steel-driver. Henry became a folk hero after successfully competing against the recently developed steam-powered hammer just before he died of exhaustion.[11] When considered in relation to Hammons's sculpture, the John Henry reference is ironically circular in its implicit reasoning, since it underscores the ways that African-Americans in the past sometimes participated in their own undoing. This downfall is evidenced by the irony that the figure of John Henry—represented in Hammons's sculpture in terms of a weathered stone—had the job of drilling into rock in order to create holes where explosives could be placed in order to blast through this material, thus detonating the type of material comprising this representation of him.

11. A number of studies have attempted to establish the identity of John Henry. One of the most recent and convincing is Scott Reynolds Nelson's *Steel Drivin' Man: John Henry, the Untold Story of an American Legend* (New York: Oxford University Press, 2006). Cf. William Grimes, "Taking Swings at a Myth, with John Henry the Man," *New York Times* (October 18, 2006), http://www/nytimes.com/2006/10/18/books/18grim.html, consulted 9/1/08.

Related to signifying but differing from it are Jacques Derrida's theories regarding the slippery nature of language and his recognition following Martin Heidegger's lead, that some terms such as *God* and *being* need to be put "under erasure" (*"sous rature"*) because they can be referenced but never known. This concept of erasure provides Gary Simmons with a modus operandi for his chalkboard drawings that employ "whitewashing" as a medium and consequently are elaborate and ironic plays on the ongoing chimera, "blackness."

In addition to seeing how signifying and *sous rature* have become viable strategies for recent African-American art, it helps to look at some of the new and far more interactive theories regarding black identity that have been advanced in the past couple of decades that have also impacted the dialectical interplays enacted by artists in "30 Americans." The most notable new concept regarding black identity is the almost two-decade-long pluralistic approach variously called the New Black, post-black, and post-soul aesthetic. This line of development focuses on post-civil rights blacks' easy access to both white and black worlds and their ability to choose their identity from a number of viable options.

The generational space marking the elitist New Black Aesthetic (NBA) was advanced in early 1989 in a namesake essay[12] written by Trey Ellis for the diasporic-oriented periodical appropriately named *Callaloo* after the Caribbean dish, which is remarkable for its many variations. An essayist, novelist, screenwriter, and, at the time, *Village Voice* critic, Ellis's biography is germane to his theorization of the NBA, which he describes in a deliberately breezy style

12. Trey Ellis, "The New Black Aesthetic," *Callaloo* 38 (Winter, 1989): 233-243.

intended to gain broad acceptance for his ideas. The son of upwardly mobile black parents educated at the University of Michigan and Yale, Ellis attended private middle school and high school before transferring to Phillips Academy Andover during his junior year. He then attended Stanford where he chose to live in the campus dorm called Ujamaa, whose website describes it as "one [of] four Ethnic theme houses" and notes that its name means "Economic Cooperation in Swahilii," thus underscoring the fact that "though it's the 'Black' dorm, Ujamaa provides a forum for diversity and unity among all ethnicities, peoples and individuals."[13] Tacitly taking this black dorm's open-ended mission as an underlying rationale for his new sensibility, Ellis describes the NBA in a stream-of-consciousness style that can be distilled into the following qualifiers, involving

13. Http://www.stanford.edu/group/resed/lagunita/ujamaa/main.htm, consulted 8/17/08.

1. A post-liberated aesthetic, free of such slave legacies as defensiveness and unencumbered with BAM's need to reify blackness in terms of black pride and group solidarity;
2. Ease of access to both black and white worlds, punctuated by the ability to freely choose being black;
3. Recognition that "racism is a hard and little-changing constant that neither surprises nor enrages . . . [and that] racism . . . [is] not an excuse";
4. Confidence in the ability of NBA adherents to change their world by breaking away from old definitions of blackness and extending diversity into heretofore unforeseen realms by demonstrating blacks to be "the intricate, uncategorizable folks we had always known ourselves to be";
5. Reliance on the opportunities afforded by upper-middle class origins, including a refusal to be limited by class barriers.

According to Ellis, initiators of the NBA are "cultural mulattoes." He explains this new category as fluid rather than fixed. "[A] genetic mulatto is a black person of mixed parents who often can get along fine with his white grandparents," Ellis writes with remarkable prescience, fully fifteen years before Barack Obama, perhaps the most famous cultural mulatto, delivered the keynote address, "The Audacity of Hope," at the 2004 Democratic National Convention and nineteen years before he became the Democratic presidential nominee and rolled out images of his white grandparents and introduced his part-Southeast-Asian sister and South Side Chicago black wife.[14] In his essay, Ellis continues by noting, "a cultural mulatto, educated by a multi-racial mix of cultures, can also navigate easily in the white world."[15] After pointing out that the members of his generation of cultural mulattoes are so numerous, confident, and self-determined that they do not need to join either black or white worlds but can "create our own," Ellis then states that, "cultural mulattoism refers to the ability of blacks to . . . take elements from different cultures to create a new diverse and pluralistic self." Moving far beyond the bourgeois politesse of political correctness that tried not to upset any constituency defined in terms of ethnicity, gender, age, and sexual persuasion, Ellis's cultural mulattoism focuses on the individuals who have the ability to forge their own hybridized identities while freeing themselves so that they can rethink blackness without being encumbered with either the shackles of New Negro idealism or BAM black pride. Similarly, it evades the straightjacket of multiculturism that tended to create equal playing fields for minorities and ended up stereotyping them according to group norms whose boundaries were then carefully policed.

14. Ibid., 236. In a February 19, 2007, blog for *The Huffington Post* entitled "Obama: Cultural Mulatto," Ellis writes:

I bit my tongue for as long as I could, reading essay after essay about Obama and his "blackness" that were about as insightful as if they'd been written in the era of Flip Wilson . . . our antebellum notions of race like the "one-drop rule" (one drop of black and you're black) no longer make any sense in this new millennium. . . .

I coined the term "cultural mulatto," to describe people like myself who, because of how we were raised, can easily navigate both the white world and the black. . . .

15. Ellis, "The New Black Aesthetic," 235.

Prominent cultural mulattoes in "30 Americans" include Iona Rozeal Brown, whose work focuses on a Japanese sub-culture of young girls intrigued with African-American rap. "Back in 1997," Brown explains, "I read an article in *Transitions* written by Joe Wood. It was titled 'The Yellow Negro,' and subsequently introduced me to a group of Japanese youth called *ganguro* who darkened their skin and paid top dollar to have their hair permed into afros."[16] In her intriguingly NBA works, Brown contrasts traditional Japanese and contemporary African-American cultural references and plays off Ukiyo-e color woodcuts from the Edo period with telling aspects of hip-hop culture, because, in her words, "we are all mirror images of each other."[17] Ironically, in a postmodern world many of these resemblances are also highly commodified.

16. Iona Rozeal Brown, "Iona Rozeal Brown," Spelman College Virtual Museum, http://www.spelman.edu/bush-hewlett/a3/artiststate.html, consulted 9/1/08.

17. Ibid.

Inflecting the NBA approach in a new direction, Kehinde Wiley deconstructs rigid Western views of power as he establishes uneasy conjunctions between the rich panoply of traditional European portraiture and the hip-hop alpha males he discovers on urban streets. Significantly, the inspiration for his series of dialectical portraits came from a mug shot that he found on the streets of Harlem while working as artist-in-residence at the Studio Museum:

> It was . . . an African-American man in his twenties that appeared sympathetic, attractive, and it had all his information on it—his name, his address, his social-security number and his infractions—and it made me begin to think about portraiture in a radically different way: I began thinking about this mug shot itself as portraiture in a very perverse sense, a type of marking, a recording of one's place in the world in a time. And I began to start thinking about a lot of the portraiture that I had enjoyed from the eighteenth century and noticed the difference between the two: how one is positioned in a way that is totally outside their control, shut down and related to those in power, whereas those in the other were positioning themselves in states of stately grace and self-possession. And the first paintings of "Passing/Posing" were the merging of those two lines.[18]

18. Kehinde Wiley, interview by Roy Hurst, "Young, Gifted and Black: Painter Kehinde Wiley," National Public Radio, June 1, 2005.

Mickalene Thomas's NBA females elaborate on the elasticity of the art of self-presentation (fashion) in the many looks assumed by one individual in *Portraits of Quanikah* (2006), and parody Black Power Afros and their cinematic appearances in coy '70s-style pinups in *Hotter than July* (2005). This latter work refers to the open-ended, playful attitude toward new and different types of identity that can be tried out within the safe confines of the kitsch bedrooms and dens in which her figures are sequestered. A similar NBA openness is evident in Lorna Simpson's many wigs printed on felt backgrounds in *Wigs (Portfolio)* (1994), which literalize and move beyond socially conditioned views of African-Americans as only being involved in soul-work and remaining closely attuned to their feelings when she pictures blackness as a series of fashions that can be as easily donned as newer styles of wigs.

Thelma Golden's highly acclaimed Studio Museum exhibition, "Freestyle," named for a particularly radical, open-ended improvisational style of rapping, proved in 2000 to be an exhilarating visual-arts celebration that has antecedents in Ellis's irreverent NBA. To characterize the new options available to African-Americans, Golden developed the term *post-black,* which she views as

> characterized by artists who were adamant about not being labeled as "black" artists, though their work was steeped, in fact deeply interested, in redefining complex notions of blackness. In the beginning, there were only a few marked instances of such an outlook, but at the end of the 1990s, it seemed that post-black had fully entered into the art world's consciousness. Post-black was the new black.[19]

19. Thelma Golden, *Freestyle* (New York: Studio Museum in Harlem, 2001), 14.

Golden views the artists, whose works make up her exhibition, as self-directed; and this view is in accord with Ellis's. Her choices include several individuals in "30 Americans," including John Bankston, Mark Bradford, and Rashid Johnson, who has succinctly summed up the overall impetus of Golden's exhibition:

> Now that we all have this knowledge and have a language to deal with it visually, it's the time to start dealing with some of the more playful things. We've accepted privilege, we're conscious of all these major issues that the generation before us laid down. Now that we have that formal language, I think we can finally talk about the smaller things.[20]

20. Rashid Johnson, interview by Barbara DeGenevieve, *Features* (April 2004), http://www.fnewsmagaine.com/2004-apr/current/2004-apr/pages/p18.html, consulted 9/1/08.

In an overview for the Modern Language Association's special 2007 issue on the post-soul aesthetic, literary specialist Bertram D. Ashe updates both the NBA and post-black with new rubrics and more culturally specific traditional black language.[21] He does not, for example, rely on philosopher Arthur Danto's term *disturbatory art*, which Ellis had referred to in his essay on the NBA as the "art that shakes you up" before he added that "the moral imperative of being black in America enrapts us with a militant juju that wards off cynical minimalism."[22] In place of disturbatory art, Bertram complements his post-soul and post-BAM rubric with the injunction to "trouble" or "worry" the category of blackness, by enacting a strategy of "blaxploration" instead of subscribing to commercial blaxploitation. (The term *blaxploitation* is notably used to describe a series of remarkable post-civil rights films like *Shaft*, *Hit Man*, and *Super Fly* [all made in the early '70s] that glamorized black street crime and successful blacks' ability to quell it.) Bertram advocates troubling or worrying conditioned ideas about blackness in order to "stir it up, touch it, feel it out, and hold it up for examination in ways that depart significantly from previous—and necessary—preoccupations with struggling for political freedom, or with an attempt to establish and sustain a coherent black identity" even though it is "done in service to black people," thus pointing to the benefits to be accrued from diversifying and mixing up black prototypes. Focusing mainly on artists and filmmakers, Ashe considers the work of such individuals as Jean-Michael Basquiat, Ellen Gallagher, Spike Lee, and Kara Walker to be exemplary of the post-soul aesthetic.

21. Bertram D. Ashe, "Theorizing the Post-Soul Aesthetic: An Introduction," *African American Review* 41, No. 4 (Winter, 2007): 609-623. Although dated Winter, 2007, this special issue devoted to the post-soul aesthetic was not published until fall, 2008.

22. Ellis, "The New Black Aesthetic," 239.

All of these artists play with stereotypical views of blacks that they then provoke to tease out additional and often latent meanings. Even though many of the stereotypes are well known paranoid white-racist determinations inflicted on the bodies and lives of blacks, their effects have continued to be felt. The artists, listed by Ashe, have consequently exaggerated stereotypical effects to make points about their racist intent. Kara Walker, for example, points out:

> When stereotypes attempt to take control of their own bodies, they can only do what they are made of, and they are made of the pathological attitudes of the Old South. Therefore, the racist stereotypes occurring in my art can only partake of psychotic activities.[23]

23. Kara Walker, lecture, School of the Arts, Virginia Commonwealth University, October 24, 2000.

Rather than subscribing to BAM's crusade to create a morally uplifting and regenerative art capable of revivifying stereotypes, as a number of mid- and late twentieth-century artists like Murry DePillars, Jeff Donaldson and Betye Saar attempted to do with the Quaker Oats Company's trademark Aunt Jemima, Walker and a number of her fellow artists wish to undermine rather than embolden racist stereotypes. Walker's above statement indicates that such well-intentioned efforts as those undertaken by BAM artists are doomed to failure because even the most seemingly benign stereotype, by its very nature, has created, in her words, an "unredeemable" form of alienation. Disapproving of efforts to reclaim and redirect such imagery, Robert Colescott—the critically attuned painter of an older generation—has noted, "the philosophy did not grow out of the paintings; the paintings grew out of the philosophy. And so they're illustrations."[24]

24. Robert Colescott, oral history interview, conducted by Paul Karlstrom for the Archives of American Art, Smithsonian Institution, 1999, http://www.aaa.si.edu/collecions/oralhistories/transcripts/colesc99.htm, consulted 9/1/08.

The almost two decade-long discourse on post-civil rights diversity enunciated by Ellis, Golden, and Ashe that this essay has just reviewed has constituted a healthy and commendable critique of earlier essentialized views such as those espoused by BAM artists. The writings of Ellis, Golden, and Ashe underscore the fact that African-Americans are no longer content to serve as the undifferentiated screens on which mainstream culture can project its biases, and are unwilling to condone reaction formations that reify blackness into an undifferentiated and monolithic whole so that it constitutes one of racism's more insidious and least understood effects. Although their combined approach provides a knowledgeable and sophisticated understanding of a great deal of art that has been made in the past few decades, including black-white interactions, it does not account for the fact that increasing numbers of artists, including those already discussed in this essay, have made concerted efforts to move beyond their personal understanding of experience in order to demonstrate a Michel Foucaultian-type consideration of the social, economic, cultural, and political discourses that frame, support, and even produce these experiences while establishing subjectivity and desire as ways of linking knowledge and representation. As Leonardo Drew explains,

> Imagine that you are a tool for creating this thing and try to remove yourself just enough, SO that you don't get too bogged down by ego or see yourself as an all-important Image.[25]

25. Lorraine Edwards, "Navigating a Sea of Chaos," *Sculpture Magazine* 16, No. 2 (February, 1997):20.

It helps to get a perspective on this type of Foucaultian critique by looking at the situation (cited above as an epigraph) that the Martiniquean expatriate psychiatrist and philosopher Frantz Fanon described in *Black Skin, White Masks* as an exile from ontology, a view that updates Du Bois's "double consciousness." Using Foucault as a means to critique both Du Bois and Fanon as well as to assess the validity of their own experiences, a number of cutting-edge black artists in recent years have relied on this French theorist's concept of the historical a priori. In doing so, they have de-centered traditional views of humanism as an immutable foundational epistemology and recognized the limits of even their own subjectivity as socially, politically, and economically produced. According to Foucault, subjectivity is framed by the broad-base assumptions comprising the archive or discursive formation of what can be said in a given historical setting.[26] It therefore reflects on the coercive role normalization assumes in establishing truth.[27] Working with Foucault's ideas, artists are keenly aware that they are functions of distinct *énonciations* that consist of both the culturally ratified position in which their articulations can be viewed as knowledge, and the resulting concomitant network that provides them with a place and a stylistic voice or métier where their works can assume authority.

26. Michel Foucault, *Archaeology of Knowledge*, trans. A.M. Sheridan Smith (New York: Pantheon Books, 1972), 127 and 129.

27. Michel Foucault, *Discipline and Punish: The Birth of the Prison*, trans. Alan Sheridan (New York: Pantheon Books, 1977), 184.

A brief look at the work of five artists in "30 Americans" indicates the relevancy of their individual énonciations and historical a priori as working premises. A decisive example of both an ongoing historical a priori as well as a majestic énonciation is evidenced in terms of the perspective provided by the appropriated image of a tribal woman with an elaborate hairstyle, seen in profile on both the right and left sides of Carrie Mae Weems's *From Here I Saw What Happened and I Cried* (1995), which serves as both the artist's and viewer's surrogate in the work. Looking as if her image has been taken from an early *National Geographic* or anthropological study, this mediated and stately profile looks at the collection of appropriated ethnographic photographs of black slaves in the center of the work who have been reduced to the tragic state of representative types. Weems reinforces this demeaning condition by branding each image with a quasi-scientific label, such as "You Became a Scientific Profile," "An Anthropological Debate," "A Negroid Type," and "A Photographic Subject." Playing on differences between African tribal culture and contemporary African-American realities, fashion designer, performance artist, and sculptor Nick Cave has created a series of full-body outfits, called "Soundsuits," in which he morphs found objects with regal African-appearing costumes to redefine race in terms of the twin legacies and dual conflicting énonciations of being American society's cast-off fringe, while invoking the more distant and romantic heritage of tribal ancestry. For Shinique Smith there are several possible énonciations that are articulated through her work: they include—but are not limited to—African-American charms, long-held views about blacks as America's cast-offs, current concerns about recycling and the plights of displaced people throughout the world, as well as the twentieth-century artistic discourse on assemblage. "There is a transient, nomadic sensibility to my work," Smith states, a "place for things that were once displaced." She continues by noting, "I see the urban terrain as nature. My work deals with my interactions with the city and popular culture and broadly with transitory phenomena and human nature."[28] Trenchant African-American artists such as Weems, Cave, and Smith then, do not attempt to achieve subjective correlations of themselves in their work; no longer believing in their experiences as legitimate origins, they aim to show how subjectivity and ideology are staged, personal insights are constructed, and individuals are represented through historical a prioris.

28. Ellen Donahue and Ronald Sosinski, "The Proposition: Shinique Smith," http://www.thepropostion.com/last/shiniquesmith_press.html, consulted 9/3/08.

Fully cognizant of the importance of moving from the subjective to the social, Kerry James Marshall in *Souvenir's Composition in Three Parts* (1998-2000), part of his tribute to the civil rights movement, and Mark Bradford in *Whore in the Church House* (2006), rely on the metonymic force of found objects and signs to locate their work in objective, on-going social and historical situations. They also attempt to diminish in these works the role played by their own combinations and articulations of these materials by foregrounding stories about the subjects and lifestyles they are re-presenting. As Bradford has pointed out, "I generally collect merchant posters because they talk about a service, and the service talks about a body and that body talks about a community, and that community talks about many different conversations."[29] On another occasion, he reinforced the role that used materials play in his work. "I don't like things that are first use. I like things that are second use. . . . I want it [found material] to actually have the memories—the cultural and personal memories that are lodged in the object."[30]

29. "Mark Bradford: "Market > Place," *Art:21 - Art in the Twenty-First Century: The Artists*, http://www.pbs.org/art21/artists/bradford/clip1.html, consulted 9/1/08.

30. Ernest Hardy, "The Eye of L.A. / Mark Bradford," *Los Angeles Times* (June 13, 2001), http://www.sikkemajenkinsco.com/markbradford_press.html, consulted 9/1/08.

In order to appreciate the value of this new emphasis on the social and historical construction of subjectivity as parallel to the ways blacks themselves have been constructed by the dominant outlooks of whites, it is necessary to clear up a basic misunderstanding about differences between ideologies in the everyday world and the roles they assume in works in art. The French Marxist Louis Althusser, whose theories are most pertinent to this difference, developed his concepts in tandem with the ideas of his friend, the noted Parisian psychoanalyst and psychiatrist Jacques Lacan. Specifically, he relied on Lacan's theory of the mirror stage in which toddlers are co-opted by images of either themselves or others as well as by language, so that their sense of reality depends on their imagined or intuited perception of themselves as wholes as well as members of the symbolic linguistic system in which they participate. Instead of viewing the toddler as the initiator of this sequence of events, Althusser ascribes agency to the mirror or language Lacan refers to, and re-conceives them as ideologies that hail or interpellate individuals as concrete subjects so that they exhibit the material effects of a particular ideology.[31] Even though Althusser's approach has proven extraordinarily useful to Marxists since it explains how ideologies are embraced by actual subjects and realized in daily life, it needed to be broadened in order to account for the competing ideologies that interpellate individuals in different and often contradictory ways. The consequent refinement of Althusser's basic approach to ideology, which does not reflect the real world but instead produces subjects involved in imaginary relations with others and thus is one step removed from the world, has been undertaken by Michel Pêcheux, his former student. Pêcheux has reworked the concept of interpellation so that it takes into consideration different subjectivities situated across the lines of race, gender, class, and other sociopolitical constructed identities.[32] Both Althusser's and Pêcheux's theories about interpellation are basic to rethinking traditional views of artists and their long-acclaimed experiences as art's primary source. Their approach enables us to re-conceive, as noted earlier, artists as ideologically constituted subjects like everyone else and to re-construe in addition their individual autonomy in terms of the ideological discourses that are channeled through them. This reconfiguration of individual artists' roles so that they are the articulators of socially constructed views that precede them and are not their creators, enables us to appreciate the ways that black artists have been interpellated in their daily lives by the ideologies of race and racial diversity, so that these and many other discourses speak eloquently through them.

31. Louis Althusser, "Ideology and Ideological State Apparatuses" in *Lenin and Philosophy and Other Essays*, trans. Ben Brewster (New York and London: Monthly Review Press, 1971).

32. An excellent example of Pêcheux's approach is in Martin Montgomery and Stuart Allan, "Ideology, Discourse, and Cultural Studies: The Contribution of Michel Pêcheux," *Canadian Journal of Communication* 17, No. 2 (1992), http://www.cjc-onlin.ca/index.php/journal/rt/printerFriendly/661/567, consulted 9/22/08.

Thus far, my discussion of Althusser and the ways ideology recruits its subjects correlates with orthodox views of his theory. But I wish to diverge from this standard interpretation of Althusser and interpellation by looking at art, which a number of critics and art historians have assumed to be a preeminently active producer of ongoing ideologies rather than being concerned with its effects, so that it recruits viewers as ideological subjects in similar ways to its functioning in everyday life. Particularly notable examples of misconceiving Althusser's approach to art and ideology are found in the writings of the eminent postmodern critic Craig Owens, who contended that "to represent is to subjugate" and who observed that the photo-based art of feminist Barbara Kruger "stages for the viewer the techniques whereby the stereotype produces subjection, interpellates him/her as subject." Owens then goes on to remark on Kruger's "*mobilization* of the spectator."[33] Such misconceptions as Owens's have been appealing and persuasive to many critics, historians, and theorists because they make art appear to be a preeminent way to inculcate and realize specific ideologies. The consequent instrumental views of art as an ideological mode, however, impoverishes art because it obviates the crucial role assumed by artistic form that distances art from the machinations of particular ideologies, thereby enabling viewers to look at them as fictive and as only reflected in art rather than actively produced by it.

33. Craig Owens, "'The Indignity of Speaking for Others': An Imaginary Interview," *Art & Social Change* (Oberlin: Allen Memorial Art Museum, 1983), 84; Craig Owens, "The Medusa Effect, or, The Specular Ruse," *Art in America* 72, No. 1 (January 1984): 104.

Although Althusser wrote little on art, he did summarize a number of his basic ideas about it in the brief yet revealing epistle known as "A Letter on Art in Reply to André Daspeŕé" (1966), which is only rarely mentioned as a cautionary note to those who would like to view art as a means for enlisting subjects on behalf of specific ideologies. Responding to Daspeŕé's question about whether or not art should be considered an ideology, Althusser unequivocably states that he does "not rank real art among the ideologies."[34] He then elucidates his position:

> I believe that the peculiarity of art is to "make us see" (*nous donner á voir*), "make us perceive," "make us feel" something which alludes to reality. . . . What art makes us *see*, and therefore gives to us in the form of "*seeing*," "*perceiving*," and "*feeling*," (which is not the form of

34. Louis Althusser, "A Letter on Art in Reply to André Daspeŕé" (1966), http://courses.essex.ac.uk/LT/LT204/althusser.htm, consulted 9/15/08.

> *knowing*), is the ideology from which it is born, in which it bathes, from which it detaches itself as art, and to which it *alludes*. . . . Balzac and Solzhenitsyn give us a "view" of the ideology to which their work alludes and with which it is constantly fed, a view which presupposes *a retreat*, an *internal distantiation* from the very ideology from which their novels emerged. They make us "perceive" (but not know) in some sense from the *inside*, by an *internal distance*, the very ideology in which they are held.[35]

35. Ibid.

Since Althusser considers knowledge (as opposed to art) to be inherently structural and involved in the articulation of systems and the implicit rules "*of arrangement and combination* that gives them their meaning," he attributes this type of analysis to science, whereas art "is 'detached' from . . . ideology and in some way makes us 'see' it from the *outside*, makes us 'perceive' it by a distantiation inside that ideology."[36] Following up on this observation, I contend that in art the wonderfully absurd opacity of its media and form preclude it from actually interpellating ideological subjects because these formal means obstruct the more direct persuasiveness necessary for this type of enlistment. The theorist Jacques Rancière comes close to ratifying Althusser's ideas about art and ideology when he views art as divided into the irreconcilable yet continually oscillating roles of its punctum (arresting form) and studium (connections with external semiotic chains of meaning that harness art to something external to itself).[37] And this oscillation, in my opinion, reinforces art's "aboutness," its distance from ideology, which it can represent as a fiction or compelling representation rather than a "reality" capable of enlisting subjects who become dedicated believers.

36. Ibid.

37. Jacques Rancière, *The Future of the Image*, trans. Gregory Elliott (London and New York: Verso, 2007).

What this Althusserian realignment of ideology and art means to African-American artists included in "30 Americans" is that their work, like all art, provides us with enough distance not to be interpellated by their ideologies so that we can recognize them to be the illusions they most assuredly are. Ideology, in this sense, becomes the subject but not the object of the art, since the object comprises the sum total of formal elements that provide us with the requisite distance for seeing the subject. We have already seen at the beginning of this essay how Hank Willis Thomas's excision of the text in his Nissan ad releases audiences from the soft-yet-persistent sell of the Nissan text and allows them to think about themselves as the empty black screen on which this corporation and others attempt to project their desires and needs. Considered in this way, art's distanced and abstracted ideology enables us to gain a much broader view of individual works and the world giving rise to them, as well as to ascertain, as in Althusser's symptomatic readings, how art comprises given problematic or discursive structures that can divulge "the undivulged even in the text it reads, and in the same movement . . . [relate] it to *a different text*, present as a necessary absence in the first."[38] This, again, is the type of reading that Thomas undertakes, and it also is a characteristic of Kara Walker's stereotypical shadows that are reflections of mainstream paranoia.

38. Louis Althusser and Etienne Balibar, *Reading Capital*, trans. Ben Brewster (London: New Left Books, 1970).

During the past few decades, the subject of race in daily life has appeared to be downgraded by the evenhandedness of multiculturalism, the widely touted diversity of the NBA, and the openness of the post-black and post-soul aesthetics whose adherents can choose to be black since race is no longer assumed to be an imperative decreed by outside forces. This de-emphasis on race is the case not only for the arts but also for such fields as anthropology, sociology, medicine, and the humanities in general. What is particularly disconcerting about this "winnowing away of racial classifications"[39] is that efforts to defuse them have a very long history. As AFRICOBRA artist and eminent historian of

39. Antonia Darder and Rodolfo D. Torres, *After Race: Racism after Multiculturalism* (New York and London: New York University Press, 2004), 9.

black art Michael D. Harris explains, the word "colored" "began to be used in the late eighteenth century as an attempt to undermine the monolithic concept of blackness, so those of mixed heritage with fairer skin would not be lumped in with their darker neighbors."[40] And yet, as anyyone who is aware of the history of twentieth-century segregation in the United States knows, "colored" assumed an almost insurmountably absolute designation that was used to differentiate black and white public facilities. Certainly, references to the genre of coloring books found in some of the works of both John Bankston[41] and Glenn Ligon play on this distinction, and ironically both artists, clearly aware of the NBA's approach, have made the decision to leave their works relying on this genre partially unfinished, to indicate that the process of providing ideological hues for ethnic groups is far from over. For his *Untitled (Malcolm X)* (2008), Ligon referenced Black Power-inspired coloring books of the 1970s. During the summer of 2000 he in fact chose images from them for his children's workshops in the Minneapolis-St. Paul area, and their involvement with this material serves as a basis for his art that focuses on this means of political indoctrination.

40. Michael D. Harris, *Colored Pictures: Race & Visual Representation* (Chapel Hill and London: University of North Carolina Press, 2003), 7.

41. In addition to coloring books, Bankston's work incorporates such sources as children's books, homoerotic sadomasochistic fantasies, nineteenth-century slave narratives, and fairy tales.

In the twentieth century, sociologists and others attempted to use the term "ethnic" as a *sotte voce* means for discussing race, but efforts to achieve widespread endorsement of this term have been at best tentative and only briefly successful. In *Racism and Cultural Studies*, E. San Juan Jr. points to early twentieth-century efforts to replace race with ethnicity:

> Among U.S. social scientists of the 1920s and 1930s, ethnicity replaced the biologically based racial paradigm of eugenics and social Darwinist theories of cultural evolution prevalent in the late nineteenth century. "Ethnic group" instead of "race" became the category that defined group-formation process based on descent and culture (religion, language, customs, nationality, and political identification). Gunnar Myrdal's *An American Dilemma* (1944) valorized ethnicity in its analysis of the African-American problem of nonassimilation and economic-political subordination.[42]

42. E. San Juan Jr., *Racism and Cultural Studies: Critiques of Multiculturalist Ideology and the Politics of Difference* (Durham and London: Duke University Press, 2002), 138.

However, despite these efforts to defuse racism's effects, the opening of the Nazi death camps at the end of World War II made the Western world painfully aware of the tragic problems that can ensue from unbridled racism. This realization was an important incentive after the war for UNESCO to commission biologists and social scientists to develop a precise and workable definition of the term "race." Biologists working on this project concluded that the species Homo sapiens has a common source and that groups previously regarded as races were far too interconnected to be segregated on this basis. Reaching a similar conclusion, sociologists decided to use the awkward yet meaningful phrase "race relations situation" when it was absolutely necessary to discuss racial problems.[43] As might be expected, their good intentions and unwieldy terminology did not gain traction.

43. John Rex, *Race and Ethnicity* (Milton Keynes: Open University Press, 1986), 18-19.

Five decades after these unsuccessful attempts to tone down prejudicial language, scholars and others were still attempting to parry race with ethnicity. In his essay "Through a Glass Darkly: Intellectuals on Race" (1999), Phil Cohen discerns a balanced equation between the two terms. "Race," he notes optimistically, "becomes ethicized and ethnicity racialised so that other terms can be used interchangeably in a way that allows their respective elements of fixity and permeability to be conjugated into more subtle idioms of attribution than either on their own could achieve."[44] Cohen's conclusion ratifies the groundbreaking work by one of the innovators of the academic discipline known as cultural studies,

44. Phil Cohen, "Through a Glass Darkly: Intellectuals on Race" in *New Ethnicities, Old Racisms?* (London and New York: Zed Books, 1999), 2.

45. Cf., Stuart Hall, "Old and New Identities, Old and New Ethnicities" in *Culture, Globalization, and the World-System*, ed. Anthony D. King (London: Macmillan Education, 1991), 19-39.

Stuart Hall, who developed in 1991 an innovative postmodern reconsideration of new and fluid groupings of people in his essay "Old and New Identities, Old and New Ethnicities."[45] In this piece and other related works, Hall explains how new global diasporic identities, predicated on the ongoing contingencies of cultural hybridity, are no longer tied to racial and national histories and are involved, in Derridean fashion, in a ongoing play of difference. His approach is similar to Ellis's NBA, except that Hall goes beyond Ellis's generational and national boundaries and also his art-based theory to explore broadly the ways that his ethnicities are global and multigenerational.

The openness and democracy promised by the term "ethnicity" as opposed to the strictures enforced by racial terminology seemed in the 1990s to portend a new worldview in which race truly could be an elective, as Ellis had suggested. But, just as in the past, the problem of race continued to reemerge, and it again became particularly timely and topical in the '90s for altogether unforeseen and very legitimate reasons as increasing numbers of impressive thinkers began to recognize that an entirely new civil rights campaign needed to be enacted. Not only were inequities between races not being addressed at the end of the twentieth century, but they were also not even being documented because specialized studies of ethnic minorities were considered undemocratic. The publication entitled *Whitewashing Race: The Myth of a Color-Blind Society* by a group of seven respected sociologists summarizes the strange reversal of circumstances in which post-civil rights language and freedom were co-opted by conservatives intent on doing away with any type of affirmative action:

46. Michael K. Brown, Martin Carnoy, Elliott Currie, Troy Duster, David B. Oppenheimer, Marjorie M. Shultz, and David Wellman, *Whitewashing Race: The Myth of a Color-Blind Society* (Berkeley and Los Angeles: University Press, 2003), http://www.ucpress.edu/books/pages/9866/9866.ch01.php, consulted 8/30/08.

> When private or public organizations set out to correct historical racial disparities, they typically institute some race-conscious remedial plan. But because such plans classify people based on race, the courts routinely strike them down. Even though these race-conscious plans aim to help subordinated groups, the courts believe they constitute reverse discrimination. Under the resulting color-blind norm, lawyers rarely succeed in justifying affirmative action plans that seek to remedy actual racial disparities and societal discrimination.[46]

In the interests of preserving color-blind equity, statistics employing racial categories were no longer permitted to be tabulated or used to buttress arguments about injustice to minorities. Thus, the following remarkable catch-22 or double bind ensued: government agencies were no longer permitted to record racial inequities because that activity would be undemocratic in a world where everyone is supposed to be equal, and since no documentation exists, no substantive arguments can be made to correct them.[47]

47. Ibid.

Sociologist Eduardo Bonilla-Silva can be credited with doing the most work to underscore the problem he calls "white racism," and is sometimes referred to as "white blindness" or "color blindness," which constitutes an almost invisible norm as the basis of institutional practices in which racial practices are deeply embedded in their structure. In "Racial Attitudes or Racial Ideology? An Alternative Paradigm for Examining Actors' Racial Views," one of his many important articles on this subject, Bonilla-Silva succinctly enumerates his basic findings regarding this new and particularly insidious form of white racism:

> Colour blindness is a formidable racial ideology because at worst, it seems like racism "lite". Yet, its frames, style, and racial stories are the main ideological elements whites use to explain and justify contemporary racial inequality. As I argued, by supporting equality,

fairness, and meritocracy as abstract principles and denying at the same time the existence of systematic discrimination and disregarding the enormous implications of existing racial inequality, whites can appear "not racist" ("I am all for equal opportunity"), safely criticize any institutional approach to ameliorate racial inequality ("Reverse discrimination?!") and blame minorities for their situation ("If minorities work hard and complain less, they would be doing much better"). Thus the political beauty of colour blindness as an ideology is that it allows whites to state their racial views in a principled, even moral manner.[48]

48. Eduardo Bonilla-Silva, "Racial Attitudes or Racial Ideology? An Alternative Paradigm for Examining Actors' Racial Views," *Journal of Political Ideologies* 8, No. 1 (2003): 79. Other important essays by this author include "Rethinking Racism: Toward a Structural Interpretation," *American Sociological Review* 62, No. 3 (June 1997): 465-480; "The Essential Social Fact of Race," *American Sociological Review* 64, No. 6 (December 1999): 899-906; and "'I Did Not Get That Job Because of a Black Man . . .': The Story Lines and Testimonies of Color-Blind Racism," *Sociological Forum* 19, No. 4 (December 2004): 555-581.

Because of the work by Bonilla-Silva and others, the American Sociological Association in August 2002 decided that efforts to dispense with the term "race" were specious and no longer tenable. It urged its members to continue using race in their research, even as they recognized that it was a dangerous and damaging ideology that continued to create differential hierarchies and exclude groups on the basis of superficial features. This respected professional group also issued in 2002 the following statement:

Those who favor ignoring race as an explicit administrative matter, in the hope that it will cease to exist as a social concept, ignore the weight of a vast body of sociological research that shows that racial hierarchies are embedded in the routine practices of social groups and institutions.[49]

49. Sally Lehrman, "Colorblind Racism," http://www.alternet.org/story/16792, consulted 8/30/08.

The American Sociological Association's decision to adopt the term "race" as one of its recommended professional practices might seem surprising in consideration of the decades of concerted work to replace it with the word "ethnicity," which seems self-selective rather than imposed from without, as is race. But its reversal should not be surprising, if one considers the great number of racial inequities that still persist. Although white racism works to minimize statistics regarding racial discrimination, some have still continued to be formulated. Sally Lehrman, an associate with the Institute for Justice and Journalism, posted on the Internet on September 18, 2003, a number of very sobering ones pertaining to racial bias.[50] The following inequities come from her list:

50. Ibid.

1. Considered demographically, twice the percentage number of blacks as whites hold low-paying jobs and are likely to be unemployed.
2. Blacks and other minorities are denied mortgages far more frequently than whites.
3. The National Cancer Institute has reported that cancer death rates are more accelerated for blacks than whites, sometimes by as much as ninety to one hundred times more.
4. Black women are more likely than white women to die of breast cancer even though the incidence of the disease is lower among blacks. According to the National Cancer Institute, "Black men have a cancer-death rate about 44 percent higher than that for white men." In fact, African-American men between the ages of fifty and seventy are nearly three times as likely to die from prostate cancer as white men, and their prostate cancer rate is more than double that of whites.
5. Exposure to environmental toxins and carcinogens, which are disproportionately located in poor and minority communities, is one important reason for the racial disparities in cancer mortality rates. Differential access to screening, prevention, and treatment is another reason for the disparities.
6. Racial differences in mortality rates for stroke and coronary heart disease are also significant. The black mortality rate for strokes is 80

percent higher than the white rate, and the black mortality rate for coronary heart disease is 40 percent higher.
7. The amputation of a lower limb is the one advanced procedure that blacks receive far more often than whites because of inadequate treatment of hypertension and diabetes.

Given this grim situation, it is not surprising that race continues to be an important topic for cutting-edge African-American artists, particularly since these problems are not being addressed by society at large. Because a number of artists also continue to celebrate the free and easy access of NBA and the new ethnicities, they find themselves facing battles on two very different fronts. At the same time they are continuing to critique monolithic racial definitions, these artists need to inject race in their work so that it will be part of the national discussion and not glossed over by the dominant yet still far too little recognized ideology of white blindness.[51] Caught between the conflicting discursive formations of self-imposed segregation and victimization by a homogenous post-civil-rights white-dominated culture, these artists must invoke race while remaining ethnic and look b(l)ack while reflecting white racism. They manage these two conflicting goals by double indexing: they demonstrate in their work ways that racism frames and makes possible their individual experiences even as they also proclaim in it their right to choose blackness among a number of equally viable options. They also balance these different initiatives by underscoring the fact that racism is a white overlay, and one of their key strategies is parody, which in their work ranges from being dry and understated to becoming ribald and hyperbolic. Because it is hierarchical, parody controls its target through the ironic detachment it effects.[52] As Robert Colescott, who paved the way for many of the other artists in the exhibition, concluded about racism:

> We've already come to understand that it's about white perceptions of Black people. And they may not be pretty. And they may be stupid. We didn't make up these images. So why should we take the heat? But it's . . . the satire that kills the serpent, you know.[53]

51. This concept that art's role in bringing racism to light is inherently political is indebted to Jacques Rancière's excellent discussion of this topic in *The Politics of Aesthetics: The Distribution of the Sensible*, trans. Gabriel Rockhill (London and New York: Continuum, 2004).

52. Lindy Hutcheon, *A Theory of Parody: The Teachings of Twentieth-Century Art Forms* (New York: Methuen, 1985), 34.

53. Robert Colescott, oral history interview.

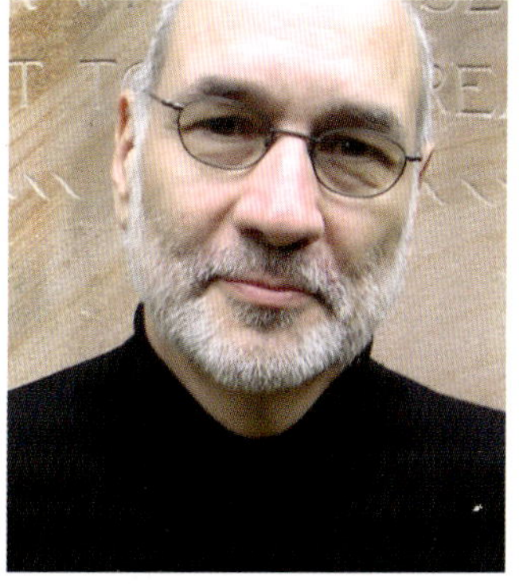

The author gratefully acknowledges the perceptive reading of this essay by Dr. Lowery Sims, formerly executive director and president of the Studio Museum in Harlem and now curator, the Museum of Arts and Design, New York City. In addition he appreciates the able and thoughtful assistance of Jessica Welton, Thalhimer Research Assistant, Virginia Commonwealth University

Robert Hobbs holds the Rhoda Thalhimer Endowed Chair of American Art at Virginia Commonwealth University and is a regular visiting professor at Yale University. Recognized as both an academic and a curator, Hobbs specializes in both later modern and post-modern art. His recent publications include (co-author with Rachel Kent), *Yinka Shonibare, MBE* (New York: Prestel, 2008); "Hernan Bas' 'Fag Limbo' and the Tactics of Reframing Societal Texts" in Mark Coetzee, *Hernan Bas: Works from the Rubell Family Collection* (Miami: RFC, 2007); and "Kelley Walker's Continuum: Consuming and Recycling as Aesthetic Tactics" in Suzanne Cotter, ed., *Seth Price / Kelley Walker: Continuous Project* (Oxford: Modern Art Oxford, 2007). He is the author of many books, including monographs on Edward Hopper, Mark Lombardi, Lee Krasner, and Robert Smithson. Hobbs divides his time between Richmond and Manhattan.

ms. or leah was a neighbor i had had growing up and i thought ms leah was alright. she was from louisiana not too educated and far from dumb. anyway, she was my mom's friend and a neighbor who i found always cordial, pleasant and lets say sincere. that image was taken from her obituary. i 'd visit miss leah on occasion after my mom died and would keep her up to date on things and she seemed to get a kick out of my "success" for lack of a better word.

Lusiana Georgescu was a girlfriend of mine who I've painted and continue to paint. this particular painting was done in her backyard in santa cruz one summer.

fuck that previous shit I wrote it was really Bigger Thomas and not me. Love Pam. That painting is of a cousin of mine by the name of Alister who was just visiting me and I had him sit for that/this portrait, but the title is the name of an old friend that I went to high school with and the only person from my graduating class that I know who majored subject-wise in art. And behind that sitter Alister Gaston was a joseph beuys postcard [original grafic seriel./Koln/Nr.16 Koln offset/edition staeck.69 heidelbergl. Postfach 471] that she sent to me in 1978 from Germany. my old friend Pam

i think we should smell/spell luciana with an s, lusiana my bad. so, i've been out but i'm back! how in the hell is Big Don? Tell em he's my frickin idol! that gyno! now you think i'm some kind of freak huh – caroline but if you only knew, when i asked Big "D" what was his occupation you should have heard him, it was classic and since then well he's become the man. i must admit i, fuck i'm trippin but really though ... i wish i could say what i wanted to say w/out someone thinking and winking. right now i'm happy i'm alive. anyway, about #3, its title is oh henry right well, that painting is of a person duh ... but caroline that day i was walking and walking's good as long as there are no landmines, anyway, i was walking and i saw this man staring up i don't remember if he had his hand out but to me even if he did what i saw was no bum but simply a being and instantly it was a more spiritual THANG! the underground kang, so it ain't and never was about me henry. it was just a sweet moment underneath "oh hennery" is a candy bar u know that so the moment was sweet even though i wish i could have helped my bro ... sorry. there's a story there somewhere i g ya tee ya. you know how they say, "angels are among us" well maybe that's whats i'm talking about, however, i'm not sure. cut the cake

Henry Taylor

 Miss Leah, 2008, acrylic on canvas, 68 3/4 x 92 1/4 in. (161.9 x 235 cm), acquired in 2008

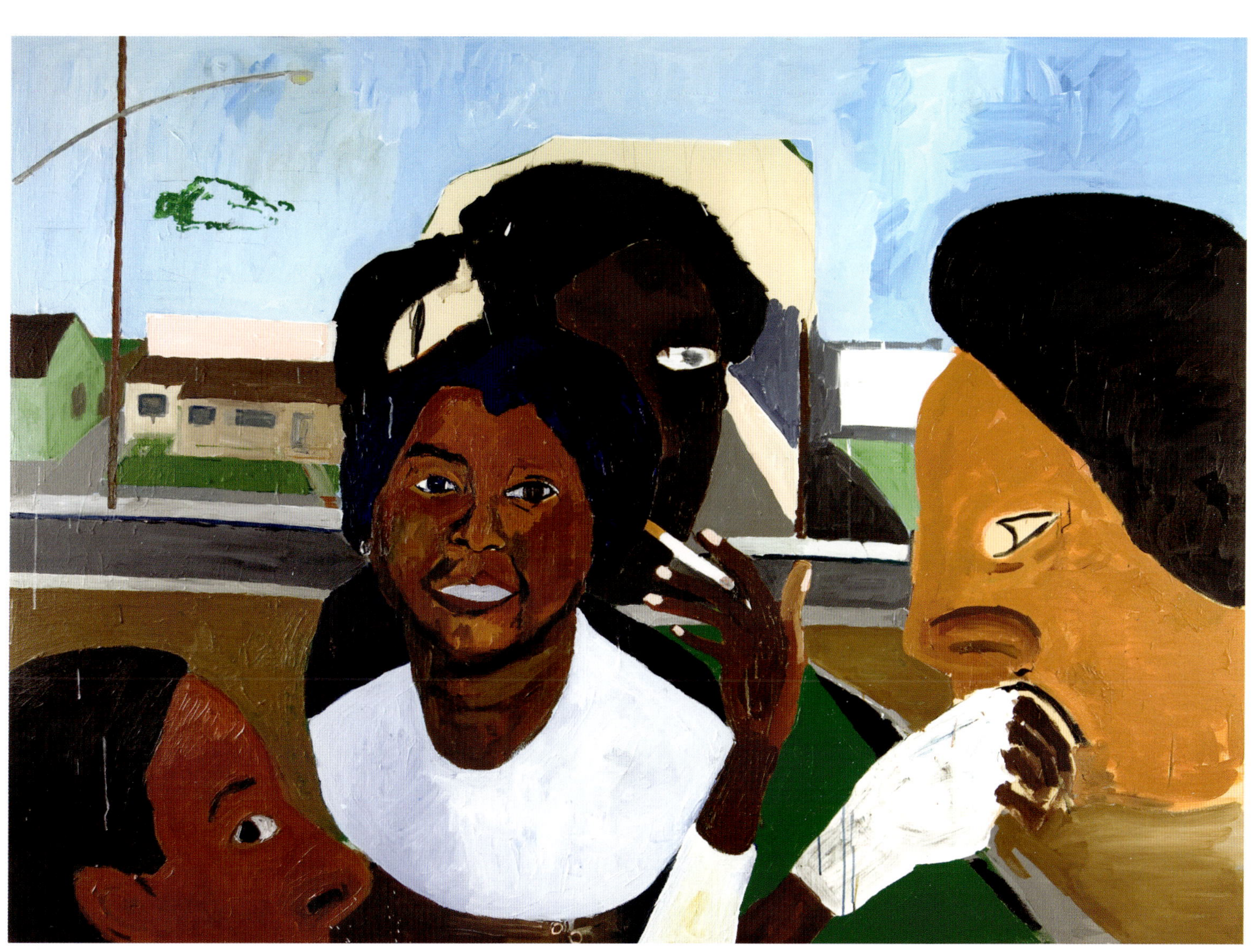

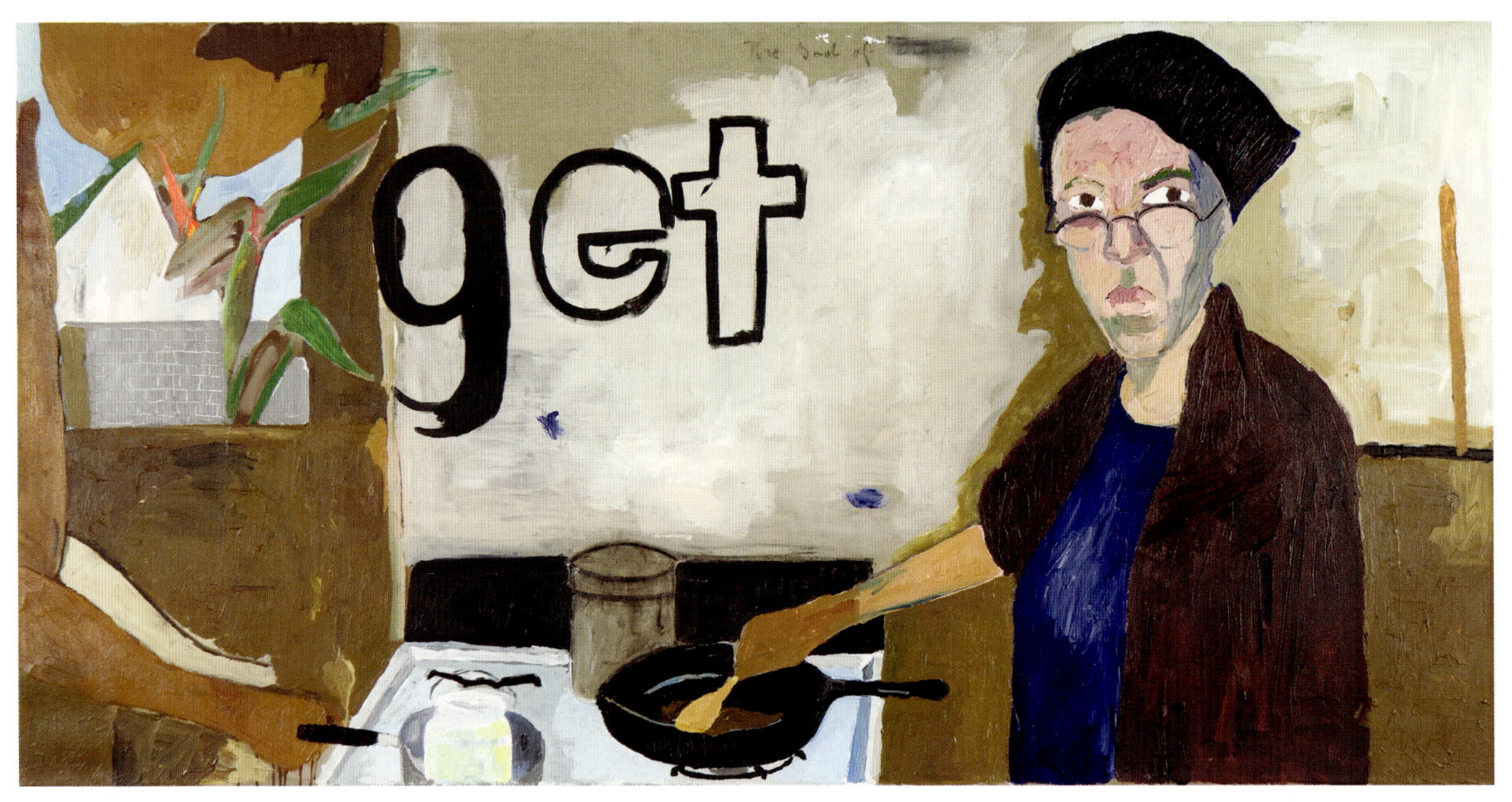

 HENRY TAYLOR *Chicago Cooks*, 2008, acrylic on canvas, 43 1/2 x 84 1/2 in. (110.5 x 214.6 cm), acquired in 2008

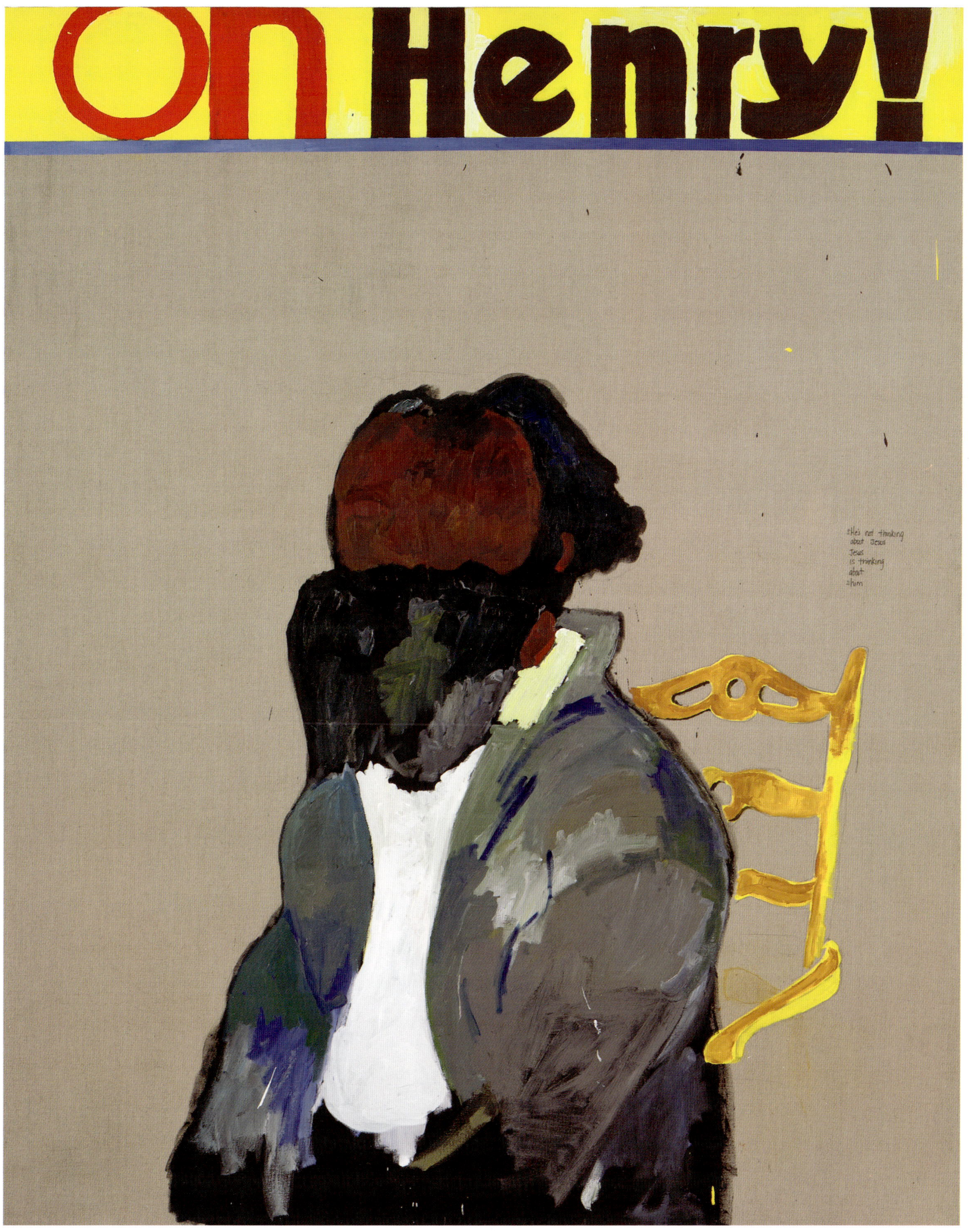

Oh Henry, 2006, acrylic on canvas, 96 x 76 in. (243.8 x 193 cm), acquired in 2006

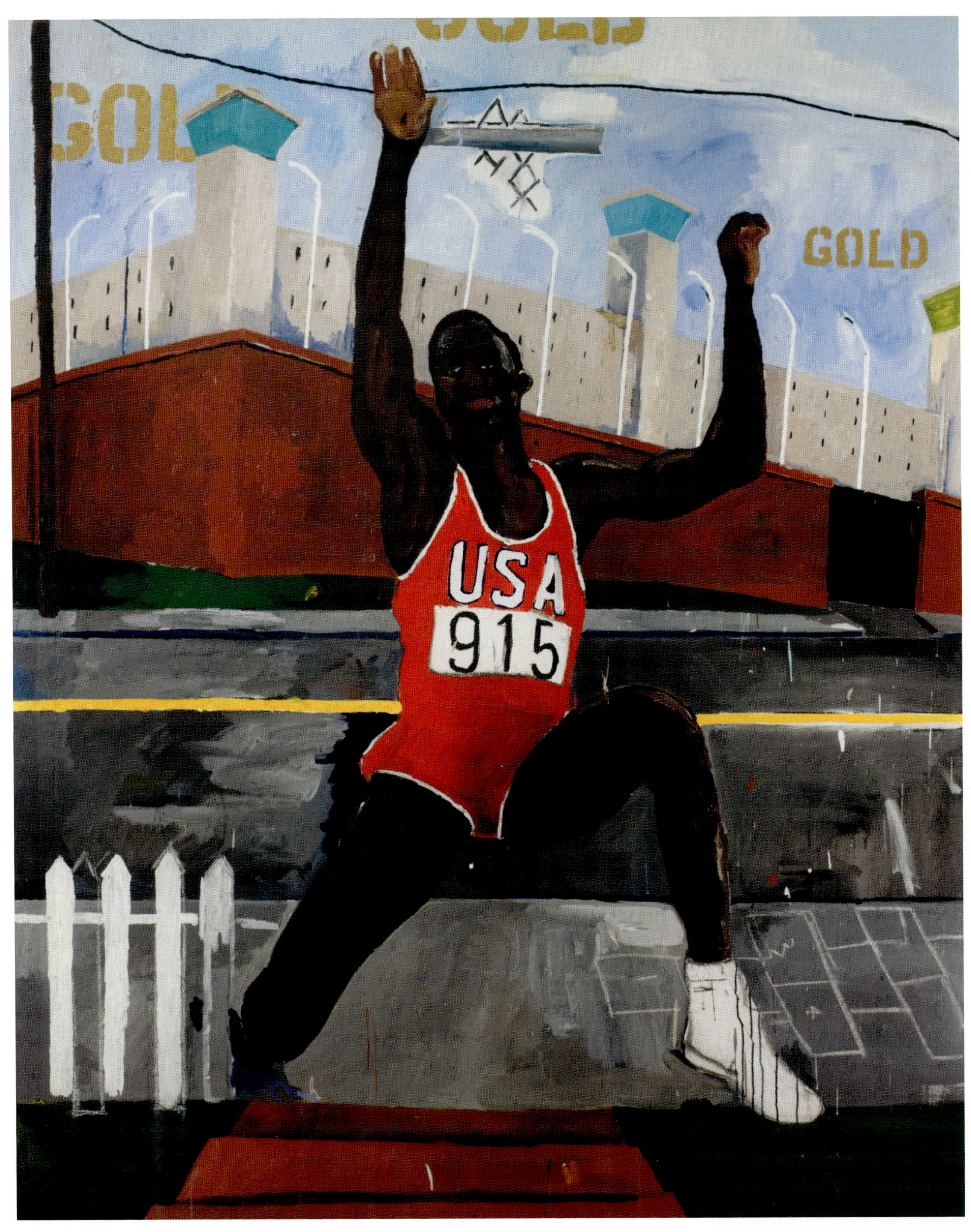

The Long Jump by Carl Lewis, 2010, acrylic on canvas, 87 1/2 x 77 in. (222.3 x 195.6 cm), acquired in 2012
Ride the White Horse Together, 2011, acrylic, wood, plastic, metal pans, yarn and hardware, 109 x 48 x 21 in. (276.9 x 121.9 x 53.3 cm), acquired in 2011

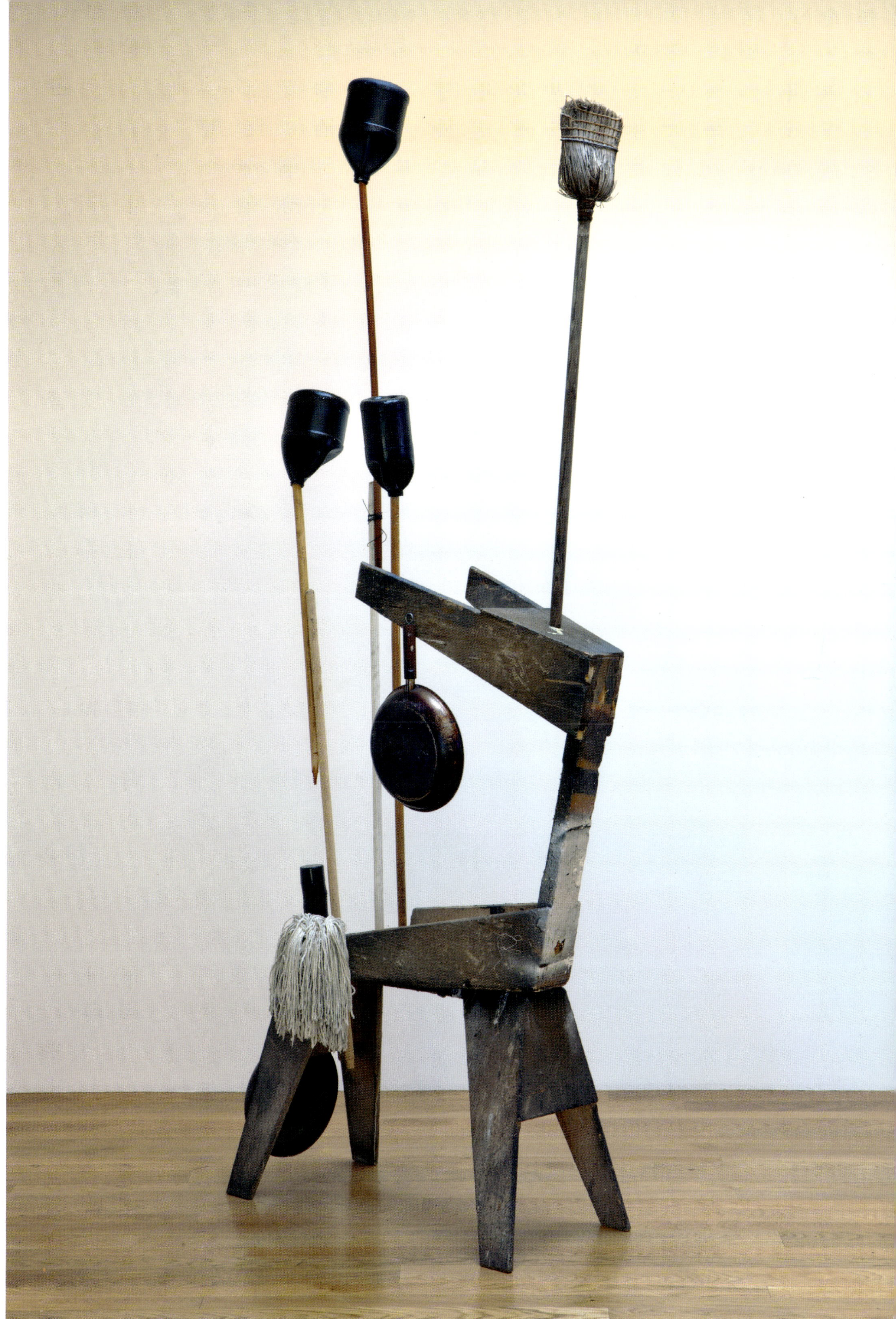

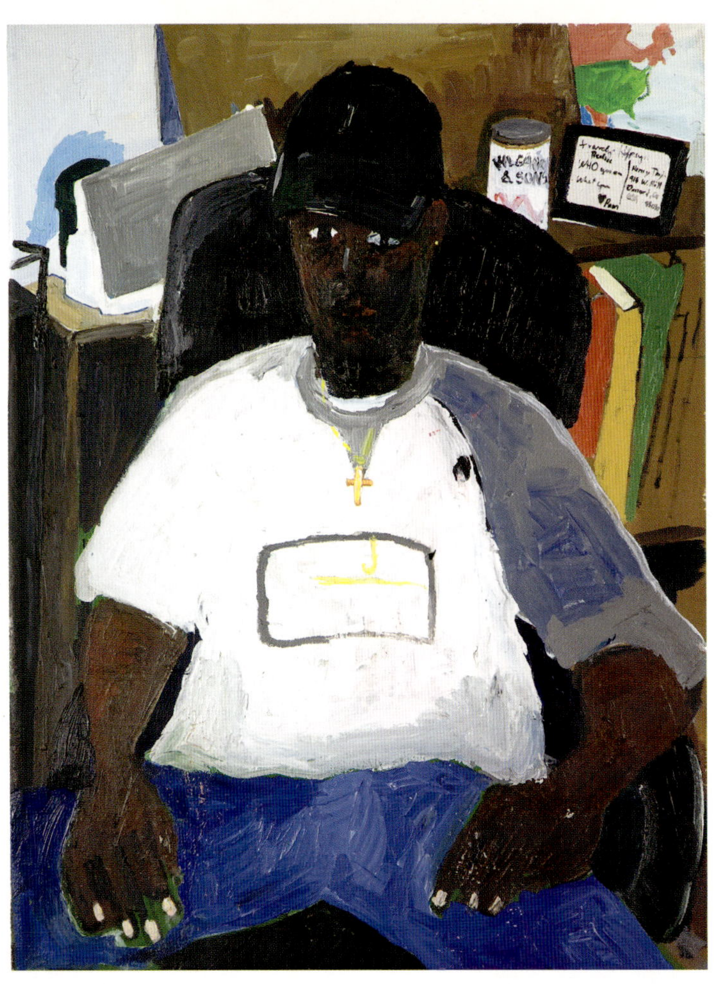

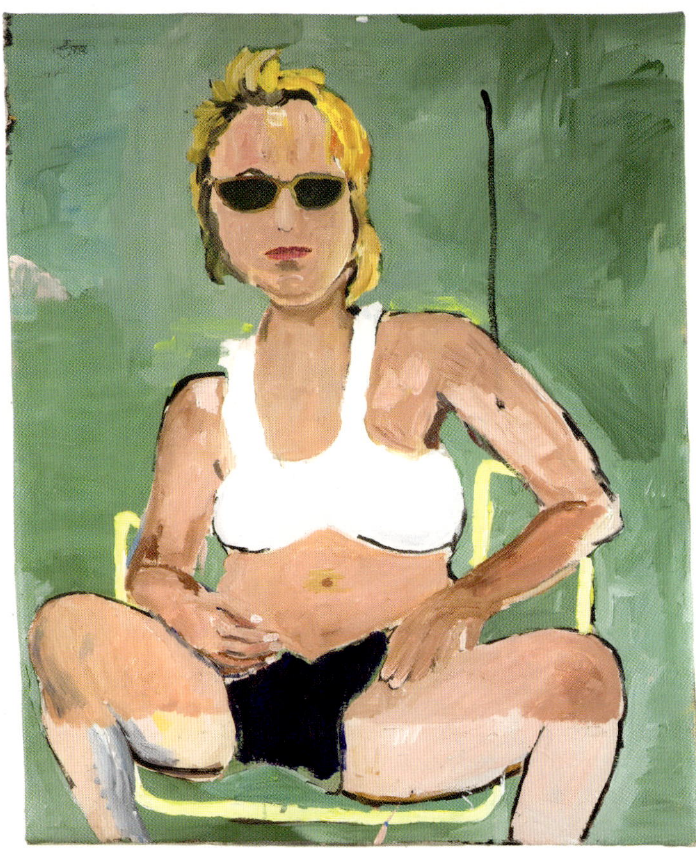

 HENRY TAYLOR

Love Pam, 2008, acrylic on canvas, 47 x 35 in. (119.4 x 88.9 cm), acquired in 2008
Lusiana, 2007, acrylic on canvas, 44 x 36 in. (111.8 x 91.4 cm), acquired in 2007

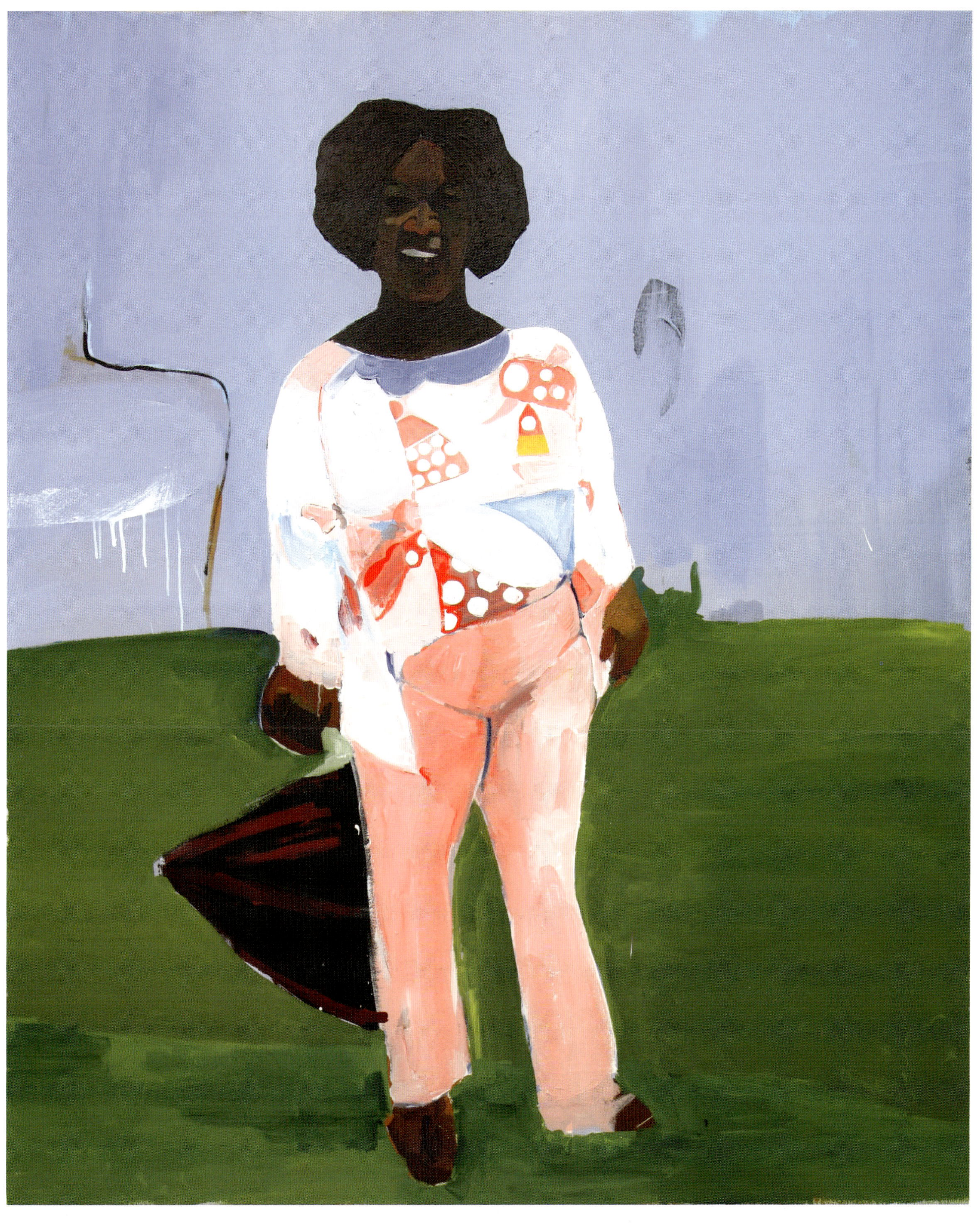

Watts County, 2004, acrylic on canvas, 76 x 61 1/2 in. (193 x 156.2 cm), acquired in 2005

I had been making a lot of images that looked like ads for a series called *Unbranded*, and they were speaking to issues related to the exploitation of primarily the black male body in popular culture, but also in history—looking at slavery and commodity culture in general. In the midst of that, I was doing a talk somewhere or maybe showing some of my work, and someone gave me an ad for a 2001 Toyota Rav4 that had an African-American male's mouth smiling with bright white teeth. In the middle was a gold tooth in the shape of the Toyota Rav4. The person who gave me the ad said, "You should do something with this." It almost seemed like the truth was better than fiction. I had been trying to make work to speak to these issues, but they were actually still very present and maybe more potent in real life. I realized that with any ad, the moment you remove the text and the logos all you're left with is the photograph, and basically the photograph tells us what's really for sale. I had been talking about the ways that black bodies were used to sell things, and then here we have Japanese cars being sold through gold teeth as kind of a value system that's attributed to African-American men.

I wanted to look at how real ads could tell stories about the way we learn identity and culture, etc. I think about advertisement as a form of social conditioning and almost brainwashing, and that it's where we learn what our values are in our society. You look at most ads and the actual image has nothing to do with the product. It's only the myths and generalizations that we have that bring to light this kind of logic that makes an ad work. I started this series that ultimately became *Unbranded: Reflections in Black by Corporate America*. I removed the text from two ads for every year from 1968 to 2008, and I really wanted to track blackness in the corporate eye over the course of forty years. I chose 1968 because it was the symbolic end of the Civil Rights Movement, when Martin Luther King and RFK were assassinated. I chose 2008 pretty randomly, but it ultimately wound up being the year that the U.S. elected its first president of African decent. That means it's bookended by these two historic events. The fact that most of the people who were making the ads for black people to consume—then and now—were white men on Madison Avenue, basically, I found fascinating. So, the values that are created, are they "black" values? Or are they just generic American—some people might call it "white"—values that are being projected onto the African-American community? By "unbranding" advertisements, I can literally expose what Roland Barthes referred to as *what-goes-without-saying* in their images, and hopefully encourage viewers to look harder and think deeper about the empire of signs that have become second nature to our experience of life in the modern world.

The piece *Priceless* is probably the most personal photograph that I've created, even though it's a mockery of an actual ad. MasterCard had this "Priceless" campaign, and this campaign was very much about nostalgia, and the fun moments of life that you share with your family. My cousin was murdered in the year 2000, and for that moment I say I stopped being a photographer and artist, because up until then I was using art and photography especially as a means to tell my stories and how I felt, and to document things. But at that point I felt like the camera couldn't document all of the feelings and complexities our family was dealing with at my cousin's funeral. For years I looked at the photographs and tried to figure out what could happen with them, and at some point I realized in thinking about the language of that MasterCard "Priceless" campaign that I could maybe speak to something that was more to the heart. There was this moment when I was in the funeral home with my family and there was the casket, my cousin was lying on the table, and they had to choose the casket. There was a $7,000 box of wood that was going to be thrown in the dirt, never to be seen again, and then there was the $2,000 box of wood to be thrown in the dirt, never to be seen again, then there was the $5,000 box of wood. There was this unspoken thing, like maybe you couldn't afford to love him enough if you bought the $2,000 box of wood; maybe you loved him more if you bought the more expensive one. It was really an impossible decision to watch my family members make, because I realized that even in mourning we're still being marketed to. So I used that to make the last lines, "Picking the perfect casket for your son: priceless." I also used the numbers for the chain—my cousin was with his friends and they were robbed. The chain that was stolen was sold in the street for $400, and then I was thinking about the price of the gun, and the price of the bullets. You have to buy a new suit for him, new socks. There are all these weird commodities, things that add up to the culmination of someone's life that I wanted to address.

Hank WIllis Thomas

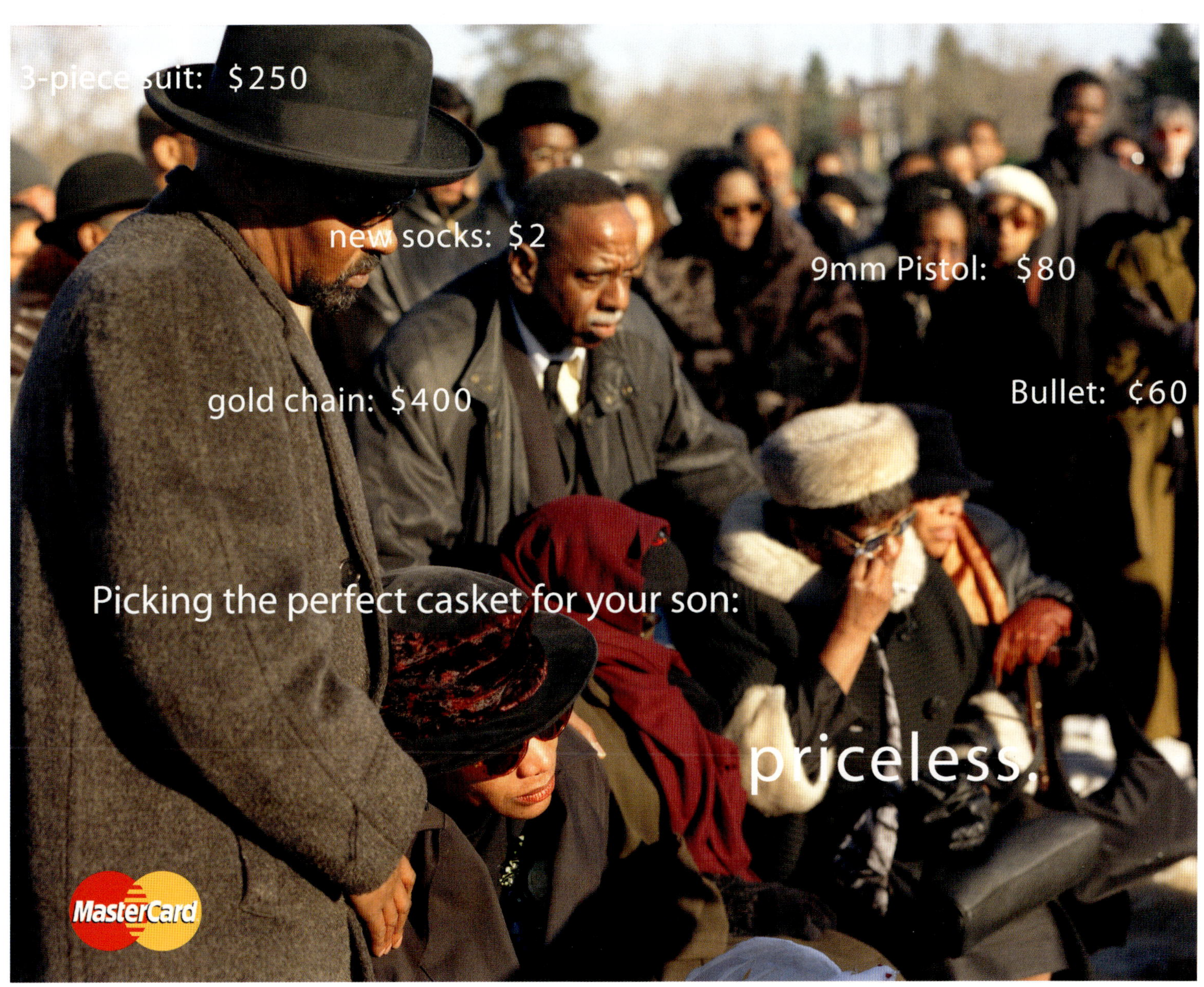

Priceless, 2004, digital chromogenic print, ed. AP, 71 x 89 in. (180.3 x 226 cm), acquired in 2007

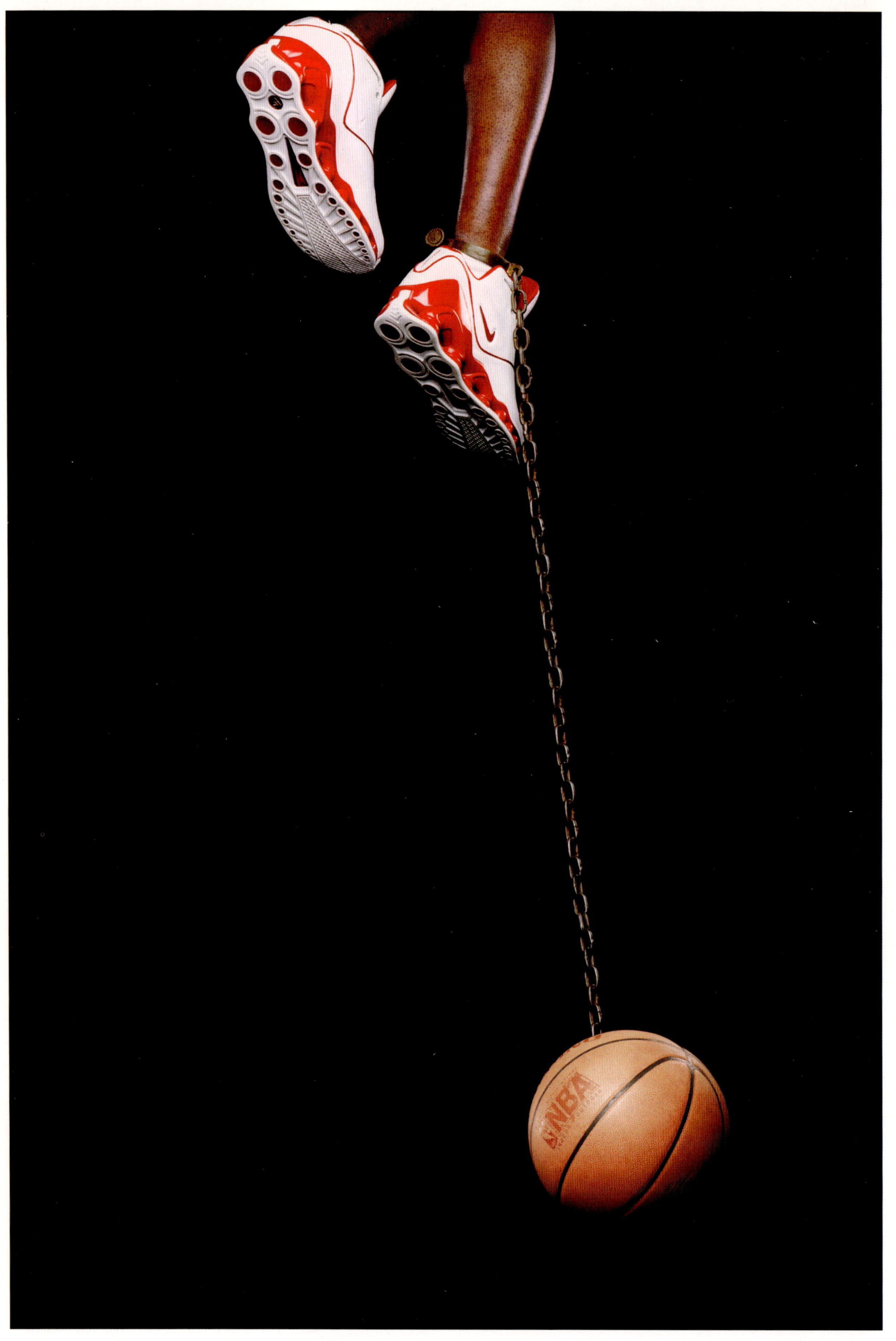

 HANK WILLIS THOMAS *Basketball and Chain*, 2003, digital chromogenic print, ed. 2/3, 99 x 55 in. (251.5 x 139.7 cm), acquired in 2007

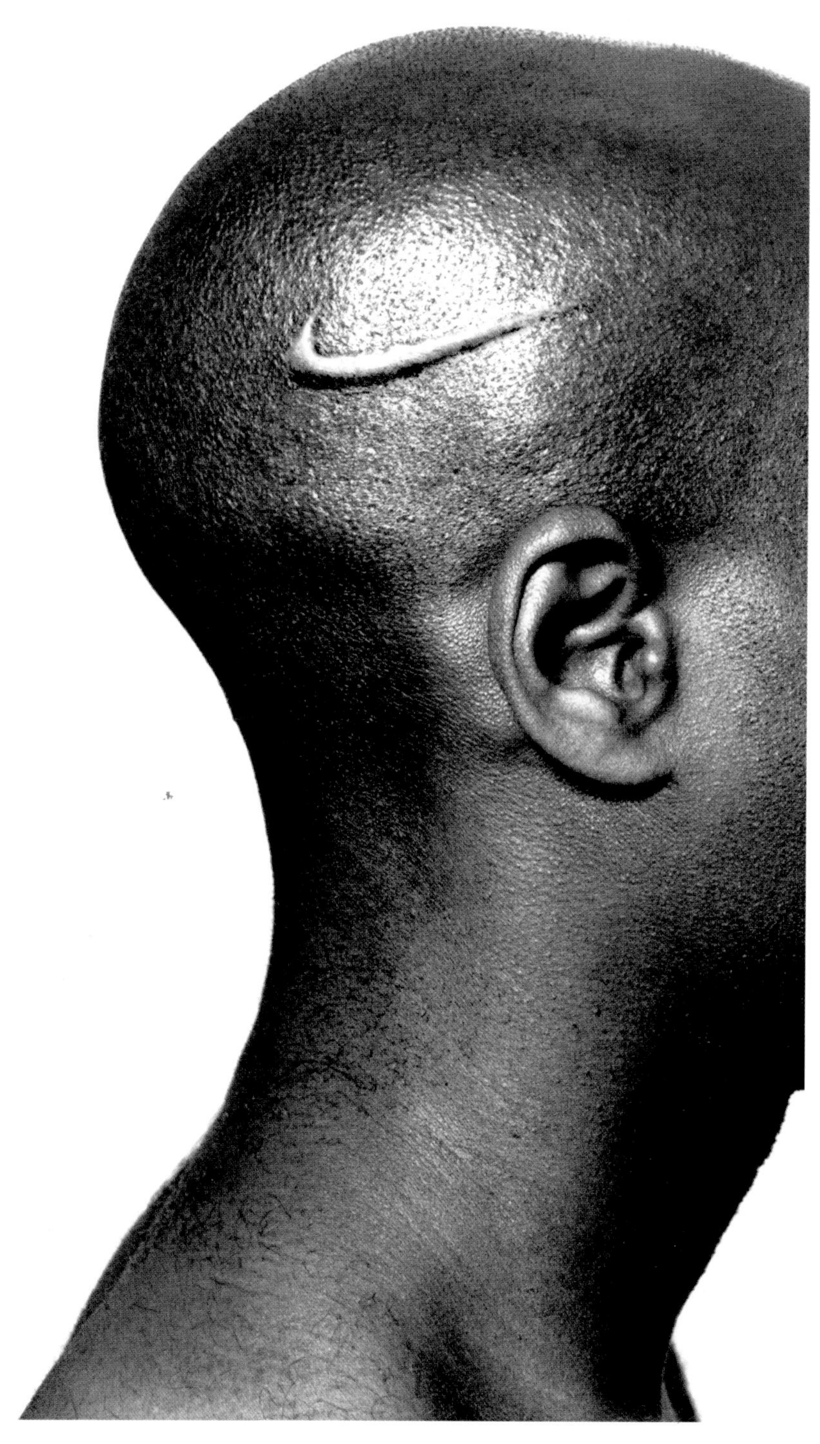

Branded Head, 2003, digital chromogenic print, ed. AP, 99 x 52 in. (251.5 x 132 cm), acquired in 2006

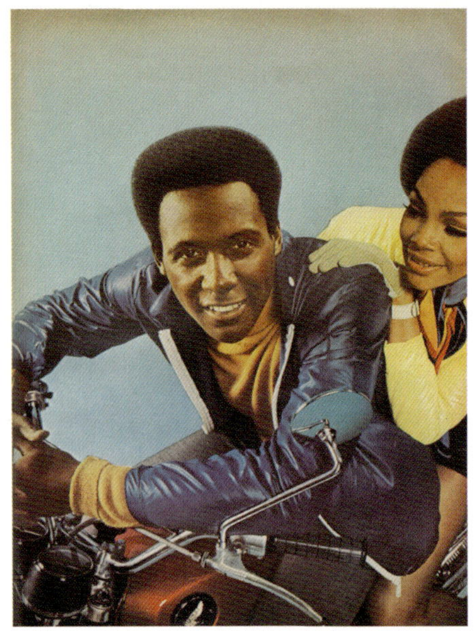

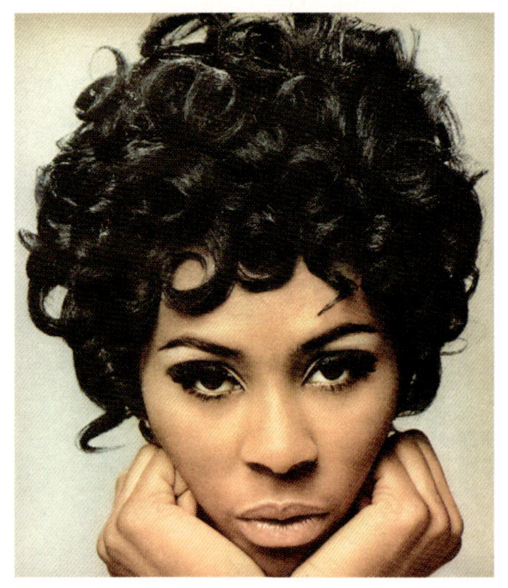

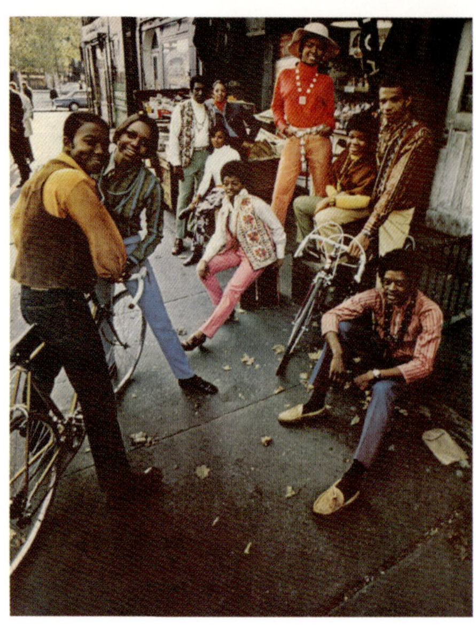

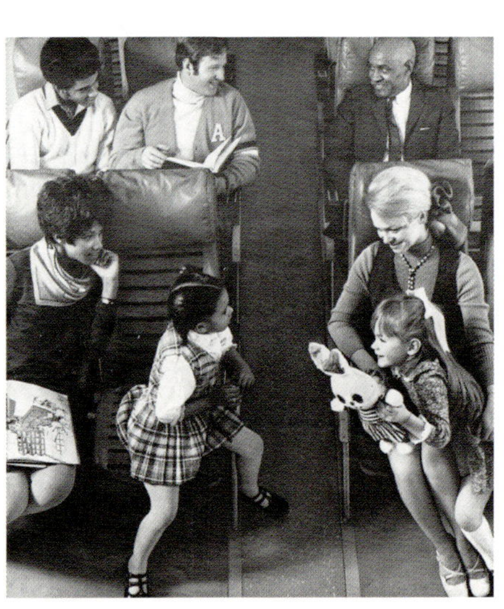

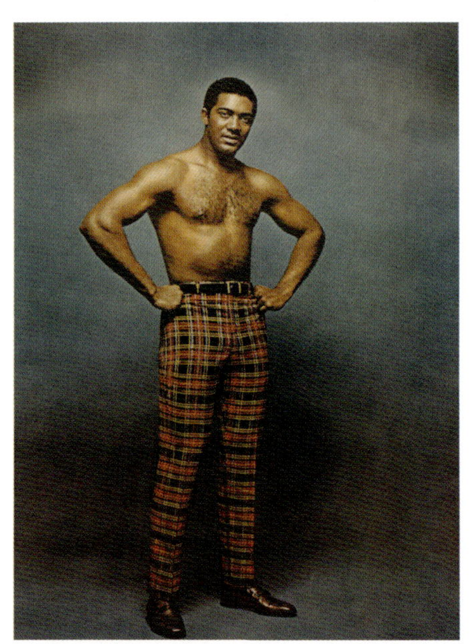

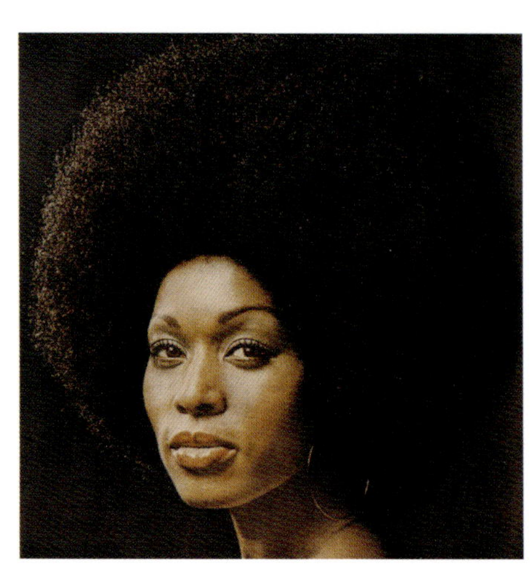

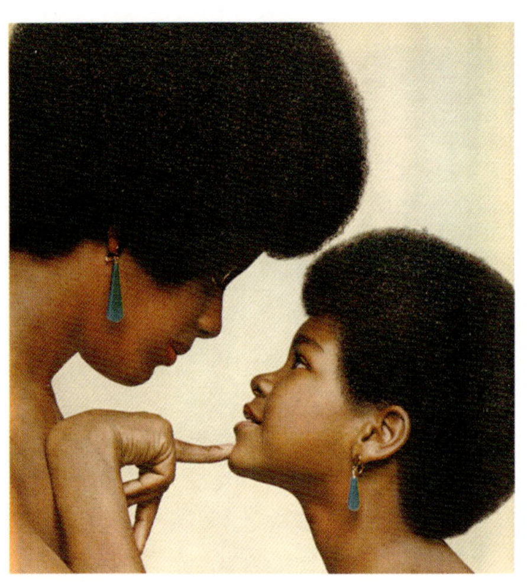

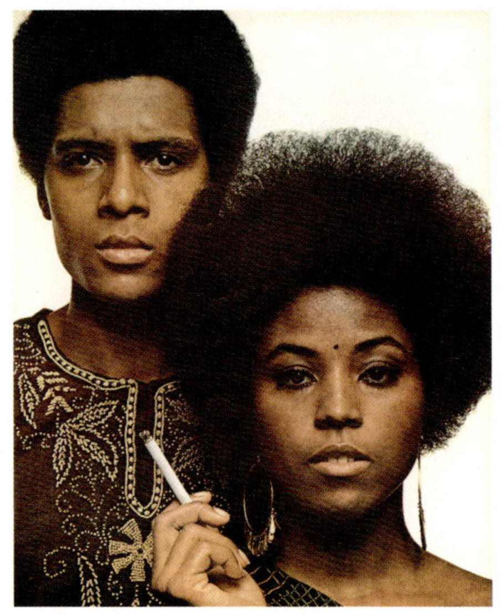

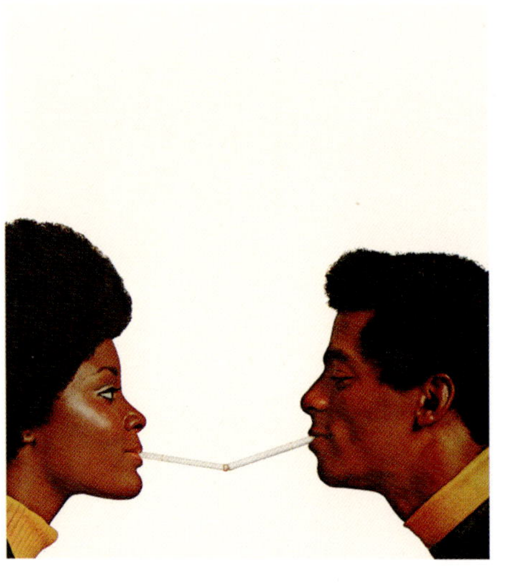

Left column, top to bottom: *Duke Natural 1968/2006*, 2006; *We Are On Our Way 1970/2008*, 2008; *Kama Mama, Kama Binti (Like Mother, Like Daughter) 1971/2008*, 2008; Middle column, top to bottom: *Why wait another day to be adorable? Tell your beautician "Relax me" 1968/2007*, 2007; *Slack Power 1969/2006*, 2006; *Farewell Uncle Tom 1971/2007*, 2007; Right column, top to bottom: *The Oft Forgotten Black Flower Children of Harlem 1969/2006*, 2006; *Who Can Say No to a Gorgeous Brunette? 1970/2007*, 2007; Pucker Up! 1972/2008, 2008, acquired in 2007

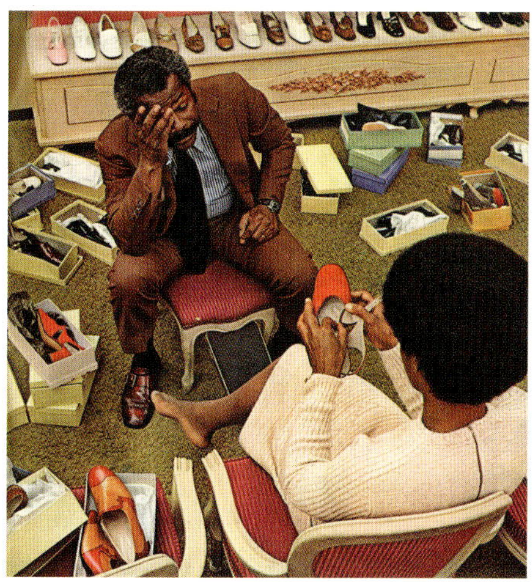
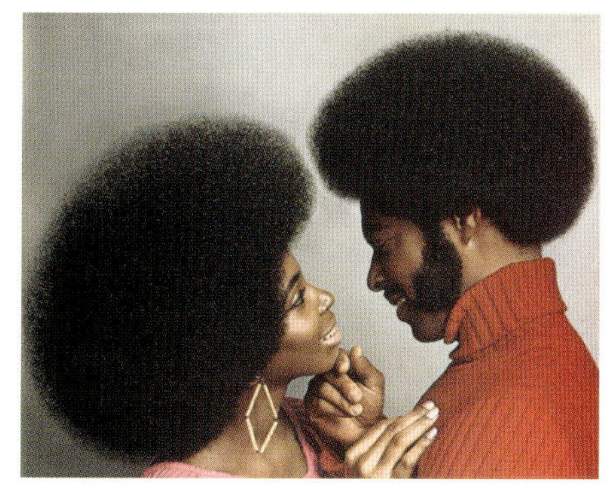
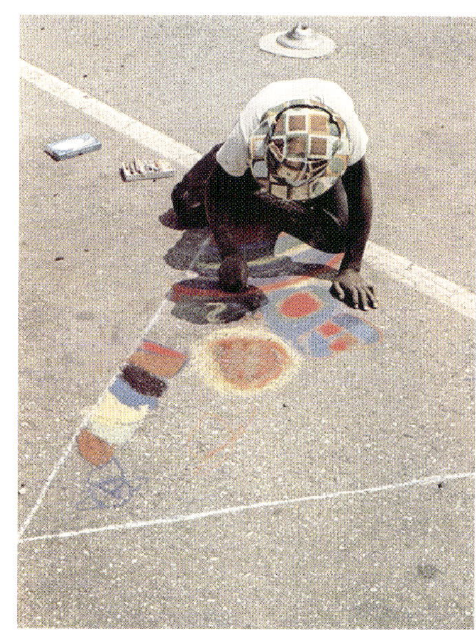
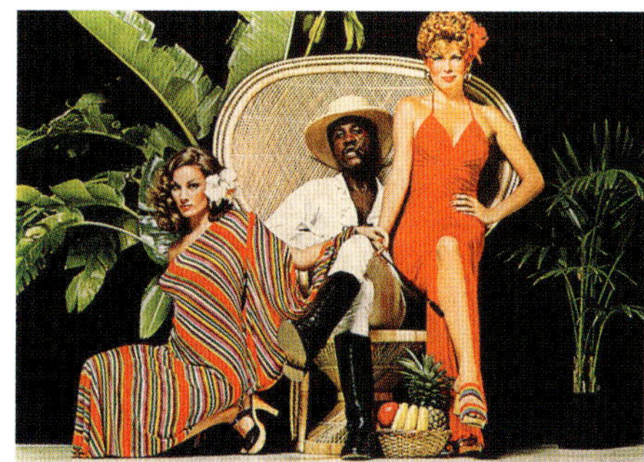
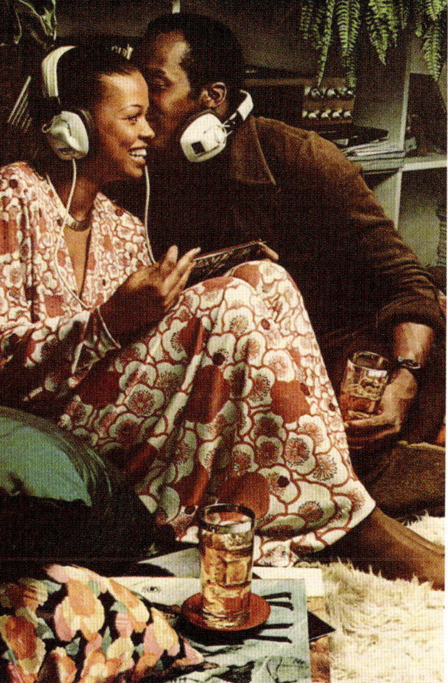
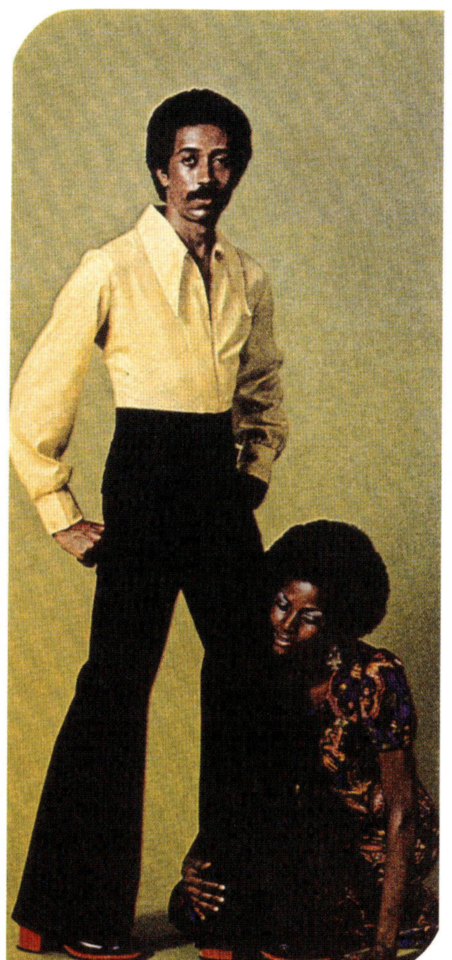
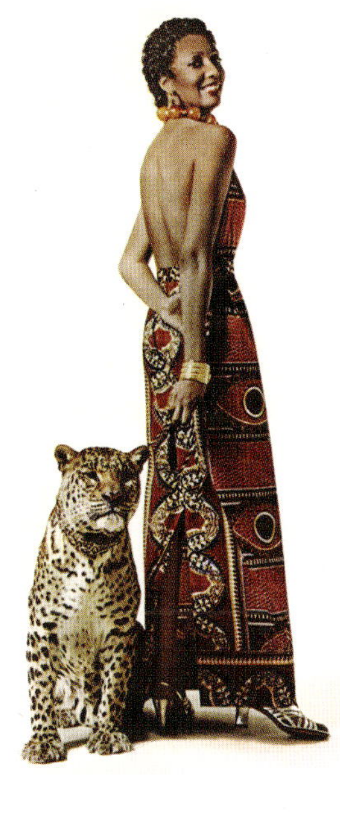
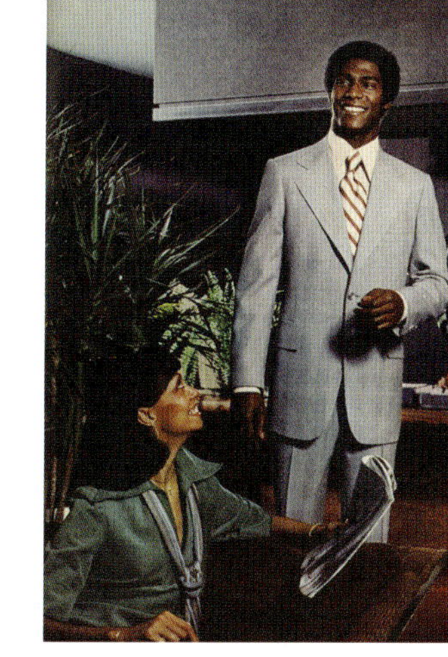
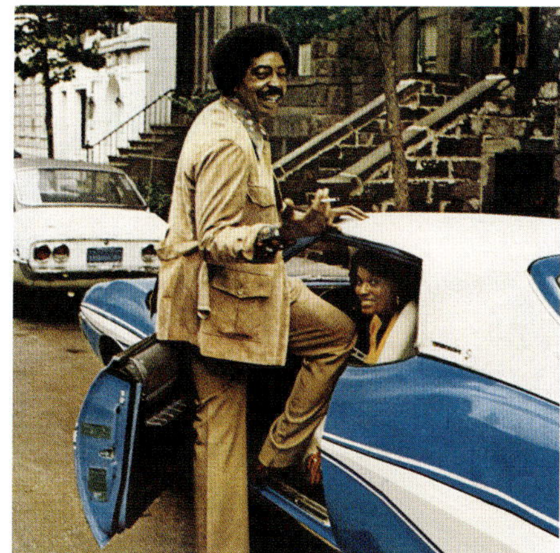

Left column, top to bottom: *When the Going Gets Hard, the Whiskey Should be Soft, 1972/2007*, 2007; *Love Hang-Over 1976/2007*, 2007; *Viceroy 1975/2008*, 2008; Middle column, top to bottom: *A Natural Exposion! Afro Sheen® Blowout Creme Relaxer, 1973/2007*, 2007; *Are You the Right Kind of Woman for It? 1974/2007*, 2007; *Can You Dig It? 1974/2007*, 2007; Right column, top to bottom: *Exxon: Black Street Art 1973/2005*, 2005; *Bleach and Glow 1975/2008*, 2008; *Movin' On Up 1976/2008*, 2008, acquired in 2007

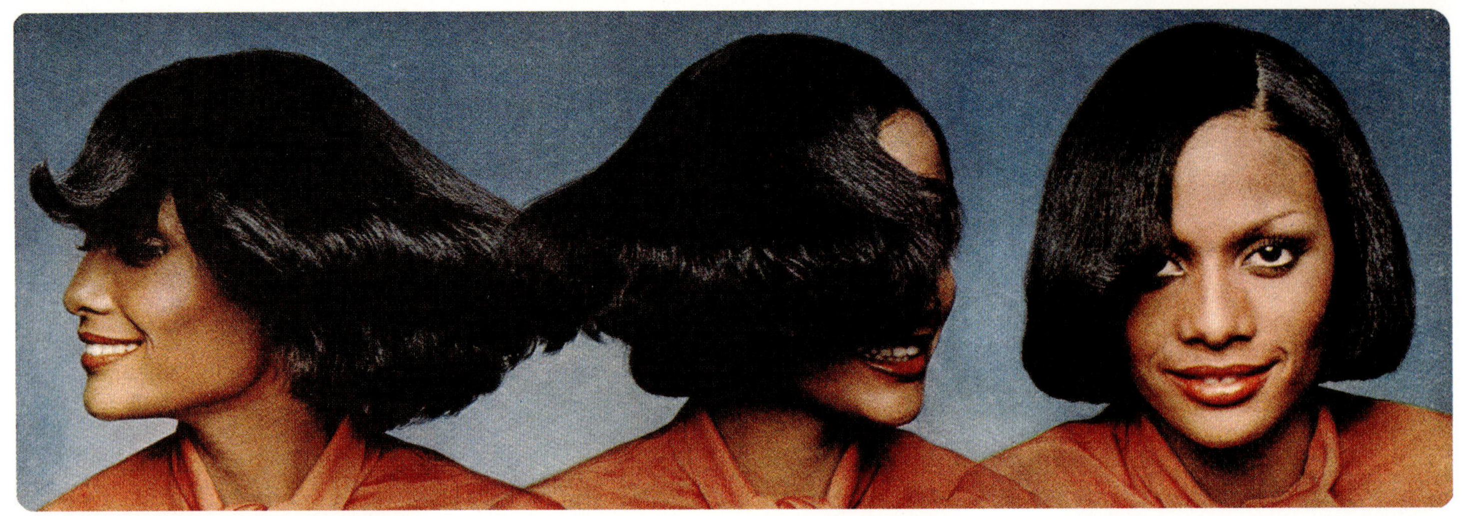

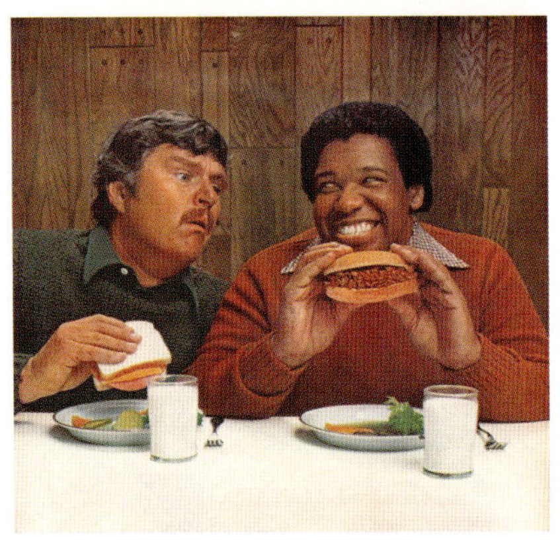

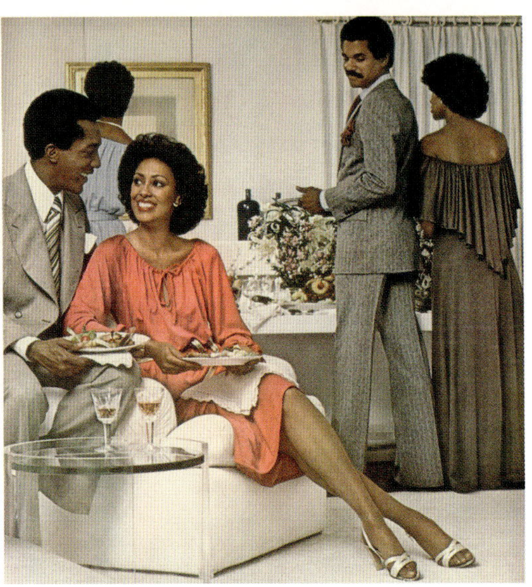

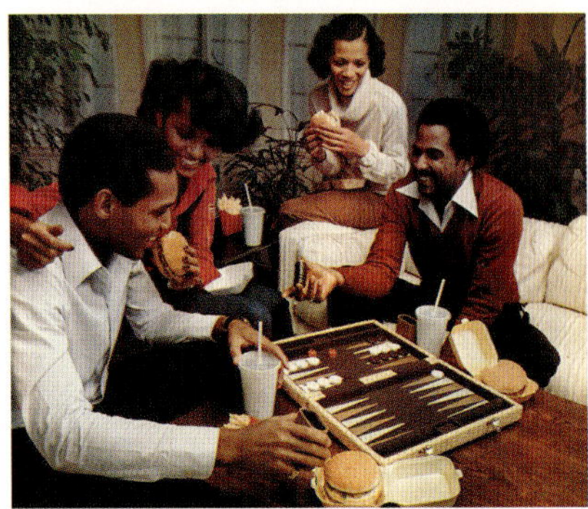

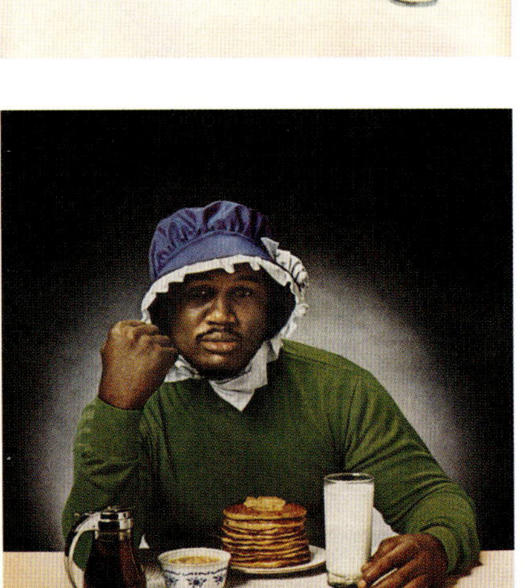

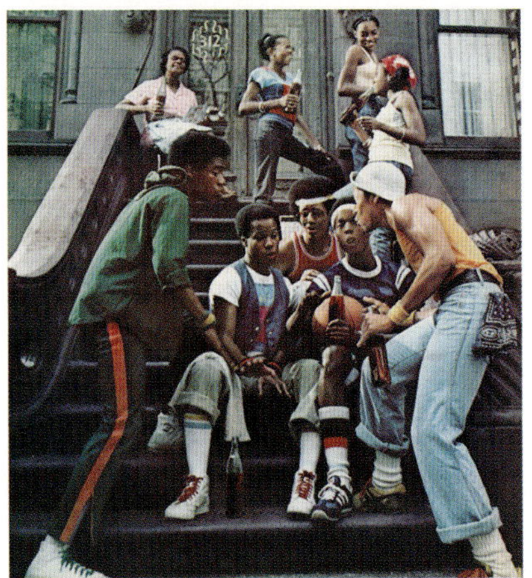

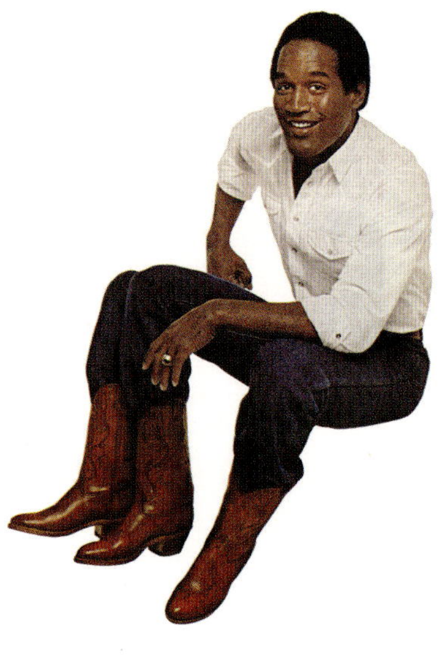

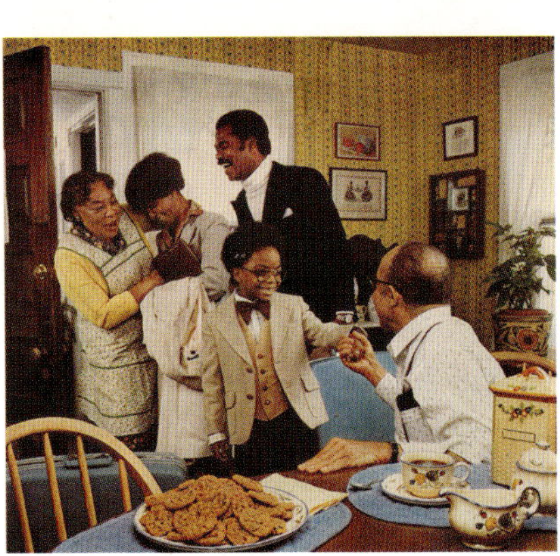

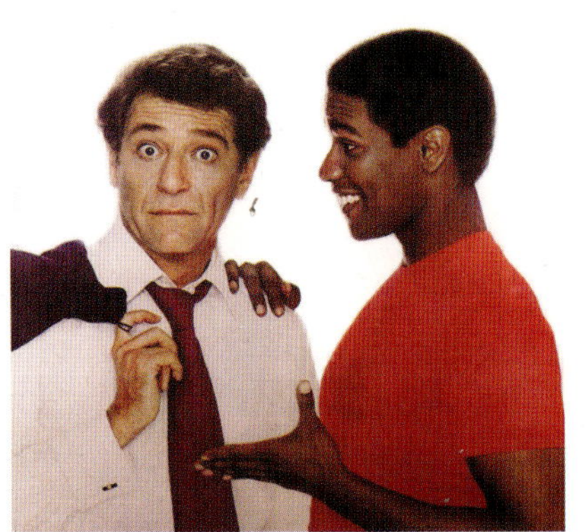

Left column, top to bottom: *The French Way 1979/2007*, 2007; *The Mandingo of Sandwiches 1977/2007*, 2007; *Smokin' Joe Ain't J'mama 1978/2006*, 2006; Middle column, top to bottom: *Available in a Variety of Sizes and Colors 1977/2007*, 2007; *O.J. Dingo 1980/2007*, 2007; Right column, top to bottom: *So Glad We Made It 1979/2006*, 2006; *It's the Real Thing! 1978/2006*, 2006; *Reparations 101: "I lost my job, my house, my Rolls Royce, my family left me...what else can go wrong?" "Hi Dad!" 1981/2007*, 2007, acquired in 2007

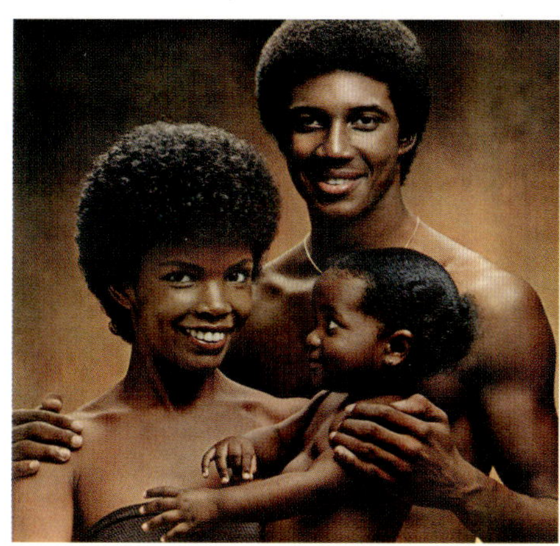

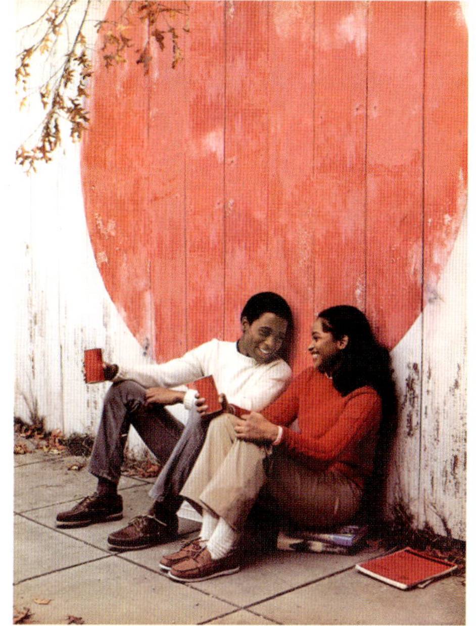

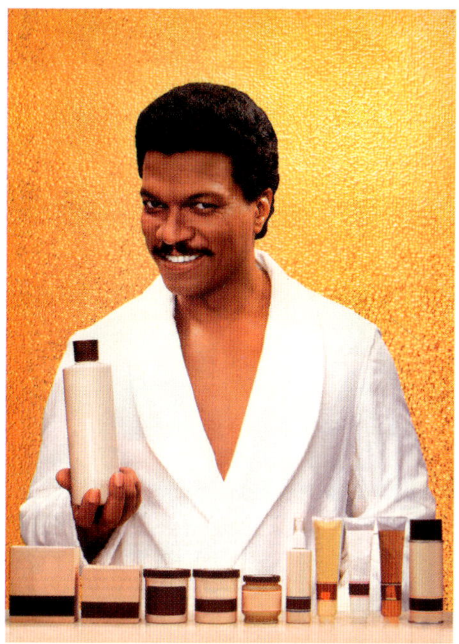

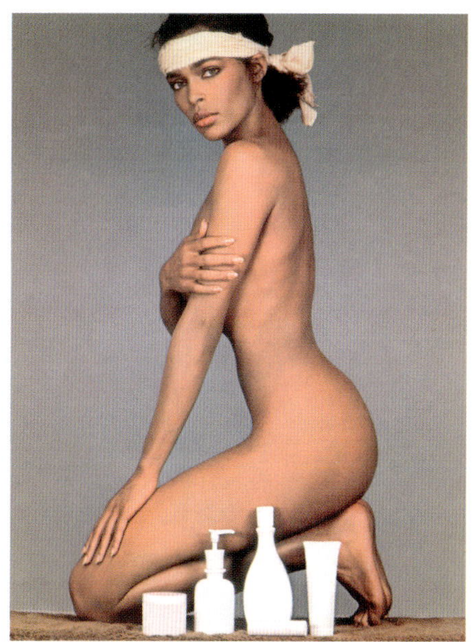

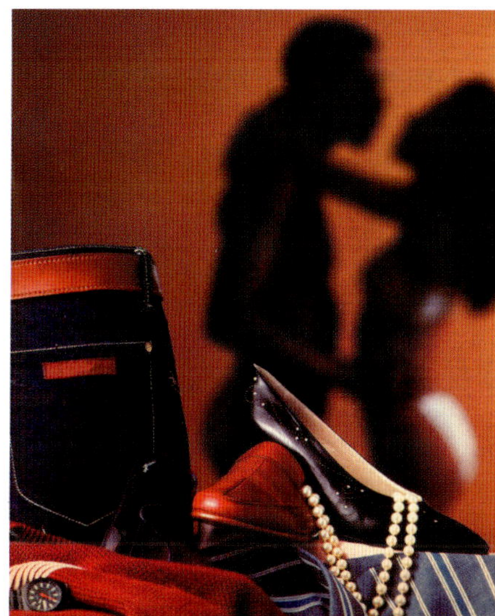

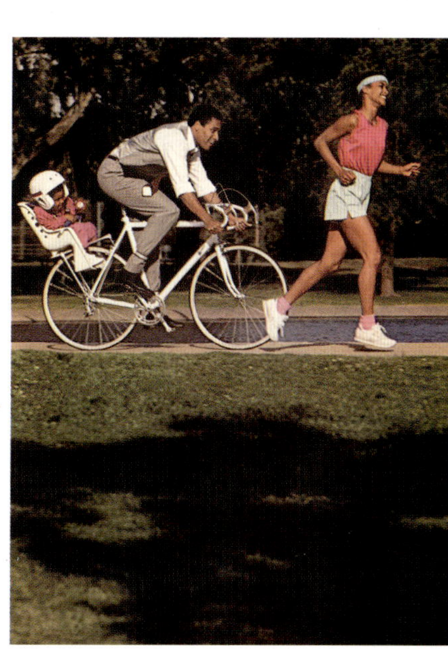

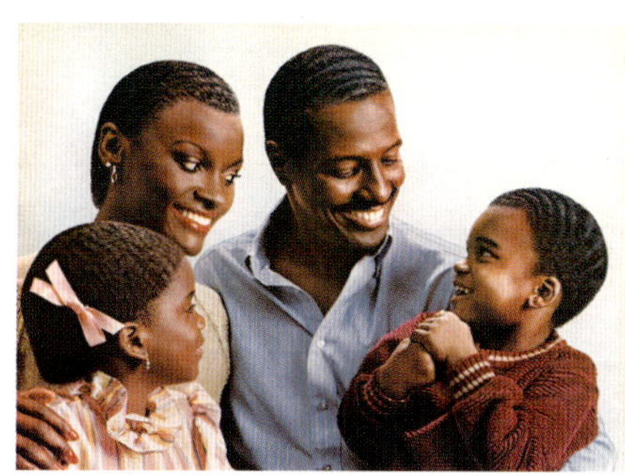

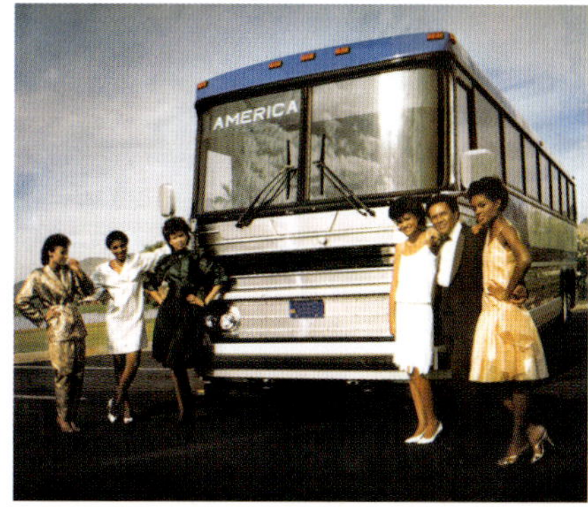

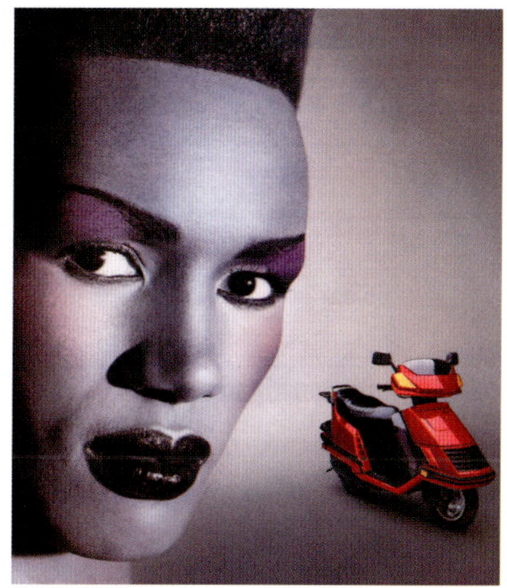

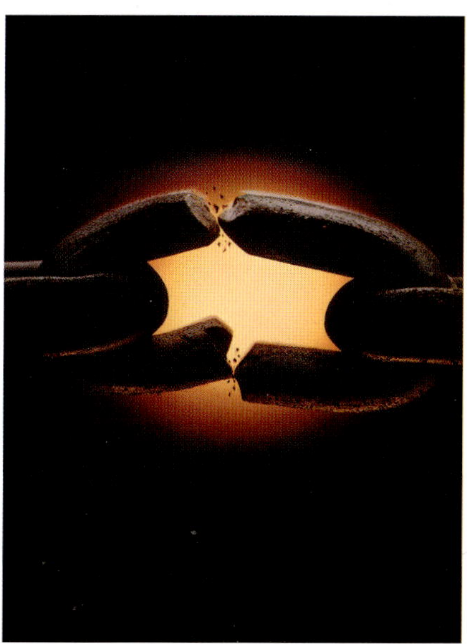

Left column, top to bottom: *The Johnson Family 1981/2007*, 2007; *And They Called It "Buppy Love" 1983/2007*, 2007; *Something to Believe In 1984/2007*, 2007; Middle column, top to bottom: *Caramel Cocoa Butta', Honey Lovah You're Like No Otha' 1982/2006*, 2006; *What's love got to do with it? 1983/2007*, 2007; *...and the rest was her story 1985/2007*, 2007; Right column, top to bottom: *Introducing New Extra Strength Fulla Waves for Course, Thick, and Unruly Hair 1982/2007*, 2007; *Ride in Style 1984/2008*, 2008; *Make a Radical Departure 1985/2007*, 2007; *Martin Luther Burger King? 1986/2007*, 2007, acquired in 2007

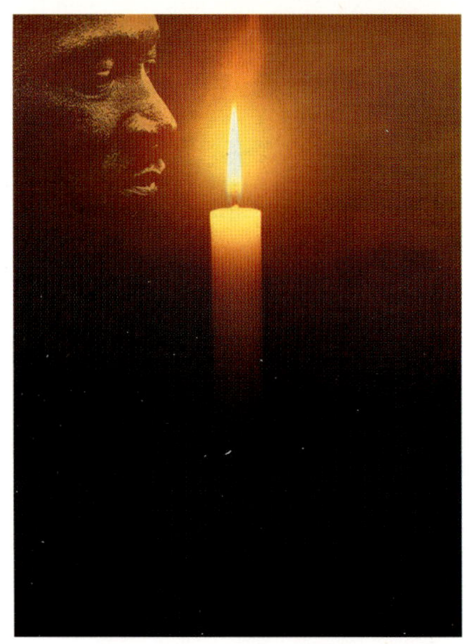

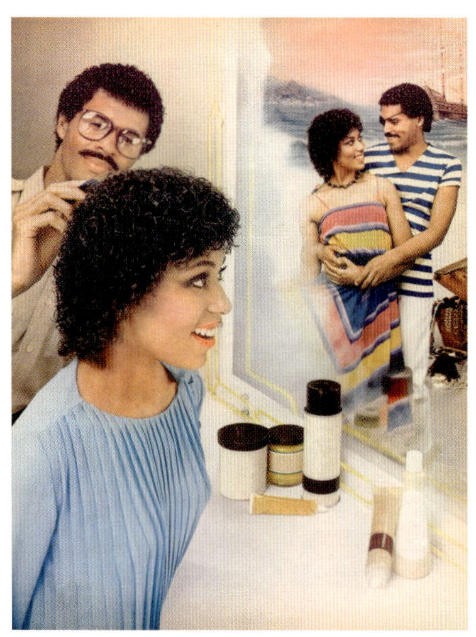

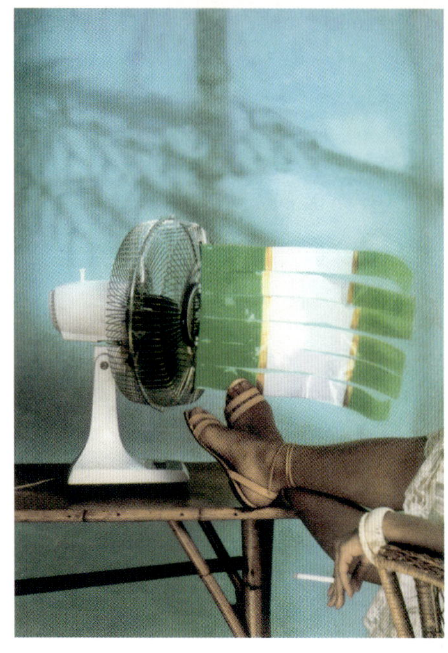

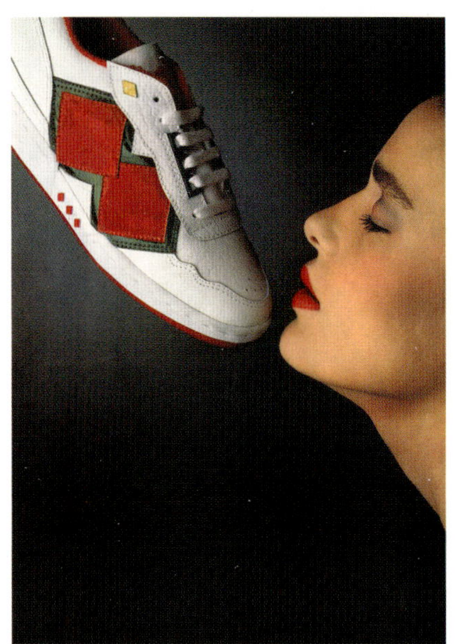

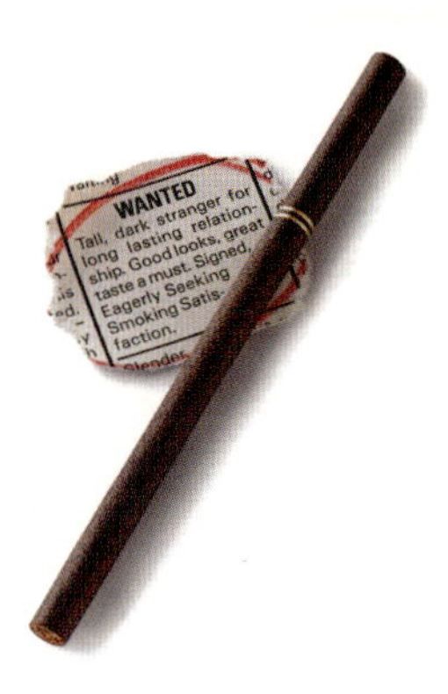

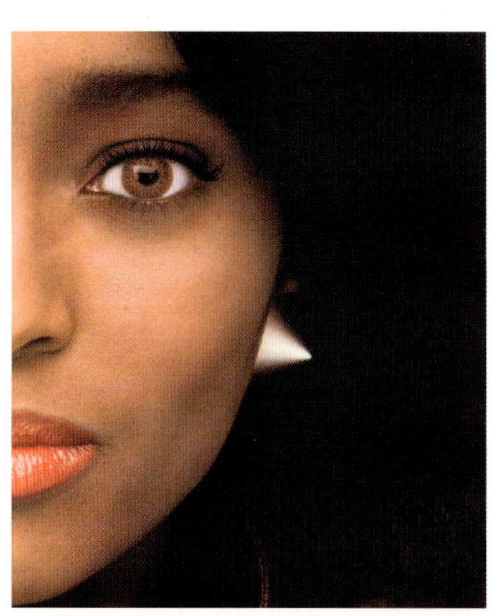

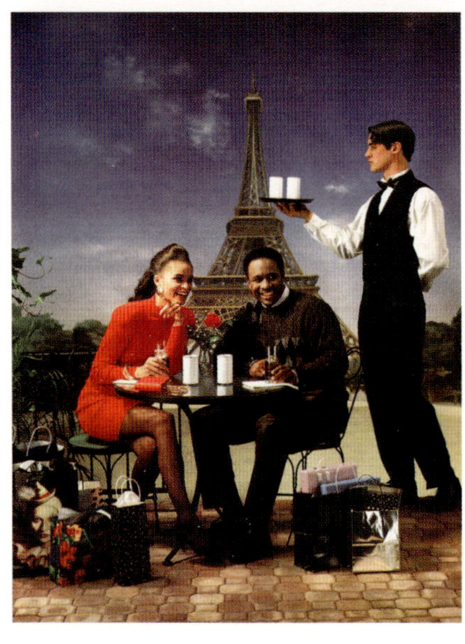

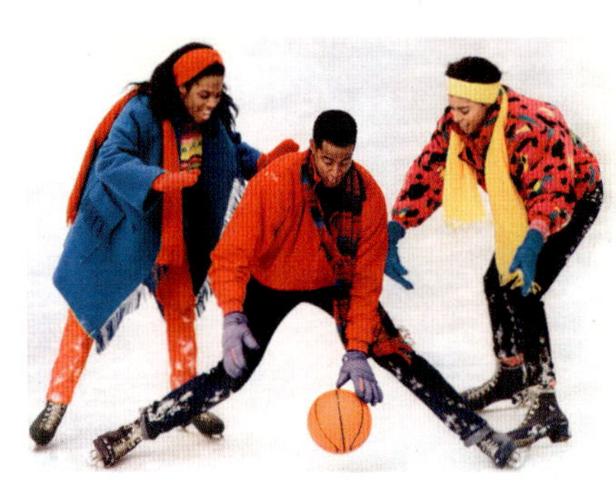

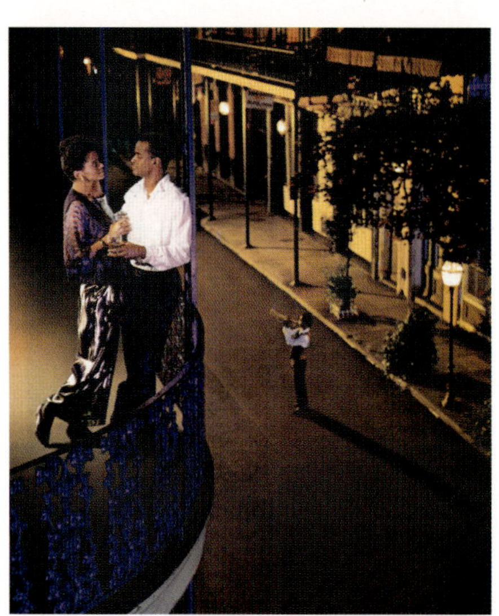

Left column, top to bottom: *McM.L.K. 1986/2007*, 2007; *Get Off On the Right Foot 1988/2007*, 2007; *Just for the Taste of It 1989/2007*, 2007; Middle column, top to bottom: *Let Beauty Go to Your Head 1987/2007*, 2007; *Wanted: Tall, dark stranger for long lasting relationship...seeking smoking satisfaction. 1988/2007*, 2007; *Alive with Pleasure 1990/2007*, 2007; Right column, top to bottom: *The Refreshest 1987/2007*, 2007; *It Could Happen to You 1989/2007*, 2007; *Late Night, Soft Lights 1990/2007*, 2007, acquired in 2007

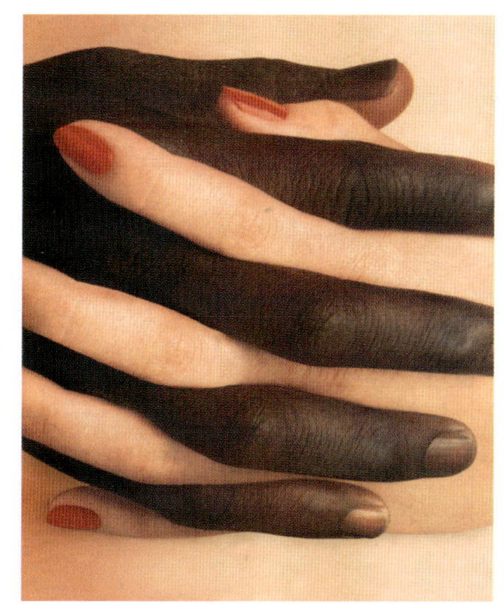

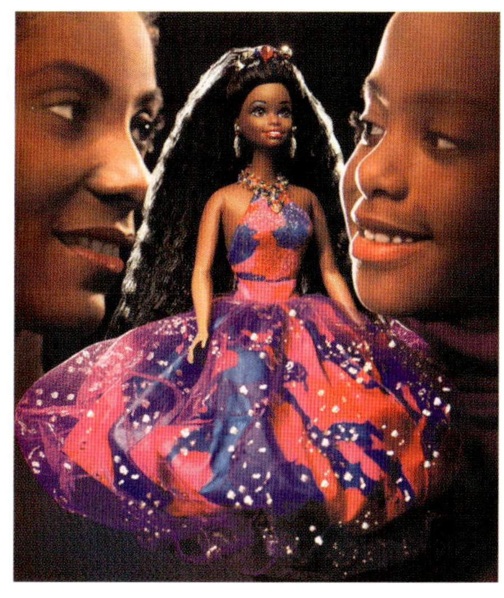

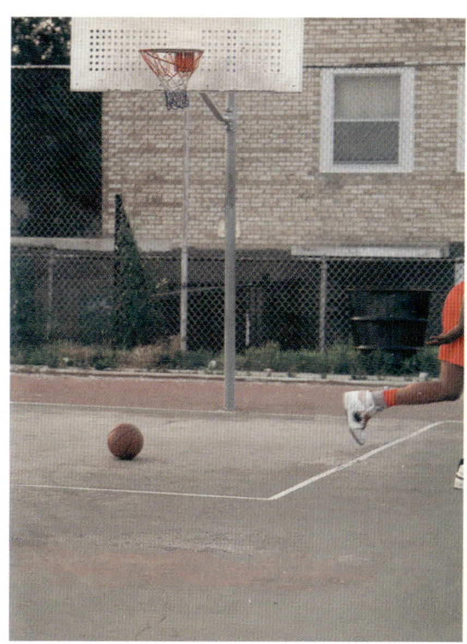

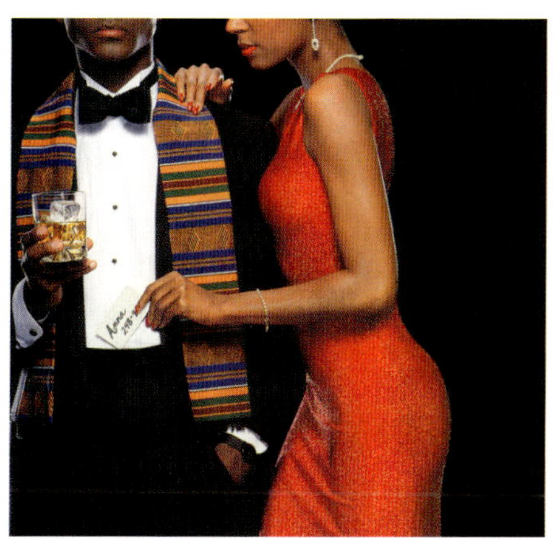

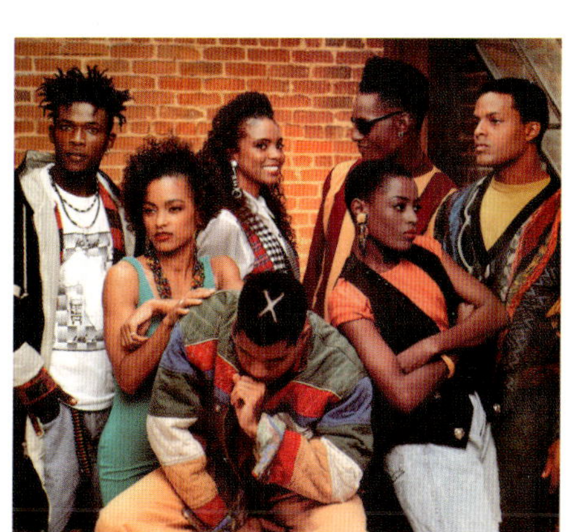

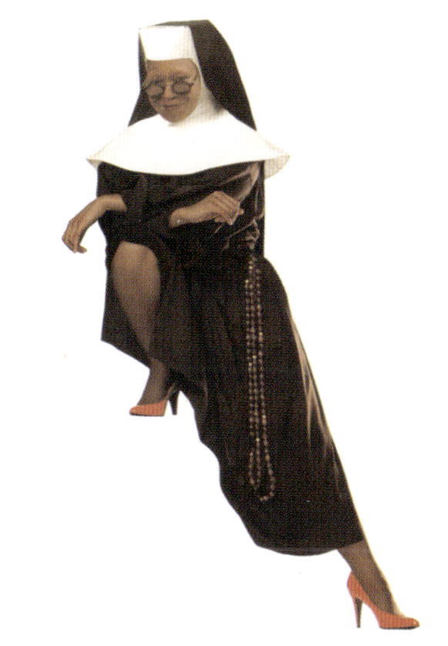

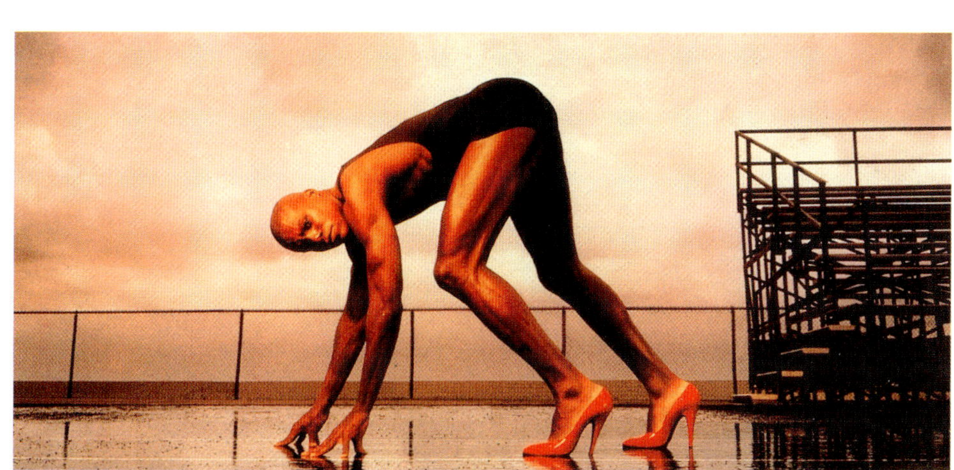

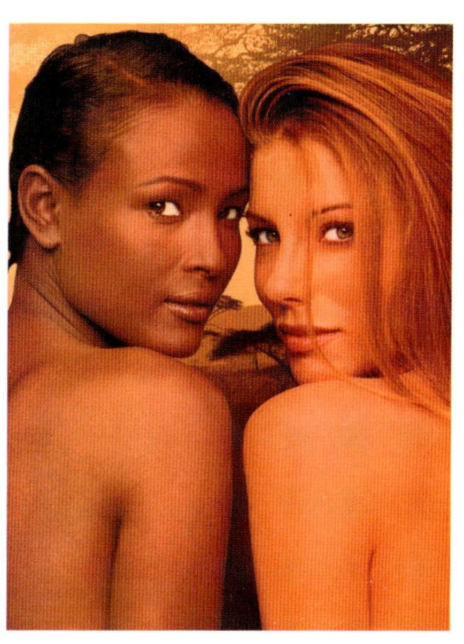

Left column, top to bottom: *Jungle Fever 1991/2007*, 2007; *Mist Behavin' 1992/2008*, 2008; *Power Is Nothing Without Control 1994/2008*, 2008; Middle column, top to bottom: *Now there's a doll that can make a real difference in her life: Shani, the first black Barbie. 1991/2007*, 2007; *By Any Means Necessary 1993/2008*, 2008; Right column, top to bottom: *Mama's Cooking Cornbread! 1992/2006*, 2006; *The Gidget of Hunter's Point 1993/2007*, 2007; *From the Heart of Africa Comes a Fragrance to Capture the Heart of Every Woman 1994/2008*, 2008, acquired in 2007

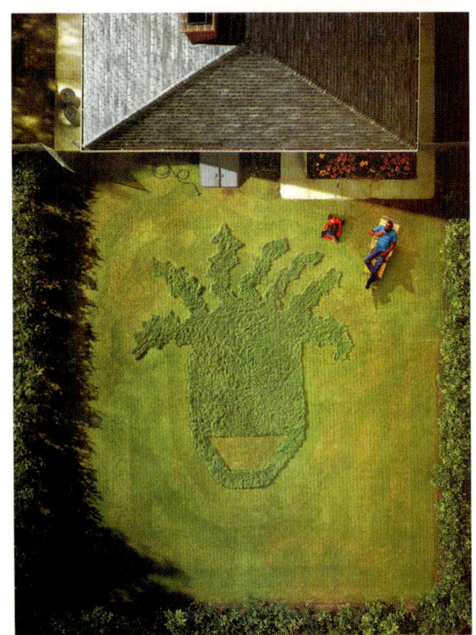

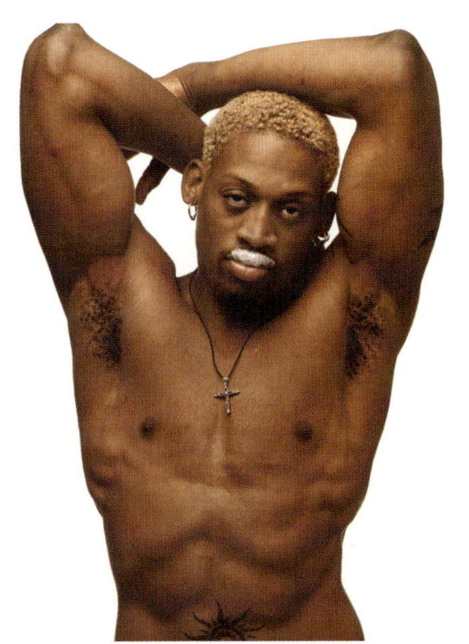

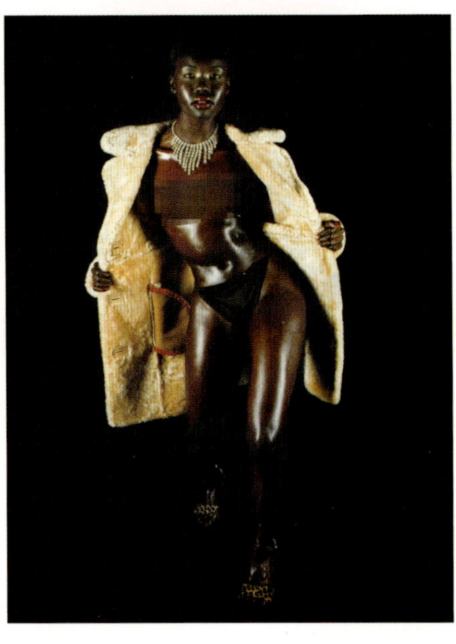

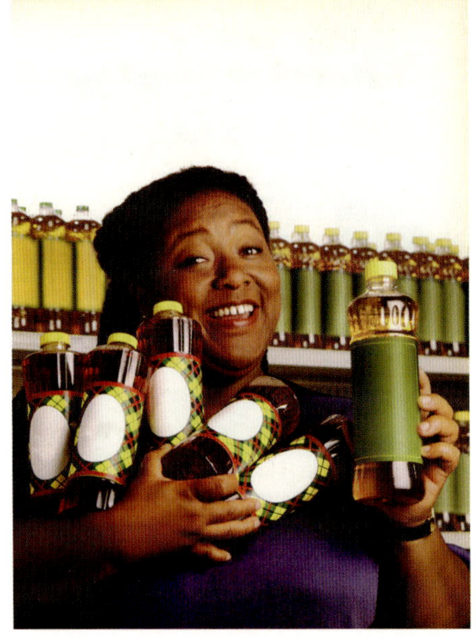

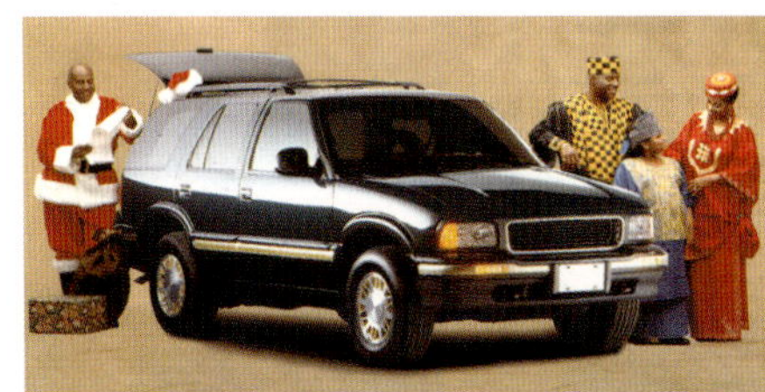

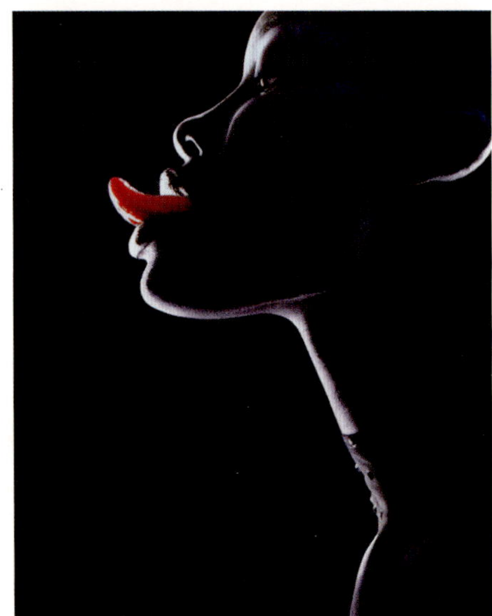

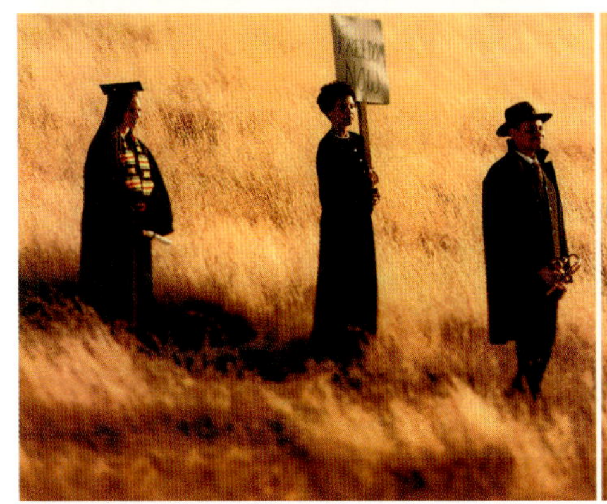

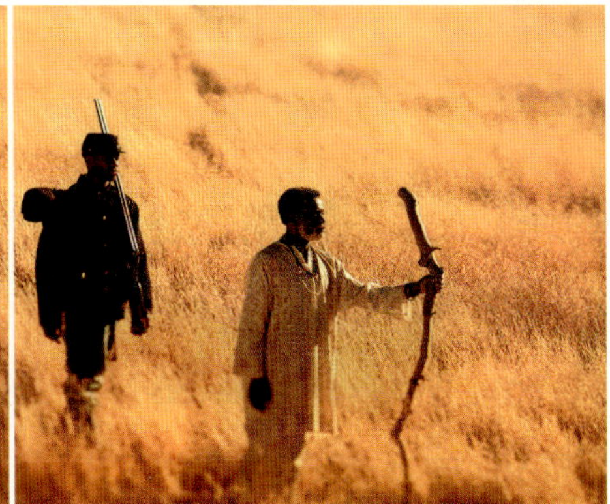

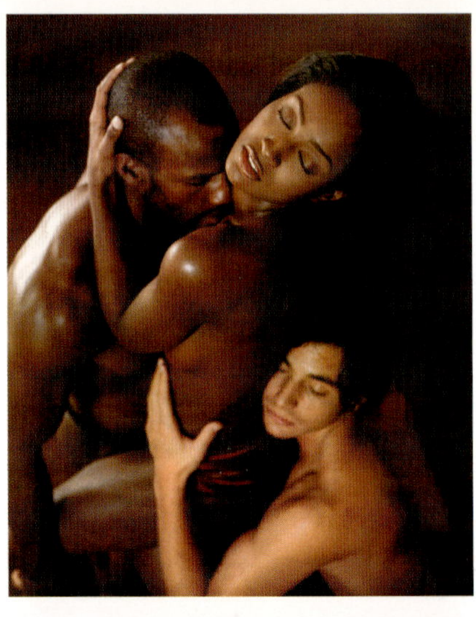

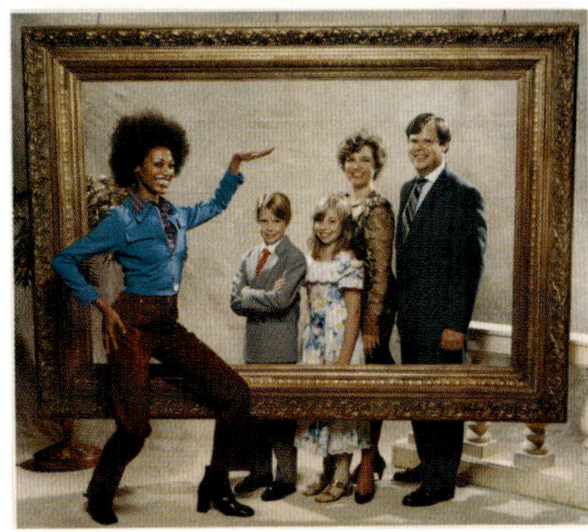

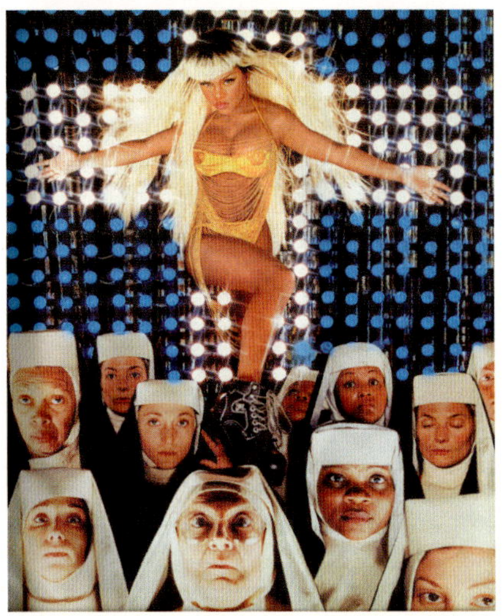

Left column, top to bottom: *It's a Great American Custom 1995/2008*, 2008; *Gotten 1996/2007*, 2007; *Ode to the Ill Nana 1998/2007*, 2007; Middle column, top to bottom: *Smell Like a Bargain 1995/2008*, 2008; *For the African and the American in You 1997/2007*, 2007; *Oh, Behave; Smooth Exotic Vivid Taste 1999/2006*, 2006; *Once upon a time in America there were no slaves 2001/2006*, 2006; Right column, top to bottom: *Be Careful What You Wish For 1996/2008*, 2008; *Celebrate Your Specialness 1997/2008*, 2008; *Holy Boot! 1998/2008*, 2008, acquired in 2007

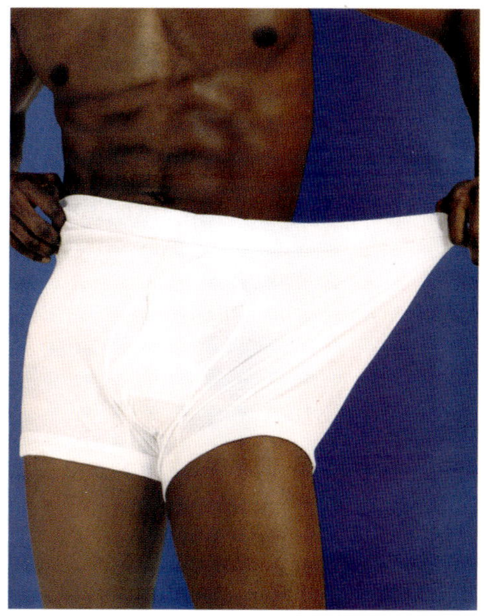

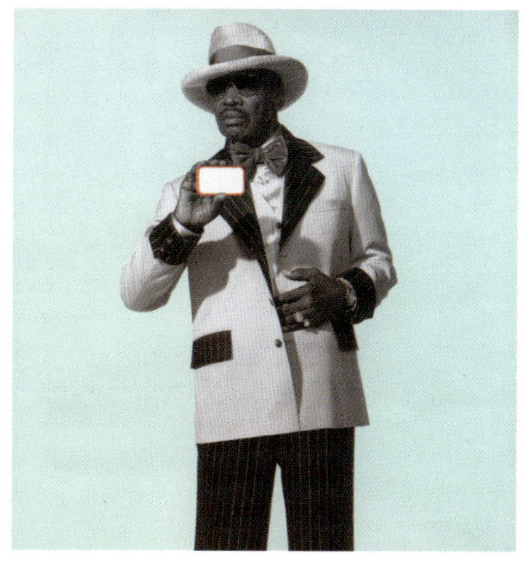

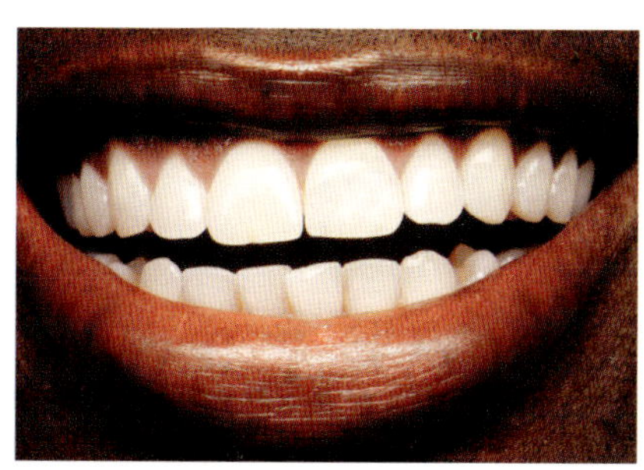

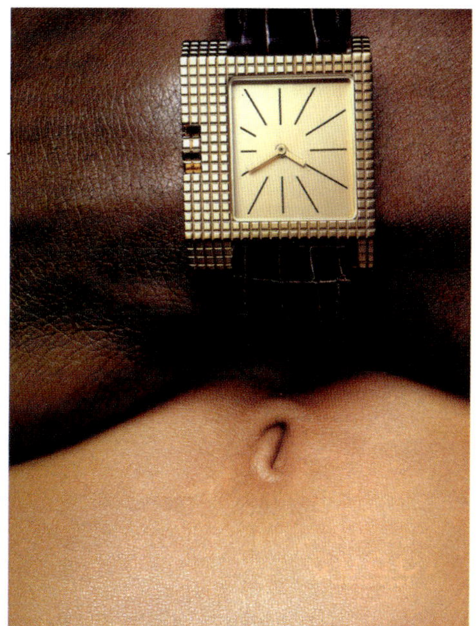

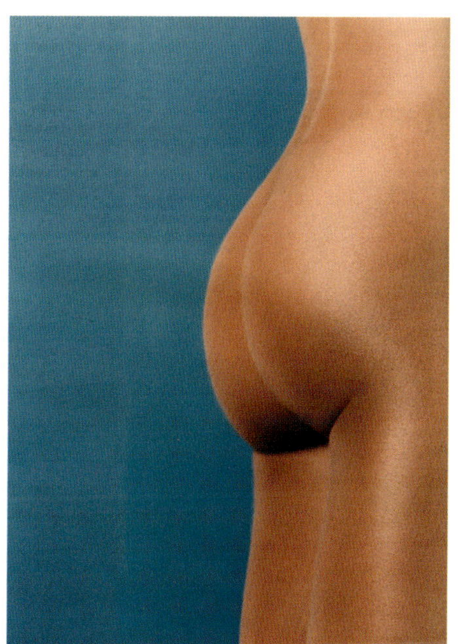

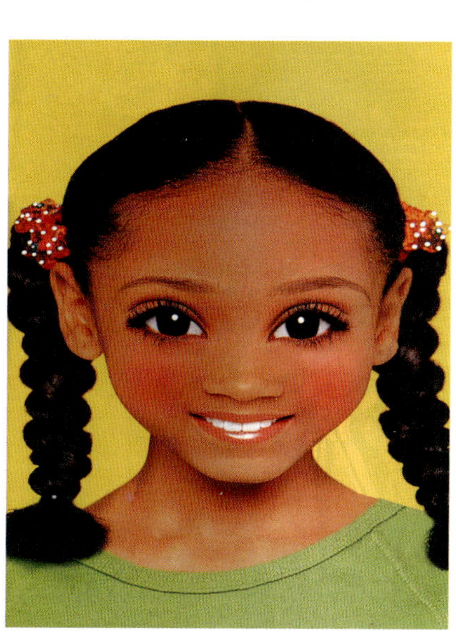

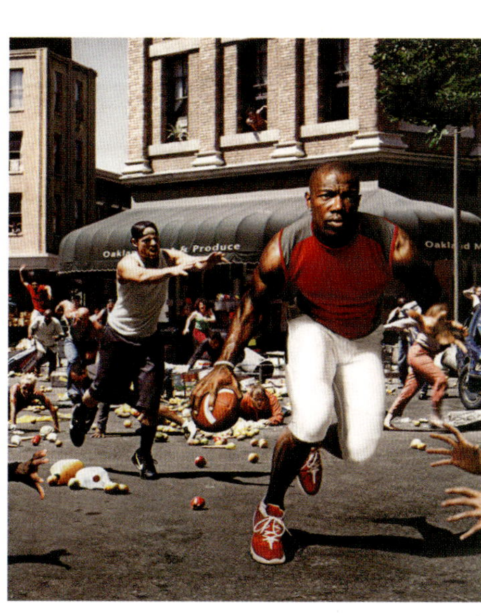

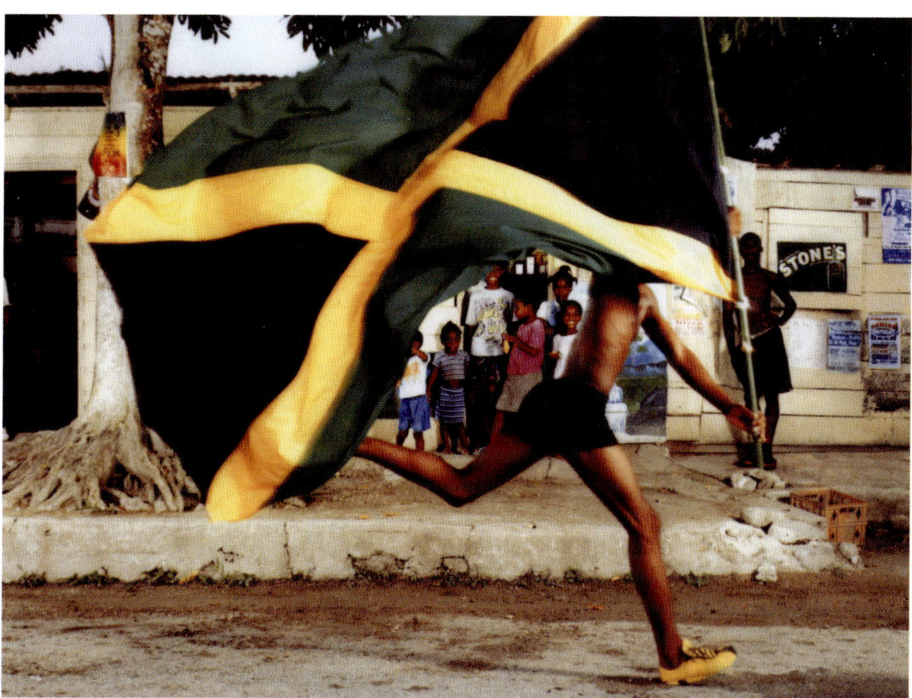

Left column, top to bottom: *Things That Make You Go Oooh! 1999/2006*, 2006; *Cucci #2: It's Time for Jungle Fever 2001/2006*, 2006; *Liberation of T.O.: "I'm not goin' back to work for massa' in dat darned field!" 2003/2005*, 2005; Middle column, top to bottom: *Petey Wheatstraw: The Devil's Son-In Law 2000/2006*, 2006; *A Moisturizer That Firms as it Tightens? Bet Your Bottom Dollar! 2002/2008*, 2008; *An Unidentified Jamaican Boy Used the Puma H Street Running Shoe to Run for his Freedom 2003/2005*, 2005; Right column, top to bottom: *Things That Make You Go Hmmmmm?!! 2000/2006*, 2006; *Motion for Kids Allows Hair to be Blown Straighter 2002/2006*, 2006, acquired in 2007

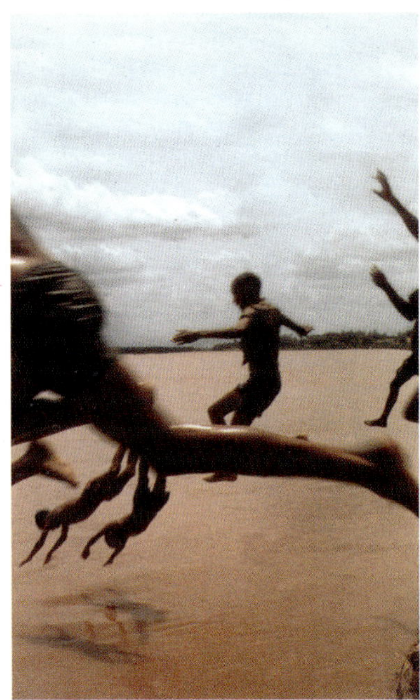

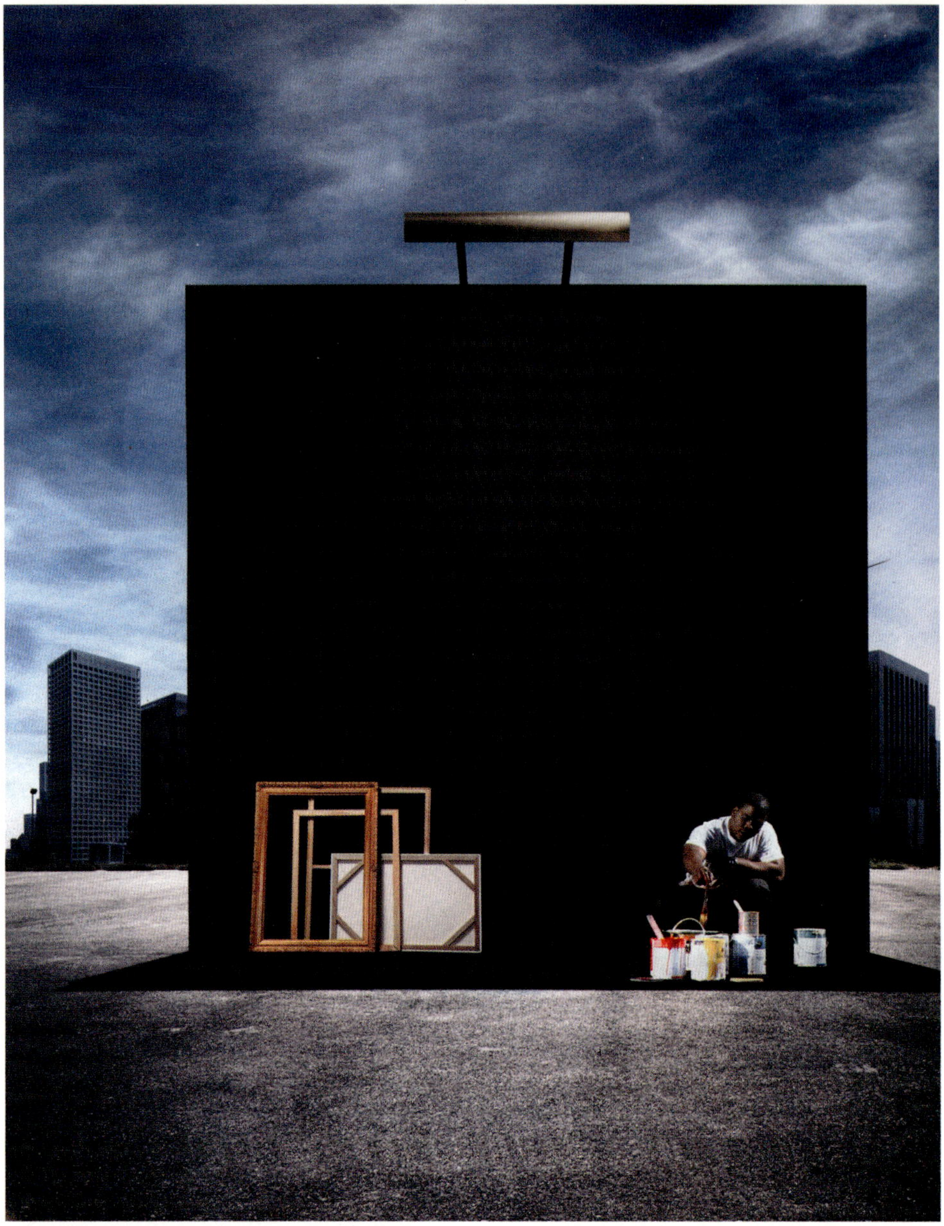

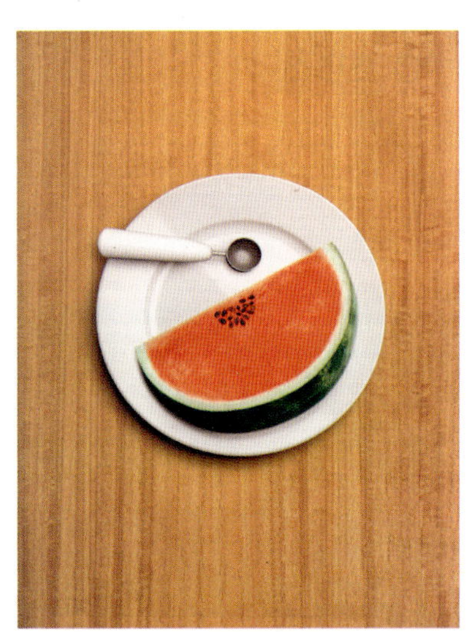

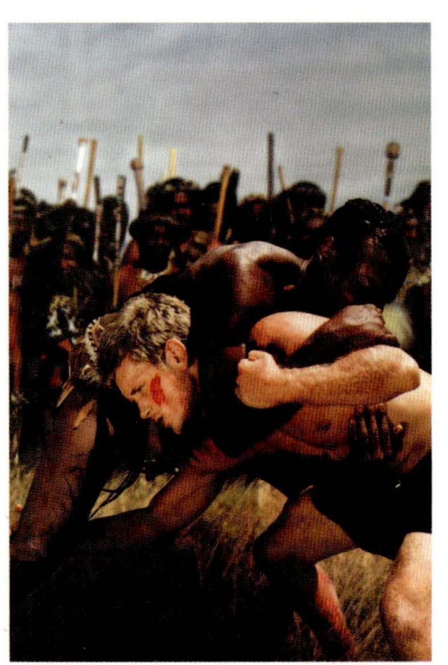

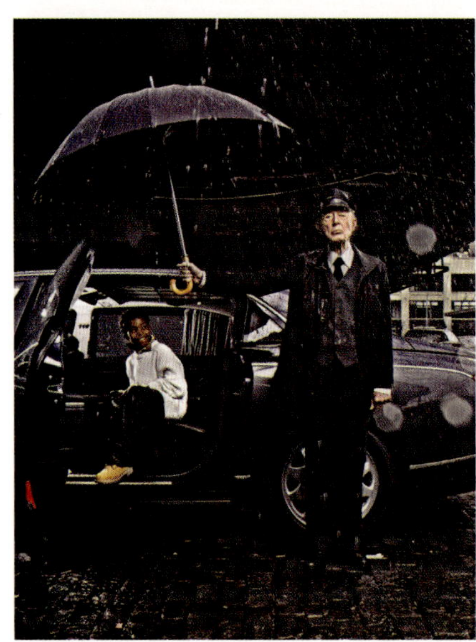

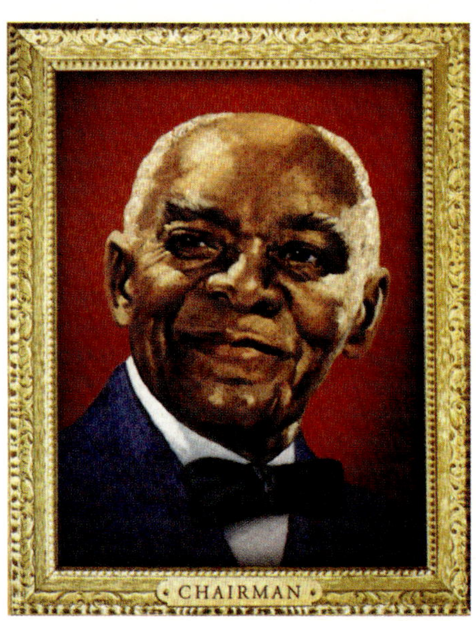

Left column, top to bottom: *Don't Let Them Catch You! 2004/2006*, 2006; *How to Market Kitty Litter to Black People: Ebony Magazine 2005/2006*, 2006; *Welcome to Full Contact Culture 2007/2008*, 2008; Right column, top to bottom: *We are the Canvas 2004/2008*, 2008; *Membership has its Privileges 2006/2008*, 2008; *After 61 Years of Service, I Ben, Promoted. 2007/2007*, 2008, acquired in 2007

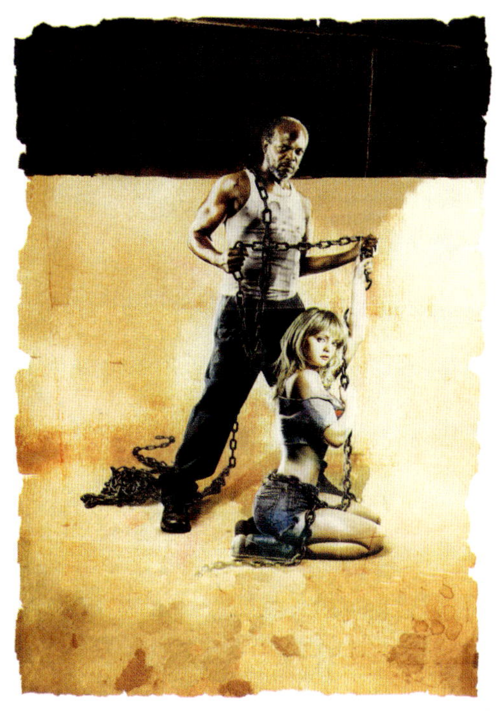

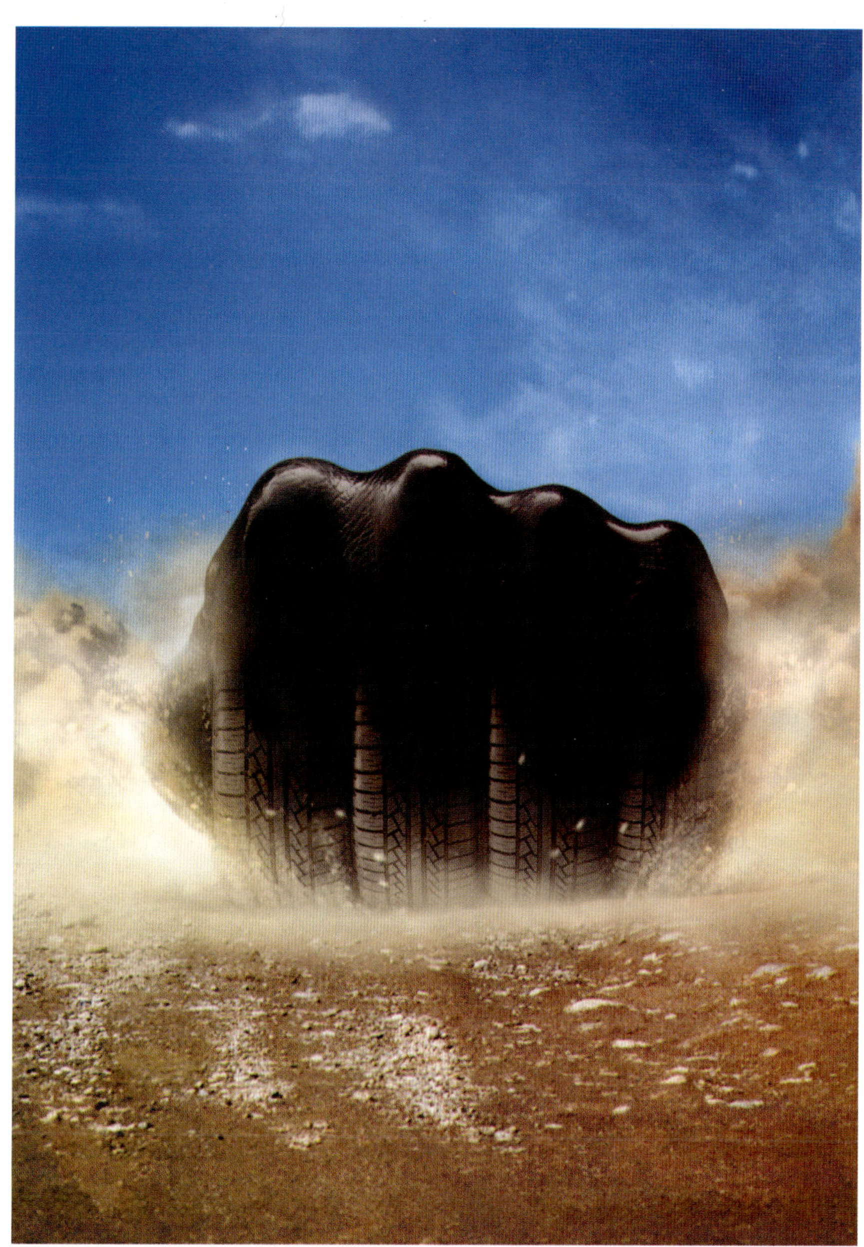

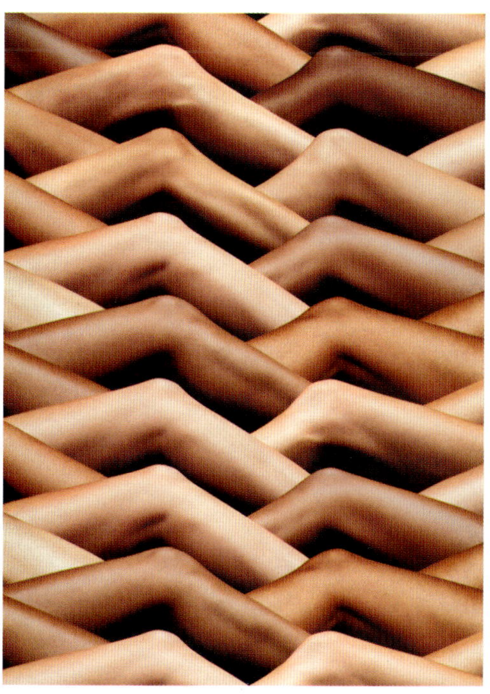

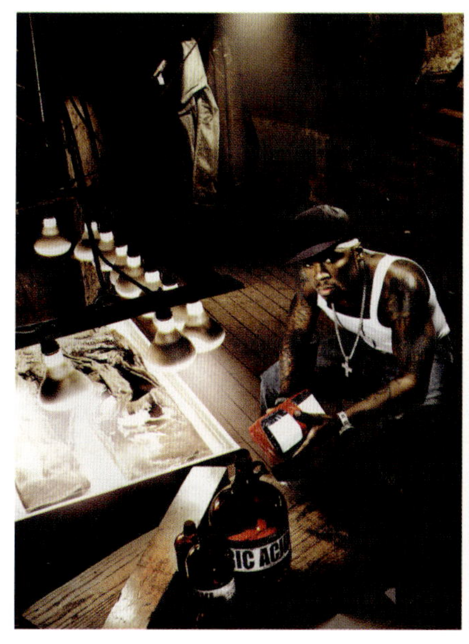

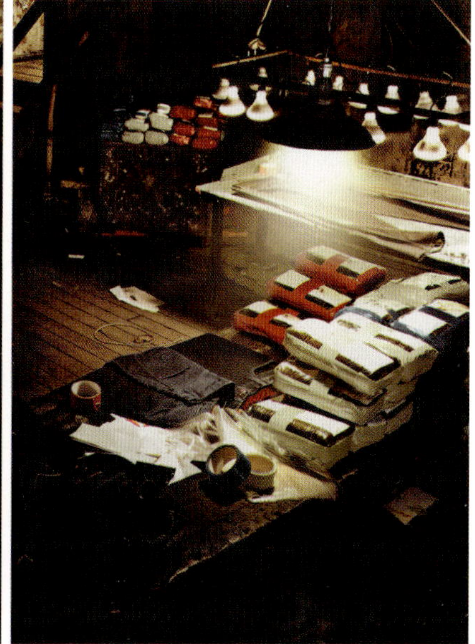

Left column, top to bottom: *Funny How Things Change 2007/2007*, 2007; *Your Skin has the Power to Protect You 2008/2008*, 2008; Right column, top to bottom: *21st Century Soul Power 2005/2006*, 2006; *Untitleable 2006/2008*, 2008, acquired in 2007

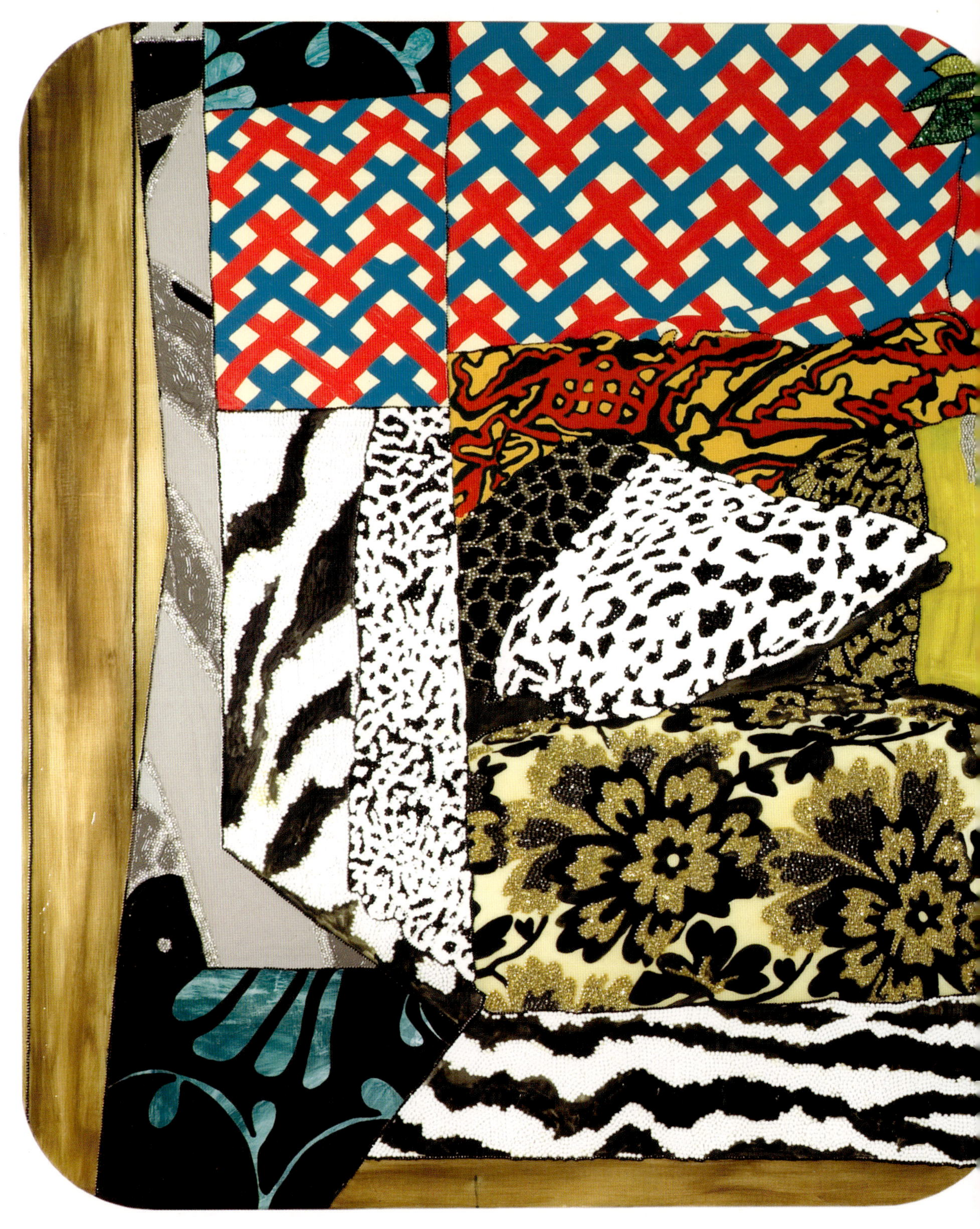

 MICKALENE THOMAS

Baby I Am Ready Now, 2007, acrylic, rhinestone and enamel on panel, diptych, overall 72 x 132 in. (182.9 x 335.3 cm), acquired in 2007

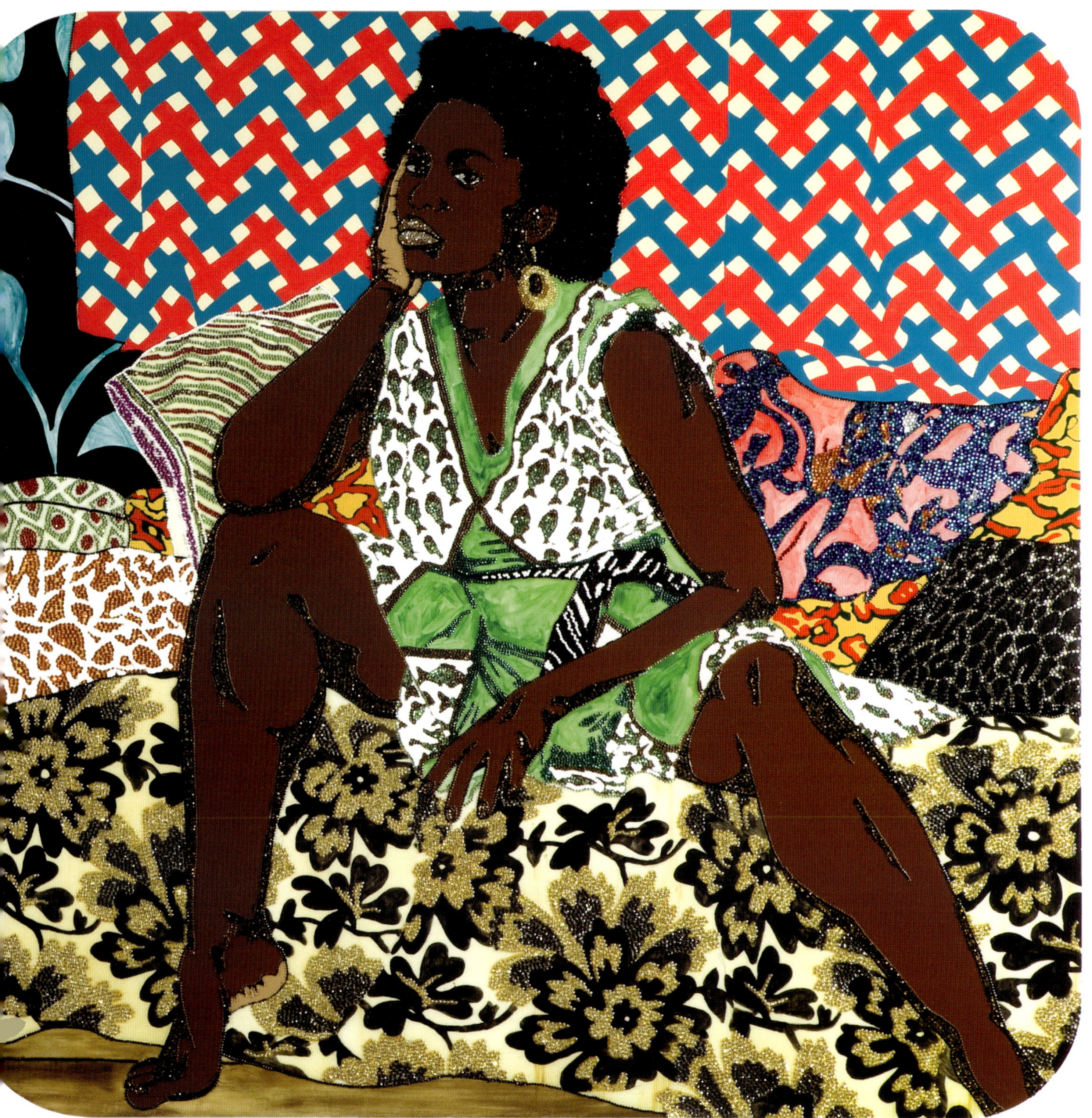

In *Baby I Am Ready Now*, the profusion of different, shifting patterns dominates. This painting is the first that I made working directly from a source collage. The method of collage naturally encourages the fracturing of spatial planes and breaks up the linear flow of composition. The basis of the work, however, rests firmly in the photograph taken in the installation I created as a specific interior space for the model. As a diptych, the piece sets up two opposing but complementary fields. On one side is a figure in an interior space, absorbed in her thoughts. On the other side the space breaks down into abstract pattern without the centering presence of the figure.

Mickalene Thomas

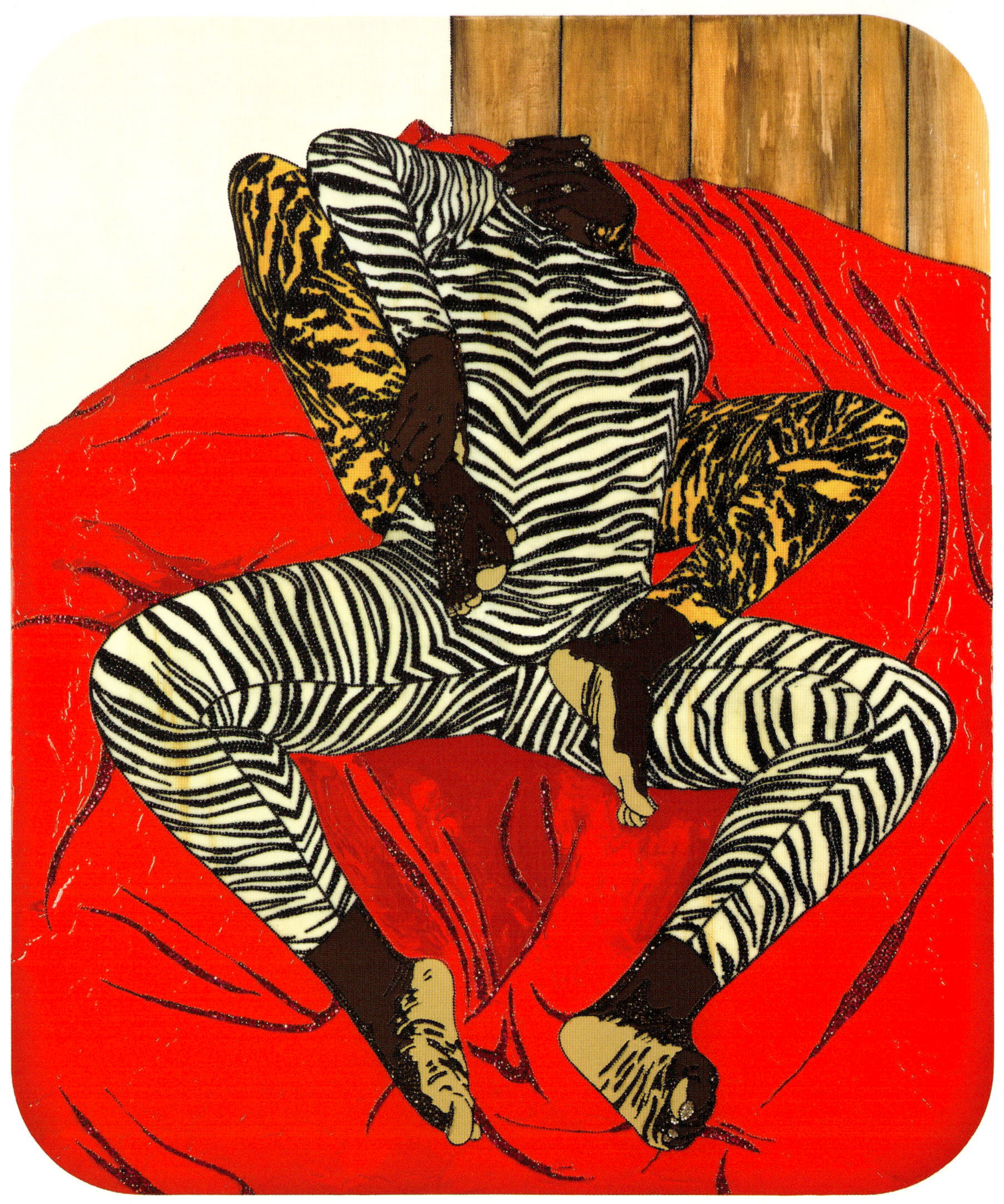

Portraits of Quanikah continues the deconstructive work of self-portraiture begun in the "Brawlin Spitfire" series. Each panel spotlights a different aspect of my own personality in the guise of my alter egos – Quanikah and the Amazonian wrestler. This piece heralds a formal shift in the paintings, breaking the pictorial space into different physical planes and using the grid as an overt reference to Pop Art and Andy Warhol in particular. These formal developments carry into my later paintings, further complicating and enriching the subject matter of self, muse, and painting. While *Portraits of Quanikah* is unmistakably a self-portrait, representative of an historical genre with specific parameters and traditions, it is a self-portrait that reflects a contemporary conception of the bifurcated self.

Mickalene Thomas

I Still Love You (You Still Love Me), 2007, rhinestones, acrylic and enamel on panel, 72 x 60 in. (183 x 152.5 cm), acquired in 2009

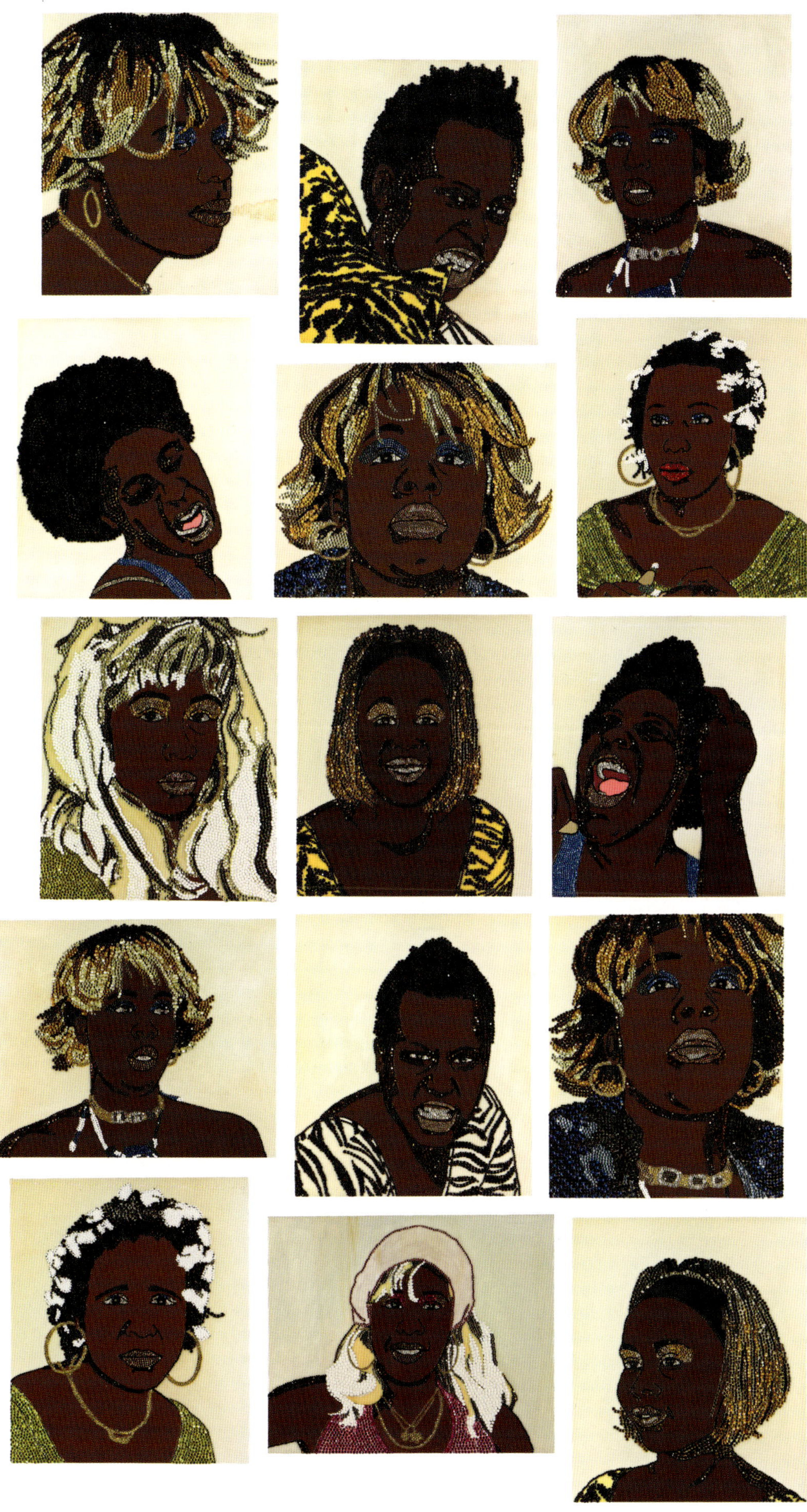

Portraits of Quanikah, 2006, acrylic, rhinestone and enamel on panel, 15 panels, overall 70 x 126 in. (178.8 x 320 cm), acquired in 2006

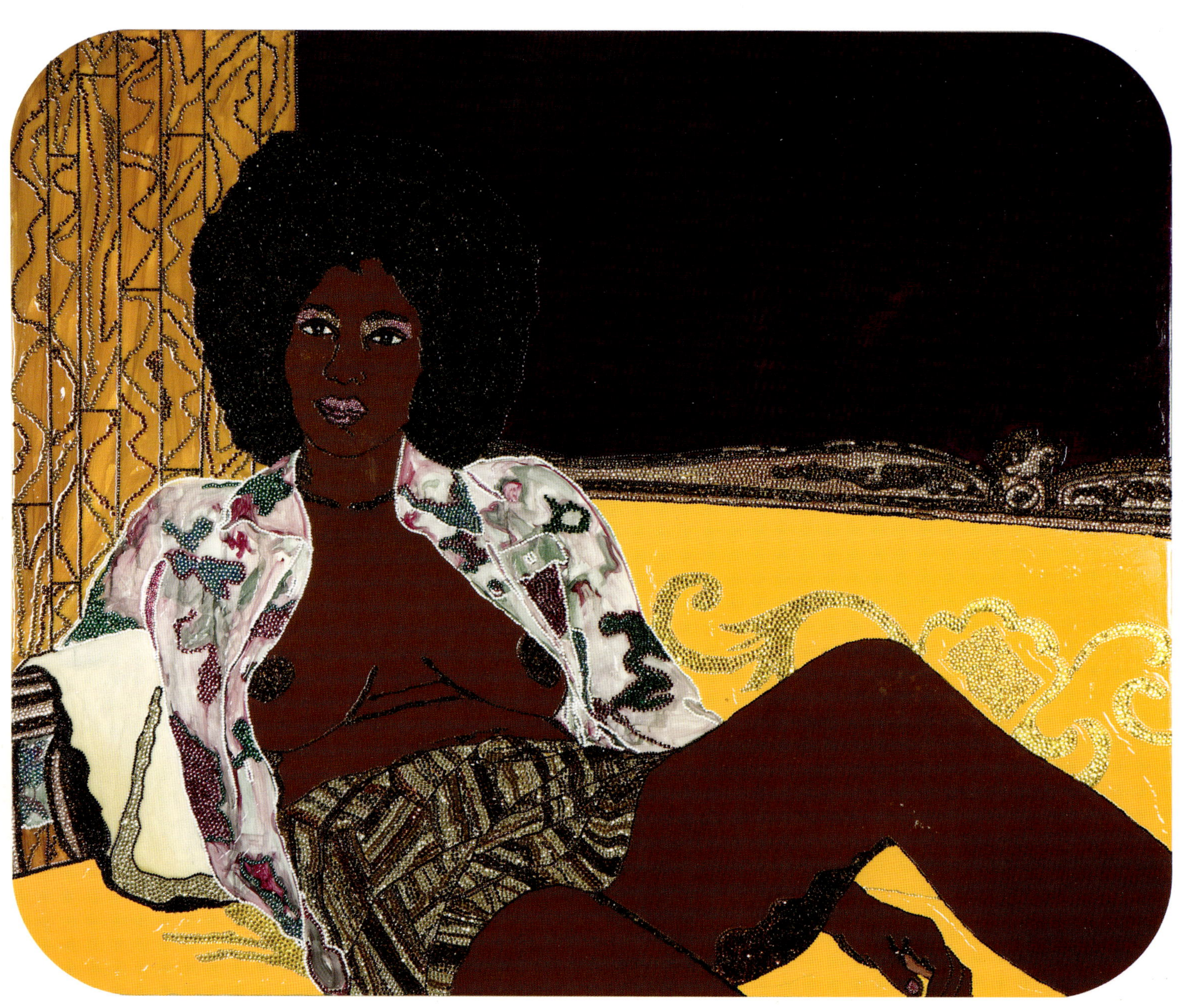

 MICKALENE THOMAS *Hotter than July*, 2005, acrylic, rhinestone and enamel on panel, 60 x 72 in. (152.4 x 182.9 cm), acquired in 2005

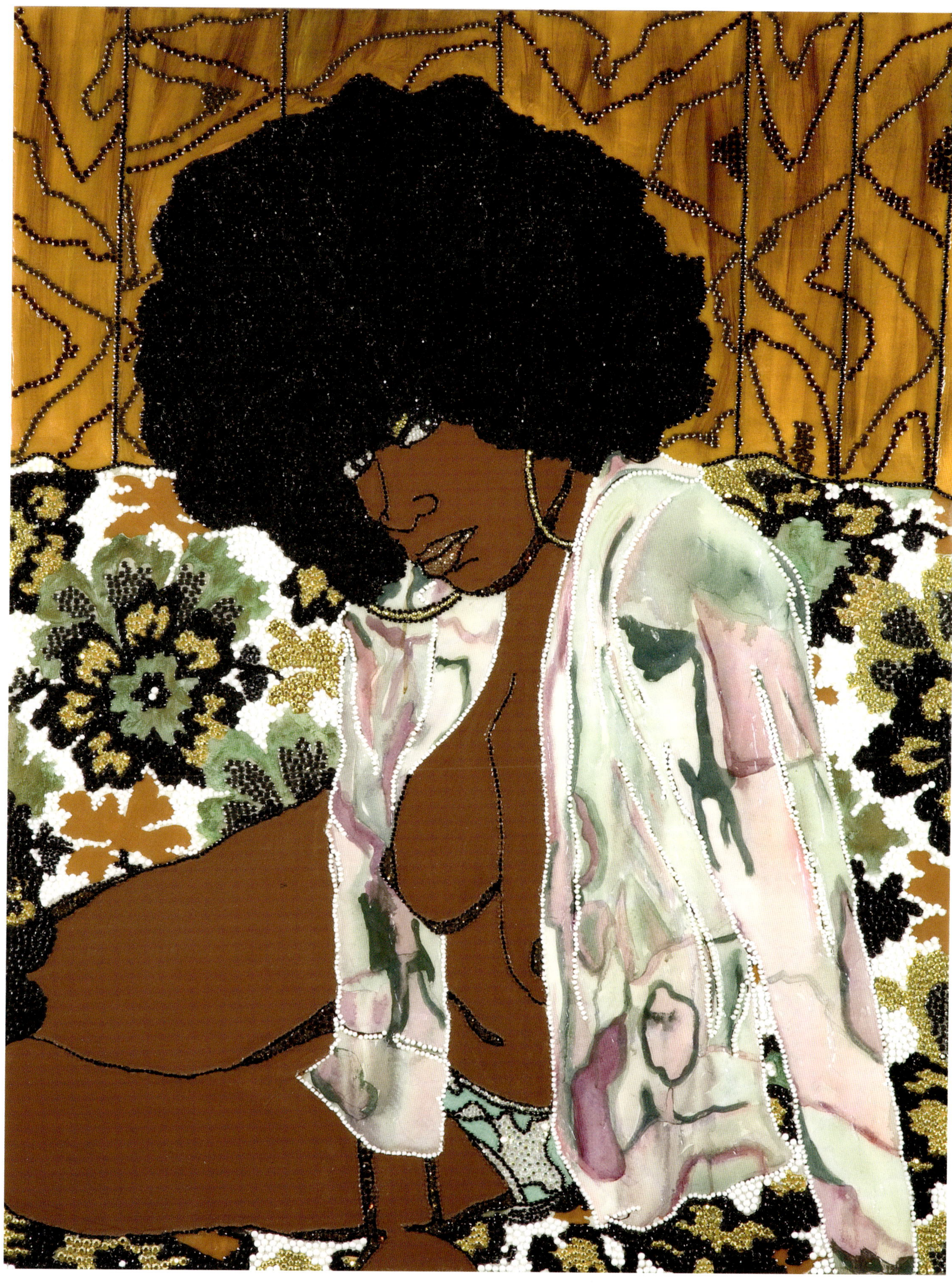

Whatever You Want, 2004, acrylic, rhinestone and enamel on panel, 48 x 36 in. (121.9 x 91.4 cm), acquired in 2005

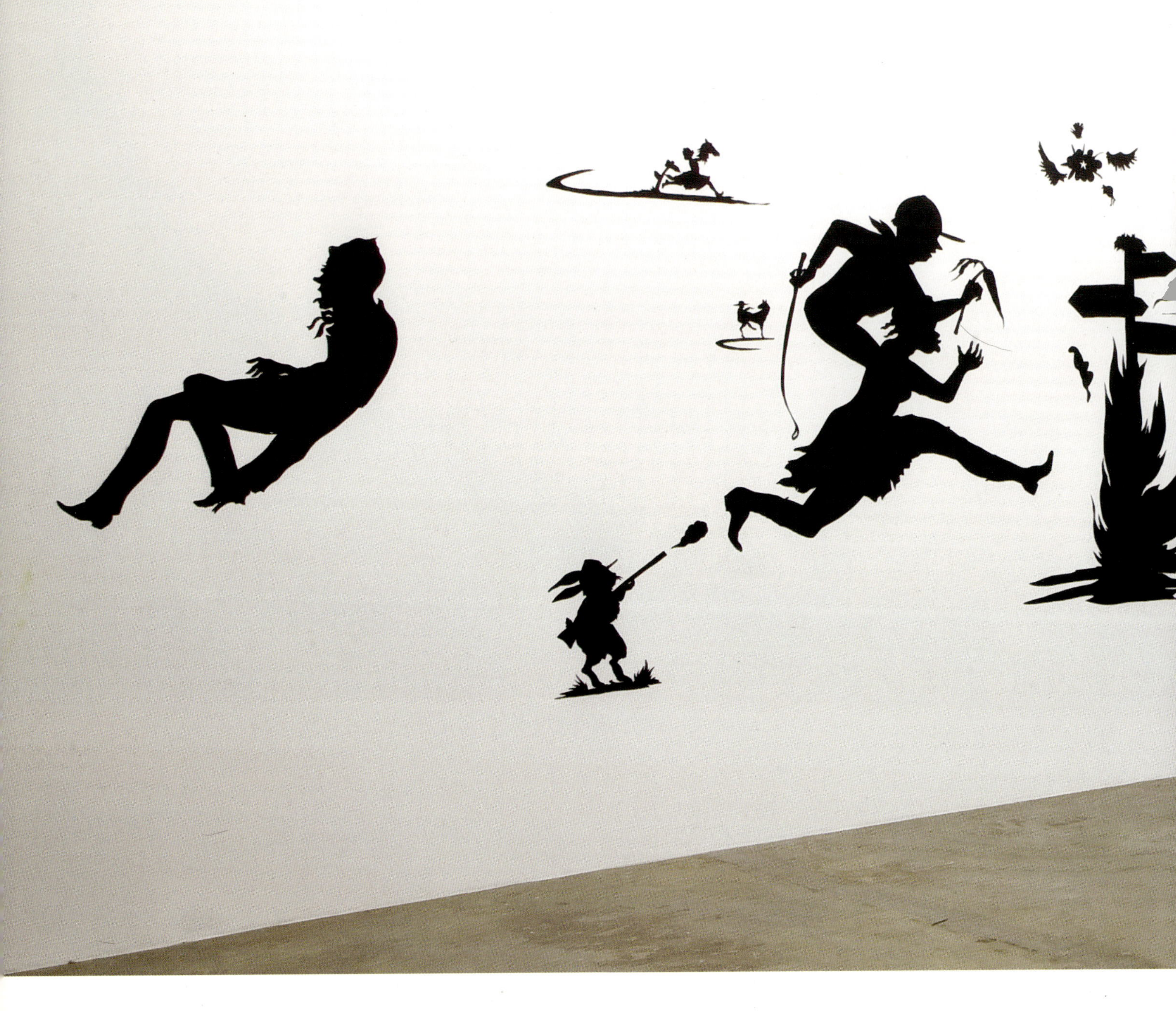

 KARA WALKER *Camptown Ladies*, 1998, paper, 8 x 55 ft (247.7 x 1691.6 cm), acquired in 1998

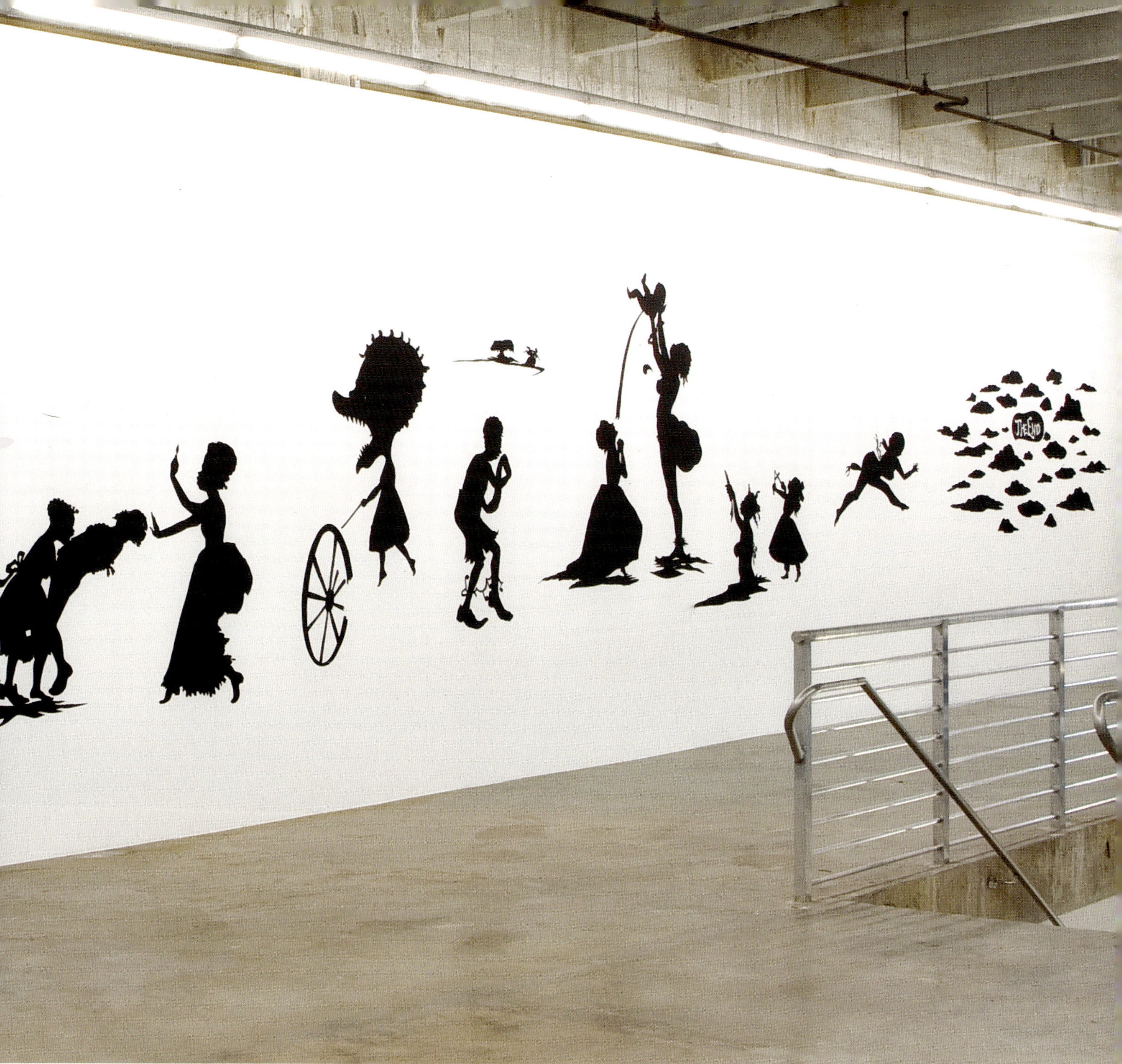

"Camptown ladies sing this song, dooh-dah! Dooh-dah! Camptown racetrack's five miles long, oh dooh-dah day!"

So goes the first line of Stephen Foster's popular minstrel nonsense song "Camptown Races," composed in 1850. A minstrel song, intended to be performed in blackface by white performers, in a raucous style intended to mimic African-American folk traditions, "Camptown Races" is about nothing but affect. It's a jaunty, jumpy sing-along. The lyrics resist meaning and so I took this opacity as a starting point for an artwork: Who are the Camptown ladies? What is doo- dah? Why do they sing it? Is it a work song for runaway slaves? A sexual allusion? Magic language? And where is Camptown? Is it someplace or anyplace? Can I take the liberty of making a nonsense piece that recasts the caricatures of the minstrel stage? Change the tune away from the fantasy of racial harmonizing?

Kara Walker

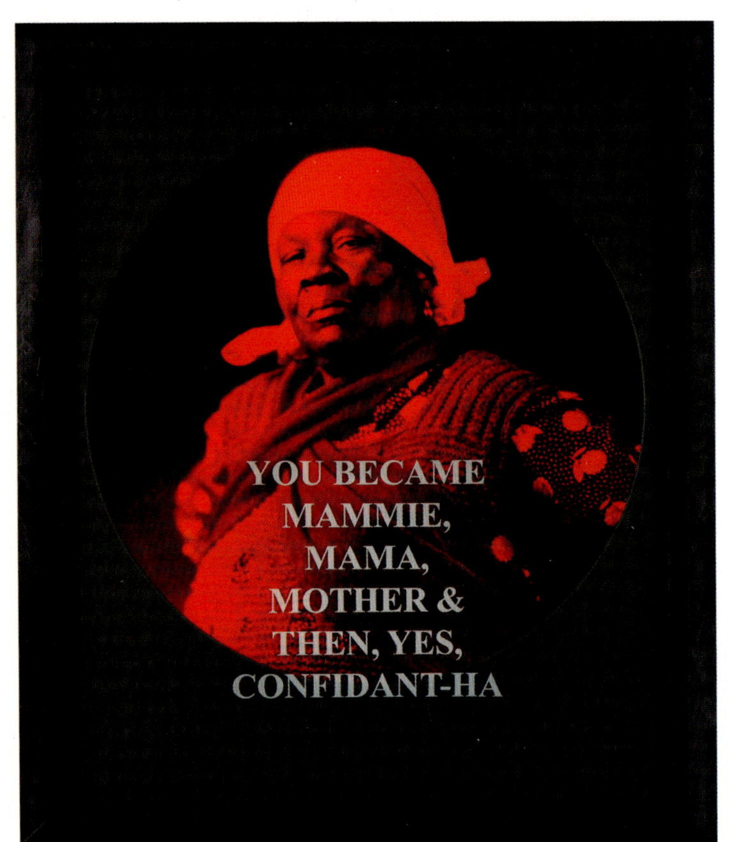

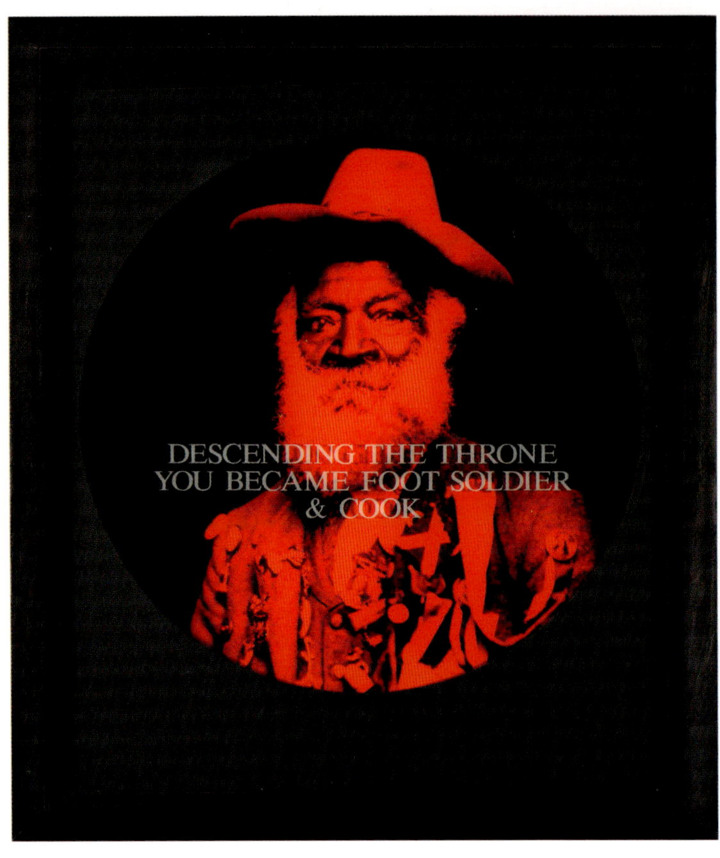

You Became Mammie, Mama, Mother, & Then, Yes, Confident-Ha/ Descending the Throne (from From Here I Saw What Happened and I Cried), 1995-1996, two chromogenic prints with sandblasted text on glass, ed. 6/10, each 26 1/2 x 22 3/4 in. (67.3 x 57.8 cm), acquired in 2008

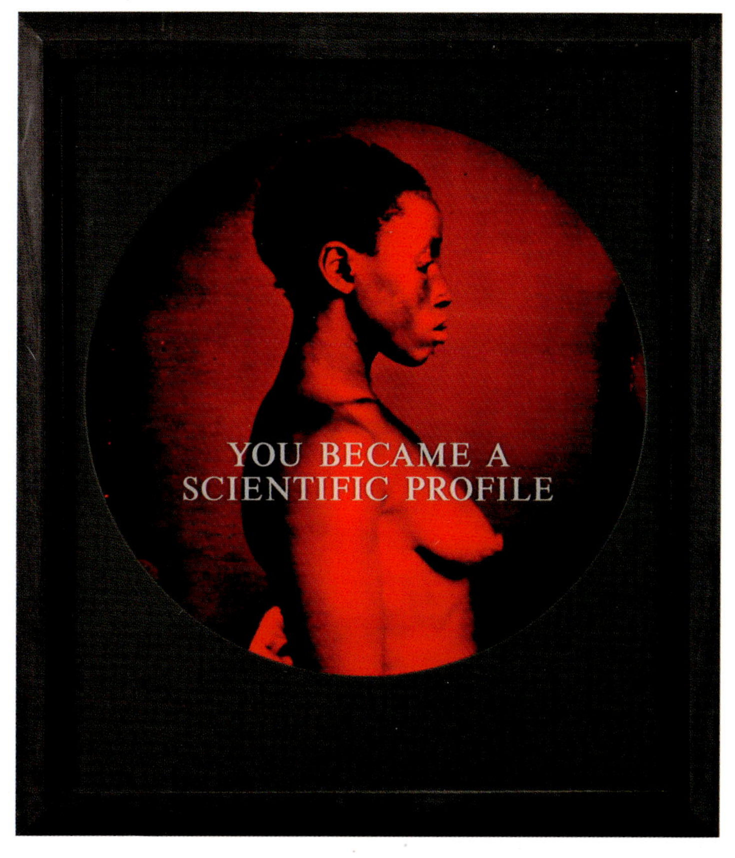

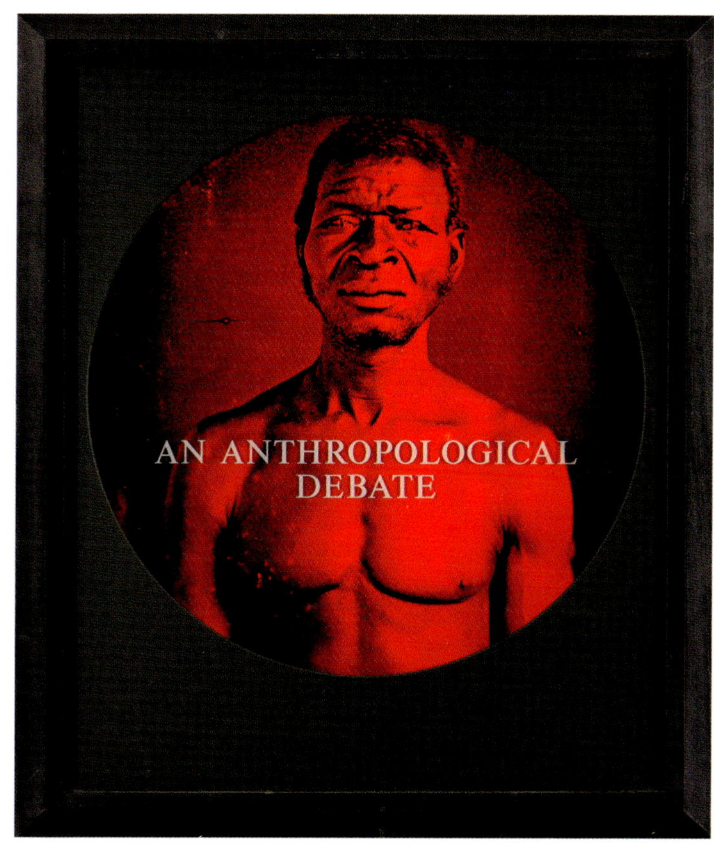

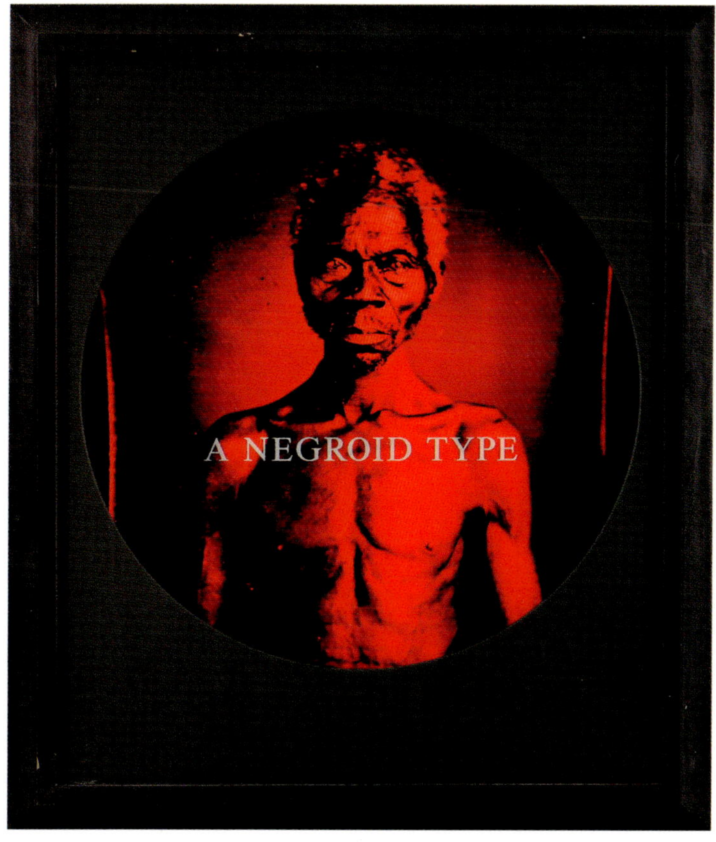

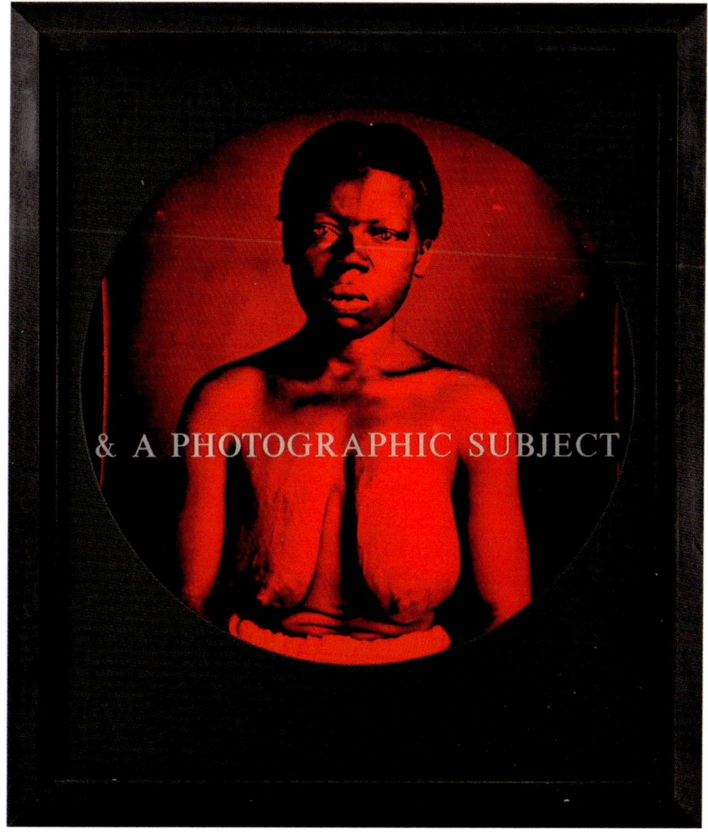

You Became a Scientific Profile/ An Anthropological Debate/ A Negroid Type/ & A Photographic Subject (from From Here I Saw What Happened and I Cried series), 1995-1996, four chromogenic prints with sandblasted text on glass, ed. 2/10, each 26 3/4 x 22 3/4 in. (68 x 57.8 cm), acquired in 2008

Equestrian Portrait of the Count Duke Olivares, is based on a Velázquez and comes out of a series of paintings titled 'Rumors of War'. Rumors of War is a body of paintings concerned specifically with the depiction of large-scale military portraiture. Much of my work is devoted to the idea of distilling masculine power down to some of its most essential components within the history of Western easel painting, and in this case military portraiture stands in for the absolute proxy of that idea. The depiction and scale shifts are oftentimes misleading. In this painting I used a real horse stand-in only to find that, in the depiction of military equestrian portraiture, the male to animal ratio was erroneous, and so I followed suit. The background components are derived from decorative wallpaper elements spanning from the late French Rococo of the 18th century, to the Arts and Crafts movement of the late 19th and early 20th centuries. Independent of period style, I chose elements that connote a sense of pedigree and Europhilia.

Kehinde Wiley

 Equestrian Portrait of the Count Duke Olivares, 2005, oil on canvas, 108 x 108 in. (274.3 x 274.3 cm), acquired in 2005

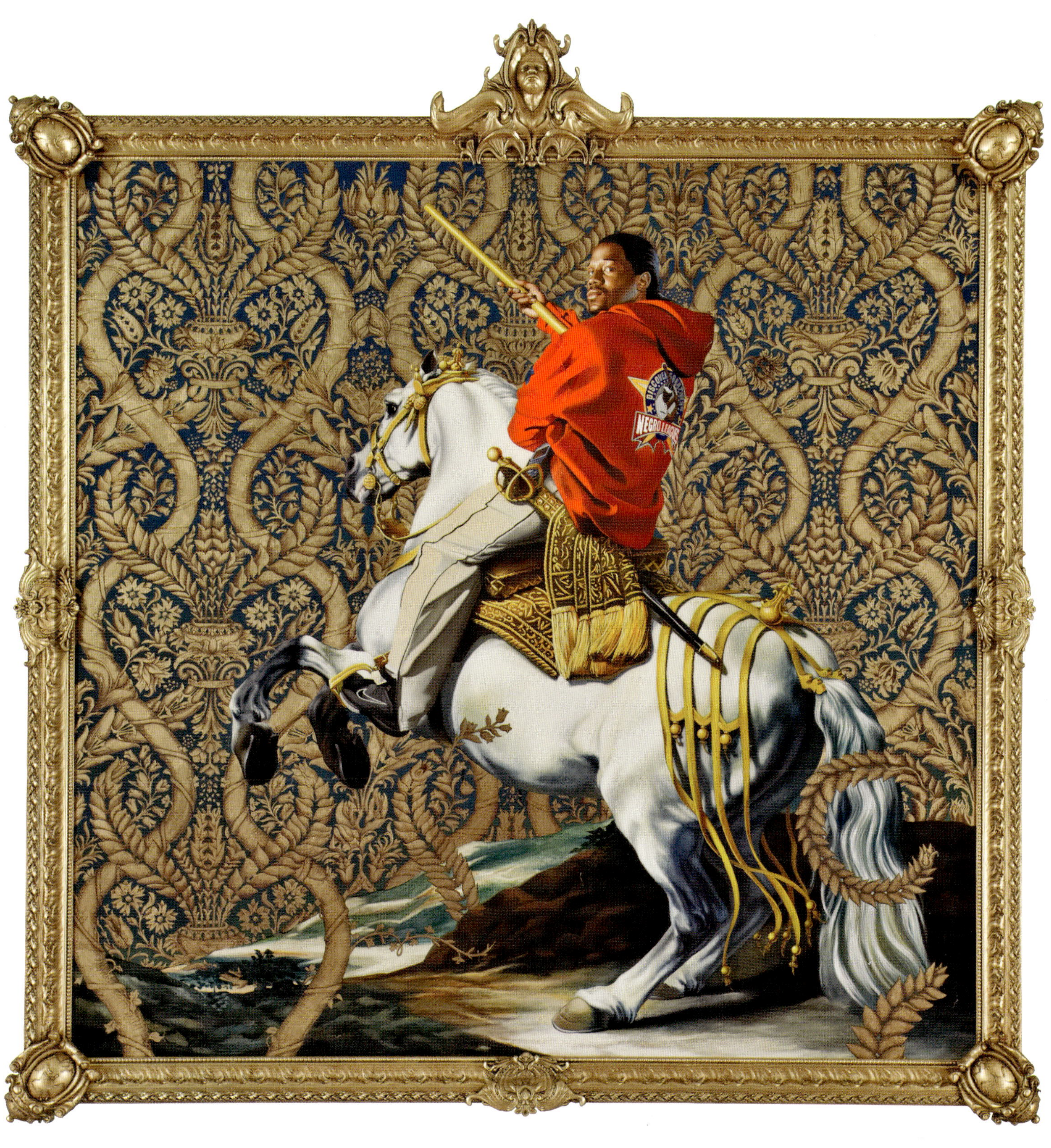
NEGRO LEAGUES

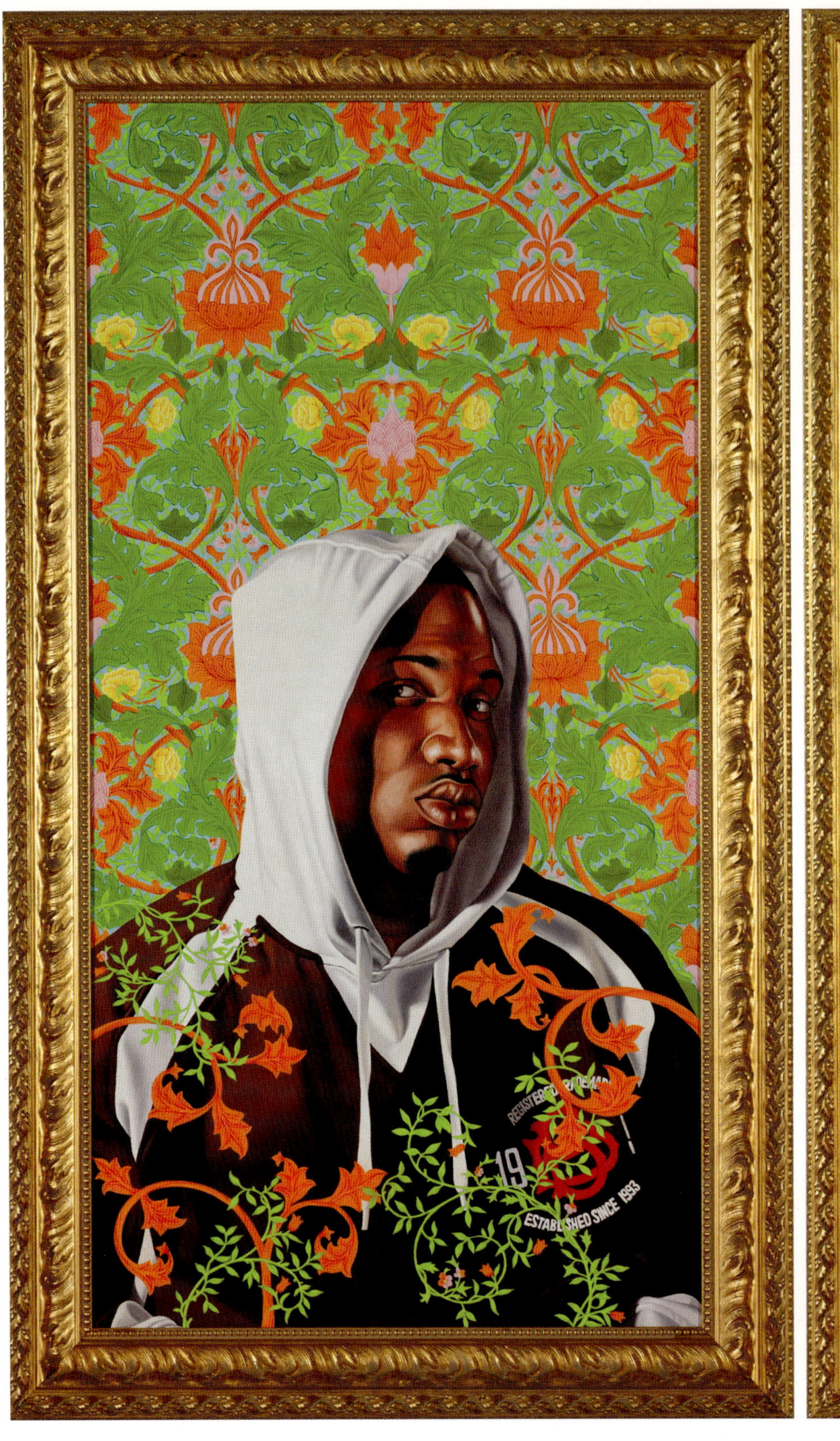

The Triple Portrait of Charles I was a preparatory painting designed to be a stand-in for use in the completion of formal portraits, be they sculptures or large paintings. In this case, three different angles were used to approximate the portrait so that other, more complicated portraits could be made. In the painting I'm actually taking a nod to the mug shot profile photograph that inspired the 'Passing/Posing' series of the early 2000s that gave rise to my career. Those were paintings

Triple Portrait of Charles I, 2007, oil and enamel on canvas, triptych, overall 82 x 135 in. (208.3 x 342.9 cm), acquired in 2007

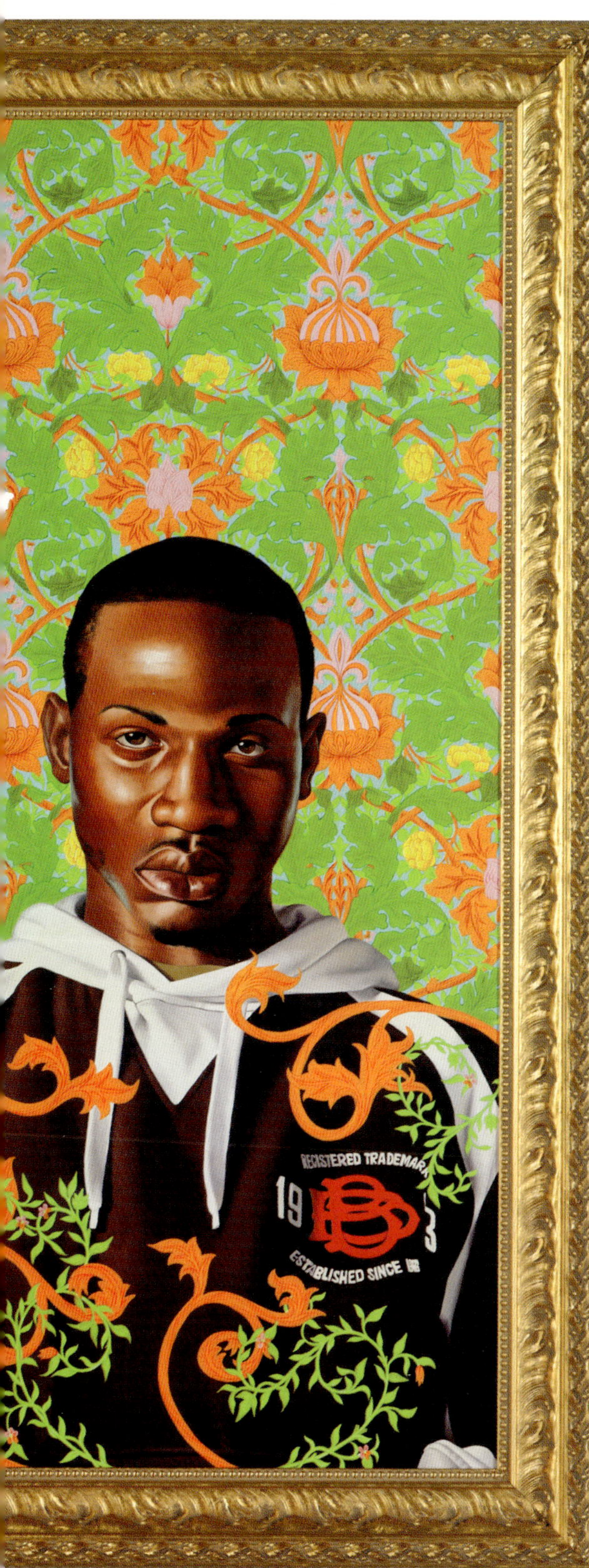

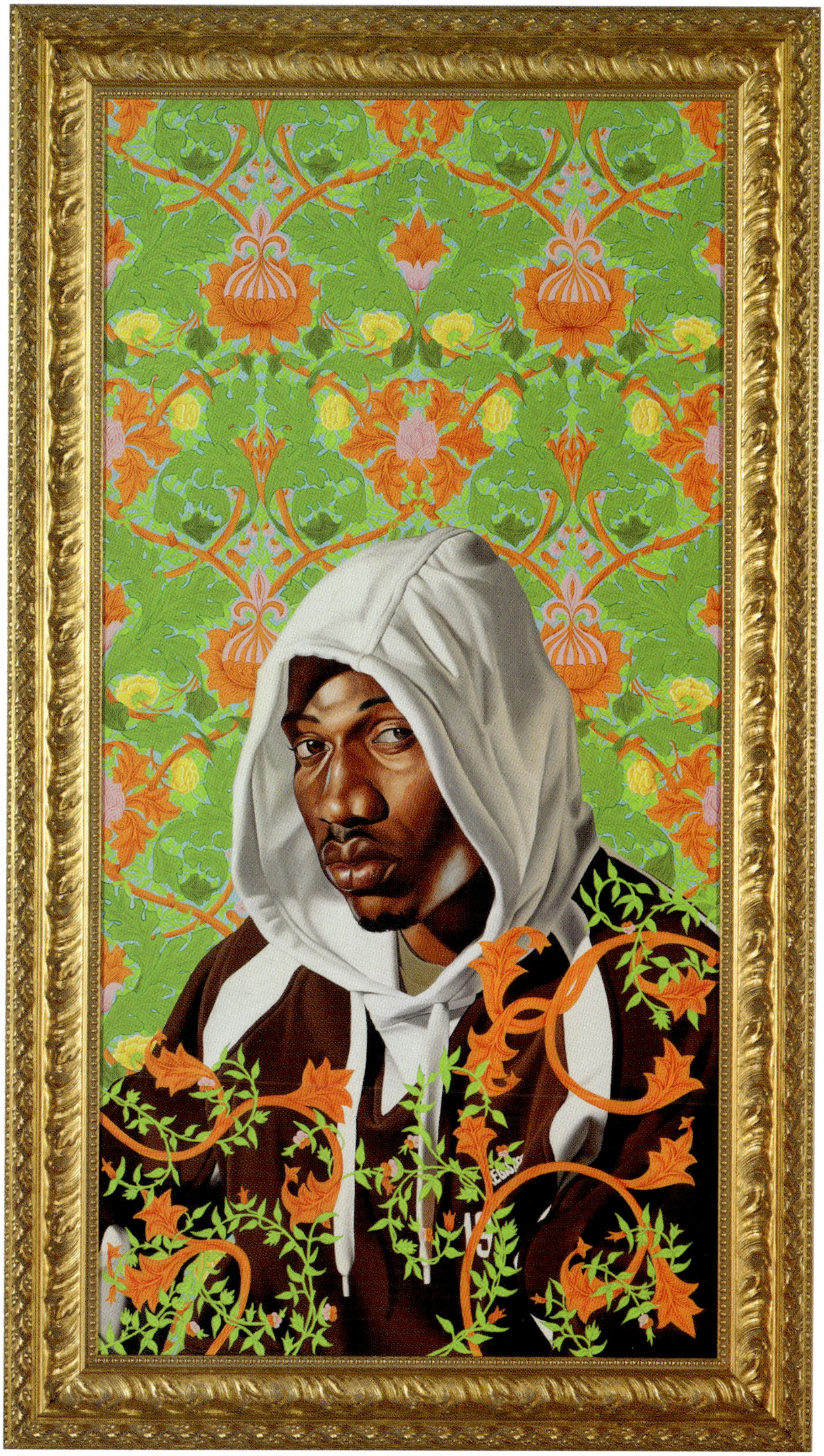

that were inspired by the mug shot photo I found on the streets of a young black man that made me question the mug shot as a type of portraiture, and whether or not portraiture connotes a certain amount of power about how you position yourself. The mug shot does not allow the model to position himself with all powers removed–side view, front view—and looking at the portraits of the land and gentry stands in stark contrast to that concept.

Kehinde Wiley

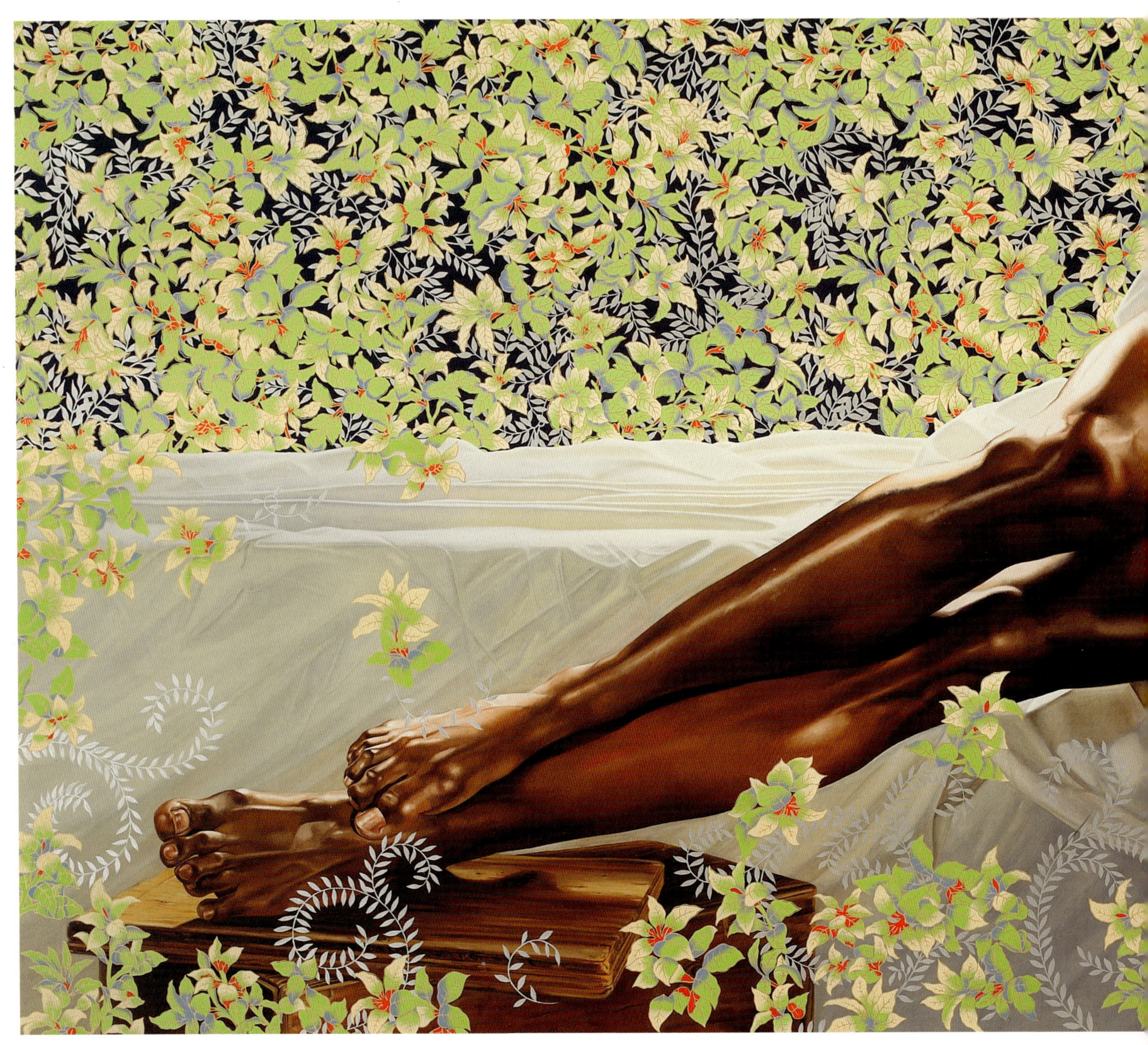

 KEHINDE WILEY *Sleep*, 2008, oil on canvas, 132 x 300 in. (335.3 x 762 cm), acquired in 2009

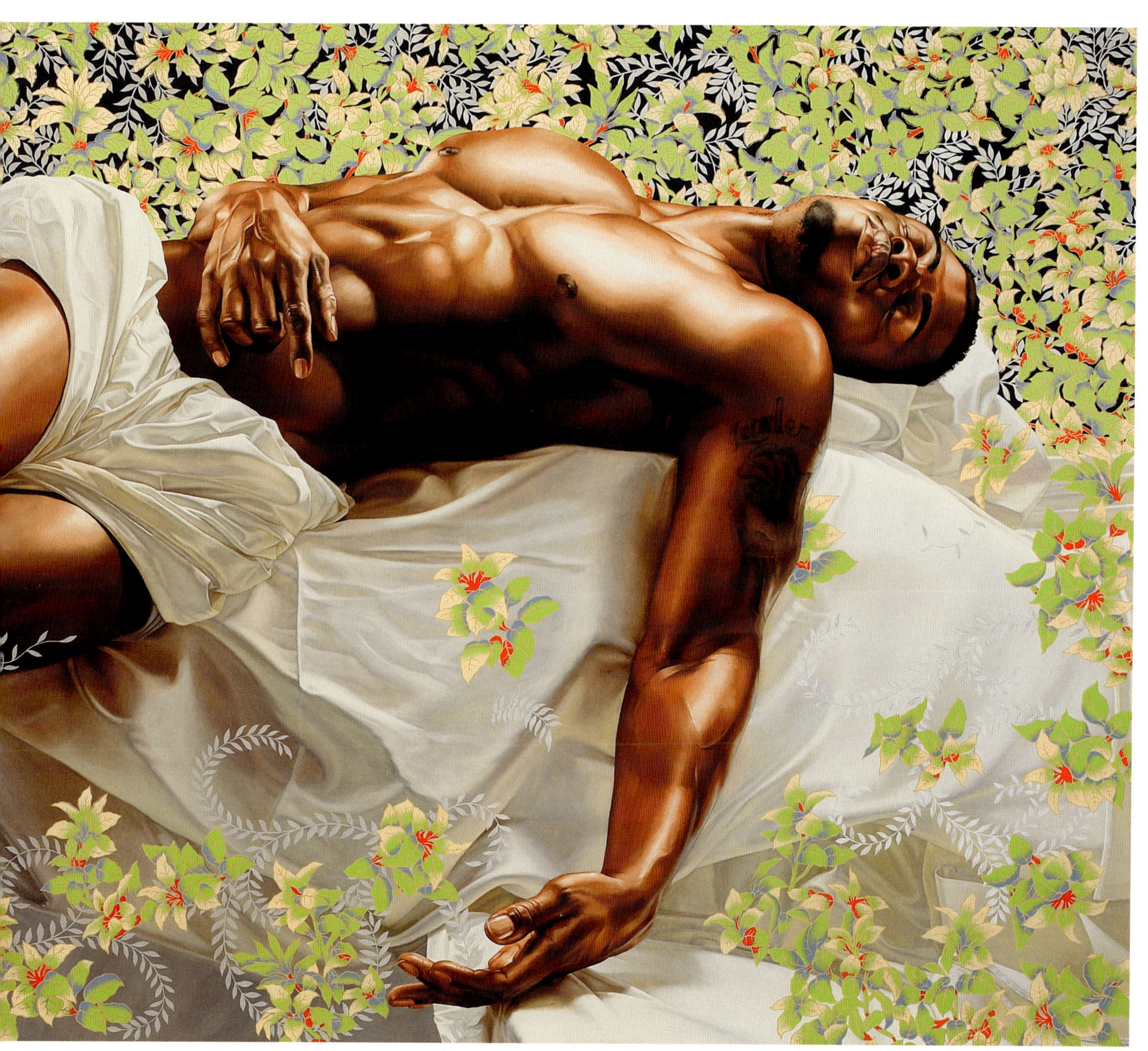

PURVIS YOUNG

Untitled, 1985-1999, paint on wood, diameter of panel: 54 in. (137.2 cm) x 2 in. (5 cm), acquired in 1999

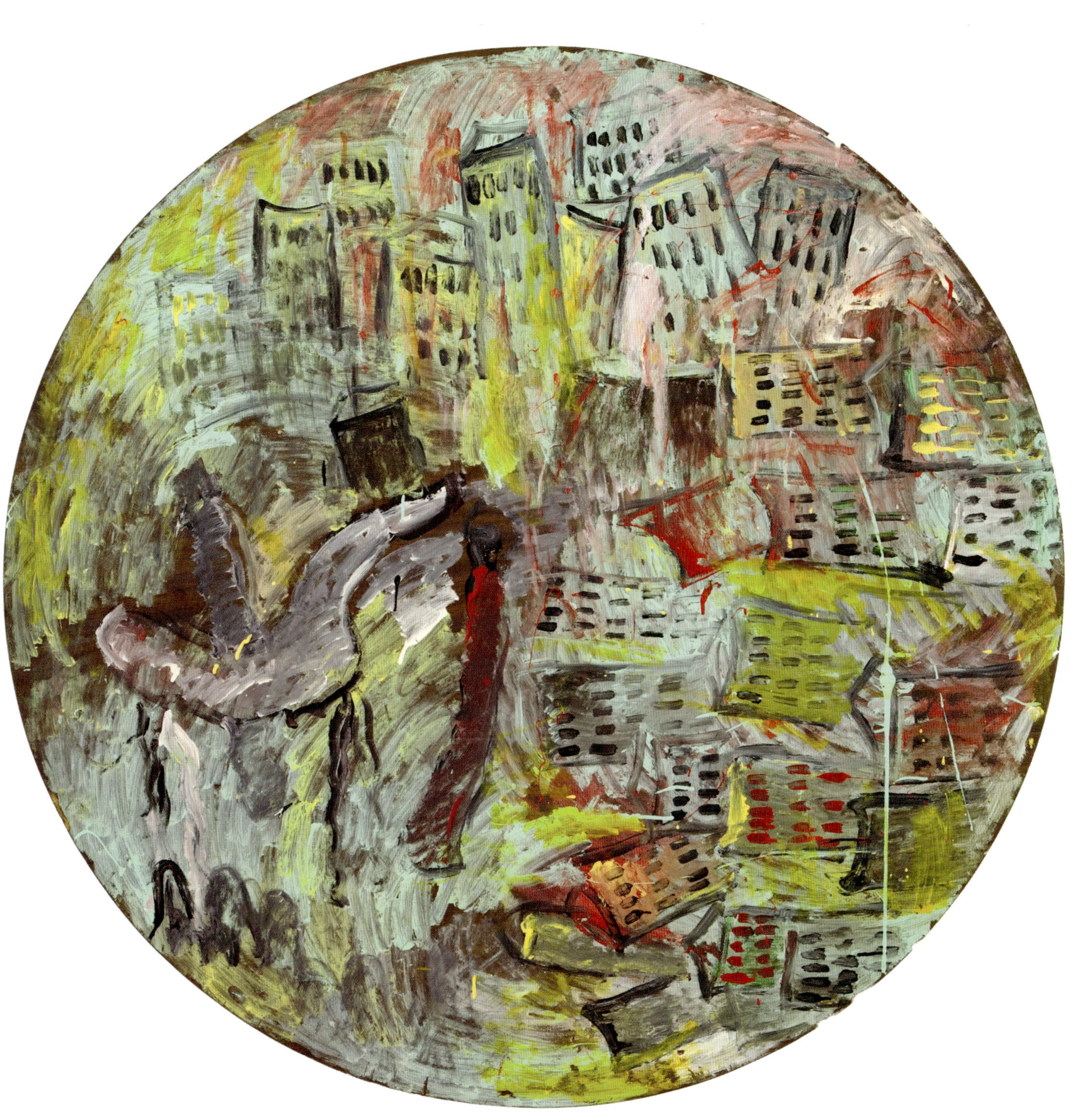

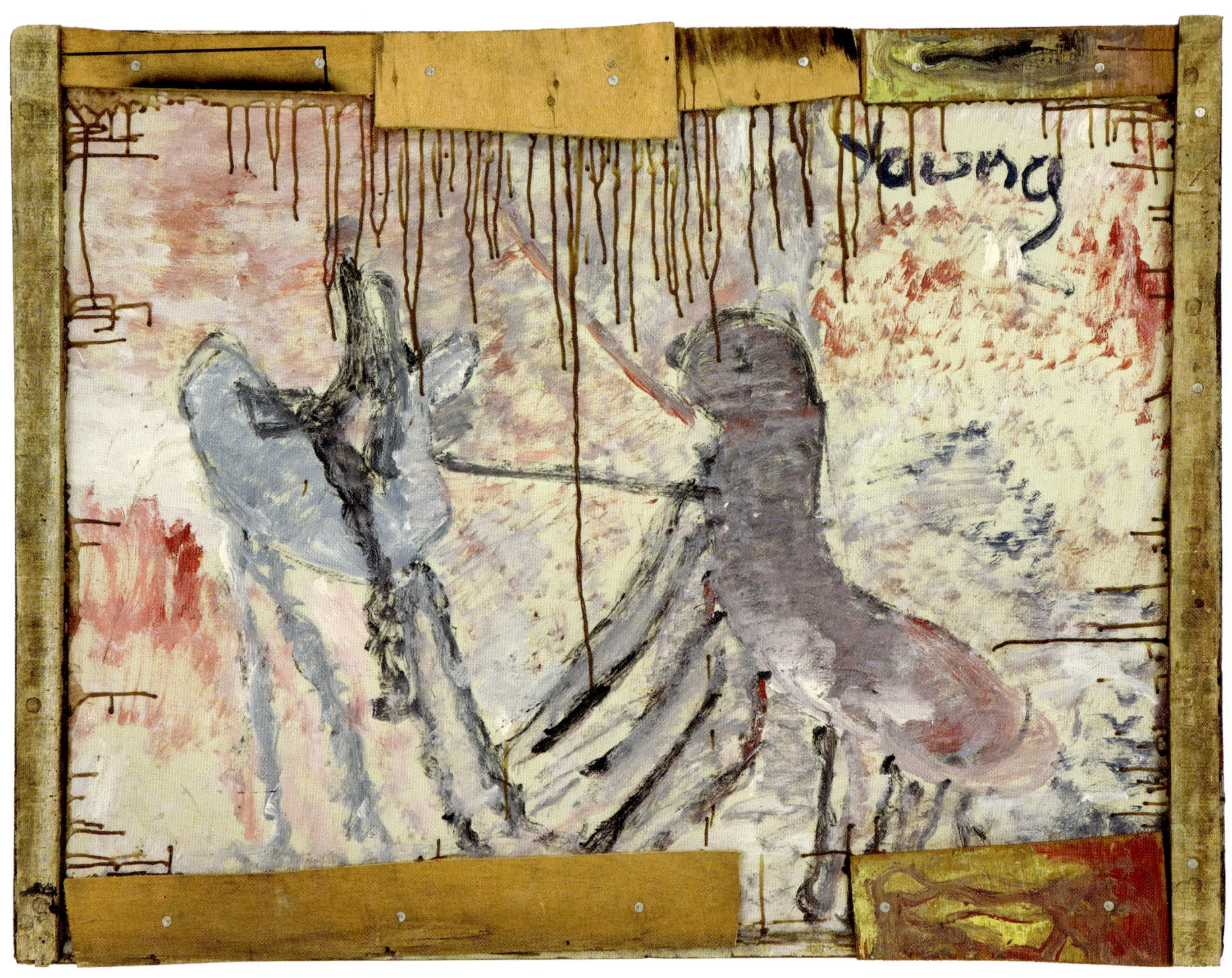

 PURVIS YOUNG *Untitled*, 1985-1999, paint on wood, 36 x 47 1/4 x 1 in. (91.5 x 120 x 2.5 cm), acquired in 1999

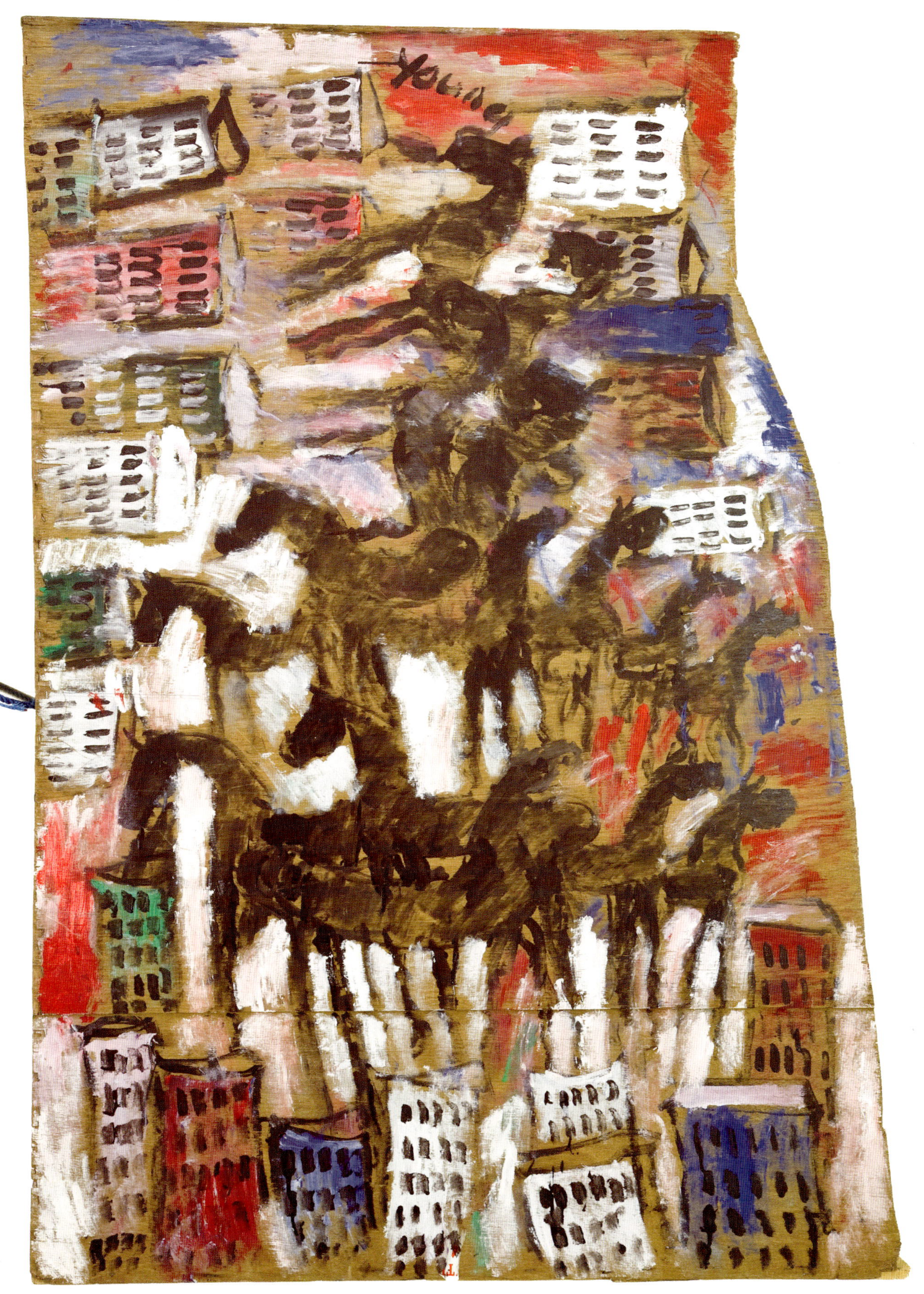

Untitled, 1985-1999, paint on wood, 60 x 42 1/4 x 7 1/4 in. (152.4 x 107.3 x 18.4 cm), acquired in 1999

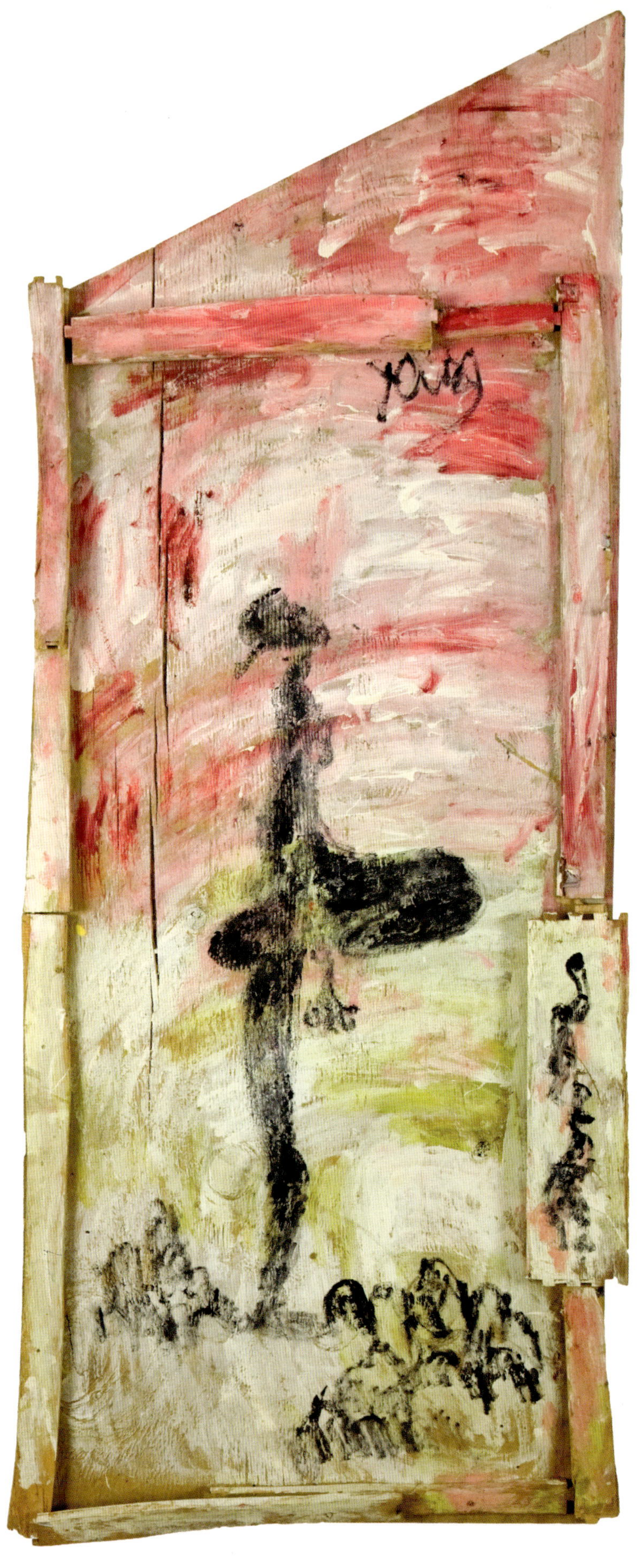

 PURVIS YOUNG *Untitled*, 1985-1999, paint on wood and canvas, 60 x 28 in. (152.4 x 71.1 cm), acquired in 1999

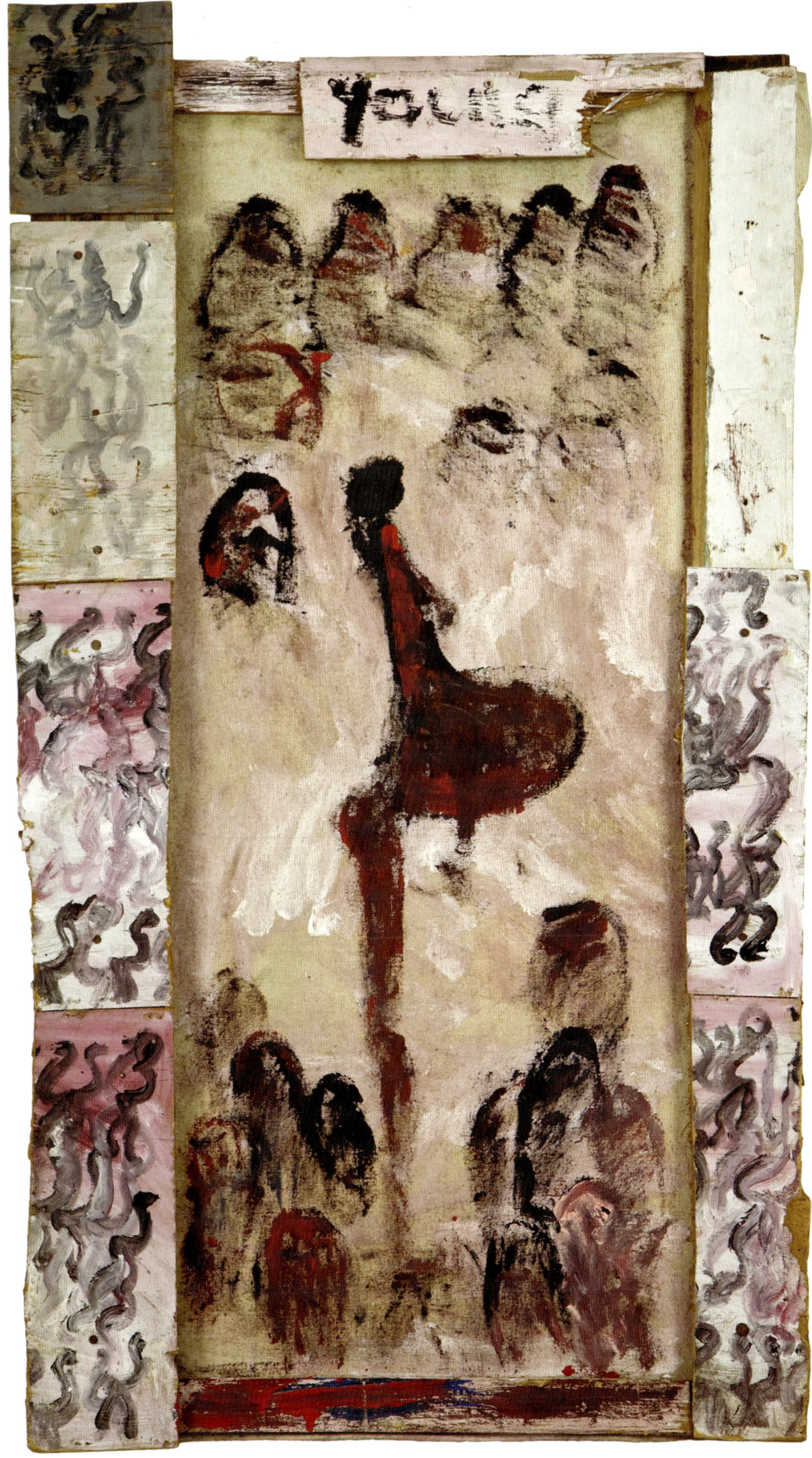

Untitled, 1985-1999, paint on wood and canvas, 50 1/2 x 28 x 2 in.(128.3 x 71.1 x 5.1 cm), acquired in 1999

CHECKLIST

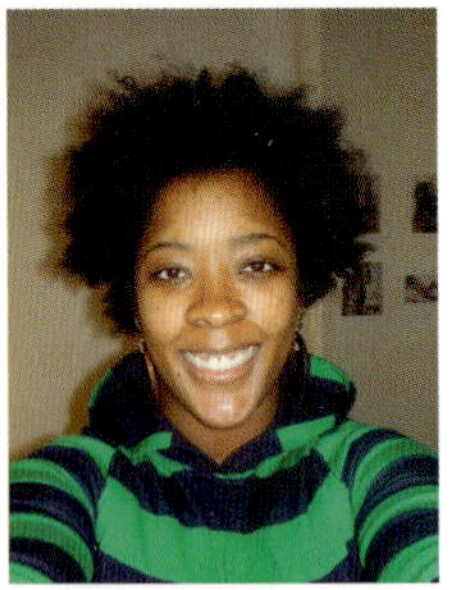

NINA CHANEL ABNEY
Born in Chicago, IL, 1982
Lives and works in New York, NY

Khaaliqua & Jeff, 2007, acrylic on canvas, 61 x 63 3/4 in. (155 x 162 cm)

Class of 2007, 2007, acrylic on canvas, diptych, overall 114 x 183 in. (289.6 x 464.8 cm)

The Boardroom, 2008, acrylic on canvas, diptych, overall 77 x 156 in. (195.6 x 396.2 cm)

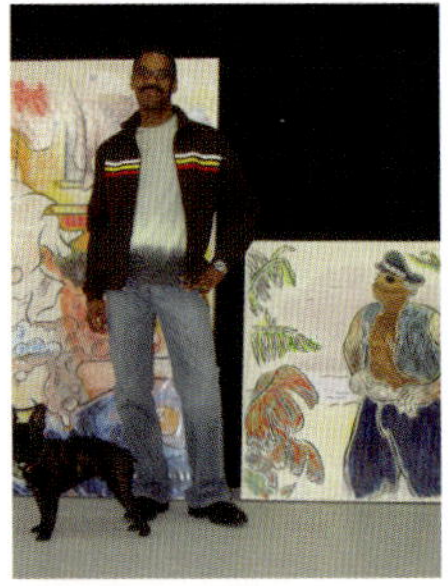

JOHN BANKSTON
Born in Benton Harbor, MI, 1963
Lives and works in San Francisco, CA

Man's Country II, 2004, oil on linen, 78 x 96 in. (198.1 x 243.8 cm)

Beginning or End, 2006-2007, oil and wax on linen, 20 x 18 in. (50.8 x 45.7 cm)

Man's Country I, 2004, oil on linen, 78 x 96 in. (198.1 x 243.8 cm)

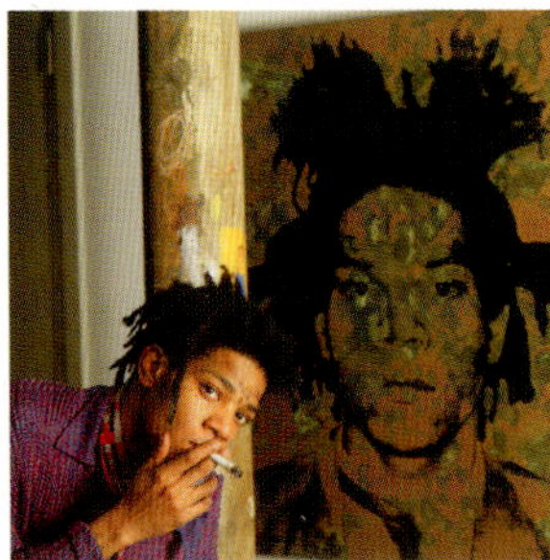

JEAN-MICHEL BASQUIAT
Born in Brooklyn, NY, 1960-1988

Bird On Money, 1981, acrylic and oil on canvas, 66 x 90 in. (167.6 x 228.6 cm)

One Million Yen, 1982, oil on canvas with wood and jute, 60 x 58 x 3 3/4 in. (152.4 x 147.3 x 9.5 cm)

Untitled (Self-portrait), 1982-1983, oil on wood, 20 x 20 in. (50.8 x 50.8 cm)

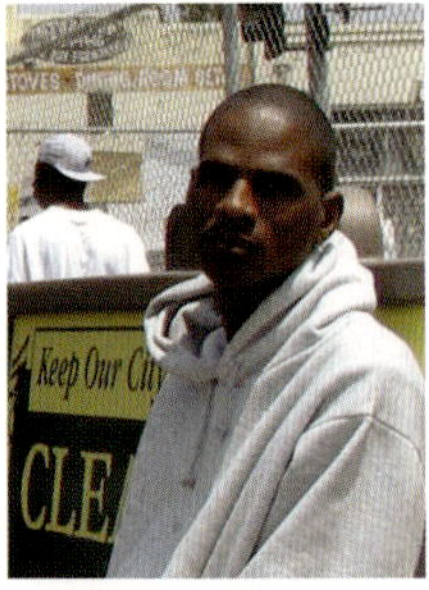

MARK BRADFORD
Born in Los Angeles, CA, 1968
Lives and works in Los Angeles, CA

Whore in the Church House, 2006, mixed media collage on canvas, 103 x 142 in. (261.6 x 360.7 cm)

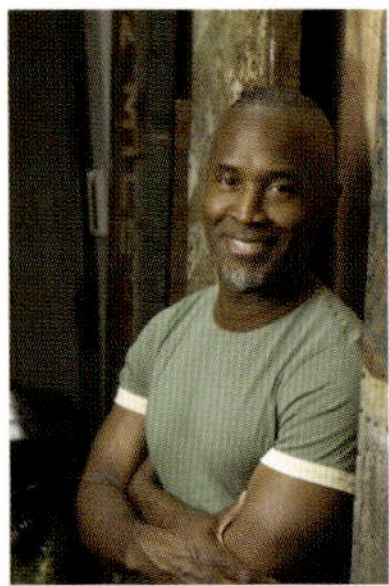

NICK CAVE
Born in Jefferson City, MO, 1959
Lives and works in Chicago, IL

Soundsuit, 2008, fabric, fiberglass and metal, 102 x 36 x 28 in. (259 x 91.5 x 71 cm)

Soundsuit, 2008, synthetic hair, fiberglass and metal, 98 x 27 x 14 in. (248.9 x 68.6 x 35.6 cm)

Soundsuit, 2008, fabric, sequins, fiberglass and metal, 100 x 25 x 14 in. (254 x 63.5 x 35.6 cm)

Soundsuit, 2006, fabric, sequins, fiberglass and metal, 100 x 26 x 13 in. (254 x 66 x 33 cm)

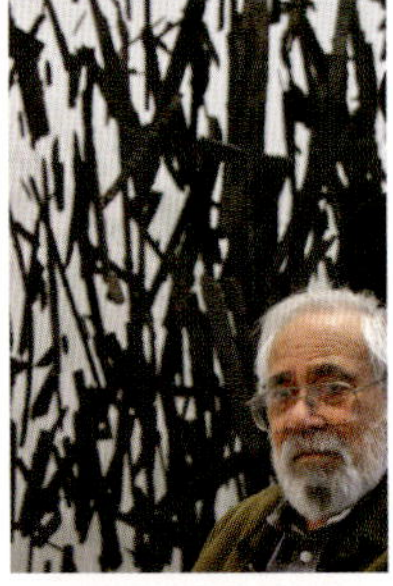

ROBERT COLESCOTT
Born in Oakland, CA, 1925-2009

Ode to Joy (European Anthem), 1997, acrylic on canvas, 90 x 114 in. (228.6 x 289.5 cm)

Arabs: The Emir of Iswid (How Wide the Gulf?), 1992, acrylic on canvas, 84 x 72 in. (213.4 x 182.9 cm)

Sunset on the Bayou, 1993, acrylic on canvas, 90 x 114 in. (228.6 x 289.5 cm)

The Sphinx Speaks, 1993, acrylic on canvas, 84 x 72 in. (213.4 x 182.9 cm)

Modern Day Miracles, 1988, acrylic on canvas, 84 x 72 in. (213.4 x 182.9 cm)

Pygmalion, 1987, acrylic on canvas, 90 x 114 in. (228.6 x 289.6 cm.)

Untitled (Adam and Eve), 1982, charcoal on paper, 83 1/2 x 29 1/2 in. (212 x 75 cm)

Untitled, 1970, graphite on paper, 19 3/4 x 26 in. (50.2 x 66 cm)

Dulacrow's Masterwork: A Mockumentary Film, 1976, digital video (color, sound), 43 min. 50 sec., ed. 1/10

Passing, 1982, charcoal on paper, 60 x 33 in. (152.4 x 83.8 cm)

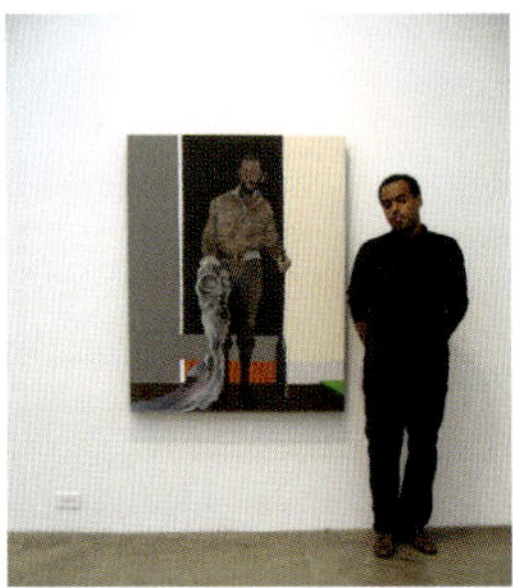

NOAH DAVIS
Born in Seattle, WA, 1983-2015

The Seven Prisoners of the Abyss, 2008, oil on canvas, 30 x 40 1/4 in. (76.2 x 102.2 cm)

American Sterile, 2008, oil on canvas, 52 x 60 in. (132.1 x 152.4 cm)

Basic Training 1, 2008, oil and acrylic on canvas, 10 x 10 in. (25.4 x 25.4 cm)

Basic Training 2, 2008, oil and acrylic on canvas, 10 x 10 in. (25.4 x 25.4 cm)

Basic Training 3, 2008, oil and acrylic on canvas, 10 x 10 in. (25.4 x 25.4 cm)

Basic Training 4, 2008, oil and acrylic on canvas, 10 x 10 in. (25.4 x 25.4 cm)

Painting for My Dad, 2011, oil on canvas, 76 x 91 in. (193 x 231.1 cm)

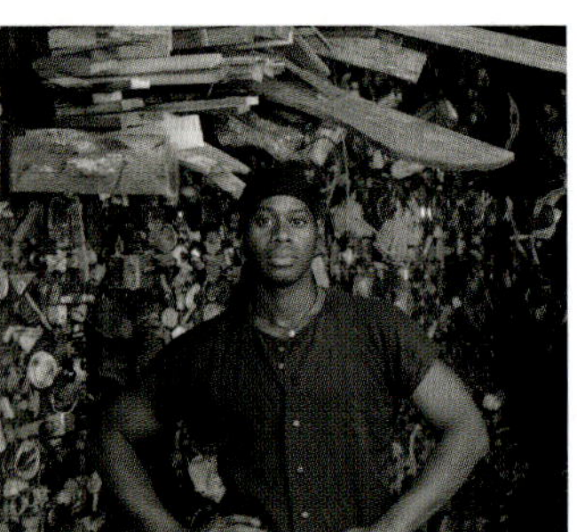

LEONARDO DREW
Born in Tallahassee, FL, 1961
Lives and works in San Antonio, TX

Untitled #25, 1992, cotton and wax, 102 x 158 x 33 in. (259 x 401.3 x 83.8 cm)

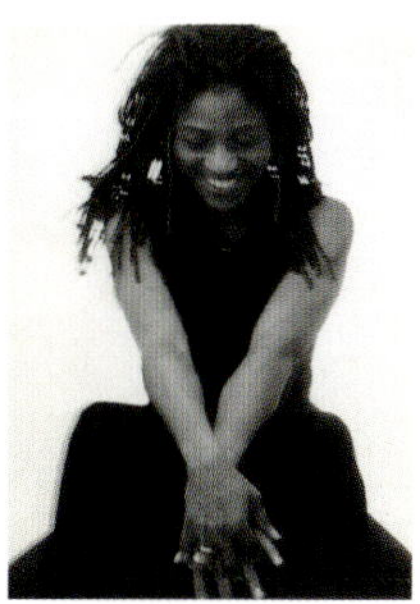

RENÉE GREEN
Born in Cleveland, Ohio, 1959
Lives and works in New York, NY, and San Francisco, CA

Between and Including, Set A (Akerman to Bogeyman), 1998, black-and-white framed photographs, framed texts and painted wall height variable; painted wall 55 in. (140 cm)

Between and Including, Set B (Un Chien Andalou to Crossdressing), 1998, black-and-white framed photographs, framed texts and painted wall, height variable; painted wall 55 in. (140 cm)

Between and Including, Set C (Dama s sobachkoi to Valie Export), 1998, black-and-white framed photographs, framed texts and painted wall, height variable; painted wall 55 in. (140 cm)

Between and Including, Set D (Earthquake to Alice Guy), 1998, black-and-white framed photographs, framed texts and painted wall, height variable; painted wall 55 in. (140 cm)

Between and Including, Set E (Marion Haensel to Invisible Invaders), 1998, black-and-white framed photographs, framed texts and painted wall, height variable; painted wall 55 in. (140 cm)

Between and Including, Set F (Journey to the Lost City to Mother's Day), 1998, black-and-white framed photographs, framed texts and painted wall, height variable; painted wall 55 in. (140 cm)

Between and Including, Set G (Mothra to Cristina Perincoli), 1998, black-and-white framed photographs, framed texts and painted wall, height variable; painted wall 55 in. (140 cm)

Between and Including, Set H (Rock 'N' Roll Highschool to Things to Come), 1998, black and white framed photographs, framed texts and, painted wall, height variable; painted wall 55 in. (140 cm)

Between and Including, Set I (Trinth T.Min-Ha to Xie Jin), 1998, black-and-white framed photographs, framed texts and painted wall, height variable; painted wall 55 in. (140 cm)

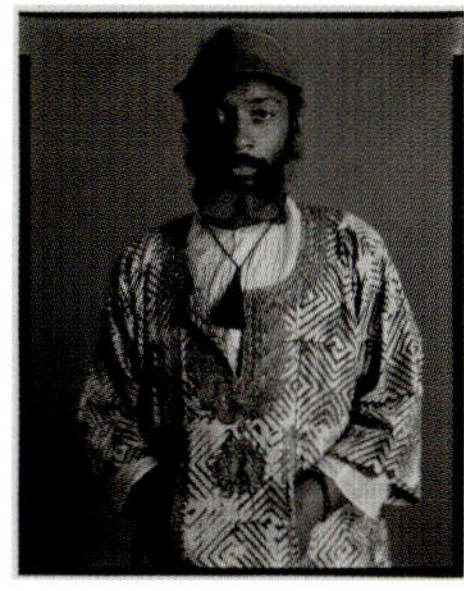

DAVID HAMMONS
Born in Springfield, IL, 1943
Lives and works in New York, NY

Esquire (or John Henry), 1990, steel, rock, human hair and tin, 45 x 9 x 5 in. (114.3 x 22 x 13 cm)

The Holy Bible, Old Testament, 2002, 1,002 page artist's book, 225 color plates, leather-bound, softcover, gilt edged, gold tooling, and slipcase, ed. 116/165, 13 1/2 x 10 1/2 x 2 1/2 in. (34.3 x 26.7 x 6.4 cm)

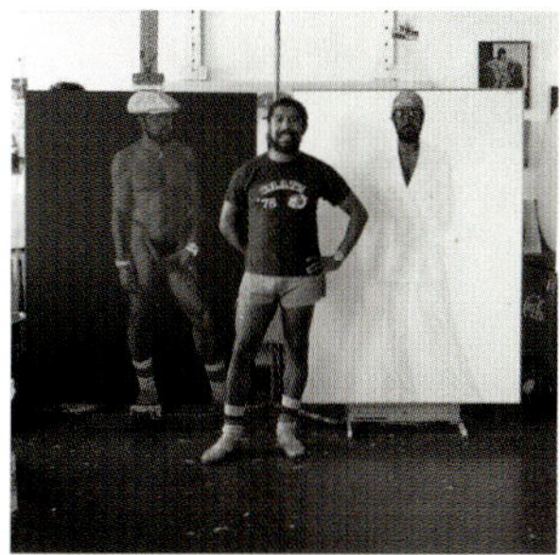

BARKLEY L. HENDRICKS
Born in Philadelphia, PA, 1945-2017

Noir, 1978, oil and acrylic on canvas, 72 x 48 in. (182.9 x 121.9 cm)

Fast Eddie Jive Niggah, 1975, oil and acrylic on linen, 48 1/2 x 36 1/2 in. (123.2 x 92.7 cm)

Thee Big Guy, 1983, oil, acrylic and gold leaf on canvas, 43 1/2 x 43 1/2 in. (110.5 x 110.5 cm)

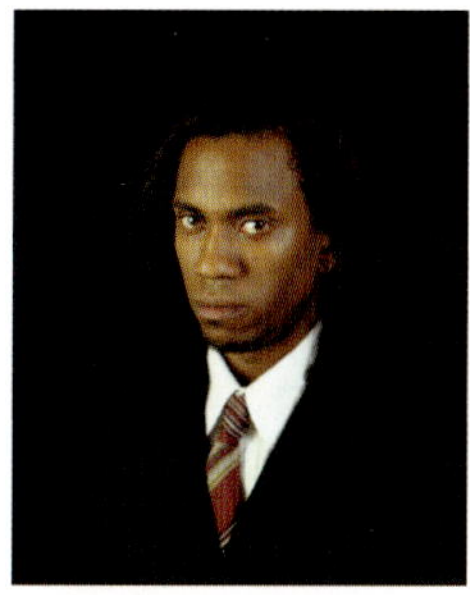

RASHID JOHNSON
Born in Chicago, IL, 1977
Lives and works in New York, NY

The New Negro Escapist Social and Athletic Club (Thurgood), 2008, Lambda print, ed. 2/5, 69 x 55 1/2 in. (175.3 x 141 cm)

Citizen Band (Explorations in Topology), 2008, wax, soap, shea butter, framed photographs and mixed media on fiberboard, 48 x 96 x 12 in. (121.9 x 243.8 x 30.5 cm)

After Medium, 2011, branded red oak flooring, black soap, wax and paint, 132 x 168 x 2 3/4 in. (335.3 x 426.7 x 7 cm)

The Shuttle, 2011, mirrored tile, black soap, wax, books, shea butter, oyster shells, plant and cb radio, 96 1/2 x 125 x 11 3/4 in. (245.1 x 317.5 x 29.8 cm)

Self-portrait as the black Jimmy Connors in the finals of the New Negro Escapist Social and Athletic Club Summer Tennis Tournament, 2008, Lambda print on dibond with stained wood frame, 60 x 48 in. (152.4 x 121.92 cm)

Barnburner, 2011, cast bronze, black soap and wax, 49 x 39 x 1 in. (124.5 x 99 x 2.54 cm)

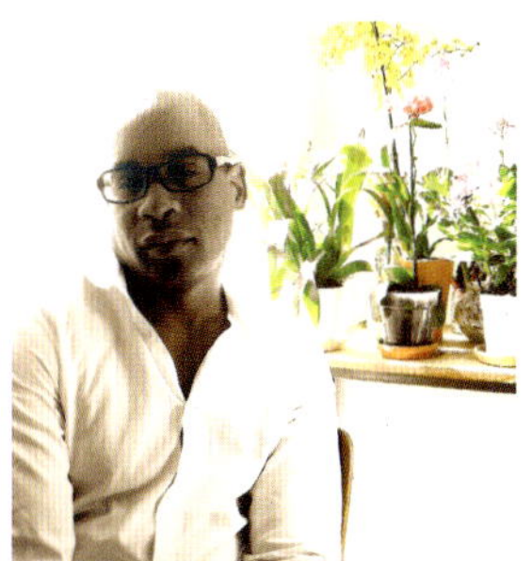

GLENN LIGON
Born in Bronx, NY, 1960
Lives and works in New York, NY

America, 2008, neon and paint, ed.of 1 plus AP, 24 x 168 in. (61 x 426.7 cm)

Untitled (Malcolm X), 2008, acrylic, vinyl-based paint and graphite on paper mounted on fiberboard, 132 x 107 in. (335.3 x 271.8 cm)

Gold Nobody Knew Me #1, 2007, acrylic and oil stick on canvas, 32 x 32 in. (81.3 x 81.3 cm)

Gold When Black Wasn't Beautiful #1, 2007, acrylic and oil stick on canvas, 32 x 32 in. (81.3 x 81.3 cm)

Stranger #21, 2005, acrylic, coal dust, screen print, gesso and oil stick on canvas, 96 x 72 in. (243.8 x 182.9 cm)

Untitled (Negro Sunshine), 2006, neon, ed. 3/7, 4 x 48 in. (10.1 x 121.9 cm)

Mirror #7, 2006, acrylic, coal dust, screen print, gesso and oil stick on canvas, 84 x 60 in. (213.4 x 152.4 cm)

Malcom X, Sun, Frederick Douglass, Boy with Bubbles # 3 (version 2), 2001, vinyl-based paint and silkscreen on paper, 23 x 16 1/2 in. (58.5 x 42 cm)

Condition Report D, 2000, iris print and iris print with serigraph, ed. 18/20, diptych, each 35 x 26 in. (88.9 x 66 cm)

Untitled (I Sell the Shadow to Sustain the Substance), 2006, neon and paint, ed. 3/3, 7 1/2 x 192 1/2 in. (19 x 489 cm)

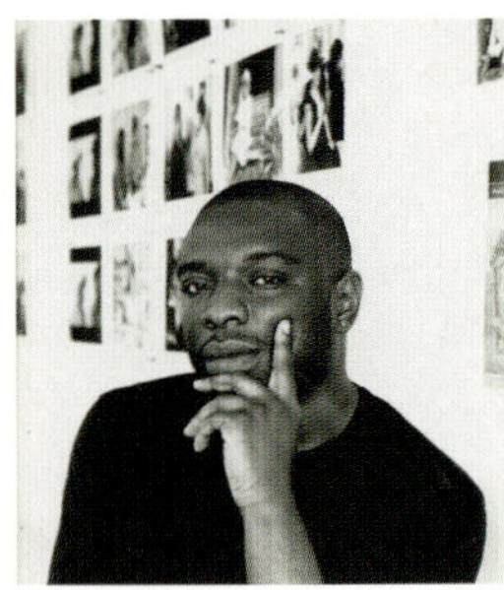

KALUP LINZY
Born in Stuckey, FL, 1977
Lives and works in Brooklyn, NY

Conversations wit de Churen IV: Play wit de Churen, 2005, digital video (color, sound), 15 min. 49 sec., ed. 1/5

Conversations with de Churen V: As da Art World Might Turn, 2006, digital video (color, sound), 11 min. 15 sec., ed. 2/5

Untitled (Golden No. 1), 2006, gouache on paper, 12 x 16 in. (38.1 x 40.6 cm)

Untitled (Golden No. 2), 2006, gouache on paper, 12 x 16 in. (38.1 x 40.6 cm)

Untitled (Golden No. 3), 2006, gouache on paper, 12 x 16 in. (38.1 x 40.6 cm)

Untitled (I'll Take You There No. 1), 2006, gouache on paper, 12 x 16 in. (38.1 x 40.6 cm)

Untitled (I'll Take You There No. 3), 2006, gouache on paper, 12 x 16 in. (38.1 x 40.6 cm)

Untitled (I'll Take You There No. 4), 2006, gouache on paper, 12 x 16 in. (38.1 x 40.6 cm)

SweetBerry Sonnet, 2008, digital video (color, sound), 37 min. 54 sec., ed. 1/5.

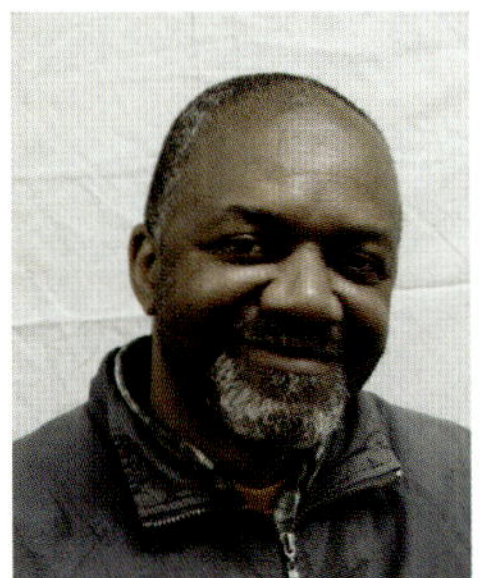

KERRY JAMES MARSHALL
Born in Birmingham, AL, 1955
Lives and works in Chicago, IL

Souvenir: Composition in Three Parts, 1998-2000, plastic, glass, paper, wood, steel and framed video still, 98 x 32 x 22 in. (248.9 x 81.3 x 55.9 cm)

Vignette #10, 2007, acrylic on fiberglass, 74 x 110 in. (188 x 279.4 cm)

Untitled, 1998-1999, 8-color unique woodcut, ed. 1/4, 12 panels, overall 98 1/2 x 608 1/2 in. (250 x 1545.6 cm)

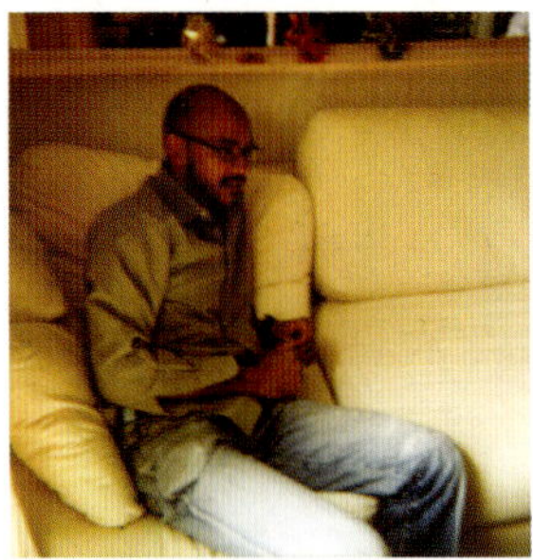

RODNEY MCMILLIAN
Born in Columbia, SC, 1969
Lives and works in Los Angeles, CA

Untitled, 2005, carpet, 139 x 178 x 114 in. (353 x 452 x 289.6 cm)

Untitled, 2007/2008, vinyl, thread, wood, metal and styrofoam, 162 x 264 x 96 in. (411.5 x 670.6 x 243.8 cm)

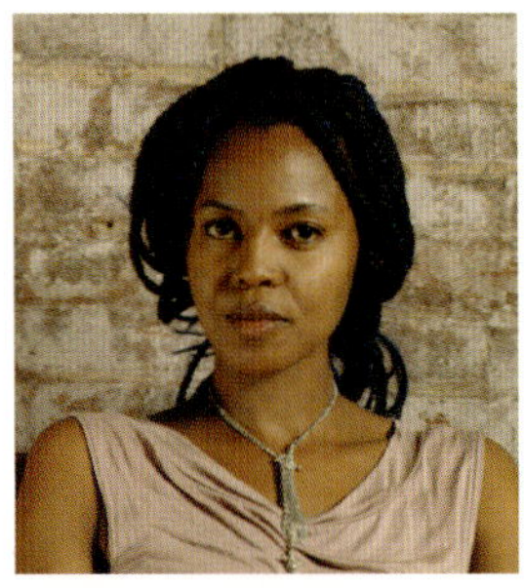

WANGECHI MUTU
Born in Nairobi, Kenya, 1972
Lives and works in New York, NY

The Evolution of Mud Mama from Beginning to Start, 2008, watercolor, gold leaf and collage on paper, 6 panels, overall 19 1/2 x 75 in. (49.5 x 190.5 cm)

Non je ne regrette rien, 2007, ink, acrylic, glitter, cloth, paper collage, plastic, plant material and mixed media on Mylar, 54 1/2 x 92 1/2 in. (138.4 x 233.7 cm)

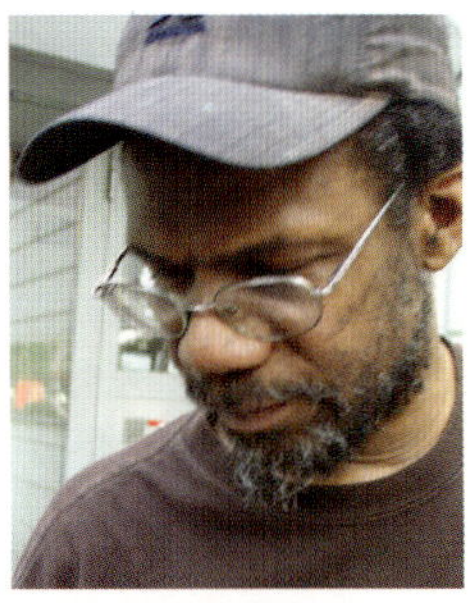

WILLIAM POPE.L
Born in Newark, NJ, 1955
Lives and works in Lewiston, ME

Skin Set: Brown People Are the Green Ray, 2008, Cray-Pas, acrylic and ink on paper, 8 1/2 x 11 in. (21.6 x 28 cm)

Skin Set: Green People Are Shitty, 2008, ink on paper, 8 1/2 x 11 in. (21.6 x 28 cm)

Skin Set: Purple People Are Reason Bicarbonate, 2006-2007, ink, Wite-Out and coffee on paper, 8 1/2 x 11 in. (21.6 x 28 cm)

Skin Set: Red People Are the Niggerss of the Canyon, 2004, ink, Wite-Out, coffee and hair on paper, 8 1/2 x 11 in. (21.6 x 28 cm)

Skin Set: White People Are Black People by Neuroses, 2008, ink on paper, 8 1/2 x 11 in. (21.6 x 28 cm)

Skin Set: Yellow People Are Hydrogenated, 2008, ink on paper, 8 1/2 x 11 in. (21.6 x 28 cm)

The Great White Way, 22 miles, 9 years, 1 street, 2001-2002, digital video (color, sound), 5 min., ed. 1/5

Foraging (asphixia version), 2008, digital chromogenic print, ed. 1/5, 23 1/8 x 24 in. (58.8 x 61 cm)

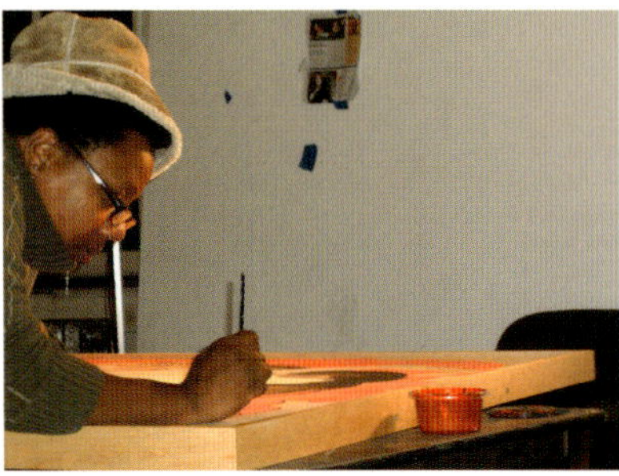

ROZEAL
Born in Washington, DC, 1966
Lives and works in Washington, DC

Untitled (after Kikugawa Eizan's "Furyu nana komachi" [The Modern Seven Komashi]), 2007, acrylic and paper on panel, 12 x 14 5/8 in. (30.5 x 37.1 cm)

Sacrifice #2: It Has to Last (after Yoshitoshi's "Drowsy: the appearance of a harlot of the Meiji era"), 2007, enamel, acrylic and paper on panel, 52 x 38 in. (132 x 96.5 cm)

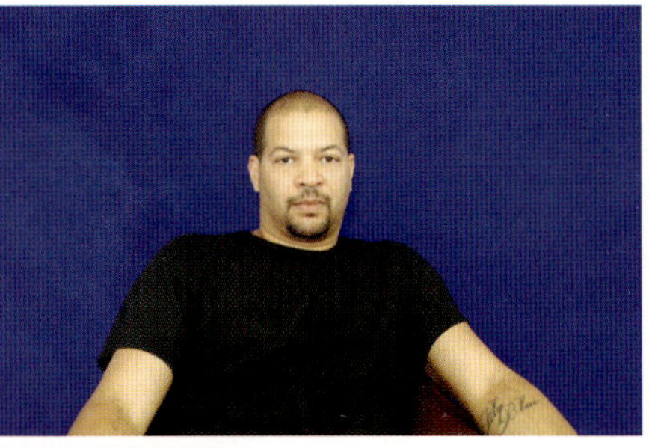

GARY SIMMONS
Born in New York, NY, 1964
Lives and works in New York, NY

Hollywood, 2008, pigment, oil and cold wax on canvas, 84 x 120 in. (213.4 x 304.8 cm)

Chalkboard Drawing #1, 1992, acrylic and charcoal on chalkboard, 47 x 60 in. (119.4 x 152.4 cm)

Chalkboard Drawing #3, 1992, acrylic and charcoal on chalkboard, 47 x 60 in. (119.4 x 152.4 cm)

Klan Gate, 1992, cast concrete, wood , brick and steel, 120 x 114 x 25.5 in. (305 x 290 x 64.8 cm)

Erasure Series (White Washed Drawings) #2, 1992, acrylic and charcoal on paper, 30 x 22 1/4 in. (76.2 x 56.5 cm)

Erasure Series (White Washed Drawings) #8, 1992, acrylic and charcoal on paper, 30 x 22 1/4 in. (76.2 x 56.5 cm)

Erasure Series (White Washed Drawings) #9, 1992, acrylic and charcoal on paper, 30 x 22 1/4 in. (76.2 x 56.5 cm)

Erasure Series (White Washed Drawings) #11, 1992, acrylic and charcoal on paper, 30 x 22 1/4 in. (76.2 x 56.5 cm)

Duck, Duck, Noose, 1992, wood, cloth, metal and hemp, dimensions variable

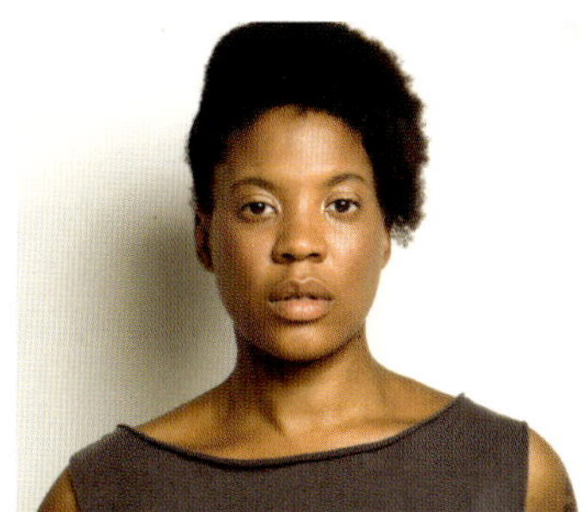

XAVIERA SIMMONS
Born in New York, NY, 1974
Lives and works in Brooklyn, NY

One Day and Back Then (Seated), 2007, color photograph, ed. 3/7, 30 x 40 in. (76.2 x 101.6 cm)

One Day and Back Then (Standing), 2007, color photograph, ed. 2/5, 30 x 40 in. (76.2 x 101.6 cm)

American Book Covers, 2007, color photograph, ed. 1/5, 30 x 40 in. (76.2 x 101.6 cm)

Make the Fist, 2004, color photograph, ed. 1/5, 30 x 40 in. (76.2 x 101.6 cm)

Appear, Appease, Applaud (Also, Perhaps, Maybe), 2008, chromira print, ed. 1/5, 30 x 40 in. (76.2 x 101.6 cm)

Beyond the Canon of Landscape (For Orhan. P, Zadie. S, Nia and Naima. M), 2008, chromira print, ed. 1/5, 40 x 30 in. (101.6 x 76.2 cm)

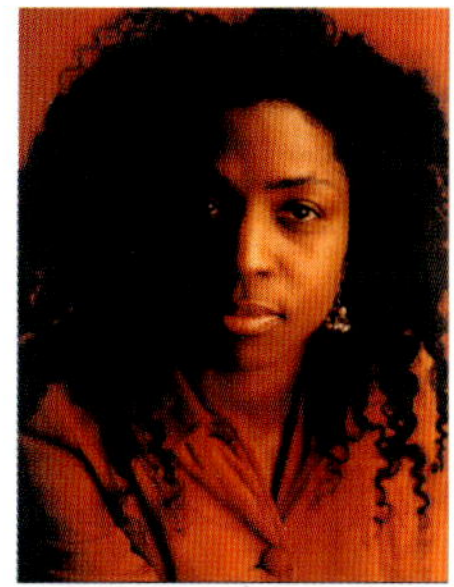

LORNA SIMPSON
Born in Brooklyn, NY, 1960
Lives and works in Brooklyn, NY

Wigs (Portfolio), 1994, waterless lithograph and felt, 38 panels, overall 72 x 162 1/2 in. (182.9 x 412.8 cm)

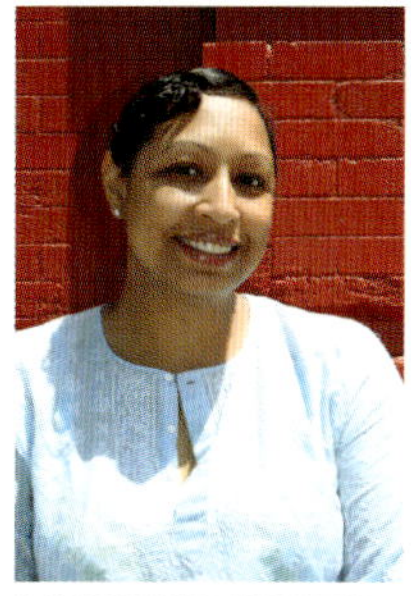

SHINIQUE SMITH
Born in Baltimore, MD, 1971
Lives and works in Brooklyn, NY

a bull, a rose, a tempest, 2007, fabric and found objects, 43 x 29 x 26 in. (109 x 73.6 x 66 cm)

Menagerie, 2007, mixed media on canvas, 72 x 48 in. (183 x 122 cm)

Crone-Huntress, 2007, wool, fabric and mixed media, 75 x 100 x 70 in. (190.5 x 254 x 177.8 cm)

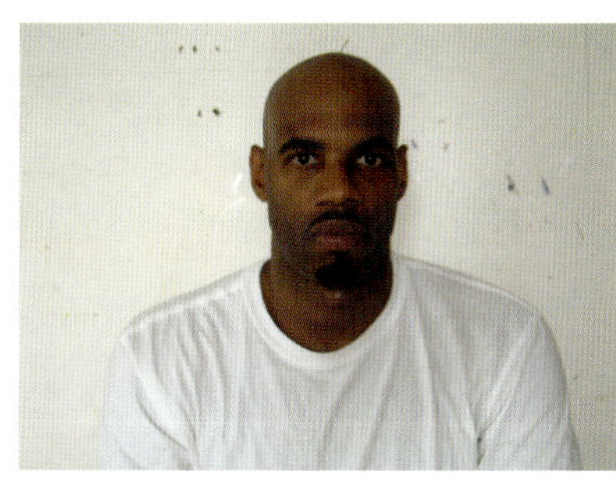

JEFF SONHOUSE
Born in New York, NY, 1968
Lives and works in New York, NY

Exhibit A: Cardinal Francis Arinze, 2005, oil and mixed media on panel, 78 x 61 in. (198.1 x 154.9 cm)

Yellow is Mellow, 2001, oil on canvas, 59 1/2 x 42 in. (151.1 x 106.7 cm)

Visually Impaired, 2008, oil on canvas, 78 x 61 in. (198.1 x 154.9 cm)

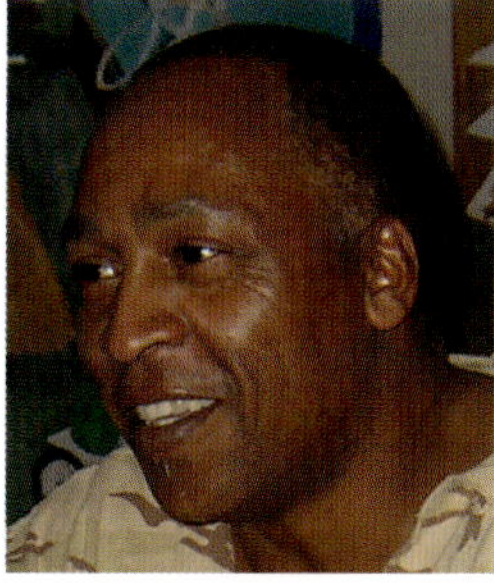

HENRY TAYLOR
Born in Oxnard, CA, 1958
Lives and works in Los Angeles, CA

Miss Leah, 2008, acrylic on canvas, 68 3/4 x 92 1/4 in. (161.9 x 235 cm)

Chicago Cooks, 2008, acrylic on canvas, 43 1/2 x 84 1/2 in. (110.5 x 214.6 cm)

Oh Henry, 2006, acrylic on canvas, 96 x 76 in. (243.8 x 193 cm)

The Long Jump by Carl Lewis, 2010, acrylic on canvas, 87 1/2 x 77 in. (222.3 x 195.6 cm)

Ride the White Horse Together, 2011, acrylic, wood, plastic, metal pans, yarn and hardware, 109 x 48 x 21 in. (276.9 x 121.9 x 53.3 cm)

Love Pam, 2008, acrylic on canvas, 47 x 35 in. (119.4 x 88.9 cm)

Lusiana, 2007, acrylic on canvas, 44 x 36 in. (111.8 x 91.4 cm)

Watts County, 2004, acrylic on canvas, 76 x 61 1/2 in. (193 x 156.2 cm)

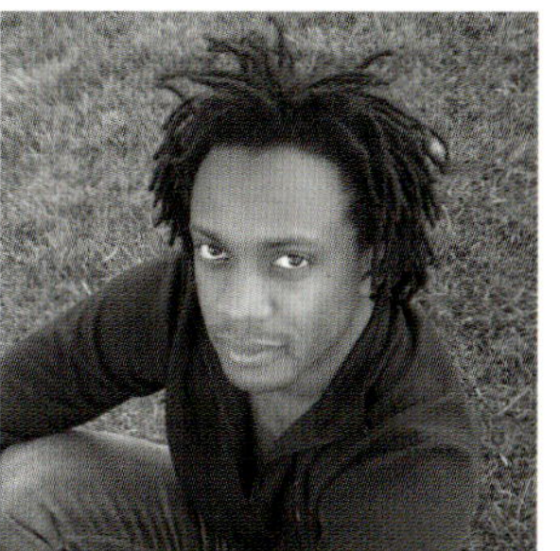

HANK WILLIS THOMAS
Born in Plainfield, NJ, 1976
Lives and works in New York, NY, and San Francisco, CA

Priceless, 2004, digital chromogenic print, ed. AP, 71 x 89 in. (180.3 x 226 cm)

Basketball and Chain, 2003, digital chromogenic print, ed. 2/3, 99 x 55 in. (251.5 x 139.7 cm)

Branded Head, 2003, digital chromogenic print, ed. AP, 99 x 52 in. (251.5 x 132 cm)

An Unidentified Jamaican Boy Used the Puma H Street Running Shoe to Run for his Freedom 2003/2005, 2005, Lambda photograph, ed. 2/5, 28 1/2 x 36 in. (72.4 x 91.5 cm)

Exxon: Black Street Art 1973/2005, 2005, Lambda photograph, ed. 1/5, 36 x 28 5/8 in. (91.4 x 72.8 cm)

Liberation of T.O.: "I'm not goin' back to work for massa' in dat darned field!" 2003/2005, 2005, Lambda photograph, ed. of 5 plus 1 artist's proof, 34 1/2 x 30 in. (87.8 x 76.2 cm)

21st Century Soul Power 2005/2006, 2006 Lambda photograph, ed. 2/5, 36 x 27 in. (91.4 x 68.6 cm)

Caramel Cocoa Butta', Honey Lovah You're Like No Otha' 1982/2006, 2006, Lambda photograph, ed. 1/5, 38 5/8 x 30 in. (98.2 x 76.2 cm)

Cucci #2: It's Time for Jungle Fever 2001/2006, 2006, Lambda photograph, ed. 2/5, 36 x 28 1/4 in. (91.4 x 71.9 cm)

Don't Let Them Catch You! 2004/2006, 2006, Lambda photograph, ed. 3/5, 36 x 24 in. (91.4 x 61 cm)

Duke Natural 1968/2006, 2006, Lambda photograph, ed. 1/5, 34 x 26 7/8 in. (86.4 x 68 cm)

How to Market Kitty Litter to Black People: Ebony Magazine 2005/2006, 2006, Lambda photograph, ed. 1/5, 36 x 30 in. (91.4 x 76.2 cm)

It's the Real Thing! 1978/2006, 2006, Lambda photograph, ed. 1/5, 32 3/4 x 30 in. (83.3 x 76.2 cm)

Mama's Cooking Cornbread! 1992/2006, 2006, Lambda photograph, ed. 1/5, 36 x 28 in. (91.4 x 71.5 cm)

Motion for Kids Allows Hair to be Blown Straighter 2002/2006, 2006, Lambda photograph, ed. 3/5, 36 x 28 3/4 in. (91.4 x 73 cm)

Oh, Behave: Smooth Exotic Vivid Taste 1999/2006, 2006, Lambda photograph, ed. 1/5, 34 3/4 x 28 3/4 (88.3 x 73 cm)

Once upon a time in America there were no slaves 2001/2006, 2006, Lambda photograph, ed. 2/5, 18 7/8 x 36 in. (48 x 91.4 cm)

Petey Wheatstraw: The Devil's Son-In Law 2000/2006, 2006, Lambda photograph, ed. 1/5, 35 3/4 x 33 3/4 in. (90.8 x 85.7 cm)

Slack Power 1969/2006, 2006, Lambda photograph, ed. 1/5, 36 x 27 3/4 in. (91.5 x 70.4 cm)

Smokin' Joe Ain't J'mama 1978/2006, 2006, Lambda photograph, ed. 2/5, 31 1/4 x 30 in. (79.9 x 76.2 cm)

So Glad We Made It 1979/2006, 2006, Lambda photograph, ed. 4/5, 30 x 34 in. (76.2 x 86.4 cm)

The Oft Forgotten Black Flower Children of Harlem 1969/2006, 2006, Lambda photograph, ed. 3/5, 34 x 27 5/8 in. (86.4 x 70.1 cm)

Things That Make You Go Hmmmmm?!! 2000/2006, 2006, Lambda photograph, ed. 1/5, 25 1/2 x 34 in. (64.6 x 86.4 cm)

Things That Make You Go Oooh! 1999/2006, 2006, Lambda photograph, ed. 1/5, 34 x 27 3/4 in. (86.4 x 70.5 cm)

...and the rest was her story 1985/2007, 2007, Lambda photograph, ed. 1/5, 36 x 28 3/8 in. (91.4 x 72.3 cm)

A Natural Exposion! Afro Sheen® Blowout Creme Relaxer 1973/2007, 2007, Lambda photograph, ed. 2/5, 30 x 36 in. (76.2 x 91.5 cm)

Alive with Pleasure 1990/2007, 2007, Lambda photograph, ed. 1/5, 30 x 40 in. (76.2 x 101.6 cm)

And They Called It "Buppy Love" 1983/2007, 2007, Lambda photograph, ed. 1/5, 36 x 28 in. (91.4 x 71 cm)

Are You the Right Kind of Woman for It? 1974/2007, 2007, Lambda photograph, ed. 1/5, 30 x 39 1/4 in. (76.2 x 99.4 cm)

Available in a Variety of Sizes and Colors 1977/2007, 2007, Lambda photograph, ed. 1/5, 32 x 30 in. (81.3 x 76.2 cm)

Can You Dig It? 1974/2007, 2007, Lambda photograph, ed. 1/5, 36 x 21 in. (91.4 x 53.3 cm)

Farewell Uncle Tom 1971/2007, 2007, Lambda photograph, ed. 1/5, 36 x 30 in. (91.3 x 76.2 cm)

For the African and the American in You 1997/2007, 2007, Lambda photograph, ed. 1/5, 23 x 39 in. (58.4 x 99 cm)

Funny How Things Change 2007/2007, 2007, Lambda photograph, ed. 1/5, 36 x 27 in. (91.4 x 68.6 cm)

Get Off On the Right Foot 1988/2007, 2007, Lambda photograph, ed. 1/5, 36 x 27 in. (91.4 x 68.5 cm)

Gotten 1996/2007, 2007, Lambda photograph, ed. 1/5, 36 x 28 1/4 in. (91.4 x 71.8 cm)

Introducing New Extra Strength Fulla Waves for Course, Thick, and Unruly Hair 1982/2007, 2007, Lambda photograph, ed. 1/5, 27 7/8 x 36 in. (70.6 x 91.4 cm)

It Could Happen to You 1989/2007, 2007, Lambda photograph, ed. 1/5, 35 x 30 in. (88.8 x 76.2 cm)

Jungle Fever 1991/2007, 2007, Lambda photograph, ed. 1/5, 35 7/8 x 30 in. (90.9 x 76.2 cm)

Just for the Taste of It 1989/2007, 2007, Lambda photograph, ed. 1/5, 28 x 36 in. (71.1 x 91.4 cm)

Late Night, Soft Lights 1990/2007, 2007, Lambda photograph, ed. 1/5, 35 x 30 in. (88.9 x 76.2 cm)

Let Beauty Go to Your Head 1987/2007, 2007, Lambda photograph, ed. 1/5, 36 x 28 5/8 in. (91.4 x 72.6 cm)

Love Hang-Over 1976/2007, 2007, Lambda photograph, ed. 1/5, 36 x 25 in. (91.4 x 63.5 cm)

Make a Radical Departure 1985/2007, 2007, Lambda photograph, ed. 1/5, 34 x 30 in. (86.4 x 76.2 cm)

Many Happy Returns 1980/2007, 2007, Lambda photograph, ed. 1/5, 30 x 32 in. (76.2 x 81.3 cm)

Martin Luther Burger King? 1986/2007, 2007, Lambda photograph, ed. 1/5, 36 x 30 in. (91.4 x 76.2 cm)

McM.L.K. 1986/2007, 2007, Lambda photograph, ed. 1/5, 36 x 27 3/4 in. (91.4 x 70.5 cm)

Now there's a doll that can make a real difference in her life: Shani, the first black Barbie. 1991/2007, 2007, Lambda photograph, ed. 1/5, 34 1/4 x 30 in. (87.3 x 76.2 cm)

O.J. Dingo 1980/2007, 2007, Lambda photograph, ed. 2/5, 36 x 27 1/4 in. (91.4 x 69.3 cm)

Ode to the Ill Nana 1998/2007, 2007, Lambda photograph, ed. 1/5, 36 x 28 3/8 in. (91.4 x 72 cm)

Reparations 101: "I lost my job, my house, my Rolls Royce, my family left me...what else can go wrong?" "Hi Dad!" 1981/2007, 2007, Lambda photograph, ed. 1/5, 31 1/4 x 30 in. (79.4 x 76.2 cm)

Something to Believe In 1984/2007, 2007, Lambda photograph, ed. 1/5, 36 x 27 5/8 in. (91.4 x 69.9 cm)

The French Way 1979/2007, 2007, Lambda photograph, ed. 1/5, 16 x 36 in. (41.1 x 91.4 cm)

The Gidget of Hunter's Point 1993/2007, 2007, Lambda photograph, ed. 1/5, 36 x 28 in. (91.4 x 71.1 cm)

The Johnson Family 1981/2007, 2007, Lambda photograph, ed. 1/5, 31 1/4 x 30 in. (79.4 x 76.2 cm)

The Mandingo of Sandwiches 1977/2007, 2007, Lambda photograph, ed. 1/5, 36 x 34 3/4 in. (91.4 x 88.5 cm)

The Refreshest 1987/2007, 2007, Lambda photograph, ed. 1/5, 36 x 26 5/8 in. (91.4 x 67.7 cm)

Wanted: Tall, dark stranger for long lasting relationship...seeking smoking satisfaction. 1988/2007, 2007, Lambda photograph, ed. 1/5, 33 3/4 x 26 in. (85.8 x 66 cm)

What's love got to do with it? 1983/2007, 2007, Lambda photograph, ed. 1/5, 33 7/8 x 28 5/8 in. (85.9 x 72.4 cm)

When the Going Gets Hard, the Whiskey Should be Soft, 1972/2007, 2007, Lambda photograph, ed. 1/5, 32 1/4 x 30 in. (80 x 76.2 cm)

Who Can Say No to a Gorgeous Brunette? 1970/2007, 2007, Lambda photograph, ed. 1/5, 31 1/8 x 30 in. (79 x 76.2 cm)

Why wait another day to be adorable? Tell your beautician "Relax me" 1968/2007, 2007, Lambda photograph, ed. 1/5, 34 1/8 x 30 in. (86.7 x 76.2 cm)

A Moisturizer That Firms as it Tightens? Bet Your Bottom Dollar! 2002/2008, 2008, Lambda photograph, ed. 1/5, 36 x 27 in. (91.4 x 68.7 cm)

After 61 Years of Service, I Ben, Promoted. 2007/2007, 2008, Lambda photograph, ed. 1/5, 36 x 29 1/4 in. (91.4 x 74.4 cm)

Be Careful What You Wish For 1996/2008, 2008, Lambda photograph, ed. 1/5, 36 x 29 7/8 in. (91.4 x 75.7 cm)

Bleach and Glow 1975/2008, 2008, Lambda photograph, ed. 1/5, 36 x 27 7/8 in. (91.4 x 70.8 cm)

By Any Means Necessary 1993/2008, 2008, Lambda photograph, ed. 1/5, 30 x 32 3/8 in. (76.2 x 82.2 cm)

Celebrate Your Specialness 1997/2008, 2008, Lambda photograph, ed. 1/5, 30 x 32 1/2 in. (76.2 x 82.7 cm)

From the Heart of Africa Comes a Fragrance to Capture the Heart of Every Woman 1994/2008, 2008, Lambda photograph, ed. 1/5, 35 3/8 x 27 7/8 in. (90.1 x 70.6 cm)

Holy Boot! 1998/2008, 2008, Lambda photograph, ed. 1/5, 35 1/2 x 30 in. (90.2 x 76.2 cm)

It's a Great American Custom 1995/2008, 2008, Lambda photograph, ed. 1/5, 36 x 28 1/8 in. (91.4 x 71.6 cm)

Kama Mama, Kama Binti (Like Mother, Like Daughter) 1971/2008, 2008, Lambda photograph, ed. 1/5, 32 x 30 in. (81.4 x 76.2 cm)

Membership has its Privileges 2006/2008, 2008, Lambda photograph, ed. 1/5, 36 x 28 5/8 in. (91.4 x 72.6 cm)

Mist Behavin' 1992/2008, 2008, Lambda photograph, ed. 1/5, 30 x 30 3/4 in. (76.2 x 77.7 cm)

Movin' On Up 1976/2008, 2008, Lambda photograph, ed. 1/5, 32 7/8 x 30 in. (83.2 x 76.2 cm)

Power Is Nothing Without Control 1994/2008, 2008, Lambda photograph, ed. 1/5, 20 x 36 in. (51.1 x 91.4 cm)

Pucker Up! 1972/2008, 2008, Lambda photograph, ed. 1/5, 33 5/8 x 30 in. (85.5 x 76.2 cm)

Ride in Style 1984/2008, 2008, Lambda photograph, ed. 1/5, 30 x 36 in. (76.2 x 91.4 cm)

Smell Like a Bargain 1995/2008, 2008, Lambda photograph, ed. 1/5, 36 x 27 5/8 in. (91.4 x 70.3 cm)

Untitleable 2006/2008, 2008, Lambda photograph, ed. 1/5, 30 x 40 in. (76.2 x 101.6 cm)

Viceroy 1975/2008, 2008, Lambda photograph, ed. 1/5, 30 x 29 5/8 in. (76.2 x 75.4 cm)

We Are On Our Way 1970/2008, 2008, Lambda photograph, ed. 1/5, 33 3/8 x 30 in. (84.9 x 76.2 cm)

We are the Canvas 2004/2008, 2008, Lambda photograph, ed. 1/5, 36 x 28 1/8 in. (91.4 x 71.4 cm)

Welcome to Full Contact Culture 2007/2008, 2008, Lambda photograph, ed. 1/5, 36 x 26 in. (91.4 x 66 cm)

Your Skin has the Power to Protect You 2008/2008, 2008, Lambda photograph, ed. 1/5, 36 x 27 1/2 in. (91.4 x 69.7 cm)

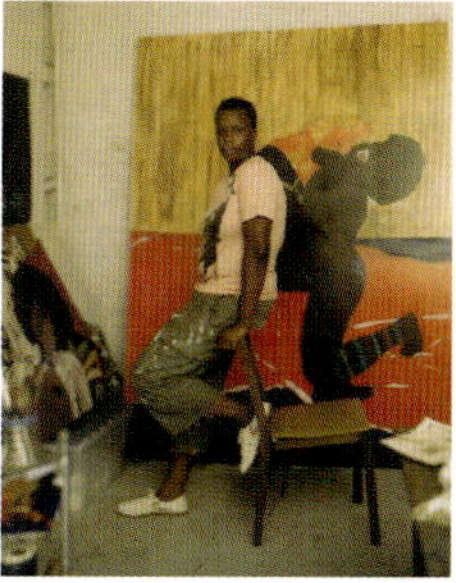

MICKALENE THOMAS

Born in Camden, NJ, 1971
Lives and works in Brooklyn, NY

Baby I Am Ready Now, 2007, acrylic, rhinestone and enamel on panel, diptych, overall 72 x 132 in. (182.9 x 335.3 cm)

Portraits of Quanikah, 2006, acrylic, rhinestone and enamel on panel, 15 panels, overall 70 x 126 in. (178.8 x 320 cm)

I Still Love You (You Still Love Me), 2007, rhinestones, acrylic and enamel on panel, 72 x 60 in. (183 x 152.5 cm)

Hotter than July, 2005, acrylic, rhinestone and enamel on panel, 60 x 72 in. (152.4 x 182.9 cm)

Whatever You Want, 2004, acrylic, rhinestone and enamel on panel, 48 x 36 in. (121.9 x 91.4 cm)

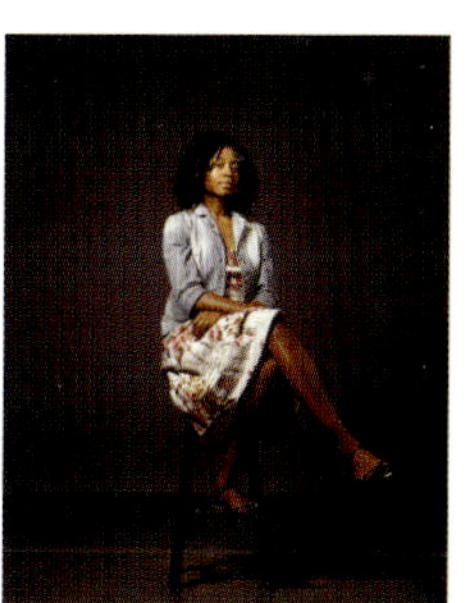

KARA WALKER

Born in Stockton, CA, 1969
Lives and works in New York, NY

Camptown Ladies, 1998, paper, 8 x 55 ft (247.7 x 1691.6 cm)

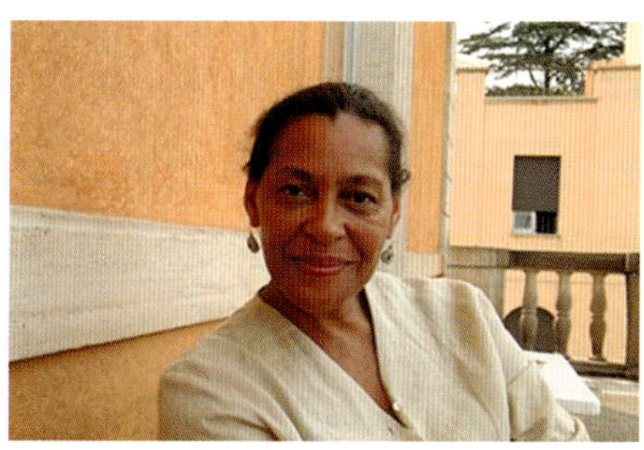

CARRIE MAE WEEMS

Born in Portland, OR, 1953
Lives and works in Syracuse, NY

You Became Mammie, Mama, Mother, & Then, Yes, Confident-Ha/ Descending the Throne (from From Here I Saw What Happened and I Cried), 1995-1996, two chromogenic prints with sandblasted text on glass, ed. 6/10, each 26 1/2 x 22 3/4 in. (67.3 x 57.8 cm)

You Became a Scientific Profile/ An Anthropological Debate/ A Negroid Type/ & A Photographic Subject (from From Here I Saw What Happened and I Cried series), 1995-1996, four chromogenic prints with sandblasted text on glass, ed. 2/10, each 26 3/4 x 22 3/4 in. (68 x 57.8 cm)

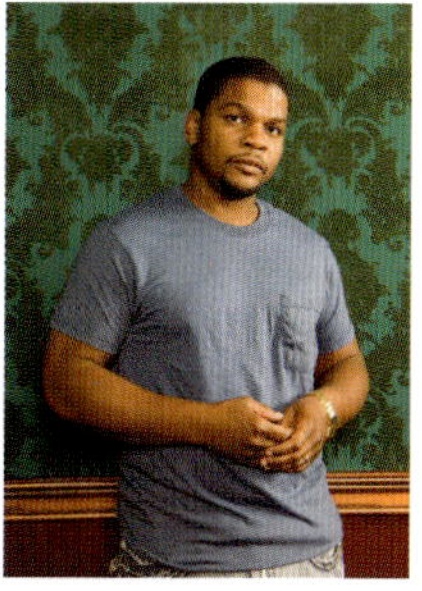

KEHINDE WILEY

Born in Los Angeles, CA, 1977
Lives and works in Brooklyn, NY

Equestrian Portrait of the Count Duke Olivares, 2005, oil on canvas, 108 x 108 in. (274.3 x 274.3 cm)

Triple Portrait of Charles I, 2007, oil and enamel on canvas, triptych, overall 82 x 135 in. (208.3 x 342.9 cm)

Sleep, 2008, oil on canvas, 132 x 300 in. (335.3 x 762 cm)

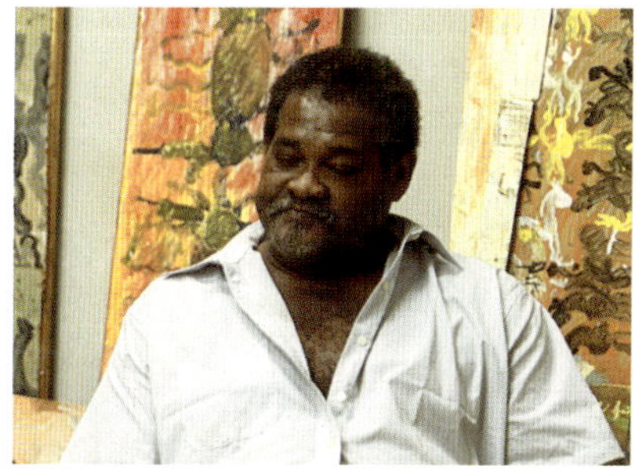

PURVIS YOUNG

Born in Miami, FL, 1943-2010

Untitled, 1985-1999, paint on wood, diameter of panel: 54 in. (137.2 cm) x 2 in. (5 cm)

Untitled, 1985-1999, paint on wood, 36 x 47 1/4 x 1 in. (91.5 x 120 x 2.5 cm)

Untitled, 1985-1999, paint on wood, 60 x 42 1/4 x 7 1/4 in. (152.4 x 107.3 x 18.4 cm)

Untitled, 1985-1999, paint on wood and canvas, 60 x 28 in. (152.4 x 71.1 cm)

Untitled, 1985-1999, paint on wood and canvas, 50 1/2 x 28 x 2 in.(128.3 x 71.1 x 5.1 cm)

CREDITS & THANKS

All images are copyright the artist. We would like to thank all those who kindly gave us their permission to reproduce material in this catalog. Every effort was made to obtain copyright permission for the images in this book. The publishers apologize for any inadvertent mistakes or omissions.

Essays: Franklin Sirmans, Photograph by George Hixson: pg. 49 | Michele Wallace, Photograph by Barbara F. Wallace: pg. 127 | Robert Hobbs, Photograph by Jean Crutchfield: pg. 173

Notes: Oral history interview with Robert Colescott, 1999 April 14. Archives of American Art, Smithsonian Institution: pg. 32

Color Plates: Jean-Michel Basquiat: © 2011 Artist Rights Society (ARS), New York / Société des Auteurs dans les Arts Graphiques et Plastiques (ADAGP), Paris | Kerry James Marshall, *Untitled*, 1998-1999, Photograph by John R. Glembin, Courtesy of the Milwaukee Art Museum, Milwaukee: pg. 110-111 | William PopeL., *The Great White Way, 22 miles, 9 years, 1 street*, 2001-2002, Photograph by Pruznick/Grey, Courtesy of the artist: pg. 130-131 | Gary Simmons, *Duck, Duck, Noose*, 1992, Photograph by Chan T. Chao, Courtesy of the Corcoran Gallery of Art, Washington, D.C.: pg. 141 | Hank Willis Thomas, *Power Is Nothing Without Control 1994/2008*, 2008, Original photograph by Annie Liebowitz: pg. 191 | *Gotten 1996/2007*, 2007, Original photograph by Annie Liebowitz: pg. 192 | *Cucci #2: It's Time for Jungle Fever 2001/2006*, 2006, Original photograph by Richard Burbridge: pg. 193 | *Liberation of T.O.: "I'm not goin' back to work for massa' in dat darned field!" 2003/2005*, 2005, Original photograph by Charlie White: pg. 193 | *Funny How Things Change 2007/2007*, 2007, Original photograph by Bruce Talamon: pg. 195

Artists' Portraits: Jean-Michel Basquiat, Photograph by Tseng Kwong Chi, Courtesy of Muna Tseng Dance Projects, Inc., New York: pg. 218 | Mark Bradford, Photograph by Juan Carlos Avedano, Courtesy of Sikkema Jenkins & Co., New York: pg. 218 | Robert Colescott, Photograph by Tasin Sabir: pg. 218 | Noah Davis, *Man with Shotgun and Alien*, 2008, Courtesy of the artist and Roberts and Tilton, Los Angeles: pg. 218 | Leonardo Drew, Photograph by Maki Kawakita, Courtesy of Sikkema Jenkins & Co., New York: pg. 218 | Renée Green, Photograph by Lina Bertucci: pg. 219 | David Hammons, Photograph by Timothy Greenfield-Sanders: pg. 219 | Barkley L. Hendricks, *Self-Portrait, New London, CT,* 1977/2008, Courtesy of the artist and The Project Gallery, New York: pg. 219 | Rashid Johnson, *Self-portrait with my hair parted like Frederick Douglass*, 2003, Courtesy of the artist and Nicole Klagsbrun Gallery, New York: pg. 219 | Glenn Ligon, Photograph by Ricardo Okaranza: pgs. 219 | Kalup Linzy, Photograph by Peter Bellamy: pg. 220 | Wangechi Mutu, Photograph by Suné Woods, Courtesy of Sikkema Jenkins & Co., New York: pg. 220 | William Pope.L, Photograph by Lydia Grey, Courtesy of the artist: pg. 220 | Gary Simmons, Courtesy of the artist and Metro Pictures, New York: pg. 220 | Lorna Simpson, *Lorna*, 1992, by Dawoud Bey, Courtesy of Dawoud Bey and Rhona Hoffman Gallery, Chicago: pg. 221 | Shinique Smith, Photograph by Kathryn Hiller, Courtesy of the artist and Yvon Lambert, New York/Paris: pg. 221 | Henry Taylor, Photograph by Simon Hare: pg. 221 | Hank Willis Thomas, Photograph by Minette Mangahas: pg. 221 | Mickalene Thomas, Courtesy of the artist and Rhona Hoffman Gallery: pg. 223 | Kara Walker, Photograph by Cameron Wittig, Courtesy of Sikkema Jenkins & Co., New York: pg. 223 | Kehinde Wiley, Courtesy of the artist and Rhona Hoffman Gallery: pg. 223

The Rubell Museum would like to especially thank all of the artists in the exhibition for their time, effort and faith in contributing to *30 Americans.*

Special thanks to: Santiago Diaz, Thelma Golden, Robert Hobbs, Christine Kim, Glenn Ligon, Louise Neri, Franklin Sirmans, Michele Wallace and Rubell Museum Staff.

Additional thanks to: Karen del Aguila | Galerie Catherine Bastide, Brussels | Atelier Cardenas Bellanger, Paris | Blum & Poe, Los Angeles | Wendy Blazier, Boca Raton Museum of Art | John Connelly Presents, New York | Paula Cooper Gallery, New York | Diego Cortez | Melissa Cueto | Deitch Projects, New York | Galleria Emi Fontana, Milan | Alina Gallo | Caren Golden Fine Art, New York | Timothy Greenfield-Sanders | Carmen Hammons | Susan Hendricks | Rhona Hoffman Gallery, Chicago | Phyllis Kind Gallery, Chicago | Nicole Klagsbrun, New York | David Kordansky Gallery, Los Angeles | Kravets|Wehby, New York | Anna Kustera Gallery, New York | L & M Arts, New York | Yvon Lambert, New York | Minette Mangahas | Elizabeth Martinez | Lehmann Maupin Gallery, New York | Galerie Hans Mayer GmbH, Düsseldorf | Monique Meloche Gallery, Chicago | Metro Pictures, New York | Fernanda Meza, Artists Rights Society | Victoria Miro Gallery, London | Annina Nosei Gallery, New York | The Project Gallery, New York | The Proposition, New York | Regen Projects, Los Angeles | Daniel Reich Gallery, New York | Rental Gallery, New York | Sandroni Rey, Los Angeles | Roberts & Tilton, Culver City | Leon Rolle | Salon 94, New York | Trevor Schoonmaker, The Nasher Museum of Art at Duke University | Jack Shainman Gallery, New York | Sho Nuff Unisex, Harlem, New York | Sikkema Jenkins & Co., New York | Lowery Simms, Museum of Arts and Design | Sister, Los Angeles | The Studio Museum in Harlem, New York | Taxter & Spengemann, New York | Jack Tilton Gallery, New York | Try Barber Shop, Harlem, New York | Untitled, New York | Susanne Vielmetter, Los Angeles Projects | Hauser & Wirth, Zurich/London | Dindy Yokel | Barbara Young, Miami-Dade Public Library